A GRAMMAR OF THE TIBETAN LANGUAGE

Literary and Colloquial

Bibliotheca Indo–Buddhica Series No. 85

A GRAMMAR OF THE TIBETAN LANGUAGE

Literary and Colloquial

Herbert Bruce Hannah

SRI SATGURU PUBLICATIONS
A Division of
INDIAN BOOKS CENTRE
DELHI — INDIA

Published by :

SRI SATGURU PUBLICATIONS
Indological & Oriental Publishers
A Division of
INDIAN BOOKS CENTRE
40/5, Shakti Nagar
Delhi- 110 007
India

First Edition : Calcutta- 1912

Reprint Delhi- 1991

ISBN 81-7030-264-1

Printed at
Mehra Offset Press
New Delhi 110 002

DEDICATED

TO

E. DENISON ROSS,

TO WHOSE INTEREST IN TIBETAN IT IS DUE THAT THIS

LANGUAGE HAS FOR THE FIRST TIME BEEN

INTRODUCED INTO THE CURRICULUM

OF A UNIVERSITY.

PREFACE.

For many centuries Tibet has been a *terra incognita*—little or nothing being known about it, as regards either its physical conditions or its inner life.

Not, indeed, till a few years ago, when a British force entered Lhasa, the "Place of the minor gods," was the veil withdrawn; and even then the withdrawal was only partial, transient, and very local.

As for the language, though there have been several gallant attempts to plunge into the labyrinthine obscurities of its construction—notably on the part of Alexander Csoma de Körös in 1834 and subsequently of H. A. Jäschke—that also, it must be confessed, remains more or less a mystery; for no one, I take it, is likely to aver that the present state of our knowledge on the subject is at all satisfactory.

Much, no doubt, has been contributed by the more recent labours of Rāi Sarat Chandra Dās Bahādur, Mr. Vincent Henderson, the Rev. Edward Amundsen, and Mr. C. A. Bell, I.C.S. But, in spite of all, even they, and every one else who has taken up the study, will admit that, wherever one treads, the ground still feels uncomfortably shaky, especially in regard to certain aspects of the so-called verb; wherever he gropes there is something that seems ever to elude him; and, amid the weird philological phantoms that flit uncertainly around in the prevailing gloom, his constant cry, I feel very sure, is still one for more light.

I do not for one moment claim for this grammar the character of a scientific work. Many years ago when I was studying the language in Darjeeling, under Kāzi Dawa Sam Dūp—a particularly intelligent and scholarly Tibetan—it was my habit during the course of my morning's lesson to make notes of what I then learnt. After a time these notes became so numerous that for my own convenience I was obliged to reduce them to some degree of order. These ordered notes themselves growing in bulk, the idea occurred to me that I might just as well put them into the form of a book, and this I did—the result being a MS which has long lain by me, but which is now about to be published.

It is merely another attempt on the part of one who has tried to profit by the works of others, to re-state (originally for his own private satisfaction) what has already been achieved in a field of obscure and somewhat difficult research; to correct or modify previous effort, wherever correction or modification seemed necessary or desirable; and even, to some extent, to supplement it in one or two respects which appeared to be susceptible of further elucidation and expansion.

Both Literary and Colloquial Tibetan have been dealt with, the particular dialect chosen for exposition being that standard one, known as the དབུས་སྐད་ or *Ǖ Kä'*, which is now spoken in and around the centre of Tibetan Civilisation—Lhasa.

This is the dialect in which, as the result of centuries of developing Lamäic culture, the phonetic values of Tibetan are found to have undergone a greater degree of change from those of the original speech than any of the other dialects.

In other regions of Tibet, it is said, the prefixes, superposed letters, and suffixes, are still more or less pronounced as of old, and the original vowel-sounds are still more or less unaltered, in a degree corresponding to the remoteness of the speakers from, or their proximity to, the Holy City.

The difficulties confronting the student of Tibetan are considerably enhanced by the fact that in addition to the Literary Language and the Modern Colloquial, it also possesses a totally different vocabulary the employment of which is *de rigueur* when one is conversing or corresponding with a person of quality. This is known as the Honorific Language; and besides that there is another called the High Honorific, which is only used when addressing exalted personages such as the Dalai Lama or the Tashi Lama. With these honorific forms of speech, however, this work is not particularly concerned. The student, if so inclined, can easily hunt them up for himself, after he has acquired a working knowledge of the ordinary literary or book language and the modern colloquial.

Attention is particularly invited to the earlier paragraphs of the Grammar dealing with the important subject of Pronunciation, in which an endeavour has been made, on principles more systematic and accurate than those hitherto in vogue, to ascertain, fix, and express in roman characters, the subtle distinctions that lurk between the numerous phonetic values of the Tibetan consonants and vowels; also to the paragraph explanatory of the use of the Tibetan Dictionary; and to the tabular statement showing what dominant consonants in a Tibetan word take particular prefixes.

A paragraph has also been exclusively devoted to an exhaustive treatment of the subject of Spelling. This is a most useful accomplishment, and one that the student should take some pains to acquire.

The so-called verb has also been elaborately treated in the body of the book; but in the appendices a novel and perhaps somewhat risky attempt has been made (how far successfully remains to be seen) to present it in the guise of skeleton conjugations or paradigms. These forms, however, should not be taken too literally, as they are not always absolute or rigid expressions, but are liable to frequent modification, or moulding, in accordance with the elusive and temporizing genius of the Tibetan sentence, the construction of which is unique, and can only be appreciated after much mental effort and distress.

As a matter of fact the only real verb in Tibetan is the verb *To be*, whether in the form of ཡིན་པ་ *Yin-pa*, or ཡོད་པ་ *Yö'pa*, and the beginner is advised to master it at as early a stage as possible in the course of his studies. He should make special note of the manner in which Literary ཡིན་པ་ differs from Colloquial ཡིན་པ་ Also of the important fact that ཡོད་པ་ is sometimes a substantive verb, meaning *To be present*, *To exist*, and sometimes a mere copula or an auxiliary, like ཡིན་པ།

All other verbs are practically a kind of noun-phrases, dependent for their significations upon the various moods and tenses of these two verbs ཡིན་པ་ and ཡོད་པ།

Throughout, the observations explanatory of each subject are followed by numerous illustrations, both Colloquial and Literary, the latter being mostly taken from the Tibetan version of the New Testament—a mine of idiomatic wealth. Amongst these illustrations will be found a few culled from Jäschke's and Das's Dictionaries, or from Amundsen's Primer. In most of such cases either the names or the initials of these authors have been given, but in one or two instances (from Amundsen) on p. 256, the reference has been omitted by an oversight.

Up to a certain stage the romanized equivalent of the Tibetan is given: but after that the student is left to discern the proper pronunciation by means of his own unaided skill.

Here it may interest others as well as students of Tibetan to mention that *Oh, the jewel in the lotus!* Lieutenant-Colonel Waddell's rendering of the celebrated formula ཨོཾ་མ་ཎི་པ་དྨེ་ཧཱུྃ། ཧྲཱིཿ༎ *Om maṇi pä'me hūm, hri*, is wholly inadequate and indeed inaccurate.

Om does not mean *Oh* at all, and the phrase as a whole, is much deeper and more complex in its signification than the above rendering would imply.

Om alone is an all-embracing expression, and stands mystically for the incarnation of the Deity, or rather for the immanence of the Supreme Being in, as well as for Its transcendence above, the phenomenal or existent world, so far as the terms 'immanence' and 'transcendence' are applicable to the relations subsisting between that world and Pure Subsistence. In other words, it stands for the never-ending kosmic process of the self-effacing involution of PARAMÂTMAN, or BRAHMAN, *into* Existence, or the world of Matter, and Its self-expressing evolution *through* Matter back to Substantial Being. This process, indeed, constitutes the famous so-called "Wheel of Life" in its Kosmic aspect.

The formula may be roughly analysed thus:—

ཨ་ - The source of all speech
ཨུ་ - ,, ,, ,, vitality
ཧྃ་ - ,, ,, ,, thrilling consciousness
} Embodiment of the Trinity.

མ་ཎི་ - Wish-granting jewel; symbolical of temporal blessings; also of the Psychical Âtman or Spiritual Ego.

པ་དྨེ་ or པད་མེ་ - Lotus; symbolical of biune man and of spiritual re-birth.

ཧཱུྃ་ It is, or I am, omnipresent.

ཧྲཱིཿ *Sct*; the universal Life Principle, or *Satyasya Satyam* of the Upanishads i.e., the Houmenal Reality underlying Empirical Reality.

The entire phrase, therefore, merely in this one limited aspect of its meaning (and it may be read in many other ways) signifies—" The Embodiment of the Trinity, or Incarnation of Deity, is my wish-granting jewel in the lotus of spiritual rebirth"; the idea apparently being that since the *Kosmical Âtman*, or *Brahman*, i.e. the first or inner principle of the universe, and the *Psychical Âtman*, or inner principle of individual Man, are essentially one and the same, our hope of spiritual rebirth is assured in and by the fact of the eternal subsistence of *Brahman* and the ceaselessness of the kosmic process above referred to—human re-incarnation being a microcosmic effect, or aspect, of the macrocosmic law.

Hence, whenever a lama is heard droning out his *Om maṇi pä' me hūm*, he is really reciting his version of one of the profoundest creeds known to philosophy—but in most cases probably with an artless ignorance that is equally profound.

Another mistake that one often meets with, especially in Theosophical literature, is that which represents the word DEVACHAN as signifying *The dwelling of the gods*, doubtless from some vague idea that it is derived from the Perso-Hindustāni words *Dewa*, 'a god,' and *Khān*, or *Khāneh*, 'a dwelling-house.' It is really the Tibetan word བདེ་བ་ཅན་ *De-wa chän*, meaning 'Blissful.'

No one will be better pleased than myself to see any errors in this book corrected, or doubts removed, by competent critics. I am conscious that there must be errors, and I know there are doubts; while the desire of all who are interested in the language cannot but be to see our knowledge of it advanced.

My acknowledgments are due to the grammarians already named, and especially to Mr. Henderson and Mr. Bell, whose respective manuals and vocabularies marked a considerable advance upon the grammars that they supplemented and, if I may say so, displaced. The earlier grammars by Csoma de Körös and Jäschke were concerned for the most part, if not solely, with archaic classical Tibetan. The former's "Colloquial Phrases" were anything but what would now be regarded as colloquial; while Jäschke's colloquial was that of Western Tibet. These grammars, therefore, were not altogether satisfactory for the purposes of modern requirements. Moreover, the manner in which they dealt with the mysteries of the verb left much to be desired. As for the late Rev. Graham Sandberg's grammar, though very elaborate and learned, it did not really constitute a bar to the successful appearance of the Manuals above alluded to. Indeed it may perhaps be said that not until the publication of Mr. Bell's book were the true forms and functions of the verb, and especially of ཡིན་པ་ and ཡོད་པ་ *To be*, stated with anything like precision and lucidity.

I desire also to acknowledge my obligations to the Hon'ble Vice-Chancellor (Sir Ashutosh Mukerji, Kt.) and Syndicate of the Calcutta University, under whose auspices this contribution to the study of Tibetan has attained the honour and privilege of publication.

Lastly, my grateful thanks are also due to Dr. and Mrs. Denison Ross for much kindness and help accorded from time to time; and perhaps most of all to my Mūnshi, Kāzi Dawa Sam Dūp, and to Mr. David Macdonald of Kalimpong (probably the first Tibetan scholar in India) who was kind enough to go through the entire MS. and to favour me with his critical comments and general approval.

H. B. H.

TABLE OF CONTENTS.

CHAPTER I.

PRELIMINARY.

			Page
§	1.	The ཀ ཁ Ka-K'a	1
		I. The ཀ་ ལི་ Kā-li	1
		II. The ཨ་ ལི་ Ā-li	3
§	2.	Romanized Equivalents	5
§	3.	Phonetic Modifications of Vowels	8
		Notes	11
§	4.	The Six Reversed Letters	15
§	5.	The Seven Consonants to which ྱ may be subjoined..	16
§	6.	The Fourteen Consonants to which ྲ may be subjoined	17
§	7.	The Six Consonants to which ླ may be subjoined ..	18
§	8.	The Six Silent Consonants to which ལ may be subjoined	18
§	9.	The Sixteen Consonants to which ྭ may be subjoined	18
§	10.	The Twelve *Ra-go* Consonants	21
§	11.	The Ten *La-go* Consonants	21
§	12.	The Twelve *Sa-go* Consonants	21
§	13.	The Five Prefixes	22
§	14.	Initial Letters and the Prefixes each may take ..	24
		Notes	28
§	15.	Peculiarities of Pronunciation	29
§	16.	The Ten Consonantal Affixes	33
§	17.	The Eleven Final Duplications	34
§	18.	Colloquial Duplications	37
§	19.	The Tone System	39
§	20.	Writing and Punctuation	45

		Page
§ 21.	Spelling	50
§ 22.	Transliteration	55
§ 23.	Use of the Tibetan Dictionary	55
§ 24.	Indicative and Differentiating Particles	57
§ 25.	*The Cases and their Signs*	61
I.	The Nominative Case	62
II.	The Vocative Case	63
III.	The Objective or Accusative Case	63
IV.	The Genitive Case	63
V.	The Dative Case	65
VI.	The Agentive Case	67
VII.	The Locative Case	69
VIII.	The Periodal or Durational Case	71
IX.	The Modal Case	73
X.	The Ablative Case	75
XI.	The Terminative or Transitive Case	77
§ 26.	NUMERALS.	
I.	*The Cardinal Numbers*	82
II.	*The Cardinals according to Alphabetical Enumeration*	85
	NOTES :—	
1.	Pronunciation	86
2.	Affixes	86
3.	Conjunctions	87
4.	The Indefinite Article	87
5.	Approximate Numbers	87
6.	Ordinal Numbers	88
7.	Distributive Numbers	88
8.	Aggregates	89
9.	Fractions	89
10.	Adverbial Cardinal Numbers ..	90
11.	,, Ordinal ,, ...	91
12	Definite and Indefinite Numerals ..	91
13	Noun Substantives	93
14.	Notation by letters	93

CHAPTER II.

ETYMOLOGY.

		Page
§ 27.	The Definite Article	95
§ 28.	The Indefinite Article	99
§ 29.	*The Noun.*	
	A.—STRUCTURE	101
	1. Monosyllables, Dissyllables, and Polysyllables ..	101
	2. The affix མཁན་	104
	3. The affix བྱེད་	104
	4. The affix རྐྱབ་	106
	5. The affix བཟོ་	106
	6. Abstract Nouns	106
	B.—INFLEXION	
	1. *Gender*	107
	2. *Number*	109
	3. *Case*	111
	I. Noun ending in a Vowel	111
	II. ,, ,, ,, ག་ or ང་	115
	III. ,, ,, ,, ད་, བ་ or ས་ ..	116
	IV. ,, ,, ,, ན་, མ་, ར་ or ལ་ ..	116
§ 30.	THE ADJECTIVE.	
	I. Form and Place	116
	II. Augmenting of Adjectives	127
	III. The Comparative Degree	129
	IV. The Superlative Degree	131
	V. Other Methods of Comparison	134
§ 31.	THE PRONOUN.	
	I. Personal Pronouns	135
	II. Declension of Personal Pronouns ..	138
	III. The Reflexive Pronouns	140
	IV. Compounds in རང་ *Rang*	143

		Page
V. *Possessive Pronouns*		
1. Ordinary Personal Pronouns	..	144
2. Reflexive Possessive Pronouns	..	145
VI. Demonstrative Pronouns	.. ..	147
VII. The Reciprocal Pronoun	..	150
VIII. Interrogative Pronouns	.. ..	151
IX. *Relative and Correlative Pronouns*		
A. Relative Pronouns	.. ..	153
B. Correlative Pronouns	.. ..	160
X. *Indefinite Pronouns*	.. ..	169
§ 32. Adverbs	.. ..	177
§ 33. Postpositions	.. ..	194
§ 34. Conjunctions	.. ..	201
§ 35. ཡོད་པ་ *To be*	.. ..	207
§ 36. ཡོད་པ་ *To have*	.. .. ..	228
§ 37. ཡིན་པ་ *To be*	.. ..	229
§ 38. The Verb.		
I. Preliminary	.. ..	239
II. Roots	.. ..	239
III. Auxiliary Verbs	.. .. ..	243
IV. Auxiliary Particles.		
(1) གི་, གྱི་, ཀྱི་, etc.	.. ..	244
(2) གིས་, གྱིས་, ཀྱིས་, etc.	.. ..	245
(3) གིན་ གྱིན་, ཀྱིན་, etc.	.. ..	245
(4) ཏེ་, དེ་, སྟེ་	.. .. ..	246
(5) ཅིང་, ཞིང་, ཤིང་	.. ..	247
6) པས། and བས་	.. .. ..	248
(7) ནས་	.. .. ..	249
(8) ལས།	.. .. ..	249
(9) ན་	.. .. ..	251
(10) ལ་	.. .. ..	252

		Page
	(11) གྲུ	254
	(12) ཡ	255
	(13) དང	255
	(14) དུ, ཏུ, ར, རུ, སུ, ལ	257
	(15) བཞིན and བཞིན་དུ	258
	(16) ཙང	259
	(17) དུས and དུས་ལ	259
V.	*Moods and Tenses.*	
	A.—Infinitive Mood	259
	B.—The Supine	263
	C.—The Verbal Noun	265
	D.—Participles	267
	E.—Gerunds	271
	F.—Indicative Mood.	
	(*a*) Present	272
	(*b*) Imperfect	275
	(*c*) Perfect	276
	(*d*) Past Indefinite	277
	(*e*) Pluperfect	279
	(*f*) Future	281
	G.—Subjunctive and Conditional Moods	283
	H.—Potential Mood	285
	I.—Probability	288
	J.—Hortative Mood	290
	K.—Purposive Mood	292
	L.—Precative Mood	292
	M.—Permissive Mood	293
	N.—Optative Mood	294
	O.—Imperative Mood	296
VI.	The Passive Voice	299
VII.	Compound Verbs	300
VIII.	Verbs of becoming, growing, changing, etc.	303
IX.	Inceptives	303
X.	Imminence	304

Page

XI. Continuatives 304
XII. Finality or Accomplishment .. . 305
XIII. Desideratives 305
XIV. Frequentatives 306
XV. Use of the PERFECT ROOT in the Colloquial .. 307

CHAPTER III.

39. Syntax 308

APPENDIX OF CONJUGATIONS.

I. COLLOQUIAL ཡོད་པ་ *To be present ; To exist ; To be* 310
II. LITERARY Ditto .. 315
III. COLLOQUIAL ཡིན་པ་ *To be* 320
IV. LITERARY Ditto 325
V. ཡོད་པ་ *To have ; to possess* 331
VI. Active, Transitive, 4-Rooted COLLOQUIAL Verb གཏོང་བ་ *To send* 331
VII. LITERARY Ditto 340
VIII. Passive, 4-Rooted COLLOQUIAL Verb གཏོང་རྒྱུ་ *To be sent* 349
IX. Active, one-Rooted COLLOQUIAL Verb མཐོང་བ་ *To see* 354
X. Neuter, one-Rooted COLLOQUIAL Verb དགའ་བ་ *To be glad, To rejoice* 360
XI. LITERARY Ditto .. 361
XII. Passive, 4-Rooted LITERARY Verb གཏོང་བྱ་ or གཏོང་བར་བྱ་བ་ *To be sent* 368
XIII. Active, 2-Rooted COLLOQUIAL Verb འགྲོ་བ་ *To go* .. 371
XIV. LITERARY Ditto 378
XV. 2-Rooted LITERARY Verb འགྱུར་བ་ *To become*, etc. 383

Page

XVI. Active, 4-Rooted COLLOQUIAL Verb བྱེད་པ་ *To do, To make*, etc. 387

XVII. LITERARY Ditto 389

XVIII. Passive, 4-Rooted COLLOQUIAL Verb བྱེད་ཀྱི་ཡོད་པ་ or ཡིན་པ་ *To be made, To be done*, etc. .. 393

XIX. Passive, 4-Rooted LITERARY Verb བྱ་བ་ *To be made, To be done*, etc... 394

XX. Passive, LITERARY Verb བྱེད་པར་འགྱུར་བ་ *To be made, or done*, etc. 395

Tibetan Grammar.

CHAPTER I.

PRELIMINARY.

§ 1.—The ཀ་ཁ་ *Ka-K'a*, or Tibetan Graphic System.

I.— ཀཱ་ལི་ *Kā-li*, or Consonantal Series of thirty letters.

Letter.	Name.	Remarks.
ཀ	Ka	Like *K* in the Urdu word کب Kab, *When*. A compact sound.
ཁ	K'a	*Kh*, forcibly aspirated. Like the Persian خ *Kh*.
ག	Ġa	Pronounced softly, from low down in the throat, rather more sharply than hard English *G*, and in a way that to English ears seems to give it the sound of *K*.
ང	Nga	Like the sound of *ng* in the English word *sing*. It often begins a word in Tibetan. As a final, often represented by a superscribed o, called o. ཀླད་ཀོར་ o LÄ'-KOR, or o *cipher*.
ཅ	Cna	Like the *Ch* in *charge*. A compact sound.
ཆ	Ch'a	*Chha*. A forcibly aspirated *ch*.
ཇ	Ja, J'a	Like the *J* in *jar*. As an initial it is slightly aspirated, and may be pronounced like ཅ *ch*.

N.B.—For the *powers* of these letters, as represented by their romanized equivalents, *see* § 2.

Letter.	Name.	Remarks.
ཉ	Nya	Like the combined sound of the *nya* in *lanyard*.
ཏ	Ta	A compact dental sound, like the Urdu or Persian ت, or the Bengali ত.
ཐ	T'a	Also dental, but forcibly aspirated.
ད	D́a	This is not exactly a dental *d*, nor is it an aspirated *d*, as sometimes described, but a dental sound, rather like the *th* in *think*, as pronounced by some Irishmen; or like the Bengali দ, but with a strong similarity to a dental *t*. A soft sound.
ན	Na	A dental *N*, softly sounded.
པ	Pa	English *P*, but more fully and compactly pronounced.
ཕ	P'a	Not *Ph* (i.e. *F*, or *Fh*), but *P-h*. A strong aspirate.
བ	Ba	Sharper than the English *B*, and rather like *P*, but softer than the latter.
མ	Ma	English *M*, sometimes abbreviated into o, written over the initial, and representing final *m*, and called o ཀླད་ཀོར་ o LÄ'-KOR, o *cipher*. It is also called སྟོད་ཀོར་ TÖ'-KOR and is the same as the Sanskrit Anuswara.
ཙ	Tsa	Like the sound of *Ts*, or Russian Tsē. A compact sound.
ཚ	Ts'a	Not *Tsh*, but *Ts-h*, strongly aspirated.
ཛ	Dz'a	Not *Dzh*, but *Dz-h*. Aspirated.
ཝ	Wa	English *W*.
ཞ	Żhya	Something like the French *J* in *jadis*, or Persian ژ, or Russian Zhē, but with a tendency towards the sound *sh*, and also with the *ya* sound. Hence, hard *z'hya*, or soft *shya*.

Letter.	Name.	Remarks.
ཟ	Za	English *Z*, but inclining to sound of *s*.
འ	'a	*Spiritus lenis*, with a vowel-sound like that in the Urdu word بس BAS, *Enough*; but soft and long, as though gently emanating from the throat. In words from Sanskrit it is used as a "mora," to denote prosodical length, i.e. a long syllable.
ཡ	Ya	English *Y*, as in *yard*, *you*, *yoke*, *ye*, *yes*, *yiddish*, *yea*.
ར	Ra	English *R*, well sounded.
ལ	La	English *L*, but, at the end of a syllable, sounded either very faintly or not at all, and sometimes changed to ར་ *Ra*.
ཤ	Sha	*Sh*. Full, strong sound.
ས	Sa	*S*. Full, strong sound, like *ss* in *hiss*, but, at the end of a syllable, not sounded at all.
ཧ	Ha	*H*. Well aspirated.
ཨ	A	Like the vowel-sound in the Urdu word بس BAS, *Enough*. Pronounced very short: but a harder, fuller and compacter sound than that of འ་ The sound of ཨ་ is inherent in all simple non-final consonants unqualified by any vowel-sign, and in all compound consonants sounding as one, when similarly unqualified. It is *not* inherent in the consonant འ་ which has a softer and more emanating sound.

II.—The ཨ་ལི་ Ā-LI, or VOWEL-SERIES, being five vowels, and four vowel-signs. For the purpose of illustrating the signs, one of the vowels, namely, ཨ་ *A*, which is also regarded as a consonant by Tibetans, is adopted as a basis. Any other consonant, however, would do equally well.

Letter.	Name.	Remarks.
ཨ	a	Like *a* in بس BAS, *Enough*. Pronunciation short, hard, compact and full. Inherent in all non-final consonants not qualified by any vowel-signs, and in single-letter and compound-letter syllables sounding as one syllable, when similarly unqualified. Thus, in ཐང་ ṬʻANG, *Path*, it is inherent in ཐ་ but not in the final ང་. So it is inherent in ང་ NGA, *I*, but not in ངོ་ NGO, *Face*; and in གླ་ LA, *Pay, salary*, but not in གླུ་ LU, *song*. It also ceases to inhere by reason of modifications other than qualifying vowel-signs, as will hereafter be shown. *See* § 3.
ཨི	i	Short, like the *i* in *is*. The sign is ི called གི་གུ་ G′I-G′U, *The Angle*, and it is placed *over* the letter it modifies. Thus, ཀྱི་ KYI, *A sign of the Genitive Case.*
ཨུ	u	Short, like the *u* in *full*. The sign is ུ called ཞབས་ཀྱུ་ ŻHYAB-KYU, *The hook*, and it is placed *under* the letter it modifies. Thus, དུ་ D′U, *A sign of the Terminative Case.*
ཨེ	e	Short, like *a* in *made*, or the Italian *e*. The sign is ེ called འགྲེང་བུ་ ḌENG-BU, *The standing stroke*, and it is placed *over* the letter it modifies. Thus, རེ་རེ་ RE-RE, *each*.
ཨོ	o	Short, like the *o* in *for*, or *rock*. The sign is ོ called སྣ་རོ་ ṄA-RO, *The horns over the nose*, and it is placed *over* the letter it modifies. Thus, རོ་ RO, *A corpse*; གོང་ ĠONG, *Price*; ཀློག་པ་ LOĠ-PA, *To read*; གློག་ LO’, *Lightning*; རྡོ་ ḌO, *Stone*.

§ 2.—The Romanized Equivalents adopted in this work, showing the Powers of the thirty consonants.

Tibetan Character.	Romanized Equivalent.	Remarks.
..	ʹ	Acute accent, used for instance with *g*, when ག་ GA, is pronounced almost like *k*; and with *d*, when ད་ DA, is pronounced almost like *T*. Thus, གོང་ ǴONG, *Price*, because it is pronounced nearly like KONG; but སྒོ་ Ğo, *Door*, pronounced like the ordinary hard English *g*. So also དེ་ ḊE, *The*, *That*, because it is pronounced almost like dental TE; but འདི་ Ď I, *The*, *This*, pronounced as dental *d*.
..	˘	This sign, placed over any letter, signifies a raising of the tone.
..	ʼ	*Spiritus lenis*, or gentle breathing. It is placed before *a*, thus *'a*, to represent འ་ For example, བཀའ་ K'A, *Order*, *Command*. For simplicity's sake, however, we shall seldom use it. It will never be used to represent འ་ as a prefix.
..	ʻ	*Spiritus asper*, or rough breathing. Thus ཁ་ K'A, for KHA. e.g., འཁྱེར་བ་ K'YER-WA, *To carry away*.
ཀ	K	Tonic pitch high.
ཁ	K'	Pitch lower than *K*.
ག	Ǵ	Pitch deep.

Tibetan Character.	Romanized Equivalent.	Remarks.
ག་ guarded	G	e.g.—སྒམ་ ĜAM, *Box, Chest*. Pitch higher than ǵ.
ང	Ng	Pitch low; sometimes represented by o LǍ'-KOR, o *cipher*.
ཅ	Ch	Pitch very high.
ཆ	Ch'	Pitch lower than *ch*.
ཇ	J, J'	When an initial, represented by J'. Thus ཇ་ J'A, *Tea*. When it has a prefix, represented by *J*. Thus, འཇུས་པ་ JÜ-PA, *To cling*; མཇལ་བ་ JǍ-WA, *To come to, To meet, To pay one's respects to*. Pitch very low.
ཉ	Ny	Pitch low.
ཏ	T	Pitch very high.
ཐ	T'	Pitch lower than T.
ད	Ď	Pitch very low.
ད་ guarded	D	*e.g.*—རྡོ་ DO, *Stone*. Pitch higher than Ď.
ན	N	Pitch low.
པ	P	Pitch very high.
ཕ	P'	Pitch lower than *P*.
བ	B, W, V	Pitch very deep.
མ་ and o		o (called *o* ཀླད་ཀོར་ LǍ'-KOR, *cipher*). Is sometimes placed on top of a letter, and stands for a final *ng*, or *m*, or *ms*. The pitch of མ་ is low.

Tibetan Character.	Romanized Equivalent.	Remarks.
ཙ	Ts	Pitch high.
ཚ	Ts'	Pitch lower than *Ts*.
ཛ	Dz'	Pitch very low.
ཝ	W	Pitch low.
ཞ	Żhy	Pitch very low. e.g., ཞྭ་མོ་ ŻHYĀ-MO, *Hat*, pronounced almost like SHĀ-MO.
ཟ	Ż	e.g.,—ཟ་བ་ ŻA-WA, *To eat*, pronounced almost like SA-WA. Pitch very low.
འ	'A	When འ་ is a prefix, it is not transliterated at all in this work. Pitch very low.
ཡ	Y	Pitch very low.
ར	R	Pitch low.
ལ	L	Lowest pitch of all.
ཤ	Sh	Pitch high.
ས	S	
ཧ	H	Pitch very high.
ཨ	A	Pitch low.

NOTE.—The remarks in column 3 regarding Tonic Pitch refer to the Rev. Mr. Amundsen's Tone-system. I would, however, advise the student to direct his attention to the *compactness or otherwise of his utterance*, and to the *shortness or length of his vowel-sounds*, rather than to Pitch of Tone. *See* § 19.

Other letters, compound and reversed, are not included in the above tables. They are dealt with in §§ 4 *et seq.*

§ 3.—PHONETIC MODIFICATIONS OF THE FIVE VOWELS. These are based on ཨ་ A, as representing any of the thirty consonants.

Tibetan Sound.	Romanized Equivalent.	Remarks.
ཨ	a	Short, hard and compact, as already explained. Ex. ཁམས་ K'AM, *Empire, Realm.* Pronounced, as regards the vowel-sound, exactly like that of the English word *Come.* ཨ་ differs from འ་ in that the latter is a long, slow and gentle emanation, while ཨ་ is uttered forcibly.
ཨ+འ་ ཨ+གས་	ā	Long, like *a* in English *far.* Ex. བཀའ་ K'Ā, *Order, Command ;* ལགས་ LĀ, *A courteous expression.*
ཨཱ ཨཱ	ā	Long, like *a* in *far.* Ex. ཀཱ་ཤ་ KĀ-SHA, *A sort of grass ;* ཏཱ་ལའི་བླ་མ་ TĀ-LE-LA-MA, *Dalai Lama,* or ĞYĀ-WA RIM-PO-CH'E ; ལྷ་ས་ L'Ā-SA.
ཨ༹	â, ā, wā,	Long, like the *o* in *corner,* or the *aw* in *Bawl,* or the Chinese *wā* as in *Kwān,* in transliterations from Sanskrit, Indian, Chinese or other foreign languages. Thus, ར་མེ་ཤ༹་ར་ RA-ME-SHÂ-RA, *A holy place near Lanka or Ceylon ;* ཐོའུ་ཀྭན་ T'O-'U-KWĀN, *Last Emperor of China of the Tartar dynasty ;* ཏཱའི་འཆིན་བཱ་དུར་ DÂI-CH'IN-B'Ā-DUR, *A Mongolian King of Tibet.* Or long, like the *a* in *far,* in Tibetan words. Thus, ཚ༹་ TS'Ā, *Salt ;* ཁ་ཏ་ K'Ā-TA, *Crow, mag-pie ;* པ་ཞྭ་ PĀ'-ŹHYĀ, *A mitre-shaped cap.* Or it serves to show that a letter is not a prefix, but an initial. Thus, དྭངས་པོ་ ḊANG-PO, *clear,* which might other-

Tibetan Sound.	Romanized Equivalent.	Remarks.
		wise have read N̆GĂ-PO ; དྭགས་པོ་ D́Ā-PO, *A district of Tibet south-east of* Ü *and Kong-po*, which might otherwise have read ǦĂ-PO.
ཨ+ན ཨ+ད	ä	Short, like *a* in *can*. Ex. གཞན་པ་ ZHYÄN-PA (pronounced ZHYÄM-PA) *other ;* or, དད་པ་ DÄ'-PA, *Faith*.
ཨ+ས ཨ+ལ	ā̈	Long, like *a* in *can't*, as pronounced by a Yankee. Ex. ཉེ་གནས་ NYE-N̈Ā, *Disciple, Pupil* : རྒྱལ་པོ་ or ǦYĀ̈-PO, *King*.
ཨི	i	Short, like *i* in *is*. Ex. ཡིན་པ་ YIN-PA (pronounced YIM-PA), *To be*.
ཨི+གས ཨི+ས ཨི+ལ	ī	Long, like *i* in *ravine*. Ex. འཇིགས་པ་ J̇Ī-PA, *To be afraid ;* གིས་ ǴĪ, *A sign of the Agentive Case ;* དཀྱིལ་ལ་ KYĪ-LA, *Among, amid, in the midst*.
ཨཱི	I	Also long, like *i* in *ravine*. Used in transliterations from foreign languages. Ex. ཤཱི་ལ་ SHĪ-LA, *Moral conduct ;* པུཎྜ་རཱི་ཀ་ PUṆ-DA-RĪ-KA, *White lotus ;* ཤྲཱི་ SHRĪ, *Glory*.
ཨེ	e	Short, like *a* in *made*, or Italian *e*. Ex. དེ་ D́E, *The, That*.
ཨེ+གས ཨེ+ས ཨེ+ལ	ē	Like the preceding, but long. Ex. བགེགས་ GE, *Devil, Demon, Evil-spirit ;* ཤེས་པ་ SHE-PA, *To know ;* སེལ་བ་ SĒL-WA, or SĒ-WA, *To absolve*.

Tibetan Sound.	Romanized Equivalent.	Remarks.
ཨེ+ན་ ཨེ+ད་	è	Short, like *e* in *get*. Ex. ཆེན་པོ CH'ÈN-PO (pronounced CH'ÈM-PO), *Great, Big, Large;* བྱེད་པ་ J'È'-PA, *To do, to act, to perform, to achieve.*
ཨཻ་	ai	Like *i* in *mind*. Ex. ཀཻ་ལཱ་ཤ་ KAI-LĀ-SHA, *A mountain on the N. shore of Lake Manasarowar;* མཻ་ཏྲི་ MAITRI, *Love, Friendship;* ཏཻ་ལིང་ག་ TAI-LING-GA, *The modern Telingana.*
ཨུ་	u	Short, like *u* in *pull*. Ex. ཧུར་པོ་ HUR-PO, *Active;* འབུ་ BU, *Worm;* ཆུ་ CH'U, *Water.*
ཨུ+གས་	ū	Long, like *oo* in *snooze*. Ex. བཞུགས་པ་ ŽHYU PA, *To sit.*
ཨཱུ་ ཨཱུ་	ū	Same as preceding. Ex. བཻ་ཌཱུར་ WAI DU-RYA, *Azure stone, Lapis lazuli;* ཧཱུྃ་ HUM, *A terrifying or angry expression.* ཀྲཱུ་ར་པ་ BRUTAL.
ཨུ+ན་ ཨུ+ད་	ü	Like *u* in French *une*. Ex. བདུན་ DÜN, *Seven;* སྐུད་པ་ KÜ'-PA, *Thread.*
ཨུ+ས་ ཨུ+ལ་	ǖ	Same as last, but long. Ex. དུས་ D'Ǖ, *Period, Time;* ཡུལ་ YǕ, *Land, Country.*
ཨོ་	o	Short, like *o* in *for*, or *rock*. This is the commonest *o* in Tibetan. Ex. ཁྲོམ་ Ṭ'OM,

Tibetan Sound.	Romanized Equivalent.	Remarks.
		Bazaar; ཡག་པོ་ YA'-PO, *Good;* བཟོ་བ་ ŽO-WA, *To build;* ལོ་ LO, *Year;* ཁྱི་མོ་ K'YI-MO, *Bitch;* ཇོ་བོ་ J'O-WO, *Nobleman, master, lord;* པོ་འོ་ PO-'O, *Grandfather.*
ཨོ+གས་	ō	Long, like *o* in *mode.* Ex. ཚོགས་ TS'Ō, *A crowd, a multitude.*
ཨཱོ་	ō	Like the last. Used only in transliterating. Ex. གཱོ་ཏ་མ་ GŌ-TA-MA, *Buddha's name.*
ཨོ+ན་ ཨོ+ད་	ŏ	Short, like *eu* in French *Jeune.* Ex. དགོན་པ་ ĞÖN-PA (pronounced ĞÖM-PA), *A monastery;* ཅོད་པན་ CHÖ'-PÄN, *Diadem.*
ཨོ+ས་ ཨོ+ལ་	ȫ	Same as last, but long. Ex. ཆོས་ CH'Ȫ, *Religion;* ཉ་དོལ་ NYA-D'Ȫ, *Fishing net.*
ཨཽ་	au, ou	Like *ou* in *Noumenon.* Ex. གཽ་རི་མ་ *Gou-ri-ma.* Sometimes also spelt ཨའུ་ or ཨཱུ་ Ex. གའུ་ཏ་མ་ or གཽ་ཏ་མ་ *Gau-ta-ma, Gou-ta-ma.*

NOTES.

1.—In the above Tabular Statement the sign + in column 1 means "as modified by the addition of." It will be seen that the basic, inherent ཨ་ *a* is subject to modifications, not only when qualified by vowel-signs, but also when followed or subjoined by འ *'a*, or when subjoined by ཧ *Ha*, or ྭ *wa-żur*, or when followed by ན *Na*, ལ *La*, ད *Da*, ས *Sa*, and གས *G'a-sa*. which last is sometimes represented by the abbreviation ཏ *Ta-log-ṭa*, i.e. ཏ *Ta* reversed, and called གསདཀྱོག *Ġa-sa-ḋa-kyo'*

2.—In words containing those vowel-modifications which are affected by ལ *la*, the ལ when pronounced, should be uttered very softly. Often it is not pronounced at all. e.g., དངུལ Ṅgüł, or Ṅgü, *Money;* གསོལཇ Söl-j'a, or Sö-j'a, *Tea*.

Where ལ, as a final, is followed by the particle བ *wa*, the latter, in the Colloquial, is often changed into ར *ra*. e.g., མཆོདཔའབུལར (instead of བ) གནངབ Ch'o'-pa ƀü-ra ṅang-wa, *To sacrifice* (Honorific form). Sometimes, however, ལ is merely duplicated. *See* § 18.

3.—In the pronunciation of words containing those vowel-modifications which are affected by ད *D'a*, or ག G'*a*, or sometimes གས *G'a-sa*, the following peculiarity should be noted. In the case of monosyllabic words or final syllables ending in one of the above letters, such letter is not exactly pronounced. Yet it is *hinted at;* for, just before pronouncing it, the speaker stops short, and, by a sharp contraction of the glottis, forms a kind of innominate sound, which perhaps is best described by reference to the Persian or Arabic ع *'ain*, or to the curious throat-sound emitted by some Glaswegians when, instead of saying *Saturday*, they say *Se'urday*, or instead of saying *water*, they say *wa'er*. This emphasized hiatus-sound will be represented by an apostrophe. Ex. བྱེདཔ J'e'-pa, *To do;* ཕྱག Ch'a', *Hand* (Honorific term);

ཉི་གདུགས་ NYI-ĎU', *Parasol.* In particular, as regards syllables ending in ག་ *G'a*, the following rules may be observed :—

(*a*) When the syllable forms a word by itself, like ཅིག་ CHI' (*Chig'*), *A, an ;* འདུག་ ĎU' (*Ďuǵ*), *Is ;* or ཤོག་ SHO' (*Shog'*), Imperative of ཡོང་བ་ YONG-WA, *To come*, the ག་ *G'a* should never be pronounced, but only *hinted* at, in manner above described.

(*b*) When the syllable in which ག་ or གས་ occurs is only one in a word of two or more syllables, and is not the final syllable, the ག་ or གས་ may be pronounced, or only hinted at, at pleasure. Ex. སྡིག་པ་ ĎIG'-PA, or ĎI'-PA, *Sin ;* རྡོག་རྡོག་ ĎOǴ-ĎOǴ, or ĎO'-ĎO', *A Lump ;* ཡག་པོ་ YAǴ-PO, or YA'-PO, *Good ;* མགྱོགས་པོ་ ĞYŌ-PO, or ĞYŌǴ-PO, *Quick*.

(*c*) Practically the same rules may be observed as regards final ལ་ *la*. Ex. ངལ་ NGÄ, *Fatigue*, and སྦྲེལ་བ་ ḌEL-WA, or ḌE-WA, *To fasten on.*

4.—A consonant, having a prefix, but no affix, nor any qualifying vowel-sign, must be supported by the lengthening affix འ་ *'a*, which prevents the prefix from being mistaken for an initial letter. Ex. བཀའ་ K'Ā, *Order, command, word ;* མདའ་ Ď'Ā, *Arrow.*

5.—བ་ *B*, is usually pronounced *W*, when, in a word of more than one syllable, it is the initial letter of the second or other following syllable, and the final letter of the immediately preceding syllable is either ང་འ་ར་ or ལ་, or if such preceding syllable does not end in a consonant, but is governed by inherent ཨ་, or one of the vowel-signs. བ་ also takes the sound of *w* when it is prefixed by ད, *Ḍa*, and has no modifying vowel-sign or *Yata* sign. In the latter case it takes the sound of the modifyng signs. Ex.:— དབང་, WANG, *Power, might, potency* (non-physical); but དབུགས་ U, *Respiration;* དབུ་སྐྲ་ U-ṬA, *Hair* (of head): དབེན་གནས་ ÈN-NÄ, *Lonely spot;* དབོན་པོ་ ÖN-PO, *Grandson, nephew* (Literary term); དབྱར་ YAR, *Summer;* དབྱིངས་ YING, *Region, Space* (e.g., heavenly expanse); དབྱུག་པ་ YUǴ-PA, or YU'-PA, *To brandish, to flourish;* དབྱེན་ཕྱེ་བ་ YÈN-CH'E-WA, *To separate;* but འབངས་ BANG, *A subject;* འབྱུང་བ་ JUNG-WA, *To happen, originate, become, arise.*

The letter བ་ *Ba*, when sounding as a *w*, and followed by འི་ *i*, is pronounced somewhat like the hard Russian vowel öɪ, but with a *w* before it, or something like the English word *way*, save that the *a* must be given the vowel-sound of ཨ་, and merged into the succeeding *i*, so as to make the two into a sort of diphthongal sound.

Second vowels, following immediately after a simple or compound consonant, whether qualified by a vowel-sign or not, are always based on འ་ *'a*, not on ཨ་ *a*. Ex. གའུ་ཏ་མ་ not ག་ཨུ་ཏ་མ་ GAU-TA-MA; ལེའུ་ LE-U, *Chapter;* མིའུ་ MI-U, *Little man.*

§ 4.—The six reversed (i.e ལོག་ lo') letters. Used chiefly in transliterations from Sanskrit, Pāli, etc.

Letter.	Name.	Romanized Equivalent.	Remarks.
ཊ	Ta-loǵ-ṭa or Ǵa-sa-ḋa Kyó	Ṭ	The dental letter ཏ་ *Ta* reversed and pronounced as a palatal. A common abbreviation for the double affix གས་. Ex. དཔུང་རྔེ་ Pung-rō, instead of དཔུང་རོགས།
ཋ	T'a-loǵ't'a	Ṭ'	ཐ་ *T'a* reversed, and pronounced as an aspirated palatal.
ཌ	Ḋa-loǵ-ḍa	Ḍ	ད་ *Ḋa* reversed, and pronounced as an unaspirated palatal, much as some Irishmen pronounce the *th* in *think*.
ཎ	Na-loǵ-ṇa	Ṇ	The dental letter ན་ *Na* reversed, and pronounced as a palatal.
ཥ	Sha-loǵ-K'a	K'	ཤ་ *Sha* reversed, and pronounced like ཁ་ *K'a*.
ཀྵ	Ka-Sha-loǵ-tā-pa (བཏགས་པ) K'ya	K'y	ཀ་ *Ka*, with a reversed ཥ་ *Sha* subjoined. Pronounced like ཁྱ་ *K'ya*, strongly aspirated.

§ 5.—THE SEVEN CONSONANTS TO WHICH ཡ་ *Ya*, IN THE FORM OF ྱ, MAY BE SUBJOINED. ཡ་ so subjoined is called ཡ་བཏགས་ or ཡ་བཏཏ་ YA-TĀ, *Ya-subjoined.*

ཀྱ	This is *Kya*, and it is so pronounced.
ཁྱ	This is *K'ya*, and it is so pronounced.
གྱ	This is *Gya*, and it is pronounced as some Irishmen pronounce *Garden*, *guide*, etc., i.e. *Gyarden*, *Gyide*, etc.
པྱ	This is *Pya*, but YA-TĀ changes the pronunciation into that of ཅ་ *Cha*.
ཕྱ	This is *P'ya*, but YA-TĀ, changes the pronunciation into that of ཆ་ *Ch'a*.
བྱ	This is *Bya* but YA-TĀ' changes the pronunciation into that o ཇ་ That is to say, when བྱ་ is an initial, it is pronounced *J'* which is practical'y like ཅ་ *Cha*; when not an initial, it i pronounced *J*. If prefixed by ད་ *Ḋa*, it is pronounced *Y* and if further qualified by a vowel-sign, it takes the *Y* soun merged into the vowel-sound. Ex. དབྱར་ YAR, *Summer*; དབྱིངས YING, *Region*, *space* (e.g. Heaven's vault); དབྱུག་པ་ YUǴ-PA or YU'-PA, *To brandish*, *flourish*; དབྱེན་ཕྱེ་བ་ YEN-CH'E-WA, *T separate*.
མྱ	This is *Mya*, but YA-TĀ changes the pronunciation to that ཉ་ *Nya*.

§ 6.—The fourteen consonants to which ར་ *Ra*, in the form of ྲ, may be subjoined. ར་ so subjoined is called ར་བཏགས་ or ར་བཏད, Ra-tā, *Ra-subjoined*.

Letter.	Name.	Romanized Equivalent.	Remarks.
ཀྲ	Ka-ra-tā-Ṭa	Ṭ	Like ཊ (All palatals.)
ཁྲ	K'a-ra-tā-Ṭ'a	Ṭ'	.. ཋ
གྲ	Ga-ra-tā-Ḍa	Ḍ	.. ཌ
ཏྲ	Ta-ra-tā-Ṭa	Ṭ	.. ཊ
ཐྲ	T'a-ra-tā-Ṭ'a	Ṭ'	.. ཋ
དྲ	Da-ra-tā-Ḍa	Ḍ	.. ཌ
ནྲ	Na-ra-tā-Ṇa	Ṇ	.. ཎ
པྲ	Pa-ra-tā-Ṭa	Ṭ	.. ཊ
ཕྲ	P'a-ra-tā-Ṭ'a	Ṭ'	.. ཋ
བྲ	Ba-ra-tā-Ḍa	Ḍ	.. ཌ
མྲ	Ma-ra-tā-Ma	M	
ཤྲ	Sha-ra-tā-Shra	Shr	
སྲ	Sa-ra-tā-Sa	S	This is the pronunciation in Literary Tibetan and in Sikhim and Būtān.
	Sa-ra-tā-Ṭa	Ṭ	This palatal pronunciation is the pronunciation in དབུས་ཕལ་སྐད Ü-p'ä-kä', *Colloquial of* Ü.
	Sa-ra-tā-Hra	Hr	Pronunciation in གཙང་ཕལ་སྐད་ Tsang-p'ä-kä', *Colloquial of Tsang.*
ཧྲ	Ha-ra-tā-Hra	Hr	

§ 7.—THE SIX CONSONANTS TO WHICH ཧ་ *Ha*, IN THE FORM ྷ (ཧ་བཏགས་ HA-TĀ), MAY BE SUBJOINED.

With the exception of ལྷ་ *L'ā* (commonly seen *Lhā*), which is frequently met with, these *Ha*-compounds are only used in transliterations from Sanskrit, Pāli, etc. The effect of subjoining ཧ་ *Ha*, is to lengthen and slightly aspirate the consonant. Ex. ལྷ་ས་ L'Ā-SA, *Lhāsa, the Capital of Tibet.*

གྷ་ *G'ā.*	དྷ་ *D'ā* (Dental)	བྷ་ *B'ā.*
ཛྷ་ *Dz'ā.*	ཌྷ་ *Ḍ'ā* (Palatal)	ལྷ་ *L'ā.*

§ 8.—THE SIX *silent* CONSONANTS TO WHICH ལ་ *La* (ལ་བཏགས་ LA-TĀ) IS SUBJOINED.

The effect of subjoining the ལ་ is to raise and emphasize the tone, and to make the sound more compact.

ཀླ་ གླ་ བླ་ རླ་ སླ་ All pronounced ལ་ *La*.

ཟླ་ Pronounced *Ḍa*.

EXAMPLES :—ཀླད་ཀོར་ LÄ'KOR, *Cipher*, such as o, the abbreviated མ་ or ང་; ཀླུ་ LU, *Serpent-demon* ; ཀློག་པ་ LŎG-PA, *To read* ; ཀླག་ཅོར་ LÄ'-CHOR, or LÄG-CHOR, *Clamour, noise*, (Literary) ; གླེན་པ་ LEN-PA *Stupid, foolish* ; ཟླ་བ་ ḌA-WA, *Month, moon* ; བླ་མ་ LA-MA, *Lama* རླུང་ LUNG, *Wind* ; སློབ་པ་ LOB-PA, *To learn, teach*.

§ 9.—THE SIXTEEN CONSONANTS TO WHICH ཝ་ཟུར་ WA-ŹUR, IN TH FORM OF ྭ, IS SUBJOINED.

ྭ is called WA-ŹUR because it is a corner of the letter ཝ་ *Wa*. When scholars from Tibet first visited India to study Buddhist

Literature, they did not realize that the Tibetan letter བ་ represented both *B* and *W* (which in Sanskrit are denoted by ब and व), just as the Bengali letter ব represents them, and that ཝ་ *Wa* was therefore unnecessary. The later scholars, however, did realize it, and since then ཝ་ *Wa* has not been much used in Tibetan. It still survives, however, in some words, and in the form of ྭ WA-ŹUR, subjoined to the consonants now under notice.

As regards Tibetan words, the effect of subjoining ྭ is merely to lengthen somewhat the sound of the vowel inherent in, or qualifying, the consonant. In the following examples the vowel-sound is the inherent ཨ་ *a*, which, when lengthened, is *ā*. Thus :—

ཀྭ་ KĀ, *Oh!*

ཀྭ་ཡེ་ KĀ-YE, *Oh! Holla!*

ཁྭ་ཏ་ K'Ā-TA, *Crow, Magpie.*

གྲྭ་པ་ ḌĀ-PA, *Mouth.*

བསླབ་གྲྭ་ LAB-ḌĀ, *School.*

དྭ་བ་ ḊĀ-WA, *A Medical plant.*

ཙྭ་ TSĀ, *Spunk, tinder.*

རྩྭ་ ṪSĀ, *Grass, herb.*

རྩྭ་ཁ་ ṪSĀ K'A, *Pasture.*

ཚྭ་ TS'Ā, *Salt.*

ཞྭ་ or ཞྭ་མོ་ ŻHYĀ, or ŻHYĀ-MO, *Hat, cap.*

ཟྭ་ ŹĀ, *Nettle.*

རྭ་ RĀ, རྭ་ཅོ་ RĀ-CHO, *Horn, sting.*

ཁྲག་རྭ་ Ṭ'AǴ-RĀ, or Ṭ'A'-RĀ, *Hartshorn.*

ལ་བ་ LĀ-WA, *A species of deer.*

ཤྭ་ SHĀ, *Flood, high water.*

ཤྭ་བ་ SHĀ-WA, *Deer.*

ཤྭ་ཕོ་ SHĀ-P'O, *Stag, buck.*

ཤྭ་མོ་ SHĀ-MO, *Doe, hind.*

ཤྭ་ཕྲུག་ SHĀ-Ṭ'U', *Young deer.*

WA-ŹUR is also used to represent the sound of *wā*, as found in old Tibetan literature, and in Sanskrit, Pāli, Chinese, and other ancient foreign languages. Ex :—

ཧྭགས་ HWĀ, *Sugared medicine like lozenges* (old Tibetan).

ར་མེ་ཤྭ་ར་ RA-ME-SHWĀ-RA, *Rameshwar*, near Ceylon.

ཐོའུ་ཀྭན་ T'O-U KWĀN, *Last Emperor of China of the Tartar dynasty.*

དྭའི་འཆིན་བྷ་དུར་ DWĀI- CH'IN-B'Ā-DUR, *A Mongolian king of Tibet.*

སྭ་བྷ་ཐན་ SWĀ-B'Ā-T'ÄN, *Name of a town.*

It also represents the sound of *â* as found in modern Indian languages, e.g. Bengali, in which that sound and *wā* seem to be interchangeable. Ex. *Swadesi*, *Shâdeshi*.

It is even met with in conjunction with the vowel-sound ~ *Na-ro*. Ex. ཀི་ ཀི་ སྭོ་ སྭོ་ དེ་རིང་ ཉི་མ་ དོ་ KI, KI, SWO, SWO, TE-RING, NYI-MA DO : *Ho, ye gods, to-day is sunny !* (Literary).

WA-ŹUR also sometimes serves to show that a letter which might possibly be mistaken for a prefix is really an initial. Ex. དྭངས་པོ་ ḌANG-PO, *Clear ;* དྭགས་པོ་ ḌĀ'-PO, *A district in Tibet.* If the WA-ŹUR had not been subjoined to the ད་ in these words, one might have read them NGĀ-PO, and ǴĀ-PO.

§ 10.—THE TWELVE CONSONANTS ON WHICH THE *silent* ར་མགོ RA-ĞO-*Ra-Heda* IS PLACED. The effect is to raise the tonic-pitch and emphasize the sound of each consonant, except those that are regarded as masculine. As to masculine letters see § 19. Sign with Romanized equivalent, ˘ above.

> རྐ་ *Ka*, རྒ་ *Ğa*, རྔ་ *N̆ga*, རྗ་ *J̆a*, རྙ་ *N̆ya*, རྟ་ *Ta*,
> རྡ་ *D̆a*, རྣ་ *N̆a*, རྦ་ *Ba*, རྨ་ *M̆a*, རྩ་ *Tsa*, རྫ་ *D̆z'a*.

It will be noticed that རྐ་ *Ka*, རྟ་ *Ta*, རྩ་ *Tsa*, have not got above them the sign for heightening the Tonic-pitch, they being masculine letters and not requiring it.

§ 11.—THE TEN CONSONANTS ON WHICH THE *silent* ལ་མགོ LA-GO, *La-Head*, IS PLACED. It has the same effect as the *Ra-Head*. Sign ˘.

> ལྐ་ *Ka*, ལྒ་ *Ğa*, ལྔ་ *N̆ga*, ལྕ་ *Cha*, ལྗ་ *J̆a*,
> ལྟ་ *Ta*, ལྡ་ *D̆a*, ལྤ་ *Pa*, ལྦ་ *B̆a*, ལྷ་ *L'ā*.

In all these the ལ་ is not pronounced, except in the case of ལྷ་ *L'ā*, and except also when there is a preceding syllable which ends in a vowel. In this latter case the ལ་ is usually carried back and given the sound of ན་ *n*. Ex. སྒོ་ལྕགས་ GÖN-CHĀ, *Lock;* ད་ལྟ་ DÄN-TA, *Now*. Sometimes, however, it is carried back as ལ་, but not sounded. Yet it modifies the preceding vowel. Ex. རྟ་ལྕག་ TĀ-CHA', *Whip*. Sometimes it even takes the sound of final བ་ *b*. Ex. བཞོ་ལྟ་ ŻOB-TA, *Mien*.

§ 12.—THE TWELVE CONSONANTS ON WHICH THE *silent* ས་མགོ SA-ĞO, *Sa-Head*, IS PLACED. It also has the same effect as the *Ra-Head*. Sign ˘.

> སྐ་ *Ka*, སྒ་ *Ğa*, སྔ་ *N̆ga*, སྙ་ *N̆ya*, སྟ་ *Ta*, སྡ་ *D̆a*,
> སྣ་ *N̆a*, སྤ་ *Pa*, སྦ་ *Ba*, སྨ་ *M̆a*, སྩ་ *Tsa*, སྫ་ *D̆z'a*.

§ 13.—སྔོན་འཇུག་ལྔ་ Ňgön-Ju' ňga, The five Prefixes, i.e. silent letters, which are prefixed to divers *Initial* (sometimes called *Radical*) letters, simple and complex, in the formation of words. Their effect is to remove the aspirate, if any, of low-toned, i.e. Feminine and Very Feminine initials, and to raise the Tonic Pitch, and make the sound more compact. Thus, take བྱུང་ J'ung, the Perfect and Imperative root of འབྱུང་བ་ J̌ung-wa, *To happen, originate, arise.* Here བ་ is a feminine letter, and therefore low-toned, and, as an initial with ྱ *Ya-tā*, it is slightly aspirated in བྱུང་. The addition of the prefix འ་ *'a* removes the aspirate, and makes the Tonic Pitch higher, and the sound more compact.

These prefixes are really a kind of Prepositive Affixes, sometimes modifying the meaning of a word, and sometimes entering into the formation of the Present, Perfect and Future Tenses of a verb. Though doubtless once upon a time actually pronounced, they are now generally silent. In the case, however, of ག་, བ་, and མ་, when the syllable in which any of them occurs is preceded by a syllable ending in a vowel-sound, the ག་, བ་, or མ་ is often carried back in pronunciation to the vowel-sound and sounded with it. The prefixes ད་ and འ་ are never sounded or carried back. As regards འ་ and མ་ the Colloquial has a curious custom of transmuting them into the sound of ན་ *N*. Ex. མེ་མདའ་ Me-ď'ā is pronounced Mèn-ď'ā, *Gun;* མི་འདུག་ Mi-ďu' is pronounced Min-ďu', *Is not;* འདྲ་འདྲ་ Ḍa-ḍa is pronounced Ḍän-ḍa, *similar.* Also བ་, as a prefix, is sometimes given the sound of མ་ *m*. Ex. ན་བཟའ་ Na-ž'ā is pronounced Nam-ž'ā, *clothes.*

No letters are ever superposed upon or subjoined to any prefix; and, as will be seen when we come to the paragraph on the Tone System (§ 19), Prefixes, as such, are of genders different from those of the same letters as Initials, or even as Affixes, save in the case of མ་ which is always Very Feminine.

གཡ་ *Ǵa.* This prefix is of COMMON GENDER, and it is found before the following Initials, namely, ཅ་ *Cha*, ཉ་ *Nya*, ཏ་ *Ta*, ད་ *Ḋa*, ན་ *Na*, ཙ་ *Tsa*, ཞ་ *Źhya*, ཟ་ *Za*, ཡ་ *Ya*, ཤ་ *Sha*, and ས་ *Sa*, all of which retain their natural sounds unaffected by the ག་ save as regards Tonic Pitch and compactness of utterance, as already explained. This prefix is found in many nouns. It also enters into the formation of the Present and Future Roots of certain verbs. Ex. གནས་ཚང་ NĂ-TS'ANG, *Inn;* གཏོང་ ŤONG, Present Root, and གཏང་ TANG, Future Root, of གཏོང་བ་ ŤONG-WA, *To send, dismiss.*

ད་ *Ḋa.* This prefix is of COMMON GENDER, and is met with before the following Initial letters, namely, ཀ་ *Ka*, ག་ *Ǵa*, ང་ *Nga*, པ་ *Pa*, བ་ *Ba*, and མ་ *Ma*, and nine other letters which are merely compounds of these with *Ya-tā'*, or *Ra-tā'*. It also enters into the formation of the Future Root of certain verbs. Ex. དབུལ་ Ü, Future Root of འབུལ་བ་ BÜ-WA, *To offer;* དགབ་ ǦAB, Future Root of འགེབས་པ་ GEB-PA, *To cover.*

བ་ *Ba.* This prefix is of MASCULINE GENDER, and occurs before the Initials ཀ་ *Ka*, ག་ *Ǵa*, ཅ་ *Cha*, ཇ་ *Ja*, ཉ་ *Nya*, ཏ་ *Ta*, ད་ *Ḋa*, ན་ *Na*, ཙ་ *Tsa*, ཛ་ *Dz'a*, ཞ་ *Źhya*, ཟ་ *Źa*, ར་ *Ra*, ཤ་ *Sha*, ས་ *Sa*, and twenty-nine other letters, compounds of the foregoing, some having one or other of the different subjuncts, and some even one or other of the three different superposed letters. It is a very common prefix, and enters into the formation of the Perfect and Future Tenses of many verbs. Ex. བསྐོར་ KOR, Perfect Root and Future Root of སྐོར་བ་ KOR-WA, *To Surround;* བཞོས་ ZHYÖ, Perfect Root, and བཞོ་ ZHYO, Future Root of འཇོ་བ་ JO-WA, *To milk.*

མ་ *Ma.* This prefix is of VERY FEMININE GENDER, and occurs before ཁ་ *Ka*, ག་ *Ǵa*, ང་ *Nga*, ཚ་ *Ch'a*, ཇ་ *Ja*, ཉ་ *Nya*, ཐ་ *T'a*, ད་ *Ḍa*, ན་ *Na*, ཚ་ *Ts'a*, ཛ་ *Dz'a* and four other letters, compounds of some of the foregoing in *Ya-tā*, or *Ra-tā*.

འ་ *'A.* This Prefix is of FEMININE GENDER, and is found before ཁ་ *K'a*, ག་ *Ǵa*, ཚ་ *Ch'a*, ཇ་ *Ja*, ཐ་ *T'a*, ད་ *Ḍa*, ཕ་ *P'a*, བ་ *Ba*, ཚ་ *Ts'a*, ཛ་ *Dz'a*, and nine other letters, compounds of some of the foregoing in *Ya-tā*, or *Ra-tā*.

The raising-power (if any) of these prefixes, as regards Tone, depends upon their gender as mentioned above, the masculine prefix བ་ *Ba* possessing the greatest power.

§ 14.—The following Tabular Statement of the consonants (in their simple form) which, as Initial Radical letters, take prefixes, and of the particular prefix or prefixes which, and which alone, each such consonant takes, may be found of use, especially in cases where the student feels some difficulty in determining whether any particular letter is or is not a prefix. For instance, no letter except ད་ *Ḍa*, or བ་ *Ba*, immediately preceding a ཀ *Ka*, can be a prefix; no letter except མ་ *Ma*, or འ་ *'A*, immediately preceding a ཁ་ *K'a*, can be a prefix; and so on.

Initial or Radical letter.	Prefix or Prefixes taken.	Example.
ཀ	ད	དཀར་པོ་ *Kar-po*, White.
	བ	བཀྲ་ཤིས་ *Ṭa-shī*, Joy, Prosperity, Blessing.

Initial or Radical letter.	Prefix or Prefixes taken.	Example.
ཁ	མ	མཁན་པོ་ *K'än-po*, Abbot.
	འ	འཁྱེར་བ་ *K'yer-wa*, or འཁུར་བ་ *K'ur-wa*, To carry away.
ག	ད	དགའ་བ་ *G'ā-wa*, Joy, Happiness.
	བ	བགེགས་ *Ğē*, Demon.
	མ	མགོ་ *Ğo*, Head.
	འ	འགྱེལ་བ་ *Ğyē-wa*, To fall, Stumble.
ང	ད	དངུལ་ *N̆gü*, Money, Silver.
	མ	མངར་མོ་ *N̆gar-mo*, Sweet.
ཅ	ག	གཅོག་པ་ *Choǵ-pa*, To break (Transitive).
	བ	བཅུག་པ་ *Chuǵ-pa*, To allow.
ཆ	མ	མཆོ་ལྟོ་ *Ch'o-to*, Beak.
	འ	འཆམ་ *Ch'am*, Masquerade.
ཇ	བ	གཟི་བརྗིད་ *Zi-ǰi'*, Glory, Splendour.
	མ	མཛལ་བ་ *J̆ä-wa*, To meet.
	འ	འཇིགས་པ་ *J̆ī-pa*, To be afraid.
ཉ	ག	གཉེར་ཚང་ *N̆yer-ts'ang*, Pantry.
	བ	བསྙེལ་བ་ *N̆yē-wa*, To ferment.
	མ	མཉེན་སད་པ་ *N̆yèn-sä'-pa*, To rouse.

Initial or Radical letter.	Prefix or Prefixes taken.	Example.
ཏ	ག	གཏམ་ *Tam*, Rumour.
	བ	བཏོན་པ་ *Tön-pa*, To cast out.
ཐ	མ	མཐའ་ *T''ā*, End.
	འ	འཐུང་བ་ *T'ung-wa*, To drink.
ད	ག	གདོང་ *D̆ong*, Face.
	བ	བདེ་པོ་ *D̆e-po*, Good, Well.
	མ	མདའ་ *D̆'ā*, Arrow.
	འ	འདམ་པ་ *D̆am-pa*, To choose.
ན	ག	གནོད་པ་ *N̆ö'-pa*, Injury.
	བ	བསྣར་བ་ *N̆ar-wa*, To lengthen, Extend.
	མ	མནའ་ *N̆'ā*, Oath.
པ	ད	དཔང་པོ་ *Pang-po*, Witness.
ཕ	འ	འཕེལ་བ་ *P'ē-wa*, To increase.
བ	ད	དབུགས་ *Ū*, Breath ; དབྱར་ཀ་ *Yar-ka*, Summer.
	འ	འབར་བ་ *Bar-wa*, To blaze up.
མ	ད	དམག་མི་ *M̆aǵ-mi*, Soldier.
ཙ	ག	གཙང་པོ་ *Tsang-po*, River.
	བ	བཙོན་ཁང་ *Tsön-K'ang*, Prison, Jail.

Initial or Radical letter.	Prefix or Prefixes taken.	Example.
ཚ	མ	མཚོ་ *Ts'o*, Lake.
	འ	འཚིག་པ་ *Ts'ig'-pa*, To burn (Intransitive).
ཛ	བ	བརྫུན་ *Dzün*, Lie, Falsehood.
	མ	མཛེས་པོ་ *Dzē-po*, Lovely.
	འ	འཛིང་ར་ *Ďzing-ra*, Fortification.
ཝ	None	
ཞ	ག	གཞན་པ་ *Żȟyän-pa* (pro. *Żȟyäm-pa*), Another.
	བ	ནང་བཞིན་ *Nang-z'ȟyin*, According to.
ཟ	ག	གཟུགས་པོ་ *Ž̌ū-po*, Body.
	བ	བཟོ་བལྟ་ *Ž'ob-ta*, Likeness.
འ	None.	
ཡ	ག	གཡག་ *Ya'*, or *Y̌aǵ*, Bull, Yak.
ར	བ	བརླ་ཤ་ *Ła-sha*, Thigh.
ལ	None.	
ཤ	ག	གཤེ་གཤེ་བཏང་བ་ *She-she tang-wa.* To rebuke.
	བ	བཤད་པ་ *Shä'-pa*. To tell.

Initial or Radical letter.	Prefix or Prefixes taken.	Example.
ས	ག	གསལ་པོ་ *Sä-po*, Bright, Clear.
	བ	བསོད་བདེ་སྐམ་པོ་ *Sö'-de kam-po*, Misfortune.
ཧ	None.	
ཨ	None.	

NOTES.

1.—Letters are either simple, like ཀ་, or complex, like ཀྲ་, སྐ་, ཀྲུ་, བཀྲ་, དཀོར་, and so forth. Syllables in which Prefixes occur may consist of two, three, or four such letters. For the purpose of ascertaining what letters are Prefixes, complex letters may be regarded as one letter. No letter that has another letter superadded to it, or subjoined to it, or which is qualified by any of the vowel-signs ི, ུ, ེ, ོ, can be a Prefix.

2.—In the case of a two-letter syllable, whenever the second letter is qualified by a vowel-sign, or is otherwise complex, the first letter, if one of the five mentioned in § 13, may be taken to be a Prefix.

Ex.—མཚོ་ TS'O, *A lake;* བཀྲ་མི་ཤིས་ ṬA-MI-SHI, *Calamity.*

3.—In the case of a two-letter syllable in which both letters are simple letters, then, even if the first letter is one of the five mentioned in § 13, it is not a Prefix, but an Initial or Radical. Ex.— བག་གག་ BA'-GA', *Cake of tea;* བབ་ཡོང་བ་ BAB-YONG-WA, *To descend.*

4.—In the case of a syllable consisting of more than two letters, the first, if one of the five mentioned in § 13, may be taken to be a Prefix. This is so whether the next letter is or is not simple.

Ex. འབབ་པ་ (the Literary form of བབ་ཡོང་བ་) BAB́-PA, *To descend*; མཁན་པོ་ K'ÄN-PO, *Abbot*; བཀོད་པ་ KÖ'PA, *To create*. Very rarely it is otherwise, as in the case of the ད་ in the word རི་དྭགས་ RI-ḊĀ, *Wild animal*. Such words are often written with a *wa-źur* under the ད, to show that it is not a Prefix, but an Initial. Thus རི་དྭགས་. It is then still pronounced RI-ḊĀ.

5.—Should the Prefix be ད, and the Initial be simple བ་, then བ་ loses its *b* sound, and is pronounced *w*, or *w* as modified by the next letter, if any, such as ན་ *Na*, ལ་ *La*, or ས་ *Sa* (*see* VOWEL MODIFICATIONS, § 3). Should, however, the བ་ be accompanied by ྱ (*ya-tā*), or any vowel-sign, it similarly loses its *w* sound, and takes that of the *ya-tā* or of the vowel-sign. Ex.—དབང་ Not ḂANG, but W̆ANG, *Authority, Power*; དབལ་ W̆Ä, *Pinnacle, Spire*; དབྱར་ Y̆AR, *Summer*; དབུར་ ŎR, *A place in Tibet*; དབོན་པོ་ ÖN-PO, *Nephew of a Lama*. If the བ་ be accompanied by ྲ (*Ra-tā*), it acquires the sound of *ḍ*, i.e. palatal *d* (*see* § 6). Ex.— དབྲ་ ḌA, *Name of a Tibetan tribe*; དབྲག་ ḌA' *Interstice*.

§ 15.—PECULIARITIES OF PRONUNCIATION.

1.—When a syllable beginning with one of the Prefixes ག་, བ་, or མ་, follows another syllable ending in a vowel-sound, the Prefix is often in the Colloquial carried back, sometimes with its own sound, sometimes with a changed sound, to the preceding syllable, and pronounced as if it were part of it. Ex.—

བཅུ་གཅིག་ CHU-CHI', pronounced CHUǴ-CHI', *Eleven*.

བཅུ་བཞི CHU-ŹHYI, pronounced CHUB-ŹHYI, *Fourteen*.

ར་བཟི་ RA-Ž'I, pronounced RAB-Ž'I, *Drunk.*

བཀའ་བཀྱོན་གནང་བ་ (*Hon.*) K'Ā-KYÖN-ÑANG-WA, pronounced K'ĀB-KYÖN-ÑANG-NGA, *To censure.*

ན་བཟའ་ (*Hon.*) NA-Ž'Ā, pronounced NAM-Ž'Ā, *Clock, Clothes.*

ཁ་མཆུ་ K'A-CH'U, pronounced K'AM-CH'U, *Law suit.*

ཡ་མཚན་པོ་ YA-TS'ĀN-PO, pronounced YAM-TS'ĀM-PO, *Astonishing.*

2.—The Prefixes ད་ and འ་ are never themselves carried back; but in the case of འ་ and also of མ་ the sound of *n* is sometimes substituted, and pronounced with the preceding syllable. Ex.—

མཐོ་འདོད་ T'O-ḌÖ', pronounced T'ÖN-ḌÖ', *Ambition.*

མི་འདུག་ MI-ḌU', pronounced MIN-ḌU', *Is not, are not.*

དགེ་འདུན་ (*Hon.*) ǦE-ḌÜN, pronounced ǦEN-ḌÜN, *Clergy.*

ཞལ་འགྲམ་ (*Hon.*) ŹHYĀ-ḌAM, pronounced ŹHYĀN-ḌAM, *Cheek.*

སྣོན་འབེལ་སྣད་པ་ ÑÖN-BE ṬĀ'-PA, pronounced ÑÖM-BE ṬĀ'-PA, *To add.*

མེ་མདའ་ ME-Ḍ'Ā, pronounced MEN-Ḍ'Ā, *Gun.*

མེ་མདག་ ME-ḌA', pronounced MEN-ḌA', *Ember.*

3.—Even when the first syllable ends in ག་, the same custom sometimes holds, probably because of the incomplete way in which final ག་ is uttered, the syllable therefore seeming to end in a vowel-sound. Ex.—

ཕྱག་མདུད་ (*Hon.*) CH'AǴ-ḌÜ', or CH'A'-ḌÜ', pronounced CH'ĀN-ḌÜ', *Knot.*

.—The sound of *n* is sometimes transmuted into that of *m*. Ex.—

མཁན་པོ་ K'ĀN-PO, pronounced K'ĀM-PO, *Abbot.*

ཡིན་པ་ YIN-PA, pronounced YIM-PA, *To be* (copula).

སྣོན་འབེལ་སྟད་པ་ ŇÖN-BĒ ṬÄ'-PA, pronounced ŇÖM-BE ṬÄ'-PA, *To add.*

གཞན་པ་ ZHYÄN-PA, pronounced ZHYÄM-PA, *Other.*

5.—The sound of ལ་ as final of first syllable is also sometimes changed into that of *m*. Ex.—

མགུལ་ཆམ་ (*Hon.*) ǦÜ-CH'AM, pronounced ǦUN-CH'AM, *Catarrh.*

རྒྱལ་མཚན་ ǦYÄ-TS'ÄN, pronounced ǦYÄN-TS'ÄN, *Banner of Victory.*

.—The sounds that are latent in superadded letters, sometimes result in audible sounds, pronounced with the preceding syllable. Ex.—

གསོལ་ལྡོང་ (*Hon.*) SÖ-ĎONG, pronounced SÖN-ĎONG, *Churn.*

ཇ་ལྡོང་ J'A-ĎONG, pronounced J'ÄN-ĎONG, *Tea churn.*

བཅོ་ལྔ་ CH'O-ŇGA, pronounced CH'Ö-ŇGA, *Fifteen.*

མཆོད་རྟེན་ CH'Ö'-TÈN, pronounced CH'ÖR-TÈN, *A monument containing the ashes of a saint or other relics.*

—ར་ *Ra* as a final is frequently pronounced so softly as to be almost unheard. Ex.—

སེར་ཀ་ SER-KA, pronounced SE-KA, *Chink.*

ཡར་ལ་ YAR-LA, pronounced ཡ་ལ་ YĀ-LA, *Above.*

དམར་ཧྲང་ང་ (བ་) MAR-HRANG-WA, pronounced MA-HRANG-NGA, *Naked.*

བར་ལ་ BAR-LA, pronounced BA-LA, *Between.*

དུར་ཁྲོད་ ĎUR-Ṭ'Ö', pronounced ĎU-Ṭ'Ö', *Cemetery.*

འུར་སྒྲ་ 'UR-ḌA, pronounced U-ḌA, *Noise.*

དཀར་ཡོལ་ KAR-YÖ, pronounced KA-YÖ, *Earthen mug or cup.*

ཚར་ TSAR, pronounced TSA, *Margin*

གསེར་ SER, pronounced SE, *Gold.*

འཁར་ངྒ་ K'AR-ŇGA, pronounced K'A-ŇGA, *Gong.*

གསར་པ་ SAR-PA, pronounced SA-PA, *New.*

8.—When the first of two syllables ends in a vowel-sound, and the next syllable consists of བ་ *wa*, the latter often takes the sound of *a*. Ex.—

ལྕུ་བ་ CHU-WA, pronounced CHU-A, *Dung of cattle.*

9.—The following is a common case of བ་ *wa*, or པ་ *pa*, being reduced to the sound of *a* :—

ཡོད་བ་རེད་ YÖ'-WA-RÈ } pronounced YAW-A-RÈ'. *Is, are, was, were* (in the sense of possibly or probably being).
ཡོད་པ་རེད་ YÖ'-PA-RÈ

10.—When the first of two syllables ends in ལ་, and the next syllable is བ་ *wa*, the latter is often pronounced as ར་ *ra*, but sometimes it is reduced to a mere *a*. Ex.—

མཇལ་བ་གནང་བ་ (*Hon.*) JĂ-WA ŇANG-WA, pronounced JĂ-RA ŇANG-NGA, *To meet.*

ཡོལ་བ་ YÖ-WA, pronounced YÖL-A, *Curtain.*

11.—The above are samples of irregularities with which one sometimes meets; practice alone will enable the student to know when other words similarly spelt follow these Colloquial customs, and when they ought to be pronounced according to the regular rules. The following are a few more specimens of irregular pronunciations :—

མ་མྱོང་ MA-NYONG, pronounced MA-NYUNG, *Never.*

སུས་ཤེས་ཀྱི་འདུག་ SÜ SHE KYI ĎU', pronounced SÜ SHIN-ĠI ĎU', *Who knows?*

ཁ་ལས་བཤད་པ་ K'A LĂ SHĂ'-PA pronounced K'AB-LĂ SHĂ'-PA, *To chat.*

ཕེབ་པ་ (*Hon.*) P'EB-PA, pronounced P'E-PA, *To arrive, depart, come, go.*

བཞུགས་འབོལ་ (*Hon.*) ŹHYU-ĎŐ, pronounced ŽHYUM-BŐ, *Mattress.*

ཞལ་འབག་ (*Hon.*) ZHYĂ-ĎA', pronounced ZHYĂM-ĎA', *Mask.*

ལྷ་བྲི་པ་ L'Ā-ḌI-PA, pronounced L'AB-RI-PA, *Painter.*

སྨོན་ལམ་ MÖN-LAM, pronounced MÖ-LAM, *Prayer.*

སྐྱབས་མགོན་ KYAB-ĞÖN, pronounced KYAM-ĞÖN, *Helper, Protector, Saviour.*

§ 16.—THE TEN CONSONANTAL AFFIXES, called རྗེས་འཇུག་བཅུ་ JE-JU' CHU, each of which, when following an Initial, simple or complex, completes the formation of a syllable.

ག་ *Ǵa,*	ང་ *Nga,*	ན་ *Na,*	བ་ *Ba,*	མ་ *Ma,*
འ་ *'A,*	ར་ *Ra,*	ལ་ *La,*	ད་ *Ḋa,*	ས་ *Sa.*

Of these ག་, ང་, བ་, and མ་ are frequently seen with an additional silent ས་, or SECOND AFFIX, called ཡང་འཇུག་ YANG-JU'. They are then called DOUBLE AFFIXES.

Another kind of DOUBLE AFFIXES is met with in old Tibetan books It is very rare, but for Literary purposes the student may as well make a note of it. It consists of ན་ *Na,* ར་ *Ra,* or ལ་ *La,* followed by ད་ *Ḋa,* here called ད་དྲག་ ḊA-ḌA', *Hard Ḍ.* Thus :—

ནད་ *nḍ,* རད་ *rḍ,* ལད་ *lḍ.*

It is used to express the Past Tense. Ex:—

གསནད་པ་ SĂNḌ-PA, *He heard.*

གྱུརད་པ་ GYURḌ-PA, *He became.*

གསོལད་པ་ SÖLḌ-PA, *He requested*

The modern Literary practice, however, is to omit the final ད, which may be regarded as obsolete.

As to the pronunciation of the affixes ག, ན, འ, ལ, ད, ས, *see* § 3, TABULAR STATEMENT of VOWEL MODIFICATIONS, and NOTES thereto.

The DICTIONARY ORDER of the above-mentioned ten Consonantal Finals, and of the four Double Finals in ས, is as follows:—

1.	ག	..	*ǵa.*	8.	བས	..	*ḃa-sa.*
2.	གས	..	*ǵa-sa.*	9.	མ	..	*ma.*
3.	ང	..	*nga.*	10.	མས	..	*ma-sa.*
4.	ངས	..	*nga-sa.*	11.	འ	..	*'a.*
5.	ད	..	*ḋa.*	12.	ར	..	*ra.*
6.	ན	..	*na.*	13.	ལ	..	*la.*
7.	བ	..	*ḃa.*	14.	ས	..	*su.*

The above, of course, is their order under each letter of the ཀ་ཁ KA-K'A; that is to say, it is their order after, or in subordination t the *Alphabetical Order*, if that term may be used in connection wit the ཀ་ཁ།

As to the Gender of the Ten Final Affixes, *see* § 19.

§ 17.—སླར་བསྡུ་བ་བཅུ་གཅིག LAR-ḊU-WA CHUǴ-CHI', THE ELEVEN D PLICATIONS in ཨོ་ *o*, of certain letters when forming the termina of verbs. The Duplication has the effect of emphasizing, or inten fying, or solemnizing the expression of a fact. It is a feature Literary Tibetan only, and is met with in nearly every senten of the existing translation into Tibetan of the New Testament.

ཀོ་ *Ǵo,* ངོ་ *Ngo,* དོ་ *D́o,* ནོ་ *No,* བོ་ *B́o, Wo,*

འ་ *'O,* རོ་ *Ro,* ལོ་ *Lo,* སོ་ *So,* ཏོ་ *To.*

EXAMPLES :—

1.—སུས་ཀྱང་ཁོང་ལ་ལག་པ་མ་རེག་གོ། *Sü-kyang k'ong-la laǵ-pa ma re'-ǵo:* And no man laid hands on him.

In the Colloquial this would be :—

སུས་ཡང་ཁོ་ལ་ལག་པ་མ་བཞག་ག་ (for བཞག་པ་) རེད་ or བཞག་མ་སོང་། *Sü yang k'o-la laǵ-pa ma źhyaǵ-ǵa* (for *źhyaǵ-pa*) *rè'* or *źhyaǵ-ma song.*

2.—ཡི་ཤཱ་ཡི་བུ་རྒྱལ་པོ་ད་བིད་བྱུང་ངོ་། *Yi-shā-yi b́u ǵyä-po D́a-wid́ j'ung ngo:* Jesse's son was king David =Jesse begat David the king.

In the Colloquial this might be :—

ཡི་ཤཱའི་བུ་རྒྱལ་པོ་ད་བིད་ཡིན། *Yi-shāi b́u ǵyä-po D́a-wid́ yin:* Jesse's son was King David.

or :—

ཡི་ཤཱ་ཡིས་རྒྱལ་པོ་ད་བིད་བསྐྱེད་སོང་། *Yi-shā-yī ǵyä-po D́a-wid́ kyè'-song:* Jesse begat King David.

3.—ཁྱོད་ཚོའི་ནང་ན་སྲོག་མེད་དོ། *K'yö'-ts'öi nang-na ṭo' mè'-d́o:* Ye have not life in yourselves.

Colloquially :—

ཁྱོད་རང་ཚོའི་ནང་ལ་སྲོག་མེད། *K'yö'-rang-ts'öi nang-la ṭo' mè'.*

4.—ཁྱོད་ཀྱི་བུ་གསོན་ནོ། *K'yö' kyi b́u sön-no:* Thy son liveth.

Colloquially :—

ཁྱོད་རེའི་བུ་གསོན་གྱི་འདུག། *K'yö' rei b́u sön-ǵyi d́u'.*

5.—ང་ག་རུ་ཡོད་ས་ལ་བསླེབ་མི་ཐུབ་བོ། *Nga ǵa-ru yö'-sa la leb mi t'ub́-b́o:* Where I am, ye cannot come.

Colloquially :—

ང་ཀ་པ་ཡོད་ས་ལ་ཡོང་ཐུབ་ཀྱི་མན་ or ཡོང་མི་ཐུབ།

Nga ǵa--pa yö'-sa la yong t'ub-kyi män, or *yong mi t'ub.*

6.—ཡང་ངས་དེ་ཐ་མའི་ཉིན་པར་སླང་བར་བྱའོ།

Yang ngä ḋe t'a-mai nyin par lang-war j'a-o : And I will raise him up at the last day.

Colloquially :—

ཡང་ངས་དེ་ཉི་མ་གཞུག་ཤོས་ལ་ཡར་ཀྱག་ཡོང་།

Yang ngä ḋe nyi-ma źhyuǵ-shö la yar kya' yong.

7.—དཀོན་མཆོག་གི་ཐུགས་འཁྲོ་བ་དེ་ལ་གནས་པར་འགྱུར་རོ་ or འབྱུང་བར་འགྱུར་རོ།

Kön-ch'o' ǵi t'ü'-ṭ'o-wa ḋe la nä-par ǵyur-ro : The wrath of God will abide on him.

Colloquially :—

དཀོན་མཆོག་གི་བཀའ་ཆད་དེ་ལ་ (or ཁོ་ལ་) ཡོང་གི་རེད།

Kön-ch'o' ǵi k'ä-ch'ä' de la (or *k'o la*) *yong-ǵi-rè'.*

8.—ཡང་ཁོང་གིས་ང་ལ་དཀོན་མཆོག་ལ་བསྙེན་བཀུར་བྱོས་ཤིག་ཅེས་གསུངས་སོ།

Yang k'ong ǵi nga-la kön-ch'o' la nyèn-kur j'ö shi' chē sung-so : Then said he unto me, worship God.

Colloquially :—

དེ་ནས་ཁོ་རེས་ང་ལ་དཀོན་མཆོག་ལ་སྨོན་ལམ་ཐོབ་དག་ག་རང་ལབ་བྱུང་།

Ḋe-nä k'o-rē nga la kön-ch'o' la mö-lam t'ob ḋaǵ-ǵa-rang lab-j'ung.

9.—དེ་ནས་ནམ་མཁའ་ན་ལྟས་གཞན་ཞིག་མཐོང་བར་གྱུར་ཏོ།

Ḋe nä nam-k''ä na tä źhyän źhyi t'ong-war ǵyur-to : And there was seen another sign in heaven.

Colloquially :—

དེ་ནས་ནམ་མཁའ་ལ་ཡ་མཚན་གཞན་པ་ཅིག་མཐོང་བྱུང་། *Ḍe-nä nam-k'ā la yam-ts'än żhyäm-pa chi' t'ong j'ung.*

N.B.—དོ་ is used only with the Literary Perfect root after final ར་, ལ་, ན་ (for རད་, ལད་, ནད་)||

The Full stop |, or ||, will henceforth be omitted. *See* WRITING AND PUNCTUATION, § 20.

§ 18.—COLLOQUIAL DUPLICATIONS.

As regards certain verbs in the Infinitive Mood, or in the Perfect tense of the Indicative Mood, i.e. verbs, the roots of which end in the final consonant ག་, གས་, ང་, ངས་, ལ་, or ར་, the following custom obtains in the Colloquial. Instead of pronouncing in the ordinary way the particle པ་ or བ་ that follows the root, the speaker merely duplicates, or emphasizes with an added *a* sound, the final consonantal sound.

Thus, as regards the Infinitive Mood, instead of saying སྒྲོག་པ་གནང་བ་ (*Hon.*) ḌOǴ-PA ŇANG-WA; the Colloquial speaker would say སྒྲོག་ག་གནང་ང་ ḌOǴ-ǴA-NANG-NGA, *To proclaim or publish.*

So, too, as regards the Perfect Indicative, instead of saying ངས་བསྒྲགས་པ་ཡིན་ ŇGÄ ḌÄ OR ḌÄǴ-PA YIN, he would say ངས་བསྒྲགས་ག་ཡིན་ ŇGÄ ḌÄǴ-ǴA YIN, *I proclaimed, I have proclaimed.*

Other Examples are :—

སེལ་ལ་ (for བ་) གནང་བ་ (*Hon.*) SĒ-LA (for WA) NANG-WA, or NANG-NGA: *To absolve.*

སྐུ་གཞོགས་ཀྱིས་སེལ་ལ་ (for བ་) གནང་ (for བ་) ཡིན་ (*Hon.*) KUSHŌ KYI SĒ-LA (for WA) ŇANG-NGA (for WA) YIN; *the master absolved or has absolved.*

གཙོ་བོས་བསལ་ལ་ (for བ་) གནང་བ་ཡིན་ (*Vulg.*) Tso-wö sä-la (for wa) nang-nga (for wa) yin ; *The lord absolved or has absolved.*

ནོར་ར་ (for བ་) གནང་བ་ (*Hon.*) Nor-ra (for wa) ňang-nga, *To err.*

སྐུ་གཞོགས་ཀྱིས་ནོར་ར་ (for བ་) གནང་ང་ (for བ་) ཡིན་ (*Hon.*) Kushō kyi nor-ra (for wa) ňang-nga (for wa) yin : or still better : –

སྐུ་གཞོགས་ཀྱིས་ཐུགས་ནོར་གནང་ང་ (for བ་) or ཐུགས་ནོར་ཤོར་ར་ (for བ་) ཡིན་ Ku-źhyō-kyi t'ū nor ňang-nga (for wa), or t'ū nor shor-ra (for wa) yin, *The master erred, or has erred.*

ངས་ནོར་ར་ (for བ་) ཡིན་ (*Vulg.*) Ngä nor-ra (for wa) yin : *I erred, I have erred.*

སྤོང་ང་ (for བ་) གནང་བ་ (*Hon.*) Pong-nga (for wa) ňang-nga : *To shun, To renounce.*

ཁོང་གིས་སྤོང་ང་ (for བ་) གནང་ང་ (for པ་) རེད་ (*Hon.*) K'ong-gi pong-nga (for wa) ňang-nga (for pa) rè' : *He shunned, He has shunned.*

ཁོ་རེས་སྤངས་ང་ (for པ་) རེད་ (*Vulg.*) K'o-rē pang-nga (for pa) rè' : *He shunned, He has shunned.*

When the root ends in final ལ་, the Colloquial sometimes resorts to a following ར་, instead of the Duplication as above. Ex.—

འགྱེལ་བ་ Ğyē-wa, *To stumble.*

འགྱེལ་ར་ (for བ) གནང་བ་ (*Hon.*) Ğyē-ra (for wa) ňang-nga : *To stumble.*

ཁོང་འགྱེལ་ར་ (for བ) གནང་ང་ (for པ་) ཡིན་ (*Hon.*) K'ong ğye-ra (for wa) ňang-nga (for pa) yin : *He stumbled, He has stumbled.*

At the same time this were better phrased thus:—

ཁོང་སྐུ་བབ་ (for སྐུ་དབ་) ཤོར་ར་ (for བ་) རེད་ K'ONG KU BAB (or KU DAB) SHOR-RA (for WA) RÈ'. *He has stumbled.*

ང་གྱེལ་ར་ (for བ་) ཡིན་ (*Vulg.*) ÑGA GYÉ-RA (for WA) YIN: *I stumbled*, *I have stumbled.*

As regards verbs the roots of which end in ད་, or ན་, or བ་, or མ་, there is no such duplicating custom. They are pronounced in the regular way.

See also § 15, 8, as to བ་ WA changing into *a* after a vowel-sound.

§ 19.—THE TONE SYSTEM.

Tone is a very important factor, a fairly correct tone being almost more desirable than absolutely correct grammar; and there exist certain rules on the subject which should be carefully studied.

The ཀ་ལི་ KĀ-LI, or CONSONANTAL SERIES of the ཀ་ཁ་ KA-K'A, is classified by Tibetan Grammarians under six heads, having reference to the respective GENDERS of the several letters.

These heads are:—

1. ཕོ་ P'O, *Masculine.*
2. མ་ནིང་ MA-NING, *Common.*
3. མོ་ MO, *Feminine.*
4. ཤིན་ཏུ་མོ་ SHIN-TU MO, *Very Feminine.*
5. མོ་གཤམ་ MO-SHAM, *Sub-Feminine*, or *Barren*
6. མཚན་མེད་ TS'ĀN MÈ', *Neuter.*

MASCULINE LETTERS.

These are pronounced with a special emphasis, fullness, compactness, and distinctness, arising from a powerful use of the vocal organs. They never undergo any modifications in this respect, even when guarded by Prefixes or Super-posed Letters, but always preserve intact their own natural sounds.

Feminine and Very Feminine Letters.

In pronouncing these the vocal organs are relaxed, and the phonetic body of the letter is not so much *sent forth* from the mouth, as *suffered to emanate from it gently and gradually.* These letters are subject to phonetic modification when guarded. For instance, the addition of Prefixed or Super-posed Letters has the effect of raising the Tonic Pitch, and softening the sound. Thus, གང་ Ǵang, is unguarded, and therefore, to an English ear, sounds very like *Kang.* But དགའ་ Ğ'ā, pronounced like the *Ga* in *Garland,* and སྒང་ Ğang, similarly pronounced, are guarded, in the first case by a Prefix, and in the second by a Super-posed Letter, and therefore the sound is no longer hard and compact like the *k* sound of unguarded ག, but softer and exactly like the sound of the English hard *g,* and the tone is moreover raised, or brought to the Pitch-level of a Masculine Letter.

Common Letters.

The manner of pronouncing these differs only in degree from the way in which Masculine and Feminine Letters are pronounced. That is, they are uttered less compactly and emphatically than the Masculine, and less softly than the Feminine Letters.

Sub-Feminine or Barren Letters.

The pronunciation of these is also only a matter of degree as compared with the pronunciation of Feminine Letters.

Neuter Letter.

This has a hard and compact sound.

The following Tabular Statement will elucidate the above remarks :–

Letter.	Gender.	Pronunciation.
ཀ་ Ka	Masculine ..	With distinctness, emphasis, fullness and compactness, effected by a special effort of the vocal organs.
ཅ་ Cha		
ཏ་ Ta		
པ་ Pa		
ཙ་ Tsa		
ཁ་ K'a	Common ..	Not so compactly as the Maseuline, and not so softly as the Feminine Letters.
ཆ་ Ch'a		
ཐ་ T'a		
ཕ་ P'a		
ཚ་ Ts'a		
ཤ་ Sha		
ས་ Sa		
ག་ Ġa	Feminine ..	A gentle and gradual *emanation* of the sound, rather than an emphatic and compact projection of it.
ཇ་ Ja		
ད་ Ḋa		
བ་ B'a		
ཛ་ Dz'a		
ཝ་ Wa		
ཞ་ Żhya		
ཟ་ Ża		
ཡ་ Ya		

Letter.	Gender.	Pronunciation.
ང་ Nga ཉ་ Nya ན་ Na མ་ Ma	Very Feminine.	More gently and gradually than the Feminine.
ར་ Ra ལ་ La ཧ་ Ha འ་ 'A	Sub-Feminine or Barren ..	Without effort.
ཨ་ A	Neuter ..	Hard, from the base of the throat.

Even the FIVE PREFIXES possess a gender of their own. Thus :—

བ་ *Ba* is *Masculine*, having been *Feminine*, as an Initial.

ག་ *Ga*
ད་ *Da* } are *Common*, having been *Feminine*, as Initials.

འ་ *'A* is *Feminine*, having been *Barren*, as an Initial.

མ་ *Ma* is *Very Feminine*, unaltered.

So, too, the TEN FINAL AFFIXES have the following genders :—

ག་ *Ga, Masculine*, having been *Feminine* as an Initial, and *Common* as a Prefix.

ད་ *Da*, Ditto. Ditto.

བ་ *Ba*, Ditto, having been *Feminine* as an Initial, and *Masculine* as a Prefix.

ས་ *Sa*, *Masculine*, having been *Common* as an Initial.

ན་ *Na*, *Common*, having been *Very Feminine* as an Initial.

ར་ *Ra* } Ditto, having been *Barren* as Initials.
ལ་ *La* }

ང་ *Nga* } *Feminine*, having been *Very Feminine* as Initials, and
མ་ *Ma* } མ་ having been *Very Feminine*, as a Prefix.

འ་ *'A*, *Feminine*, having been *Barren* as an Initial, and *Feminine* as a Prefix.

Thus, the only Letter which undergoes no change in gender, whether as Initial, Prefix, or Final Affix, is མ་ *Ma*.

In his PRIMER OF STANDARD TIBETAN the Revd. Mr. Edward Amundsen, when dealing with the Tone system, gives prominence to the *Pitch* and *Length*, rather than to the *Compactness*, *Emphasis*, and *Distinctness* of the tone. His classification may be represented thus :—

1. ཀ་ ཅ་ ཏ་ པ་ ཧ་	High and short.
2. ཙ་ ཤ་ ས་	High and long.
3. ཁ་ ཆ་ ཐ་ ཕ་ ཚ་	Medium and short.
4. ང་ ཉ་ ན་ མ་ ཟླ་ ར་ ཨ་	Medium and long.
5. ག་ ཇ་ ད་ བ་ ཛ་ ཞ་ ཟ་ འ་ ཡ་	Descending but re-ascending and long.
6. ལ་	Very low and long.

We have seen that the LENGTH OR SHORTNESS of the TONE is governed by rules of its own (*see* § 3) : hence we need not consider it here in connection with PITCH. So far, therefore, as Pitch alone is concerned, Mr. Amundsen's system may be reduced to only three classifications, namely :—

1. High	consisting of Mr. A.'s	1. High and short. 2. High and long.
2. Medium		3. Medium and short. 4. Medium and long.
3. Low		5. Low and ascending. 6. Very low.

Now, if, instead of regarding this question of Tone from the point of view of Pitch, we regard it from that of emphasis, fullness, compactness and distinctness, we shall find that the subject again arranges itself under three heads namely, utterances that are very compact and full, those that are only moderately so, and those that are soft and gradual emanations.

To sum up: for all practical purposes it will be found that (1) words beginning with the Masculine Initials ཀ་, ཅ་, ཏ་, པ་, ཙ་, should be pronounced compactly and fully, and in a high key; (2) words beginning with the Common Initials ཁ་, ཆ་, ཐ་, ཕ་, ཚ་, ཤ་, ས་, should be pronounced with moderate emphasis and in a moderately high key; (3) while words beginning with the Feminine Initials ག་, ཇ་, ད་, བ་, ཛ་, ཝ་, ཞ་, ཟ་, ཡ་, or with the Very Feminine Initials, ང་, ཉ་, ན་, མ་, or with the Barren Initials ར་, ལ་, ཧ་, འ་, or with the Neuter Initial ཨ་, should be pronounced softly and in a low key. It should also be remembered that when an Initial has a Prefix, or a Surmounting Letter, the utterance according to these three rules is somewhat intensified as regards Masculine and Common Initials, and heightened and rendered more compact as regards all the others.

It would appear, however, to be doubtful whether Prefixes have much to do with *the raising of the Tonic Pitch.* What is more certain is that they are used (1) for modifying the meaning of a word, e.g., ཆོད་པ་ Ch'ö'-pa, *To be cut off, To be decided*, but མཆོད་པ་ Ch'ö'-pa

To honour ; གྲོང་བ་ ḌONG-WA (for གྲང་བ་ ḌANG-WA, *Cold*), but བགྲོང་བ་ ḌONG-WA, *To count*, and འགྲོང་བ་ ḌONG-WA, *To die* ; (2) in the formation of the tenses of verbs, as already explained (§ 13); and (3) to effect changes in the pronunciation of Initial Letters. Thus ག, as an Initial, is pronounced almost like *K* in English ; but, when prefixed by ད, བ, མ, or འ, it is pronounced like hard *G* in English Again བ, as an Initial, is pronounced almost like *P* in English ; but when prefixed by ད, it is pronounced as *W*, when unqualified by any vowel-sound, and as the vowel-sound only, when so qualified ; or, if prefixed by འ, it takes the sound of *B* in English. Again, as regards ཝ, *see* § 13. Again, ད, as an Initial, is pronounced as a dental *T* ; but if prefixed by ག, བ, མ, or འ, it takes the sound of a dental *D*. Again, ཇ and ཛ, when Initials, are pronounced with a slight aspirate ; but, when prefixed by བ, མ, or འ, they lose the aspirate. Again ཟ, as an Initial, is pronounced almost like *S* in English ; but, when prefixed by ག or བ, it is pronounced like *Z* in English. Lastly, ཞ, as an Initial, is pronounced almost like *shya* ; but, prefixed by ག or བ, it takes the sound of *zhya*.

§ 20.—WRITING AND PUNCTUATION.

Originally, Tibetan was a monosyllabic language. Nowadays, however, its words are mostly dissyllabic. There is no attempt in the written or printed language to divide off *words* from one another, either by spacing or by punctuation. Hence, they all succeed and seem to run into each other in one continuous line, and the reader's knowledge is all that enables him to recognize them individually. It is otherwise, however, with *syllables*. A syllable may consist of a single consonant, simple or complex, or of two or more such consonants, silent or pronounced. But, be its consonantal structure what it may, the whole collocation of letters possesses only *one vowel-sound*, inherent or expressed by vowel-signs. Every such collocation or syllable must be marked off from its successor by a dot (·) placed at the right-hand top corner of the final consonant. This dot is called ཚེག་ Ts'ᴇ'. To mark the termination of clauses such as those for which we generally use a comma, a semi-colon, or a colon, another sign is used in the shape of a vertical stroke (|), called ཀྱང་ཤད་ Kyang-Shä'. Whenever this sign is used, the ཚེག་ after the last consonant is omitted, except in the case of final ང་ *nga*, which always retains it. A double vertical stroke (||), called ཉིས་ཤད་ Nyi-Shä', is used where we would use a full stop. At the end of a paragraph, or of a chapter, a fourfold vertical stroke (||||), called བཞི་ཤད་ Žhyi-Shä', is placed. Instead of the four plain strokes the following may be used: , or , or , or , or . Instead of the two plain strokes the following, . Instead of the one plain stroke the following, 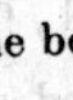. In some books the comma is seen thus, . Sometimes the dot (˙) or ཚེག་ is seen ❛, and sometimes even larger, ❛. In Book-letter and in Running-hand the ཚེག་ is seen thus, ᑦ.

At the commencement of printed and written matter symbols like the following may often be seen :—

This is called Swasti or the *Auspicious Benediction.* It may begin any work dealing with Ethics and Morality. The top figures are the Double Flame, or Radiance, the next are the Double Gem, and the lowest are the Double Lotus. On the right is ཉིས་ཤད།

Triple ditto, for writings on Philosophy and Theology.

Radiance, Gem, Triple Lotus, and Stalk. Beginning chapters in Religious works.

Lotus and Stalk. Used with official correspondence proverbs, maxims, etc., to indicate a fresh beginning.

Ordinary Block Print.

The proper method of writing this is first to make the thick horizontal stroke at the top of each letter, and then the rest of the character, working from left to right as in English, and adding the *Ya-tas*, *Ra-tas*, and vowel-signs last. The straight vertical strokes should be long, fairly thick at the top, and tapering to the bottom.

In writing ག, the vertical stroke on the left may first be made downwards, and then the rest, never omitting clearly to define the loop in the centre. Or, a horizontal stroke may first be made, then the vertical stroke on the left downwards, and then the remainder, from the right-hand end of the horizontal stroke. The down-stroke from the loop must be long, quite vertical, and tapering, otherwise the beginner is apt to produce something which might be mistaken for ཤ, which has no central loop, and whose final down-stroke is short, and instead of being vertical slopes off to the right.

Other letters which the beginner is apt to mix up with each other when attempting to write them, are ང *Nga*, ཏ *Ta*, and ད *Da*. The down-strokes in *nga* and *da* begin at or near the right end of the horizontal line, and curve well to the left, whereas the down-stroke of *Ta* begins at the left end of the horizontal line, and comes straight down, or even with a slight slant to the right. The final stroke of *nga* is short and thick, while those of *Ta* and *Da* are long and tapering. *Ta's* final down-stroke, moreover, takes a bend to the left, while that of *Da* bears well to the right. Both, too, are brought well down, whereas *Nga's* final stroke is stunted.

In writing ཀ the little stroke on the left should first be made, then the thin stroke next to it, then the top horizontal stroke and undercircle, and finally the long vertical down-stroke.

ཐ may be written by first making the top horizontal stroke, then the whole left side of the letter, and finally the vertical down-stroke on the right. Or, after the horizontal stroke, first the little curved stroke in the top left-hand corner, then a straight diagonal line from right to left downwards, and finally the vertical stroke on the right downwards.

In writing letters like ཧ་ and ཨ་, the down-stroke containing the loop is usually commenced from near the right-hand end of the horizontal stroke.

The vertical stroke of ད་ should project down slightly beyond the point of junction with the curve on the right.

ཅ་ First the horizontal, then the thin curving down-stroke, beginning it from the centre of the horizontal, and lastly the thick curving stroke on the right, the top end of which should meet the thin down-stroke a little below the letter's junction with the horizontal. Or thus, ཅ, that is, first the horizontal stroke, then the short down stroke, and lastly the curving stroke, somewhat after the way we write the figure five.

ཆ་ First the horizontal, next from the centre of that stroke the down-stroke, then the loop on the left, working upwards, and then by carrying on the pen, the loop on the right working downwards.

ལ་ First make an འ་ That is to say, a vertical down-stroke, then the rest of the figure. Lastly make a straight down-stroke, meeting the end of འ་, ལ་ has no loop.

ཉ་ First the dot, or thick short stroke on the left at the top, then the half circle to the right, then the thick short stroke slanting from left to right, and finally the long hook. Or else, first a horizontal stroke, then the dot or short thick stroke on the left at the top and then the rest as stated.

ཨ་ First the horizontal, then from its centre or from near its right-hand end the short thin lines loping downward to the left, then the hook with the tail brought up level with but clear of the horizontal stroke; next, from near the top of the second stroke a straight or curving line downwards with a slant to the right; and lastly the vertical down-stroke

ཡ First a short horizontal, then a sort of ᑌ with another horizontal over the right-hand limb, then the stroke slanting to the right, and finally the vertical down-stroke. Or, first two parallel vertical strokes of equal length, with a horizontal on each, then another parallel vertical stroke a little longer than the others. Then join the first two with an under-curved stroke ; and lastly, with a slanting stroke from left to right, join the second and third vertical strokes, at the bottom. The first way is the better.

ཡྲ First write an elongated ཡ, thus ཡ, and then add the bar across the middle.

Or first write an ordinary ཡ, and then subjoin a ར without its horizontal stroke.—Thus ཡྲ།

ཤ First a short horizontal, then the thin short down-stroke, slanting to the left, then the thick stroke up the end of it, slanting to the right. Then, from near the top of the second stroke, make the long down-stroke, sloping to the right, and lastly the vertical down-stroke.

ར First a horizontal, then the short thin down-stroke from near the right-hand end of the horizontal, and slanting to the left, then the thick stroke at the bottom, beginning it from well to the left of the down-stroke and carrying it boldly across the end of the latter, with a good sweep to the right and with a downward trend.

In making ར the beginner should see that he does not make it look like ས.

ས First a fairly long horizontal. Then from near the left-hand end a thin downward stroke slanting to the left, then a thick downward-stroke slanting to the right, and finally the vertical down-stroke, commencing it from the right-hand end of the horizontal.

ཧ First a fairly long horizontal. Then to the first half of it subjoin a small ཀ without its horizontal. Then, from the right-hand end of the horizontal, make the long vertical down-stroke.

ཁ This is the same as ཀ reversed.

ཏ First the horizontal. Then the two little strokes, and finally the long vertical down-stroke.

BOOK-LETTER and RUNNING-HAND.

These are very much alike, the Running Hand, however, being the more difficult of the two to read and write. Specimens of both, in all possible combinations, are given in Csoma de Körös's Grammar (1834).

§ 21.—SPELLING.

Tibetan spelling may be described as a cumulative process, one only of the component parts of a syllable being taken up at a time. Next, the sound so taken up is repeated, but with the addition in advance, or by way of assumption, of the second component part. Then this second component part is pronounced by itself. Finally, the phonetic effect of *all* that has thus been taken up is pronounced together, and that effect represents the literal expression of the syllable.

A knowledge of how to spell is most useful, and it is quite worth the student's while to take the trouble to acquire it.

The following examples are intended to exhibit the process progressively, through most of the stages from simple to complex syllables :—

I.—*Simple Consonants.*

ཏ (for example), and one final affix.

ཏག Ka, Kaǵ-ga, *Ka'*.

ཏང Ka Kang nga, *Kang*.

ཏད Ka, Kä'-da, *Kä'*.

ཏན Ka, Kän-na, *Kän*.

ཏལ Ka, Kä-la, *Kä*.

ཏས Ka, Kä-sa, *Kä*.

II.—*Consonant and Double Affix.*

གངས་ Ġa, Ġang-nga-sa, *Ġang.*

ཁམས་ K'a, K'am-ma-sa, *K'am.*

ཁཾས་ K'a, K'am-ma (Lä'-kor)-sa, *K'am.*

III.—*Consonant with Prefix and Affix.*

དཀའ་ Ḍa-wo: Ka, K'ā-'ā, *K'ā.*

མཁའ་ Ma-wo: K'a, K''ā-'a, *K''ā.*

IV.—*Consonant and Single Vowel-sign.*

ཀི་ Ka, ġi-ġu, *Ki.*

ཀུ་ Ka, źhyab-kyu, *Ku.*

ཀེ་ Ka, ḍeng-bu, *Ke.*

ཀོ་ Ka, na-ro, *Ko.*

V.—*Consonant with double Vowel-sign and Subjunct.*

གཽ་ Ġa, na-ro, ġo; 'ā, na-ro, oû; *Ġoû.*

VI.—*Consonant with Vowel-sign and Affix.*

ཀོང་ Ka, na-ro, ko; kong, nga, *Kong.*

རེད་ Ra, ḍeng-bu, re; rè'-da, *Rè'.*

VII.—*Consonant with Vowel-sign and Double Affix.*

ཁོམས་ K'a, na-ro, K'o; k'om, ma, sa, *K'om.*

VIII.—*Reversed Letters.*

ཊཾཁ་ Ta-loġ-Ṭa; Ṭam-ma (Lä'-kor) Ṭam; k'a; *Ṭam-k'a.*

ཌམ་རུ་ Ḍa-loġ-Da; ma; Ra, źhyab-kyu, Ru; *Ḍa-ma-ru.*

IX.—*Ya-tās.*

ཀྱ་ Ka, Ya-tā, *Kya.*

པྱ་ Pa, Ya-tā, *Cha.*

ཕྱ་ P'a, Ya-tā, *Ch'a.*

བྱ་ Ḃa, Ya-tā, *J'a.*

མྱ་ Ma, Ya-tā, *Nya.*

X.—*Ya-tā with Vowel-sign.*

ཀྱི་ Ka, ya-tā, kya; kya, ǵi-ǵu, *kyi.*

XI.—*Ya-tā with Vowel-sign and Affix.*

ཀྱིས་ Ka, ya-tā, kya; kya, ǵi-ǵu, kyi; kvī, sa, *kyi*:

XII.—*Ya-tā with Vowel-sign and Double Affix.*

ཁྱེབས་ K'a, ya-tā, k'ya; k'ya, ḍeng-bu, k'ye; k'yeb, ba, sa, *k'yeb.*

XIII.—*Ya-tā with Prefix and Affix.*

དཀྱར་ Ḋa-wo: ka, ya-tā, kya; kyar, ra, *kyar.*

དཔྱལ་ Ḋa-wo: pa, ya-tā, cha; chä, la, *chä.*

XIV.—*Ya-tā with Prefix, Vowel and Affix.*

དཀྱིལ་ Ḋa-wo: ka, ya-tā, kya; kya, ǵi-ǵu, kyi; kyī-la, *kyī.*

དཔྱོད་ Ḋa-wo: pa, ya-tā, cha; cha, na-ro, cho; chö', ḋa, *chö'.*

XV.—*Ya-tā with Prefix, Vowel and Double Affix.*

བཀྱིགས་ Ba-wo: ka, ya-tā, kya; kya, ǵi-ǵu, kyi; kyi, ga-sa, *kyī.*

XVI.—*Ya-tā and Affix, each with Vowel-sign.*

ཁྱེའུ་ K'a, ya-tā, k'ya; k'ya, ḍeng-bu, k'ye; 'ā, ẑhyab-kyu, 'u; *k'ye-'u.*

XVII.—*Ra-tās and Ha-tās.*

Spelt like ya-tās, but the following would be new:—

བན་དྷཱུ་ཀ Ba, bän, na, bän; d́a, ha-tā, d'ā; d'ā, ẑhyab-kyu, d'ū; ka; *Bän-d'ū-kā.*

བྷྲཱུཾ་ཧྲི་ Ba, ha-tā, b'ā; b'ā, ra-tā, br'ā; br'ā, ẑhyab-kyu, br'ū; br'um, ma, br'ūm; ha, ra-tā, hra; hra, ǵi-ǵu, hri; *Br'ūm-hri.*

XVIII.—*La-tās.*

ཀླ་ Ka,
གླ་ Ǵa,
བླ་ Ba, } la-tā, *La.*
རླ་ Ra,
སླ་ Sa,

ཟླ་ Ża, la-tā, *Da.*

ཀློག Ka, la-tā, la; la, na-ro, lo; loǵ-ǵa, *Lo'.*

XIX.—*Wa-żurs.*

ཚྭ་ཁུག Ts'a, wa-żur, ts'ā; k'a, ẑhyab-kyu, k'u; k'uǵ, ǵa, k'u': *Ts'ā-k'u'.*

ཞྭ་མོ་ Žhya, wa-żur, ẑhyā; ma, na-ro, mo; *ẑhya-mo.*

བོ་དྷི་སཏྭ Ba, na-ro, bo; d́a, ha-tā, d'ā; d'ā, ǵi-ǵu, d'ī; sa; ta, wa-żur, tâ: *Bo-dī-sa-tâ.*

XX. *Ra-gos, La-gos, and Sa-gos.*

རྐ་ Ra, ka-tā, *Ka.*

རྒ་ Ra, ǵa-tā, *Ǵ'a.*

རྔ་ Ra, nga-tā, *Ňga.*

ཀླ་ La, ka-tā, *Ka.*

གླ་ La, ga-tā, *Ğa.*

ལྔ་ La, nga-tā, *Ňga.*

སྐ་ Sa, ka-tā, *Ka.*

སྒ་ Sa, ga-tā, *Ğa.*

སྔ་ Sa, nga-tā, *Ňga.*

In spelling, the Prefix is taken first, then the surmounting letter, then the *ya-tā*, or *ra-tā*, or other subjunct, then the vowel, then the affix or affixes. Thus :—

བསྒྲུངས་ Ba-wo : Sa, ga-tā, ğa ; ğa, ra-tā, ḍa ; ḍa, źhyab-kyu, ḍu ; ḍung, nga, sa, *Ḍung.*

XXI. *Miscellaneous Examples.*

པཎ་ཆེན་རིན་པོ་ཆེ་ Pa, päṇ, ṇa, päṇ ; ch'a, ḍeng-bu, ch'e ; ch'én ; na, ch'èn ; ra, ģi-ģu, ri ; rin, na, rin ; pa na-ro, po ; ch'a, ḍeng-bu, ch'e : PÄṆ-CH'ÉN, RIN-PO-CH'E, The Grand Lama of Ṭashī L'ümpo in Tsang, usually called the Ṭashī Lama, and an incarnation of 'Ö'-*paģ-mè*'.

འོད་དཔག་མེད་ 'A, na-ro, 'o ; 'ö', ḍa, 'ö' ; ḍa-wo ; pa, paģ, ģa, paģ ; ma, ḍeng-bu, me ; mè', ḍa, mè' : 'Ö'-PAĠ-MÈ', Buddha Amitabha, or, Boundless Light.

ཏཱ་ལའི་བླ་མ་ Ta ; La ; 'ā, ģi-ģu, 'ī ; laī ; Ba, la-tā, la ; ma : TA-LAI LA-MA, The Dalai Lama, or Spiritual Head of Tibet until Sir Frank Younghusband's entry into Lhassa.

འབྲས་སྤུངས་ 'A-wo ; ba, ra-tā, ḍa ; ḍä, sa, ḍä ; la, ja-tā, ʝa ;

ja, na-ro, jo; jong, nga, sa, jong: ĎÄ-JONG (pronounced ĎÄN-JONG), Sikkim.

རྡོ་རྗེ་གླིང་ Ra, d́a-tā, ḑa; ḑa, na-ro, ḑo; ra, ja-tā, ja; ja-ḍeng-bu, je; ga, la-tā, la; la, ǵi-gu, li; ling, nga, ling: DO-JE-LING, or DOR-JE-LING, Darjeeling, or the Place of Ecclesiastical Sway; literally the Place of the Sovereign Stone.

བོད་སྐད་ Ba, na-ro, bo; bö', d́a, bö'; sa, ka-tā, ka; Kä', d́a, Kä': BÖ'-KÄ', Language of Tibet.

§ 22.—TRANSLITERATION.

For the system adopted in this work of transliterating Tibetan words into Romanized Equivalents *see* § 2.

The best method, no doubt, is the one that was adopted at the Vienna Congress of Orientalists, and which may be found exemplified in Rai Sarat Chandra Das Bahadur's TIBETAN-ENGLISH DICTIONARY. By that system each letter in a Tibetan word is transliterated, but a line is drawn under every letter that is not pronounced, or it is distinguished by special type from the letters that are pronounced. It is not adopted in this work, as it is really only necessary for purposes of scientific precision.

§ 23.—USE OF THE TIBETAN DICTIONARY.

The following appears to be the way in which the words in a Tibetan Dictionary (ཚིག་མཛོད་ T'SIǴ-ĎZÖ') are arranged.

1.—According to the order of the ཀཱ་ལི་ KĀ-LI, or Consonantal Series of the ཀ་ཁ་ KA-K'A, regarded as *Initials*, or as they are sometimes called, *Root letters*, with the inherent vowel-sound of ཨ་ *A*. The first thing, therefore, that the student has to do, when he wants to look up a word, is to ascertain what its Initial letter is.

Then the words under each consonant, beginning for instance with ཀ་ *Ka*, are arranged thus :—

2.—The simple consonant, e.g. ཀ།

3.—The simple consonant with subjuncts like འ་ *'ā*, ཿ *wa-żur*, or ཕ་ *Sha-loġ-K'a*—e.g. བླ་ LĀ-WA, *Woollen Blanket.*

4.—The simple consonant with affixes, single and double, for the order of which as amongst themselves, see § 16.

Then the same with subjuncts.

5.—Next, according to the foregoing order as regards their consonants, words qualified by the vowel-signs ི *ġi-ġu*, *żhyab-kyu*, ེ *Ḍeng-bu*, and ོ *Na-ro*, in that order.

6.—Simple consonant qualified by *ya-tā* alone.

7.—*Ya-tā* words in all orders down to 5, inclusive.

8.—Simple consonant qualified by ྲ *Ra-tā* alone.

9.—*Ra-tā* words in all orders down to 5, inclusive.

10.—Simple consonant qualified by ཧ *Ha-tā* alone.

11.—*Ha-tā* words in all orders down to 5, inclusive.

12.—Simple consonant qualified by *la-tā* alone.

13.—*La-tā* words in all orders down to 5, inclusive.

14.—Foreign or other special words formed with the Reversed letters.

15.—Words with the Prefixes ག, ད, བ, མ, and འ, in that sequence, and each sequence arranged according to the foregoing orders.

16.—Consonant qualified by *Ra-ġo.*

17.—*Ra-ġo* words according to foregoing orders.

18.—Consonant qualified by *La-ġo.*

19.—*La-ġo* words according to foregoing orders.

20.—Consonant qualified by *Sa-ġo.*

21.—*Sa-ġo* words according to foregoing orders.

22.—No words with ལ *La*, as an Initial, and having any Superposed letter like ར or ས, need be looked for under ལ *La.* They will only be found under the head of the Superposed letter.

Words in ལ་ *La*, however, are found with qualifying vowel-signs, and such words may be looked for under ལ་ *La*.

N.B.—Csoma de Körös's Dictionary is differently arranged.

§ 24.—Indicative and Differentiating Particles.

ཀ་ *Ka*. Used both in Literary Tibetan and in the Colloquial, and may have any of the following meanings, namely: *The*, *All*, *Both*, *Together*, *The very*, *Just*, *Exactly*, etc. Ex.:— དཔྱིད་ཀ་ *The Spring*; དབྱར་ཀ་ *The Summer*; སྟོན་ཀ་ *The Autumn*; དགུན་ཀ་ *The Winter*. Sometimes, in this connection, ཁ་ is seen instead of ཀ།

གཉིས་ཀ་ *Both*, *The two together*; གསུམ་ཀ་ *All three*, *The three together*. In this connection ཅ་ sometimes replaces ཀ།

དེ་ཀ་ *The very*, *That very*; དེ་ཀ་ལྟར་ *Just so*; དེ་ཀ་ཡོད་ (as a reply) *Yes*, *exactly*, *precisely*, *to be sure*.

Sometimes its sole use is to differentiate between words that resemble each other, e.g. གདེང་ *Confidence*; but གདེངས་ཀ་ *Hood of a snake*; སྟོན་པ་ *To show*, *To teach*; but སྟོན་ཀ་ *Autumn*.

ཀ, when used, is generally found attached to words ending in ག་, ད་, བ་, ས་ and also in མ་ and in vowels.

ཁ་ *K'a*. When this particle is used, it is generally found attached to Literary words ending in ན་, ར་, and ལ་, and to Colloquial words ending in ང་, or ངས།

Ex.:—དང་ཁ་ (properly དང་ག་) *Appetite*; གྲངས་ཁ་ (properly གྲངས་ཀ་) *Number*, *Enumeration*.

Also sometimes used instead of ཀ་ as above explained.

ཁ་ also indicates the top, upper surface, or front of anything inanimate. Ex.:— ཁ་ or ཁ་གཅོད་ *Lid*; སྒང་ཁ་ *Ridge, or Summit of a hill*; ལ་ཁ་ *Top, or head of a mountain, or pass*; བྲག་ཁ་ *Head of cliff.*

ག་ *Ga.* Used after vowels, or after ང་, མ་, འ་, and ལ་ It is used as a Differentiating Particle with many roots. Ex.:—ཡལ་བ་ *To disappear*; but ཡལ་ག་ *Branch*; ཐང་ *Plain or Steppe*; but ཐང་ག་ *Painted Scroll*; ཁྱོ་ *Husband*; but ཁྱོ་ག་ *A man, as distinguished from an effeminate person.*

ཆ་ *Ch'a.* Apart from its meanings as a word by itself, this Particle is often seen added to roots. Ex.:—བྲག་ཆ་ (Literary), or བ་ཆ་ (Colloquial), *Echo*; སྐད་ཆ་ *Conversation*; སྒྲིག་ཆ་ *Negotiations.*

པ་ *Pa.* Used after ག་, ད་, ན་, བ་, མ་, ས་ expresses ownership, or possession, or the connection subsisting between a person and some thing, action, employment, place, etc. Ex.:— ཁྱིམ་ *A house*, but ཁྱིམ་པ་ *A married man, or householder*; རྟ་ *A horse*, but རྟ་པ་ *Horseman*; ཆུ་ *Water*, but ཆུ་པ་ *Water-carrier*; མདའ་ *Arrow*, but མདའ་ལྔ་པ་ *A title of Cupid as holder of five arrows*; ཀ་ཁ་ *The Tibetan Alphabet*, but ཀ་ཁ་པ་ *A child learning its letters*; ལྷ་ས་ *Lhassa*, but ལྷ་ས་པ་ An inhabitant of Lhassa.

2.—When added to all Cardinal Numbers except གཅིག་ *One*, it forms the Ordinal Numbers. Thus, གཉིས་ *Two*, but གཉིས་པ་ *Second.*

3.—It is used also in connection with other enumerational expressions. Ex.:— སུམ་ཅུ་པ་ the ཀཱ་ལི་ *or consonantal series of* 30 *letters* ; ཕྲུ་གུ་ལོ་གཉིས་པ་ *A two-year-old boy* ; ཁྲུ་གང་པ་ *Measuring a cubit.*

4.—It is the sign of the Infinitive Mood, the Verbal Substantive, and the Participle. Ex. :— སྒྲོག་པ་ (Lit.) and ཆོས་བཤད་པ་ (Coll.) *To preach. The or A preaching, Preaching, Preached.* ཁོ་རྒྱ་གར་ལ་ཆོས་བཤད་པ་ཕྱིན་པ་རེད་ *He went to India to preach* : འོན་པ་ཞིག་ལ་ཆོས་བཤད་པ་ཕན་ཐོགས་ཀྱི་མ་རེད་ *(The) preaching to the deaf is useless* ; ཆོས་བཤད་པའི་མི་ཞིག་ཐུགས་དྲང་དགོ་གི་རེད་ *A preaching man must be sincere* : སྔར་དངོས་ནས་ཆོས་བཤད་པ་རེད་ *The truth was preached a long time ago.*

The last example shows that པ་, added to a root, and helped out by the auxiliary ཡིན་པ་ *To be*, goes to form the Perfect Indicative Tense.

5.—པ་ is also used to distinguish the different meanings of homonymous roots. Ex. :— ཀང་ *Marrow*, but ཀང་པ་ *Foot.*

6.—In the Colloquial it is often used instead of the supinal particle པར་ (much used in Literary Tibetan). Ex. :— ཁོ་སྒམ་འཁྱེར་ཡོང་བར་ཕྱིན་པ་རེད་ *He has gone to bring the box.* This is Literary. Colloquially it would be, ཁོ་སྒམ་ཁྱེ་ཡོང་བ་ཕྱིན་པ་རེད་ ང་ཕྱུག་པོ་མེད་པར་དྲན་གསོ་སྟེ་ (Literary) *Remembering that I was not rich*, or *Remembering myself not to be rich.* Colloquially, ང་ཕྱུག་པོ་མེད་པ་དྲན་གསོ་ཙང་ །

པོ་ *Po.* Indicates an agent. It is then sometimes, e.g. when annexed to the Infinitive, preceded by པ་ *pa.* Thus, ཐོས་པ་པོ་ *A or the hearer.*

It also expresses the idea of the Definite or Indefinite Article in connection with Noun Substantives. Ex. མིག་པོ་ *An or the eye ;* ཡུལ་པོ་ *A or the country ;* ཤིང་པོ་ *A or the tree*, or *piece of wood :* ལམ་པོ་ *A or the road ;* མེད་པོ་ *The poor.*

Used with numerals it also performs the functions of the Definite Article, or of the word *aforesaid.* Ex. :— གསུམ་པོ་ *The three together.*

ཕོ་ *P'o.* An affixed or prefixed particle, signifying *Male*, or *paternal.* Ex. :— བྱ་ཕོ་ *Cock-bird ;* ཝ་ཕོ་ *Male fox ;* ཕོ་གཡག *Bull Yak ;* ཕོ་ཁྱི་ *Dog.*

བ་ *Wa.* The form assumed by པ་ when the root to which it is annexed ends in a vowel, or in ང་, ལ་, ར་ or འ་ In many noun-substantives, however, its place is taken by པ་. Ex. :— ཤར་པ་ *An oriental ;* ལུང་པ་ *Valley ;* ཡུལ་པ་ *A provincial or rustic ;* མཐའ་པ་ *A frontiers-man.*

བོ་ *Bo*, or *Wo.* The form assumed by པོ་ when the root to which it is annexed ends in a vowel, or in ང་, ལ་, ར་ or འ་ Ex. :— ཆུ་བོ་ *A river ;* མཐེ་བོ་ or ཐེ་བོ་ *Thumb ;* དཔའ་བོ་ *Brave.*

མ་ *Ma.* An immovable particle after various roots of substantives. Ex. :— ཉི་མ་ *Sun ;* བླ་མ་ *Monk ;* འོ་མ་ *Milk.* Sometimes, though not always, it indicates the Feminine Gender. Ex. :— རྒོད་མ་ *A mare.*

མོ་ *Mo.* Affixed or prefixed to noun roots, it generally indicates the Feminine Gender. Ex. :— ཁྱི་མོ་ or མོ་ཁྱི་ *Bitch.* But not always. Ex. :— རོལ་མོ་ *Music ;* རྩེ་མོ་ *Top-point.*

Attached to adjectives, it does not always indicate gender. Ex. ཆེན་མོ་ *Great ;* ལེགས་མོ་ *Good, fine.*

ཙ་ *Tsa.* A differentiating particle. Ex.:— དཀན་ *A steep declivity*, but དཀན་ཙ་ *A staircase.*

ཙེ་ *Tse.* A *point, top, or edge.* Also, however, an affix of Chinese origin. Ex.:— དཀྲག་ཙེ་ *Polish, lustre, brilliant to a point or degree ; dazzling* ; ཡ་ཙེ་ *A duck* ; ཏོང་ཙེ་ *A brass coin* ; ཀོང་ཙེ་ *Tibetan name of Confucius.*

ནི་ *Ni.* See § 27, 2, on the Definite Article.

ང་ *Nga.*
ཤེ་ *Śe.*
ངེ་ *Nge.*
} Indicate the Definite or Indefinite Article, but are not much met with. Ex.:— སྒོ་ང་ *The or an egg* ; སེང་གེ་ *The or a lion* ; ཏིང་ངེ་ *The deep.*

ཀུ་ *Ku.*
ཁུ་ *K'u*
གུ་ *Gu.*
ངུ་ *Ngu.*
ནུ་ *Nu.*
བུ་ *Bu. Wu.*
རུ་ *Ru.*
ལུ་ *Lu.*
འུ་ *'u*
ཡུ་ *Yu.*
} Definite or indefinite and diminutive particles. Apparently a re-duplication in ུ (źhyab-kyu) of the final letter of the root. Ex. :— ཆུང་ངུ་ *A or the mite* ; ཕྲུག་གུ (ཕྲུ་གུ་) *A or the child* ; གཞོན་ནུ་ *A or the youth.* But not always. Ex. :— མི་འུ་ *A or the mannikin* ; ཐིགས་བུ་ *A or the little drop.*

§ 25.—The Cases and their Signs.

(N.B.—*The student is advised to glance at the paragraphs and conjugations relating to the verb* To Be. *See post.*)

The various relations in which a Tibetan Noun and Pronoun may tand to some other word in the sentence are nearly all expressed by means of divers monosyllabic primitive particles, and words compounded therewith, which perform the same functions as are performed by English Prepositions, but which, save for sundry Vocative Signs, are all Post-positional. These relations or cases are as follow :—

I.—The Nominative Case.

Except in connection with Intransitive Verbs (Active ; Neuter or Inactive ; and Inceptive, *i.e.*, implying a beginning or change of state), and also with the verbs ཡིན་པ་ *To be* (the mere copula which is used attributively) ; མིན་པ་ or མན་པ་ its negative form ; ཡོད་པ་ *To be to exist, to be present ;* མེད་པ་ its negative form ; མོད་པ་ its emphatic or intensive form (hardly ever used), and one or two other forms of the verb *To be* used in Literary Tibetan ; there is practically no such thing in Tibetan as a verb governed by the Nominative Case. The following is an instance in which, though the practice is irregular, it is allowable and common in the Colloquial to use the Nominative in the usual European way :—

ཁྱོད་རང་ཇ་འཐུངས་ཡོང་ངས། *Will you drink tea ?*

The more correct way would be :—

ཁྱོད་ཀྱིས་ (or ཁྱོད་རང་གིས་) ཇ་འཐུངས་
ཡོང་ངས་ (or ཇ་འཐུང་གི་ཡིན་པས་
or འཐུང་གི་རེད་པས་)།

Honorifically :—

ཁྱེད་ཀྱིས་གསོལ་ཇ་བཞེས་ཡོང་ངམ་ or
གནང་ཡོང་ངམ།

The subject, however, is always put in the Nominative Case sentences like the following, where, though the verb is Transitive, is also Passive :—

ང་ (ལ་) རྡུང་གི་ཡོད། *I am being beaten.*

བུ་མོ་ (ལ་) བྱམས་པོ་བྱེད་ཀྱི་འདུག། *The girl is loved.*

In such cases ལ་ *la* is optional, and may be omitted if desired.

The subject is always put in the Nominative Case in sentences like the following, where the verbs are Intransitive (active, neuter, or inceptive) :—

རྟ་ཚོ་རྒྱུག་གི་འདུག།	*The horses run.*
ང་ཁྲོམ་ལ་མར་འགྲོ་གི་ཡོད།	*I am going down to the bazaar.*
ཆར་པ་བབ་ཀྱི་འདུག།	*It is raining.*
ཉི་མ་ཤར་གྱི་འདུག།	*The sun shines.*
ཕྲུ་གུ་ཉལ་སྡོད་ཀྱི་འདུག།	*The child sleeps.*
ཕྲུ་གུ་གཉིད་སད་ཀྱི་འདུག།	*The child wakes, or breaks from slumber.*

Where, however, the verb is transitive, the Nominative Case is never used, but always the Agentive Case. *See* § 25, VI.

II.—The Vocative Case.

There is practically no Vocative Case, but several polite expressions are often used by way of assent, dissent, or address. The commonest is ལགས་ LĀ, and its variants.

III.—The Objective or Accusative Case.

This is the same as the Nominative, with or without ལ་ LA, signifying *As regards.* Ex. :—

ཁོས་བུ་མོ་ (ལ་) བྱམས་པོ་བྱེད་ཀྱི་འདུག།	*He loves the girl.* Literally, *By him, as regards the girl, a loving is.*
ཁྱེད་ཀྱིས་ང་ (ལ་) མ་བརྗེད་པ་བྱེད།	*Do not forget me.*

IV.—Genitive Case.

The signs are :—

གི་ Ġi, used after words ending with ག་, or ང་

ཀྱི་ Kyi, used after words ending with ད་, བ་, or ས་, or in the Colloquial after འདི་ Ḋi, *This.*

གྱི་ Ġyi, ,, ,, ,, ,, ན་, མ་, ར་, or ལ་

འི་ i } ,, after vowels.
ཡི་ yi }

ཡི་ yi ,, in verse.

N.B.—གི་, ཀྱི་, and གྱི་ may all alike be pronounced Ġi in conversation.

1.—*Possessive Aspect.*

When the word to which the sign is annexed is in that part of the sentence which contains the subject, it should precede the chief substantive of the subject. Ex. :—

ལྷ་སའི་སྐད་གྲགས་ཆེན་པོ་འདུག། — *The fame of Lhassa is great.*

ཀུན་དབང་མཁྱེན་གྱི་ཐབས་མཁས་ཐུགས་རྗེ་ གས་གལ་ (or ཕྱོགས་ཐམས་ཅད་དུ་) ཁྱབ་ཞིང་འདུག། — *The gracious wisdom of the Almighty is everywhere pervading.*

2.—*Qualificative Aspect.*

When the word to which the sign is annexed is indicative of some quality, it may be regarded as an adjective; but, unlike Tibetan adjectives in general, it should *precede* whatever it qualifies. Ex. :—

ལྷ་ས་འཇོལ་མོའི་གྲོང་ཁྱེར་རེད། — *Lhassa is the city of the Jōlmo* (a sweet-singing bird).

སྔོན་ལ་བོད་ཡུལ་ནི་སྦས་པའི་ (or གསང་བའི་) ཡུལ་ཞིག་རེད། — *Tibet was formerly a hidden (or secret) land.*

N.B.—The particle ནི་ Ni (*see* § 27, 2) has the effect of singling out and laying stress on the word བོད་ཡུལ་ Bö'-yü, *Tibet.* This

English word TIBET seems to have originated from some phrase such as འདི་བོད་ DI-BÖD, whence *Ti-bōt*=TIBET; for, to a European (i.e., Continental, e.g. German) ear the sound of ད་ is very like *t*.

As to the adjectival use of the Genitive case-sign, see also § 30, I, (vi).

3.—*Purposive Aspect.*

སྨན་གྱི་སྒམ།	*For medicine the box, The medicine box.*
ཐ་མག་གི་ཁུག་མ་ or རྒྱ་ཁུག་ or, better still, simply ཐ་ཁུག།	*For tobacco a bag—A tobacco pouch.*
དངུལ་ཁུག།	*Money-bag.*
ཙམ་ཁུག།	*A leather bag for dry barley flour.*

V.—THE DATIVE CASE.

1.—The only genuine Dative sign is ལ་ LA, which should be used in this sense after verbs of *giving*, *shewing*, *speaking* or *telling*, and *teaching*, and some others.

Ex. :—

ངས་ཁྱོད་ལ་དཔེ་ཆ་དེ་སྟེར་གྱི་ཡིན།	*I will give you the book.*
ངའི་ཆིབས་དཔོན་གྱིས་ཁོ་ལ་ལམ་ཀ་བསྟན་པ་རེད་ or བསྟན་སོང་ or འདུག།	*My syce showed him the way.*
མི་ལ་ཤོག་ལབ་དང་།	*Tell the man to come.*
ཁོང་གིས་ཁོ་ཚོ་ལ་ཁོ་རང་གི་ཆོས་ཁྲིམས་བསླབ་ཡོང་།	*He will teoch them his (religious) law.*
ཁྱོད་ཀྱིས་གཡོག་པོ་ལ་མ་འགྲོ་ལབ་པ་ or ཟེར་ར་ (for པ་) ཡིན་པས།	*Did you tell the servant not to go?*

2.—When the verb *To be* is used impersonally; for instance, in sentences intended to be the equivalent of English sentences beginning with the phrases, *There is*, *There was*, *There has been*, Tibetan requires that the word to which ལ་ LA, when used, is annexed, should precede the chief substantive of the subject. With regard to the idiom for expressing the verb *To have*, Tibetans use the verb ཡོད་པ་ YÖ'-PA, *To be present*, *To exist*, in connection with the Dative in ལ་ LA, after the manner of the Russians when the latter, instead of saying YA IMĒYU, *I have*, say U MENYA YEST, *To me is*, or *To me there is*. Ex:—

རི་རྩེ་དེའི་སྟེང་ལ་གངས་ཡོད། — *There is snow on that hill-top.*

If the speaker has some uncertainty regarding the fact to which he is speaking, he will use the verb འདུག་ instead of ཡོད་ Thus:—

རི་རྩེ་དེའི་སྟེང་ལ་གངས་འདུག། — *There is (I am almost sure) snow on that hill-top.*

If he is not at all sure, but is only hazarding the statement, he will use the phrase ཡོད་པ་རེད་ YÖ-PA-RÈ', pronounced YAW-A-RÈ', instead of either ཡོད་ or འདུག་, or he may even use ཡོང་ YONG. Thus:—

རི་རྩེ་དེའི་སྟེང་ལ་གངས་ཡོད་པ་རེད་ (or ཡོང་)། — *There is (I understand) snow on that hill-top.*

When *There is*, *There was*, etc., is used indefinitely, ཡོང་ YONG, *Will be*, takes the place of the above, much as the future is employed by a Highlander in Scotland to express the present tense. Thus:—

ལུང་པས་གི་དེའི་ནང་ལ་ཤིང་སྡོང་ཧ་ཅང་མང་པོ་ཡོང་། — *There are (I expect), or There will be, very many trees in that valley down there.*

3.—The following examples also illustrate the verb *To have*:—

མི་འདི་ལ་ཕ་མ་ཡོད། — *This man has parents.*

ལགས་ཁོ་ལ་ཕ་མ་མེད། (མོད་ is not used now.) — *No, he has no parents.*

ལགས་ཁོ་ལ་ཕ་མ་ཡོད་ — *Yes, he has parents* (emphatic).

4.—The Dative instead of the direct construction may also be used thus :—

ངའི་སེམས་ལ་ཁྱོད་ཀྱི་ཨ་མ་རྒན་མོ་ཡིན་པ་འདྲ། — *I suppose your mother is aged.* Literally, *To my mind your mother seems aged.*

The Honorific form of this would be :—

ངའི་སེམས་ལ་ཁྱེད་ཀྱི་ཡུམ་སྐུ་གཞོགས་
དགོང་ལོ་བགྲེས་པོ་ཡིན་པ་འདྲ།

ལ་, La, is used to express for in sentences like the following :—

རྟ་འདི་སྒོར་མོ་བརྒྱ་ལ་འཚོང་གི་ཡིན། — *I will sell this horse* for Rs. 100.

About, or concerning, is also expressed by ལ་ la. Thus :—

ལས་ཀ་མང་པོ་ཡོད་པའི་དོན་ལ་དཀའ་
ལས་བྱུང་ང་ (བ) རེད་ or སོང་། — *I was or have been troubled about many affairs.*

VI.—The Agentive Case.

This case, which expresses the idea of anything being done by a person or thing, should always be used instead of the Nominative case with Transitive Verbs. The case-signs are as follow, and are annexed to the subject, that is to say, to the noun-substantive, the adjective if any, the definite or indefinite article, if any, or to the phrase constituting the subject.

ས་ Sa, usable after vowels, or after a consonant sounding in inherent ཨ་ *a*. This ས་ is silent, but modifies the immediately preceding vowel-sound. *See* § 3.

གིས་ Ǵi, used after words ending with ག་ or ང་

ཀྱིས་ Kyi, ,, ,, ,, ,, ,, ད་, བ་, or ས་

གྱིས་ Ǵyi, ,, ,, ,, ,, ,, ན་, མ་, ར་, or ལ་

(*N.B.*— གིས་, ཀྱིས་, and གྱིས་ may all be pronounced གིས་ Ŝt.)

འིས་	I	used after words ending with vowels.
ཡིས་	Yi	
ཡིས་	Yi	used in versification after vowels.

EXAMPLES :—

བླ་མ་ཚོས་ཡང་དང་ཡང་གསོལ་ཇ་བཞེས་ཀྱི་འདུག། — *Lamas often drink tea.*

ཁྱེད་ཀྱིས་ང་ལ་དངོས་གནས་བཤད་ཡོད་ན་ ངས་ཁྱེད་ལ་སྙིང་རྗེ་བལྟ་བ་ཡོད། — *If you had told me the truth I would have forgiven you.*

ངས་ཁོ་ལ་ལས་ཀ་དེ་སྤྲོར་ཐུབ་ཀྱི་མེད། — *I cannot give him the work.*

མོས་མོ་རའི་ཁ་ལག་ཟ་གི་མ་རེད། — *She will not eat her food.*

དེ་ནས་མི་སྐྱ་གཡོག་པོས་ (or གཡོག་པོ་ཞིག་གིས་) ཁ་ལག་ཁེ་ཡོང་གི་རེད་ or ཁེ་སླེབ་ཡོང་ or ཁེ་སླེབ་ཀྱི་རེད། — *Then a serving layman will bring food.* (Amundsen).

དེ་ནས་བང་ཆེན་དེས་བུ་མོའི་ཕ་མ་གཉིས་ ལ་སློང་ཆང་བླུག་གི་འདུག། — *Then the messenger pours out the wooing-beer for both the parents of the girl.* (Amundsen).

བུ་དེའི་ཕ་མ་གཉིས་པོས་སྐད་ཆ་འདི་འདྲས་ བྱས་སོང་། — *The two parents of the boy thus consulted (conversed).* (Amundsen).

2.—In connection with the Agentive Case it is convenient here to notice the affix མཁན་ K'ÄN, which in various ways is extensively used in Tibetan, much as کار *Kār*, or گار *Gār*, is used in Persian to indicate a *Doer*. It may also be likened to the English affix ER, in words such as *Behold*ER, *Murder*ER, etc. Later on it will be fully dealt with in connection with the Verb. Here it is only briefly alluded to as a sort of Active Participle annexed to Verbal Roots. Ex.—

འགྲོ་མཁན་	Ḍo-K'än,	*The goer, He who goes.*
ཡོང་མཁན་	Yong-K'än,	*The comer, He who comes.*
འབྲི་མཁན་	Ḍi-K'än,	*The writer, He who writes.*

It is found thus in the Literary Tibetan into which the New Testament has been translated :—

དངོས་པོ་ཐམས་ཅད་བཀོད་མཁན་ནི་དཀོན་མཆོག་ལགས་སོ། *He who built all things is God* (Heb. iii. 4).

སྐུས་ཀྱང་རང་བཏང་མཁན་གྱི་གྲགས་པ་འདོད་པ་དེ་ནི་བདེན་པ་ཡིན་ནོ། *But he that seeketh the glory of him that sent him, the same is true* (John vii. 18).

It is also used adjectively, thus :—

ལུག་རྐུ་མཁན་གྱི་མི། *The man who steals sheep.*

The way in which it is used with the different tenses will be found explained in the paragraphs on The Pronoun (§ 31, IX, A), and The Verb (§ 38, V., D.), and in the Appendix of Conjugations.

VII.—The Locative Case.

This case expresses relations of *Space*, but implies also the idea of *Rest*.

The common case-signs are the following primitive particles :—

ལ་ La }
ན་ Na } : *In, On, At, By*, etc.

so བརྒྱུད་ནས་ Gyü'-nä : *Through.*

Sometimes the more Literary particles ཏུ་, Tu, དུ་, Ḍu, རུ་ Ru, ར་ R., སུ་ Su, are also met with.

Examples :—

ཁོ་ལྷ་ས་རང་ལ་སྡོད་ཀྱི་འདུག། *He lives in Lhassa proper.*

ངས་ཞབས་པད་དེ་ཡིབ་ལམ་ལ་མཐོང་བྱུང་། *I saw the Shā-pe on the road.*

བོད་སྐད་ལ་གསུང་རོགས་གནང་།	*Please speak in Tibetan.*
ངས་ཁོ་ཁོའི་སྤུན་གྱི་ཙར་ (for ཙ་ར་) བསྡད་པ་མཐོང་བྱུང་།	*I saw him sitting next his brother.*
མཆོད་རྟེན་དེ་ལུག་རྫིའི་ཤིང་སྡོང་གི་འགྲམ་ལ་འདུག་གམ།	*Does the chhörten remain by the shepherd's tree?*
ཁོ་རང་གི་ཁང་པ་ལ་ཡོད་།	*He will be at his own house.*
ངས་དེ་ལོ་རྒྱུས་ལ་ (or ན་) བཀླགས་བ་ཡིན།	*I have read it in a history-book.*
ཁོའི་ཨ་མས་ཁོའི་དྲོད་པ་ལ་ཁ་བསྐྱིལ་སོང་།	*His mother kissed him on the forehead.*

The following Colloquial examples illustrate the use of compound postpositions as expressive of the same Locative idea:—

གཡོག་པོས་ཕྱི་ཕྱོགས་ལ་སྒུག་གི་རེད་པས་ or སྒུག་ཡོང་ངམ།	*Will the servant wait outside?*
ངའི་སྔོན་ལ་མ་བཞུགས་རོགས་གནང་།	*Please do not stand in front of me.*
བོད་ཡུལ་འབྲས་ལྗོངས་ཀྱི་ཡར་ཕྱོགས་ལ་འདུག།	*Tibet is beyond Sikhim.*
འབྲས་ལྗོངས་བལ་ཡུལ་དང་འབྲུག་ཡུལ་གྱི་བར་ལ་འདུག།	*Sikhim is between Nipāl and Butān.*
ཁང་པ་ཆུའི་འགྲམ་ལ་འདུག།	*The house is near the river.*
རི་རྩེ་ཚོའི་སྤྱེང་ལ་ (or སྤྱེང་དུ་ or སྟང་ལ་) སྟངས་རྒྱབ་ཀྱི་འདུག།	*It is snowing on the hill-tops.*

དངུལ་རྐྱལ་པའི་ནང་ལ་འདུག།	*The money is inside the leather bag.*
སྤྱང་ཀུ་ལུག་ཁྱུའི་དཀྱིལ་ལ་ (or ནང་ན་) འདུག།	*The wolf is in the midst of the flock of sheep.*
གྲོང་ཁྱེར་དེ་གཙང་པོ་ཆེན་པོ་ཞིག་གི་རྩ་ལ་ ཆགས (or གནས་) འདུག།	*The city stands beside a big river.*
ཁྲིམས་ཁང་དེ་ལྡུམ་ར་སྐྱིང་ཛེ་པོ་ཞིག་གི་ཐག་ ཉེ་པོ་ལ་འདུག།	*The court of justice is near a pretty garden.*
ཕྲུ་གུ་དེ་རྟ་དེའི་རྐང་པའི་འོག་ལ་ཁ་བུབ་ནས་ གོག་པ་རྒྱབ་ཀྱི་འདུག།	*The child creeps under the pony's legs.*

It will be seen that the above Locative postpositions are used with the Genitive Case, that is, they are connected by means of the Genitive sign with the substantive or other part of speech to which they refer.

Notice, however, the following constructions :—

ཁྱི་གིས་བྱ་མོ་ཁང་པ་སྐོར་ར་རྒྱབ་ནས་ གཞུག་དེད་འགྲོ་གི་འདུག།	*The dog chases the hen round the house.*
ཁལ་ (or དོ་པོ་) ཀ་བ་གཉིས་ཀྱི་བར་ བརྒྱུད་ནས་འགྲོ་དགོས་ཀྱི་རེད།	*The load must pass through between the two posts.*
རེ་ལི་དེ་བྲག་རིའི་དཀྱིལ་བརྒྱུད་ནས་ལམ་ བཅོས་པའི་ནང་ལ་བརྒྱུགས་སོང་།	*The train, passing through the midst of the rocky hill, inside the constructed path, ran = The train ran through the rock by the tunnel.*

VIII.—The Periodal or Durational Case.

This case expresses relations of *Time.* Its common signs are the same primitive particles as those which denote the Locative Case, namely :—

ན་ NA	}	*At*, *In*, *During*, etc.
ལ་ LA		

There are also others, like རུ་ Ru, ར་ Ra, དུ་ Ḋu, དུས་ Ḋü, etc.

Sometimes the sign is used alone, and sometimes it forms part of compound postpositions, or even of precedent adverbial expressions.

Examples :—

ཁོ་ཆུ་ཚོད་གསུམ་ལ་འགྲོ་དགོས་ཀྱི་རེད།	*He must go at three o'clock.*
ཁོ་ཁོའི་ལོ་ཉི་ཤུའི་དུས་ལ་རྒྱ་གར་ལ་སླེབས་འདུག།	*He came to India in his twentieth year.*
ངས་ཁྱོད་ལ་ཟླ་བ་གསུམ་གྱི་ནང་ལ་སྤྲད་ཡོང་།	*I shall pay you within three months.*
ཕྱག་འབུལ་དང་པོ་ལ་བོད་པ་ཚོས་གཅིག་ལ་གཅིག་གིས་ཁ་བཏགས་བཏགས་ཀྱི་འདུག།	*At* (or *during*) *the first salutation Tibetans present ceremonial scarfs to each other.*
གདོང་འདྲི་ (or ཕྲདུད) དེ་ས་རིབ་ལ་ (or མཚན་ལ) ཡལ་སོང་།	*The devil disappeared at dusk.*
སྔར་ངས་སངས་རྒྱས་ཀྱི་ཆོས་ལུགས་ཤེས་ཀྱི་ཡོད།	*I knew the doctrine of Buddha a long time ago.*
སྔོན་ལ་ངས་ཤང་དའི་ཟེར་མཁན་གྱི་ཨམ་བན་ངོ་ཤེས་ཀྱི་ཡོད།	*I knew the Amban named Shangtāi a short time ago.*
དུས་གཅིག་ལ་ཁོ་ རྡོ་རྗེ་གླིང་དུ་རྒྱ་མིའི་སྐུ་ཚབ་ཡིན།	*At the same time* (or *At a certain time*) *he was Chinese Ambassador in Darjeeling.*
དུས་དེའི་རྗེས་ལ་ (or གཞུག་ལ་) ངས་འདི་འདྲ་གོ་བྱུང་ཁོ་ཤི་སོང་ (or ཤི་ཚར་) འདུག།	*Since that time, so I have heard, he has died.*

ཆུ་ཚོད་ལྔའི་བར་ལ་ (or བར་དུ་) མ་ཡོང་ རོགས་གནང་།	*Please do not come till five o'clock.*
དེ་དུས་ངས་ཁྱོད་ལ་མཇལ་ཁ་བཏང་གི་ཡིན།	*Then* (or *At that time*) *I will receive you*, i.e., *grant admittance.*
ཁྱོད་གཞུག་ལ་སླེབས་པ་རེད།	*At last you have arrived!*
རིའི་རྩེ་ལ་མ་སླེབས་ (or སླེབས་སླེབས་ without the མ་) གོང་ལ་ཁྱོད་ཐང་ཆད་ཀྱི་རེད།	*On the way up to* (i.e. *before reaching* or *getting to*) *the hill top, you will be tired.*

In sentences like the following, where the durational signification is obvious, the case-sign (say དུས་ལ་ D́Ū-LA) is omitted :—

ཆུ་ཚོད་གཉིས་ཆར་པ་བབ་པ་རེད།	*It has rained for* (or *during*) *two hours.*

That is to say, it is unnecessary to say ཆུ་ཚོད་གཉིས་དུས་ལ་, just as in English it suffices to say *It has rained two hours*, instead of *for two hours.*

IX.—The Modal Case.

This Case is intended to include all that is connoted by the term *Instrumental Case*, and some other additional significations. The signs are :—

ནས་ NĂ : *By, Through, By way of, Via.*

དང་ Dang : *With, Against.*

ས་ Sa (silent) : *With, Because, Since*, etc. Also the *Participial idea.*

རྐྱེན་གྱིས་	Kyèn-gyi	*By, Through, On account of, By reason of*, etc.
ཕྱིར་	Ch'ir (Literary)	
ཕྱིར་དུ	Ch'ir-d́u (Literary)	

EXAMPLES :—

ཁོ་ལ་མིང་ནས་སྐད་བཏང་ (or བརྗོད་)།	*Accost* (or *call to*) *him by name.*
རྟ་དེ་སྲབ་ཐག་ནས་འཛུས།	*Seize the horse by the reins.*
བྱ་བཟུང་ན་རྐང་པ་ནས་བཟུང་།	*If you catch the fowl, catch it by the legs.*
ཉ་བཟུང་ན་མགོ་ནས་བཟུང་།	*If you grasp the fish, grasp it by the head.*
བླ་མ་དེ་ཚོས་དུང་ནས་ལབ་བྱུང་།	*The lamas spoke through trumpets.*
ང་ཚོ་ལ་ལམ་ཀ་ལ་ཇག་པ་དང་ཐུག་བྱུང་།	*We met* (or *fell in*) *with robbers on the road.*
ཞབས་པད་ཚོས་རྒྱལ་པོ་དང་མཇལ་བ་རེད།	*The Shyab-pä's (Żhāpés) have had an interview with the Regent.*
རྒྱལ་པོས་བཀའ་བློན་ཚོ་འི་བསམ་པ་དང་ བསྟུན་ཡོང་ངམ།	*Will the Regent agree with the opinion of the Kā-lōns ?*
ང་ཚོ་འི་དམག་མི་ཚོས་དགྲ་དང་འཛིང་ང་ (for བ་) རེད།	*Our soldiers have fought with the enemy*, or *against the enemy.*
གཟེར་ (ལ་) ཐོ་བས་བརྡུང་།	*Strike the nail with the hammer.*
ཆང་ཁང་གི་རྐྱེན་གྱིས་ཁོ་མེད་པ་སོང་བ་རེད།	*He was ruined by, through*, or *on account of, the beer-house.*
བཀྲ་ཤིས་བླ་མ་འམ་པཎ་ཆེན་རིན་པོ་ཆེའམ་ གཙང་པཎ་ཆེན་ཡང་ཟེར། ཁོང་བཀྲ་ཤིས་ ལྷུན་པོ་ནས་རྡོ་རྗེ་གླིང་བརྒྱུད་འཆིབ་རྒྱུ་ གནང་སོང་།	*The Päṇ-chhen-rim-po-chhe*, *or Tsang-päṇ-chhen, called the Ṭashi Lama, came from Ṭashi lhümpo via Darjeeling.*

The following is Literary from the New Testament :—

ཁྱེད་ཚོ་གང་གི་སྐོར་ལ་འདི་དག་དང་རྩོད་པ་ བྱེད།	*What question (dispute) ye wit them ?*

Colloquially :—

ཁྲོད་ཆོས་ག་རེའི་སྐོར་ལ་འདི་ཚོ་དང་རྩོད་པ་རྒྱབ་ཀྱི་ཡོད།

Again :—

ང་ཡིན་པས་མ་འཇིགས་ཤིག། — *It is I : be not afraid :* Literally, *It being I*, etc.

Colloquially :—

ང་ཡོད་ཙང་ (ཅིང་) མ་ཞེད་ཅིག།

The following also is Literary :—

ཅིའི་ཕྱིར་ཁོ་བརླག་སོང་ or མེད་པ་སོང་། — *Through* or *by what was he ruined?*

X.—The Ablative Case.

Postpositions such as དང་ Ḋang, ནས་ Nǎ, and ལས་ Lǎ, all signifying *From*, *From amongst*, *From amidst*, *Out of*, etc., are usually assigned to this case ; but inasmuch as, when carrying those significations, they really express the idea of *Direction from*, they have been placed under the heading Terminative Case.

ལས་ Lǎ, however, possesses meanings other than *Direction from*.

Accordingly, ལས་ Lǎ, and ན་ Na, may be taken as the signs of the Ablative Case, as expressive of significations such as the following :—

ལས་ Lǎ : *Than*, *Except*, *Save*, *But*, *But for*, *Besides*, etc.

ན་ Na (with negative) : *Unless*, *If..not*.

Examples :—

ཞབས་པད་དེ་རྒྱ་གར་ལ་ཟླ་བ་ཁ་ཤས་ལས་སྡོད་མི་ཡོང་། — *The Shapé will not stay in India except for a few months*, i.e. *longer than a few months.*

རྫོང་གི་ནང་ལ་དམག་མི་གཅིག་ལས་མི་འདུག། — *There was nobody in the fortress except one soldier.*

ཤར་པ་ལ་རས་གོས་གཅིག་ལས་མེད་ཀྱང་ མང་ཤོས་ཁོ་སྐྱིད་པོ་འདུག།	*When the Oriental possesses nothing but one piece of cotton cloth he is often happy.*
འདི་ལས་གཞན་མེད།	*Besides this there is no other.*
ལས་ཀ་ཐམས་ཅད་མ་ཚར་ན་གླ་ཐོབ་ཀྱི་མ་ རེད།	*Unless all the work is done you will get no pay.*
འགྲུལ་པ་ཚོ་ཇག་པ་རྒྱབ་ན་ཁྱེད་ཚོ་ཐམས་ ཅད་ཉེས་པ་བཏང་ཡོང་།	*Unless travellers are not robbed*, i.e. *If travellers are robbed, you will all be punished.*

Resort may also be had to the phrase གལ་ཏེ་ (or གལ་སྲིད་) .... ན་ ǴĂ-TE (or ǴĂ-ṬI')..NA, with a negative, *If..not*, or even the ན་ NA alone, as above, without the གལ་ཏེ་ Thus :—

གལ་ཏེ་ཁྱེད་ཚོ་སེམས་མི་སྒྱུར་ན།	*Unless ye repent*, or *If ye repent not* (Literary. I Luke xiii. 3, 5).

Colloquially :—

ཁྱེད་ཚོ་འགྱོད་པ་མི་སྐྱེད་ན།	*Unless you repent.*
ཁྱི་ཁང་པའི་རྒྱལ་སྒོ་ལ་མེད་ན།	*Unless the dog is at the entrance door.*
སྙན་ཞུ་མ་ཕུལ་ན།	*Unless the petition is presented.*
གན་རྒྱ་ལ་རྟགས་མ་བཞག་ན།	*Unless the agreement (bond) has been signed.*

The following are Literary expressions used in the New Testament :—

མི་སྣ་རྣམས་མ་གཏོགས་པར་དེ་དག་ཐམས་ ཅད་ etc.	*Except the apostles they all*, etc. (Acts viii. 1).
དེ་མ་ཟད་ངེད་དང་ཁྱེད་ཀྱི་བར་ལ་གཡང་ས་ ཆེན་པོ་ཞིག་ཡོད་དེ།	*Besides all this, between us and you is (being) a great gulf*, (Luke xvi. 26).

སུས་ཀྱང་རང་གི་ཆུང་མ་ལོག་གཡེམ་མ་ བྱས་པར་དེ་དང་བྲལ་ནས་ etc.	*Whosoever shall put away his wife, except it be for fornication,* i.e. *fornication not having been committed.* (Matt. v. 32).

These may be rendered Colloquially thus :—

མི་སྣ་ཚོ་མ་གཏོགས་ (or མིན་པ་) དེ་ཚོ་ ཐམས་ཅད་ etc.	*Except the apostles they all*, etc.
སུས་ཀྱང་རང་གི་སྐྱེ་དམན་ལོག་གཡེམ་མ་ བྱས་ནས་ཁ་བྲལ་ན།	*Whosever shall put away his wife, except it be for fornication=If anybody divorces his wife, fornication not having been committed.*
དེ་མ་གཏོགས་ (or དེ་མིན་པ་) ང་ཚོ་དང་ ཁྱོད་ཚོའི་བར་ལ་གཡང་གཟར་པོ་ཆེན་ པོ་ཞིག་ཡོད་ཙང་།	*Besides all this, between us and you is (being) a great gulf*, etc.

The expressions *Apart from*, and *Rather than*, are rendered thus :—

ང་ལ་སྒོར་མོ་གཉིས་ཡོད་དེ་དེ་མ་གཏོགས་ ངས་ཁྱོད་ལ་ག་གས་སྤྲེར་གྱི་མིན།	*I have two rupees, but apart from that I will give you nothing.*
ཁྱོད་ལ་དངུལ་སྤྲེར་བ་ལས་ཁ་ལག་སྤྲེར་ར་ དགའ་བ་ཡིན།	*I would rather give you food than money.*
Or བསྤྲེར་ར་ཡིན།	*Would give.*

XI.—The Terminative or Transitive Case.

This case denotes the relations of a noun or pronoun with reference to its *Direction* in *Time* or *Space*, either *towards* or *from* something mentioned in the sentence, and it may imply the idea of *motion* as well as that of *rest*. Under it come, as already stated, many expressions signifying *direction from*, which in other books are assigned to the Ablative Case.

The signs of the case as thus defined are :—

དུ་ Ḍu : after final ང, ད, ན, མ, ར, ལ		DIRECTION TOWARDS.
ཏུ་ Tu : after final ག, ད་དྲག, བ		
ར་ Ra, རུ་ Ru : after final vowels.		
སུ་ Su : after final ས་		
ལ་ La : commonly used in the Colloquial after anything, and possessing the significations of all the above signs.		

དང་ Ḍang	DIRECTION FROM.
ནས་ Nä	
ལས་ Lä	

EXAMPLE :—

1.—DIRECTION TOWARDS.

བར་དུ་ Ḅar-ḍu : *Up to, Until, As far as, As long as..not.*

ད་ལྟའི་བར་དུ་ངས་ཁོ་མ་མཐོང་ *Up till now, I have not seen him.*

ད་བར་དུ་ *Hitherto.*

དེའི་བར་དུ་ or དེ་བར་དུ་ *Until then, Up to that time.*

མ་ཐོབ་པའི་བར་དུ་ *As long as it has not been obtained*, i.e. *Until it has been obtained.*

ཁོ་མ་ཤི་བའི་བར་དུ་ *As long as he does not die*, i.e. *Until he dies*

འདི་ནས་ལྷ་ས་ག་རེ་བར་དུ་འདུག *How far is Lhasa from here?*

དང་མཉམ་དུ་ Dang Ñyam-ḍu : *Together with, Along with, In Company with.*

ཁོ་བྱེ་ཐང་ལ་རི་དྭགས་དང་མཉམ་དུ་བསྡད་པ་རེད *He has been dwelling with wild beasts in the desert.*

དཀྱིལ་དུ་ KYI-ḌU : *Amongst, Amidst, Into the midst of.*

ཞི་མི་ཙ་ཙི་ཡོད་པའི་བྱིའུ་སྐྱ་ཚོ་ནི་དཀྱིལ་དུ་མཆོངས་ཀྱི་འདུག *The cat springs in amongst the twittering sparrows (little gray birds.)*

གན་དུ་ ǴÄN-ḌU : *Towards.*

མི་ཚོགས་དེ་ཕོ་བྲང་གི་གན་དུ་འགྲོ་གི་འདུག *The crowd is going towards the palace.*

ནང་དུ་ NANG-ḌU : *Into.*

ཁྱི་དེ་ཆུའི་ནང་དུ་མཆོངས་པའི་འདོད་པ་འདུག *The dog wishes to jump into the water.*

ཐོག་ཏུ་ T'OǴ-TU : *In the direction of ; Towards.*

གོ་བོ་ཉི་མའི་ཐོག་ཏུ་ལྡིང་གི་འདུག *The eagle soars towards the sun.*

ར་ RA }
རུ་ RU } *To.*

བུ་གུ་རྒྱ་མཚོ་རུ་ (or ལ་, or མཚོར་) བཏང་ང་རེད *The boy has been sent to sea.*

ཁོ་ཡ་ནས་ཚུར་ཡོངས་པ་རེད *He has come from up there hitherward.*

ཁོ་མ་ནས་ཚུར་ཡོངས་པ་རེད *He has come from down there hitherward.*

ཁོ་ཕ་ནས་ཚུར་ཡོངས་པ་རེད *He has come from over there, or yonder, hitherward.*

གྲོག་མ་དེ་ཚོ་ངའི་རྐང་པའི་རྩར་ (or more Colloquially ཙྲོ་) སྦྲུང་ཡོང་གི་འདུག *The ants are swarming near my feet.*

མ་རུ་ MA-RU : *Down to.*

ང་ཁྲོམ་མ་རུ་འགྲོ་གི་ཡོད་ *I am going down to the bazaar.*

མར་ MAR : *Downwards, Down ;* ཡར་ YAR, *Upwards, Up.*

ང་ཡར་འགྲོ་མར་འགྲོ་བྱེད་ཀྱི་ཡིན་ *I shall travel up and down.*

སུ་ Su : *To, Towards.*

དུས་སུ་ (or ལ་) འབབ་ཀྱི་འདུག *It is getting towards the time.*

ཁོ་རང་གི་གནས་སུ་སོང་ *He has gone to his own abode.*

ཕྱོགས་ལ་ Ch'ō-la, or ངོས་ལ་ Ngö-la : *Towards, On,* etc.

ལམ་ཀའི་ཚུར་ཕྱོགས་ལ་ཁང་པ་ཚོ་ཡོད་ཕར་ཕྱོགས་ལ་སྤང་ཡོད་ *On this side of the road there are houses, on that side meadows.*

དམག་དཔུང་དེ་བོད་ཡུལ་ངོས་ལ་ (or ཕྱོགས་ལ་) སྐྱིབས་བྱུང་ *The army marched towards Tibet.*

དུས་ལ་ Ďü-la : *To the time ; at the time of.*

དུས་ལ་བབ་སོང་ *It came down to the time,* i.e. *The time arrived*

དུས་ལ་བབ་ཡོང་ *The time will come.*

བར་སྣང་དུ་ Ďar-ňang-ďu ? or བར་ལ་ Ďar-la : *Over, above.*

ཕྱེ་མ་ལེབ་དེ་ངའི་མགོ་འི་བར་ལ་འཕིར་གྱི་འདུག *The butterfly flits over my head.*

སྔོན་ལ་ Ngön-la : *Ahead, In front.*

ངའི་སྔོན་ལ་རྒྱུག *Go on ahead* (or *in front*) *of me.*

2.—Direction from.

དང་ Ďang : *From.* This is Literary.

མཚོ་དེ་ས་མཚམས་དེ་དང་ཐག་རིང་པོ་ཡོད་ *The lake is far from the frontier.*

པགས་པ་དེ་འབྲུ་དེ་དང་ཕྲལ་བ་ཡིན་ *The husk was separated from the grain.*

ནས་ Nä : *From.*

སྦྲུལ་དེ་ཤིང་སྡོང་ཚང་ཚང་གི་བར་ནས་ཁ་བུབ་གོག་པ་རེད་ *The snake has crawled from between the bushes.*

ཞི་མི་དེ་ཀྲུ་ལྕོག་གི་འོག་ནས་ཁ་བུབ་གོག་གི་འདུག *The cat creeps from under the table.*

ཁྲིམས་ཁང་དེ་ལྡུམ་ར་སྐྱིད་རྗེ་པོ་ཞིག་ནས་ཐག་ཉེ་པོ་འདུག *The Court of Justice is close to* (literally *from*) *a pretty garden.*

ཁོ་ཡ་ནས་ཕར་ཕྱིན་པ་རེད *He has gone from up there thitherward.*

ཁོ་མ་ནས་ཕར་ཕྱིན་པ་རེད *He has gone from down there thitherward.*

ད་ནས་ཕྱིན་ཆད་ངས་ཁྱོད་ལ་ལབ་ཀྱི་མིན *Henceforth I shall not speak to you.*

དེ་ནས་ངས་ཁོ་ལ་མ་ལབ་པ་ཡིན *After that*, or *thenceforth, I did not speak to him.*

ཁྱོད་འདི་ནས་དེ་ཐུག་འགྲོ་ཆོག་གི་འདུག *You may walk from here to there*, or *to that.*

ཐོག་མ་ནས་དེ་ལྟར་མེད་པ་ཡིན *From the beginning it was not so.* —(New Testament).

Colloquially :—

སྔོན་དང་པོ་ནས་འདི་འདྲས (or དེ་ག་ཟེ་, or དེ་ག་རང) མེད་པ་རེད *From the beginning it was not so.*

ཁོང་པད་མ་ནས་བྱུང *He originated from the Lotus.*—(S. C. Das.)

དེ་དུས་གཞོན་པ་ཚོ་དཔེ་ཆ་བློ་ནས་སྐྱོར་དགོས *Meanwhile the younger ones must recite their books by* (literally *from*) *heart.*—(Amundsen).

ལས LĀ : *Out of.*

མི་བརྒྱད་ལས་གཉིས་གཅིག་པོ་སླེབས་བྱུང *Out of eight men only two arrived.*

ཁོས་ཁ་ཏི་ཞྭ་མོ་ཆུ་ལས་འཐེན་སོང *He drew his cap out of the water.*

§ 26.—Numerals.

I.—*The Cardinal Numbers*, according to གྲངས་ཀྱི་ (or རྩིས་ཀྱི་) རྣམ་གྲངས་ Ḍang-kyi (or Tsī-kyi) Ňam-ḍang, *Arithmetical Enumeration.*

English Figure.	Tibetan Figure.	Tibetan Name.	Romanized Equivalent.
1	༡	གཅིག་	Chi'.
2	༢	གཉིས་	Ňyī.
3	༣	གསུམ་	Sum.
4	༤	བཞི་	Žhyi.
5	༥	ལྔ་	Ňga.
6	༦	དྲུག་	Ḍu'.
7	༧	བདུན་	Ďün.
8	༨	བརྒྱད་	Ǧyä'.
9	༩	དགུ་	Ǧu.
10	༡༠	བཅུ་, or བཅུ་ཐམ་པ་	Chu, or Chu t'ampa.
11	༡༡	བཅུ་གཅིག་	Chuǵ-chi'.
12	༡༢	བཅུ་གཉིས་	chuǵ-ňyī.
13	༡༣	བཅུ་གསུམ་	Chuǵ-sum.
14	༡༤	བཅུ་བཞི་	Chub-žhyi.
15	༡༥	བཅོ་ལྔ་	Chŏ-ňga.
16	༡༦	བཅུ་དྲུག་	Chu-ḍu'.
17	༡༧	བཅུ་བདུན་	Chub-ďün.

English Figure.	Tibetan Figure.	Tibetan Name.	Romanized Equivalent.
18	༡༨	བཅོ་བརྒྱད	Chob-ğyä'.
19	༡༩	བཅུ་དགུ་	Chu-ğu.
20	༢༠	ཉི་ཤུ, or ཉི་ཤུ་ཐམ་པ་	Nyi-shu, or Nyi-shu t'am-pa.
21	༢༡	ཉི་ཤུ་རྩ་གཅིག, or ཉེར་གཅིག, or རྩ་གཅིག	Nyi-shu tsaǵ-chi'. Nyer-chi'. Tsaǵ-chi'.
22	༢༢	ཉི་ཤུ་རྩ་གཉིས, or རྩ་གཉིས་	Nyi-shu tsaǵ-ňyī. Tsaǵ-ňyī.
30	༣༠	སུམ་ཅུ, or སུམ་ཅུ་ཐམ་པ་	Sum-chu, or Sum-chu t'am-pa.
31	༣༡	སུམ་ཅུ་སོ་གཅིག, or སོ་གཅིག་	Sum-chu soǵ-chi'. Soǵ-chi'.
40	༤༠	བཞི་བཅུ, or བཞི་བཅུ་ཐམ་པ་	Žhyib-chu, or Žhib-chu t'am-pa.
41	༤༡	བཞི་བཅུ་ཞེ་གཅིག, or ཞེ་གཅིག་	Žhib-chu źhye-chi. Źhye-chi'.
50	༥༠	ལྔ་བཅུ, or ལྔ་བཅུ་ཐམ་པ་	Ňgab-chu, or Ňgab-chu t'am-pa.
51	༥༡	ལྔ་བཅུ་ང་གཅིག, or ང་གཅིག	Ngab-chu nga-chi'. Nga-chi'.
60	༦༠	དྲུག་ཅུ, or དྲུག་ཅུ་ཐམ་པ་	Ḍuǵ-chu, or Ḍuǵ-chu t'am-pa.
61	༦༡	དྲུག་ཅུ་རེ་གཅིག, or རེ་གཅིག་	Ḍuǵ-chu re-chi'. Re-chi'.

English Figure.	Tibetan Figure.	Tibetan Name.	Romanized Equivalent.
70	༧༠	བདུན་ཅུ་, or བདུན་ཅུ་ཐམ་པ་	Ďün-chu, or Ďün-chu t'am-pa.
71	༧༡	བདུན་ཅུ་དོན་གཅིག་, or དོན་གཅིག་	Ďön-chu ďön-chi'. Ďön-chi'.
80	༨༠	བརྒྱད་ཅུ་, or བརྒྱད་ཅུ་ཐམ་པ་	Ǧyä'-chu, or Ǧyä'-chu t'am-pa.
81	༨༡	བརྒྱད་ཅུ་གྱ་གཅིག་, or གྱ་གཅིག་	Ǧyä'-chu ǵya-chi'. Ǵya-chi'.
90	༩༠	དགུ་བཅུ་, or དགུ་བཅུ་ཐམ་པ་	Ǧub-chu, or Ǧub-chu t'am-pa.
91	༩༡	དགུ་བཅུ་གོ་གཅིག་, or གོ་གཅིག་	Ǧub-chu ǵo-chi'. Ǵo-chi'.
100	༡༠༠	བརྒྱ་, or བརྒྱ་ཐམ་པ་	Ǧya, or Ǧya-t'am-pa.
101	༡༠༡	བརྒྱ་དང་གཅིག་	Ǧya Ǧdang chi'.
200	༢༠༠	ཉི་བརྒྱ་, or ཉིས་བརྒྱ་	Nyib-ǧya, or Nyīb-ǧya.
300	༣༠༠	སུམ་བརྒྱ་	Sum-ǧya.
400	༤༠༠	བཞི་བརྒྱ་	Žhyib-ǧya.
500	༥༠༠	ལྔ་བརྒྱ་	Ňgab-ǧya.
1000	༡༠༠༠	སྟོང་, or སྟོང་ཕྲག་	Ťong, or Ťong-ṭ'a'.
5500	༥,༥༠༠	སྟོང་ཕྲག་ལྔ་དང་ལྔ་བརྒྱ་	Ťong-ṭ'a' ňga ďang ngab-ǧya.
10,000	༡༠,༠༠༠	ཁྲི་, or ཁྲི་ཕྲག་	Ṭ'i, or Ṭ'i-ṭ'a'.
100,000	༡༠༠,༠༠༠	འབུམ་, or འབུམ་ཕྲག་	B̌um, or B̌um-ṭ'a'.
1,000,000	༡,༠༠༠,༠༠༠	ས་ཡ་	Sa-ya.
10,000,000	༡༠,༠༠༠,༠༠༠	བྱེ་བ་	J'e-wa.

English.	Tibetan.	Romanized equivalent.
100 millions	དུང་ཕྱུར་	Ḍung-ch'ur.
1000 millions	ཐེར་འབུམ་	Ṭ'er-ḃum.
10,000 millions	ཐེར་འབུམ་ཆེན་པོ་	Ṭ'er-ḃum ch'em-po.
100,000 millions.	ཁྲག་ཁྲིག་	Ṭ'aǵ-t'i'.
A billion	ཁྲག་ཁྲིག་ཆེན་པོ་	Ṭ'aǵ-ṭ'i' ch'em-po.
10 billions	རབ་བཀྲམ་	Rab-ṭam.
100 billions	རབ་བཀྲམ་ཆེན་པོ་	Rab-ṭam ch'em-po.
1000 billions	གཏམས་	Ṭam.
10,000 billions	གཏམས་ཆེན་པོ་	Ṭam-ch'em-po.
100,000 billions	དཀྲིགས་	Ṭī'.
1,000,000 billions	དཀྲིགས་ཆེན་པོ་	Ṭī ch'em-po.

N.B.—To the above succeed progressive numbers increasing by multiples of ten up to sixty enumerations, counting 100 millions as the ninth. These sixty enumerations are used for astronomical and astrological purposes. Sanskrit equivalents exist only up to the fifty-first enumeration. *See* Rai Sarat Chandra Das Bahadur's Dictionary, article གྲངས་ GRAṄGS (*Ḍang*).

II.—*The Cardinal Numbers*, according to ཀ་ཁའི་རྣམ་གྲངས་ KA-K'AI ŇAM-ḌANG, *Alphabetical Enumeration.*

The following system of Numerical Notation is employed by Tibetans in their Registers, Indices, and the like. It only goes up to 300, and consists of an adaptation of the ཀ་ལི་. It may be regarded as the equivalent of our own method of Notation by means of the Roman letters.

1 to 30	ཀ,	ཁ,	ག,	and so on to	ཨ
31 ,, 60	ཀི,	ཁི,	གི,	,, ,, ,, ,,	ཨི
61 ,, 90	ཀུ,	ཁུ,	གུ,	,, ,, ,, ,,	ཨུ
91 ,, 120	ཀེ,	ཁེ,	གེ,	,, ,, ,, ,,	ཨེ
121 ,, 150	ཀོ,	ཁོ,	གོ,	,, ,, ,, ,,	ཨོ
151 ,, 180	ཀཱ,	ཁཱ,	གཱ,	,, ,, ,, ,,	ཨཱ
181 ,, 210	ཀཱི,	ཁཱི,	གཱི,	,, ,, ,, ,,	ཨཱི
211 ,, 240	ཀཱུ,	ཁཱུ,	གཱུ,	,, ,, ,, ,,	ཨཱུ
241 ,, 270	ཀཱེ,	ཁཱེ,	གཱེ,	,, ,, ,, ,,	ཨཱེ
271 ,, 300	ཀཱོ,	ཁཱོ,	གཱོ,	,, ,, ,, ,,	ཨཱོ

NOTES.

1.—Pronunciation.

The Colloquial custom of pronouncing the prefix of a second syllable with, and as though it were part of, the preceding syllable, is really incorrect, and is not followed in Literary Tibetan. Thus, བཅུ་གཅིག *Eleven*, pronounced CHUǴ-CHI' in Colloquial, is pronounced CHU-CHI' in Literary Tibetan. So བཅུ་བཞི *Fourteen*, pronounced CHUB-ŽHYI in Colloquial, is pronounced CHU-ŽHYI in Literary Tibetan.

2.—Affixes.

ཐམ་པ་ T'AM-PA, signifies *full*, or *complete*, and is almost exclusively used with the full tens, up to and inclusive of a hundred; meaning thereby a collective body, or whole lot, of any of those numbers. It is, however, similarly, but much less frequently, applied to numbers *below* ten.

After a hundred and with thousands ཕྲག T'A' is used. Also after expressions denoting periods of time, such as བདུན་ཕྲག ḌUN-Ṭ'A', *a week*; ཟླ་ཕྲག ḌA-Ṭ'A', *a month*.

With numbers above thousands ཚོ་ Ts'o ; is used.

As regards all these affixes, however, their use or non-use is quite optional.

3.—CONJUNCTIONS.

Note that where units are connected with some multiple of ten, the conjunction used is different for each series. In the 20 series it is ཙ་ TSA ; in the 30 series, སོ་ So ; in the 40 series, ཞེ་ ŻHYE ; in the 50 series, ང་ NGA ; in the 60 series, རེ་ RE ; in the 70 series, དོན་ ḊÖN ; in the 80 series, གྱ་ ǴYA ; in the 90 series, གོ་ ǴO. With the hundreds it is དང་ ḊANG. It would not, however, be wrong to use དང་ ḊANG in all cases. In Literary Tibetan both དང་ ḊANG, and one of the other conjunctions (usually) ཙ་ TSA, are used together. Thus སྟོང་དང་ཙ་གསུམ་ TONG ḊANG TSA SUM, 1003. This is not done in the Colloquial.

In the Colloquial the short forms ཙ་གཅིག་ TSAǴ-CHI', 21 ; ཙ་གཉིས་ TSAǴ-ŃYI, 22 ; སོ་གཅིག་ SOǴ-CHI', 31 ; སོ་བཞི་ SOB-ŻHYI, 34 ; and the like, are very often heard instead of the longer forms, ཉི་ཤུ་ཙ་གཅིག་ NYI-SHU-TSAǴ-CHI', 21, etc.

When dates are being stated or enumerated, the ཙ་ TSA, or དང་ ḊANG in the 20 series is dropped, and the form with ཉེར་ NYER is used, e.g. ཉེར་བརྒྱད་པ་ NYER-ǴYË'-PA, *the 28th.*

4.—THE INDEFINITE ARTICLE, *see* § 28.

5.—APPROXIMATE NUMBERS.

Expressions like *two or three, nine or ten*, are rendered by putting the numbers in immediate juxtaposition. Ex. གཉིས་གསུམ་ ŃYI-SUM *two-three* ; དགུ་བཅུ་ GUB-CHU, *nine-ten*. If the speaker likes, he may add ཅིག་ CHI', *a or an*, to any of these expressions. Thus, གཉིས་གསུམ་ཅིག་ ŇYI SUM CHI', *Two* or *three*.

Another method is to employ the adverb ཙམ་ TSAM, *About*, *Just about*, *As many as*. Ex. སོ་གཅིག་ཙམ་ SOǴ CHI' TSAM, *About* 31, or *As many as* 31; or the adverbs ཧ་ལམ་ HA-LAM, ག་ཆེན་ ǴA-CH'EN, ཙར་ TSAR, or འགྲམ་ལ་ ḌAM-LA, signifying *nearly*, *almost*. In these cases the adverb follows the numeral it qualifies.

6.—ORDINAL NUMBERS.

The first is rendered དང་པོ་ ḊANG-PO, and *The very first* ཇེ་དང་པོ་ JE-ḊANG-PO. With these exceptions the ordinals are merely the cardinals plus the particle པ་ PA. Ex. གཉིས་པ་ ŇYI-PA, *The second*; བཅོ་ལྔ་པ་ CHÖ-ŇGA-PA, *The fifteenth*; ཉེར་གསུམ་པ་ NYER-SUM-PA, or ཉེ་ཤུ་གསུམ་པ་ NYE-SHU SUM-PA, *The twenty-third*.

7.—DISTRIBUTIVE NUMBERS.

When simple numerals are repeated in juxtaposition, e.g. གསུམ་གསུམ་ SUM-SUM, *Three-three*, the meaning may be either *three each*, or *three at once*, or *three at a time*, or *in threes*, according to the way the sentence is framed. For instance, phrases like *Three at a time*, or *In threes*, or *One at a time*, are rendered by help of the expression བྱས་ནས་ J'Ă-NĂ, or CHĂ NĂ, literally *Having done* or *Having made*. Thus:—

ཁོ་ཚོ་སུམ་སུམ་བྱས་ནས་ཐོན་སོང་།	*They set out in threes*, or *three at a time*.
ཁོ་ཚོ་རེ་རེ་བྱས་ནས་ཕེབས་བྱུང་།	*They arrived one by one*, or *one at a time*.

Expressions like *Three each*, *Two each*, *One each*, are rendered by རེ་རེ་ RE-RE and a repeated numeral, but without the བྱས་ནས་ J'Ă-NĂ.

Thus :—

མི་རེ་རེ་ལ་སྒོར་མོ་སུམ་སུམ་ཐོབ་སོང་། *Each man got three rupees.*

དོས་པ་རེ་རེ་ལ་སྒོར་མོ་རེ་རེ་སྟེར། *Give each coolie one rupee.*

In the case of composite numerals like དོན་གཅིག་ DÖN-CHI', *Seventy-one*, only the last number of the compound is repeated. Ex. :— དོན་གཅིག་གཅིག་ DÖN-CHIǴ-CHI', *Seventy-one each, seventy-one at a time,* or *In seventy-ones.*

8.—AGGREGATES.

Expressions like *The two together*, or *Both*, or *All three*, or *The whole ten*, may be rendered with the aid of the particles ཀ་ KA, or ཅ་ CHA, or པོ་ PO, affixed to the cardinal. Ex. :—གཉིས་ཀ་ NYÍ-KA, *Both*, or *The two together* ; གསུམ་པོ་ SUM-PO, *All three*, or *The three together* ; དགུ་ཅ་ GU-CHA, *The whole nine.*

པོ་ PO, thus affixed, may also signify *the aforesaid*, if the context so requires.

9.—FRACTIONS.

These are usually expressed by adding the word ཆ་ CH'A, *Part*, to the cardinal, which is sometimes put in the Genitive Case. Thus :—

⅓rd	is rendered by			གསུམ་ཆ་ SUM-CH'A.
¼th	,,	,,	,,	བཞི་ཆ་ ŻHYI-CH'A.
$\frac{1}{32}$nd	,,	,,	,,	སོ་གཉིས་ཆ་ SOǴ-ŇYİ CH'A, or སོ་གཉིས་ཀྱི་ཆ་ SOǴ-ŇYİ KYI CH'A.
$\frac{1}{100}$th	,,	,,	,,	བརྒྱ་ཆ་ GYA-CH'A or བརྒྱའི་ཆ་ GYÄI-CH'A.
$\frac{1}{1000}$th	,,	,,	,,	སྟོང་ཆ་ TONG-CH'A, or སྟོང་གི་ཆ་ TONG-ǴI-CH'A.
⅔rd	,,	,,	,,	གསུམ་ཆ་གཉིས་ SUM-CH'A NYİ.
¾th	,,	,,	,,	བཞི་ཆ་གསུམ་ ŻHYI-CH'A SUM.

As regards ½, there is a special expression, namely, ཕྱེད་ཀ་ CH'E'-KA.

1½. may be rendered two ways: either གཅིག་དང་ཕྱེད་ཀ་

CHI' ḌANG CH'E'-KA, or ཕྱེད་དང་གཉིས་ CH'E' ḌANG ÑYI, *With a half, two.* The latter is the commoner usage in the Colloquial.

3¼ is rendered གསུམ་དང་བཞི་ཆ་ SUM ḌANG ŹHYI-CH'A, or བཞི་ཆ་གསུམ་དང་བཞི་ ŹHYI-CH'A SUM ḌANG ŹHYI, *With ¾ths four.*

མགོ་པས་ཅ་ལག་ཁྱུན་མ་ཁྱ་བའི་བཅུ་ཆ་ཐོབ་བྱུང་། *The leader received one-tenth of the booty.*

10.—ADVERBIAL CARDINAL NUMBERS.

Expressions like *Once, Twice, Thrice, Four times*, etc., are rendered by the word ཚར་ TS'AR, or ཐེངས་ T'ENG, *Time*, followed by the desired cardinal number. EX. :—ཚར་གཅིག་ TS'AR-CHI', or ཐེངས་གཅིག་ T'ENG-CHI', *Once* ; ཚར་གཉིས་ TS'AR-ÑYI, or ཐེངས་གཉིས་ T'ENG-ÑYI *Twice* ; ཚར་གསུམ་ TS'AR-SUM or ཐེངས་གསུམ་ T'ENG-SUM, *Thrice* ; ཚར་བཞི་ TS'AR-ZHYI or ཐེངས་བཞི་ T'ENG-ZHYI, *Four times*.

Another word with the same signification, as ཚར་ T'SAR and ཐེངས་ T'ENG is ལན་—LĀN, but it is not so much used in the Colloquial.

Other expressions that may here be mentioned are :—

ལམ་སང་ LAM-SANG : *At once. Forthwith, Straightway, Immediately.*

ད་རུང་ཚར་གཅིག་ ḌA RUNG TS'AR-CHI' : *Once more.*

ད་རུང་ཚར་གཉིས་ ḌA-RUNG TS'AR-ÑYI } *Twice more.*
ད་རུང་ཐེངས་གཉིས་ ḌA-RUNG Ñ'ENG-ÑYI }

ཚེར་ TS'ER, *A separate time* or *occasion*, or *instance*.

ཚེར་ཚེར་ TS'ER TS'ER, *Many times, On separate occasions, Repeatedly.*

ཤུག་ཚེར་ SHUǴ-TS'ER, *A separate time* or *occasion*.

ཚར་མང་པོ་ TS'AR MANG-PO : *Many times.*

ཚར་མང་པོ་རང་ TS'AR MANG-PO RANG (with negative) : *Not many times.*

Once upon a time, or *Once*, or *One day*, referring either to the past or the future, may be rendered དུས་ཚར་ (or ལན་, or ཐེངས་) གཅིག་ (ཞིག or ཤིག་) D́Ü TS'AR (or LÄN, or T'ENG) CHI' (ZHYI', or SHI'); or དུས་རེ་ཞིག་ D́Ü-RE-ZHYI', or དུས་རེ་ཞིག་གི་ཚེ་ D́Ü-RE-ZHYIǴ-ǴI TS'E.

11.—ADVERBIAL ORDINAL NUMBERS.

These are formed by adding ར་ RA, to the པོ་ PO, or པ་ PA, of the ordinals. Ex. :—

དང་པོར་ D́ANG-POR: *Firstly.*

གཉིས་པར་ ŃYI-PAR: *Secondly.*

ཙ་གཅིག་པར་ TSAǴ-CHIǴ-PAR: *Twenty-one'thly* (= *Twenty-firstly.*)

12.—DEFINITE AND INDEFINITE NUMERALS.

Among these may be classed the following :—

གཉིས་ཀ་ ŃYI-KA, *Both*, e.g., འདི་གཉིས་ཀ་དེ་གཉིས་ཀ་ *Both this and that.*

བུ་མོ་མཛེས་པོ་གཉིས་ཀ་སླེབས་པ་རེད་ *Both the pretty girls have arrived.*

སུ་ཡང་ SU-YANG, *Anybody* ; (with a negative) = *None, Nobody.*

ག་གའི་ ǴA-ǴÄI, *Anything* ; (with a negative) = *None, Nothing.*

The Literary forms of ག་གའི་ ǴA-ǴÄI, are གང་ཡང་ ǴANG-YANG, and ཅི་ཡང་ CHI-YANG.

Another expression is གཅིག་ཡང་ CHIǴ-YANG, *Even one* ; (with a negative)—*None, Nobody, Nothing.*

EXAMPLES.

ཁོ་ཚོའི་ནང་ནས་སུ་ཡང་སླེབས་མ་བྱུང་། *None of them arrived.*

ངས་ཁོ་རོའི་ནང་ནས་སུ་ཡང་ངོ་ཤེས་ཀྱི་མེད། *I know none of them.*

ཅ་ལག་དེ་ཚོ་འི་ནང་ནས་ང་ལ་ག་གའི་འོས་ཀྱི་མ་རེད་ or འོས་པོ་མ་རེད།	*None of these things will suit me.*
འདི་གཉིས་ཀའི་ནང་ནས་གཅིག་གིས་ཡང་མི་ཡོང་།	*None*, or *neither of these two will do.*

Expressions like *A whole* (something), *An entire* (something), *A complete* (something), *A full* (something), are rendered by གང་ག་ ǴANG-ǴA, སྒང་ཁ་ ĞANG-K'A, or simply གང་ ǴANG, or སྒང་ ĞANG; and the word གཅིག་ CHI', *one*, or ཅིག་ CHI', *A*, *An*, is not made use of at all in such cases. Ex.:—

དམག་མི་ཚོས་གླང་གོག་སྒང་ཁ་ (or སྒང་) རྗོད་ཀྱི་འདུག།	*The soldiers are roasting a whole ox.*
འདི་སྒྲུང་སྒང་ཁ་མ་རེད།	*This is not a complete story.*
ང་ལ་གསོལ་ཇ་ཞལ་དཀར་གང་གཞང་རོགས་གནང་།	*Please give me a full cup of tea.*

Entirely is rendered by ཐད་དེ་ B̆Ä'-ǴE, used only with a negative. Thus:—

རྩིས་དེ་ཚོ་ཁྲིག་ཁྲིག་ཐད་དེ་མ་རེད།	*Those accounts are not altogether* (or *entirely*) *accurate.*

All, *whole*, *entire*, may also be rendered by ཐམས་ཅད་ T'AM-CHÄ', ཚང་མ་ TS'ANG-MA, and སྒང་ཁ་ ĞANG-K'A, or གང་ག་ ǴANG-ǴA. Ex.:—

ལམ་སང་ཚོགས་ཐམས་ཅད་ཡལ་སོང་།	*Suddenly the whole crowd disappeared.*
སྐྱེས་དམན་དེ་ཐམས་ཅད་ཞེད་སོང་།	*All the women were frightened.*

དེ་ཐམས་ཅད་ ǴE T'AM-CHÄ', not དེ་ཚོ་ཐམས་ཅད་ ǴEN-TSO T'AM-CHÄ': *They all.*

སྒང་ ǴANG, or གང་ ǴANG, is also used in connection with weights and measures instead of གཅིག, or ཅིག་ CHI', *One*, *A*, *An*.

So also, in connection with weights and measures and the Tibetan monetary system, དོ་ ḌO, is used instead of གཉིས་ NYI, *Two*, and signifies *A couple*. Otherwise the word for *a couple* is ཆ་ CH'A.

But a phrase like *Two-legged*, or *Three-legged*, is rendered with the particle པ, thus:—རྐང་གཉིས་པ་ or རྐང་གསུམ་པ་ Here པ་ means *possessed of*.

Other expressions are: གཉིས་ལྡབ་ *Double*, or *Two-fold;* གཉིས་སྐྱེས་ *Twice-born;* གཉིས་ཚར་གྱིས་ *Every second day.*

13.—NOUN SUBSTANTIVES.

ཚོ་ Ts'o, the Plural-sign used in the Colloquial, is never expressed, either in speech or in writing, after a numeral adjective, or numeral adjectives, the noun-substantive thereby qualified always remaining in the singular. Ex.:—

མི་གསུམ་ (not མི་ཚོ་གསུམ་) ཁྱོད་དང་ མཉམ་དུ་ཕྱིན་ཡོང་། *Three men will go with you.*

14.—NOTATION BY LETTERS.

The use of the ཀ་ཁའི་རྣམ་གྲངས་ KA-K'AI ŇAM ḌANG, or *Alphabetical Enumeration*, has already been explained (*See* § 26 II). In this connection, when references in Indices, or Registers, or to quotations from learned works are being cited, it is customary to qualify the numeral letter by affixes such as པ་ PA, པར་ PAR, and པ་ལ་ PA-LA, of which the first denotes the Book, Register, Index, or the like, to which reference is being made, and the last two denote that the particular quotation or citation is to be found *in* some particular Book, etc.

Ex.:—

ཐོ་ཨ་པ་ T'O A-PA : *Register No.* 30.

པོ་ཏི་ཁ་པར་ PO-TI K'A-PAR : *In Volume No.* 2.

ཐོ་ག་པ་ལ་ T'O ǴA-PA-LA : *In Index No.* 3.

CHAPTER II.

ETYMOLOGY.

§ 27.—The Definite Article.

1. The Definite Article The (which is really only an abbreviation of That) is represented in Tibetan in various ways, the principal being the words འདི་ Ḋi, and དེ་ Ḋe, of which the former is usually said to mean *This*, and the latter *That*.

Properly, འདི་ or དེ་ when used at all, should always follow the noun or adjective which it distinguishes.

As a rule it is only used when the distinguishing or demonstrative idea is intended to be conveyed.

Examples :—

མི་འདི་དང་པོ་སླེབས་བྱུང་།	*This man arrived first.*
ཁྱོད་ཀྱིས་བཏང་བའི་མི་བཟང་པོ་དེ།	*The good man whom you sent.*
བུ་མོ་མཛེས་མོ་དེ།	*That pretty girl.*

As a matter of fact Tibetans altogether discard the article in conversation, unless they really desire to express the demonstrative or distinguishing idea.

Examples :—

མི་ཡོང་གི་འདུག།	*The man is coming.*
སྒོ་རྒྱབ།	*Shut the door.*
སྒོ་ཁུང་ཕྱེས།	*Open the window.*

A distinction, however, in the use of འདི་ and དེ་ is made between the *nearer* and the *remoter* relation, in regard both to *time* and *space*.

For instance, when the article is intended to distinguish some person or thing already referred to, but to whom or to which reference is again being made, then, on the occasion of the second or any subsequent reference, Tibetans use དེ་ ḊE ; འདི་ ḊI having been used on the occasion of the first reference.

EXAMPLE :—

མི་དེ་སླེབས་བྱུང་། *The man has arrived* (referring to somebody already mentioned).

Notice also how འདི་ and དེ་ are used in a phrase like this :—

འདི་ཁས་ས་ (or ཁ་སང་) ཡོངས་མཁན་གྱི་བང་ཆེན་དེ་རེད། *This is the messenger who came yesterday.*

(*N.B.*—ཁས་ས་ *yesterday*, is Colloquial, ཁ་སང་ is Literary).

So, if on the occasion of the first reference, the object distinguished was a distant object, then དེ་ would be used ; འདི་ being employed to distinguish a near or present object. Ex. :—

མི་དེ་ཁས་ས་ (or ཁ་སང་) ཡོངས་མཁན་གྱི་བང་ཆེན་དེ་རེད། *That man* (referring to somebody at a distance) *is the messenger who came yesterday.*

When, moreover, the article distinguishes first one and then another of two objects, both of which are present, and which are being contrasted, or to which an alternative reference is being made, then, in the case of the one, འདི་ would be used, and, in the case of the other, དེ་ Ex. :—

མི་འདི་འགྲོ་མ་ཐུབ་པ་དང་མི་དེ་འགྲོ་གི་རེད། *This man cannot go, but that man can go (will go).*

Practically, therefore, in addition to representing the article THE, འདི་ and དེ་ respectively also represent the distinguishing adjectives THIS and THAT. They also respectively represent THIS ONE and THAT ONE ; HE, SHE, IT.

PLURAL.

The Colloquial plural of འདི་ is འདི་ཚོ་ (pronounced DIN-TS'O), *The, These, They*: and that of དེ་ is དེ་ཚོ་ (pronounced DEN-TS'O) *The, Those, They.*

Both articles, however, are often used in the singular to distinguish collective nouns. In such cases they precede the word they distinguish. Ex. :—

འདི་གསུམ།	*These three*
དེ་ལྔ།	*Those five.*
འདི་ཐམས་ཅད།	*All these.*
དེ་སྐྱང་ཁ།	*All those.*

The following is Literary :—

གསུང་དེ་ཀུན་སེམས་ལ་ཤིན་ཏུ་འཐད་པ་ཞིག་བྱུང་།	*All these sayings pleased greatly.*

Where a plural noun is qualified by an adjective, and the whole is distinguished by the article, it is the article which takes the plural sign ཚོ་ Ts'o, and it is the ཚོ་ which takes whatever case-sign there may be.

Ex. :—

ངས་བླམ་ཡོན་ཏན་ཅན་པོ་འདི་ཚོ་ལ་ལབ་ཀྱི་ཡིན།	*I shall speak to these learned lamas.*

2. Another method by which the Definite Article is represented is by using the particle ནི་ NI; but this is rather Literary than Colloquial. In a long and involved sentence it may be placed after the principal noun, or noun-phrase, so as to distinguish it prominently. It may also be used to emphasize a particular word or expression, and may even be employed in addition to འདི་ or དེ་.

Ex. :—

ར་མགོ་བཅུ་གཉིས་ནི།	*The twelve ra-gos* (or *ra-heads*).
མི་ནི་སེམས་ཅན་ཀུན་ལས་ཁྱད་དུ་འཕགས།	*Mankind are the noblest of all. animals.*
བཀའ་དེ་ནི་དཀོན་མཆོག་དང་མཉམ་དུ་བཞུགས་པ་དང་།	*And the word was with God* (*John i.* 1.)

3. The functions of the Definite Article are sometimes performed by the particles པ་ PA and པོ་ PO, when affixed to numerals. (*See* § 26, *Notes* 6, 8, 14.)

4. The particles པོ་ PO, པ་ PA, ཁ་ K'A, etc., as performing the function of the Definite Article in connection also with nouns and adjectives, are used when the idea of *individuality*, or *definiteness*, is particularly desired. Thus, རྒྱལ་པོ་ཆེན་པོ་ *The great king.* But they are also sometimes discarded. Thus, རྒྱལ་ཆེན་བཞི་ *The four great kings.* They are also discarded in enumerations like the following :—

ཆེ་ཆུང་།	*Great and small.*
སྐྱེ། རྒ། ན། འཆི།	*Birth, Old age, Sickness, Death.*

The conjunction དང་ DANG, *And*, is also discarded in such expressions.

The particles under notice and conjunctions are also discarded in enumerations of nouns that are in apposition or contrast. Ex. :—

རེ་དོགས།	*Hope and Fear.*
དགེ་སྡིག།	*Virtue and Vice*
གནམ་ས།	*Heaven and Earth.*

In a sentence like རེ་གི་ཀ་བ་ (otherwise རེ་བའི་ཀ་བ་) *The pillar of hope*, the particle is omitted from the first noun, རེ་བ་ *Re-wa*, and annexed only to the second.

Sometimes however a phrase is contracted and the particle omitted in both its members. Ex.: རེ་ཀ་ *The pillar of hope.*

5. The student may also be reminded of the various affixes set out at the end of § 24, since they too occasionally perform the functions of the Definite Article.

§ 28.—The Indefinite Article.

1. ཅིག་ *A, An, Some,* is a modification of གཅིག་ *One*, and is seen in the following forms, which may be used even in the Colloquial, if it is desired to be very correct, though as a matter of fact the form ཅིག་ Chi' is the one most favoured:—

   ཅིག་ after final ག་, ད་, or བ།

   ཞིག་ after all vowels, or after final ང་, ན་, མ་, ར་, or ལ།

   ཤིག་ after final ས།

2. Being an adjective when it qualifies a noun, and an adverb when it qualifies an adjective, its place in the sentence is immediately after the noun, or noun and adjective, that it qualifies. Ex.:—

རྟ་ཞིག་ (or ཅིག)།	*A horse.*
མི་བཟང་པོ་ཅིག།	*A virtuous man.*
རྟ་ཅིག་དང་ཤིང་རྟ་འཁོར་ལོ་ཅིག།	*A horse and a carriage.*

3. ཅིག་ and not the noun or adjective to which it is annexed, takes the case-sign, but only in what we would call the Nominative. In the other cases ཅིག་ is usually dropped. Ex.:—

ཁྱད་མཚར་པོ་ཅིག་གིས་ང་ཚོའི་གཟན་པ་བཟས་པ་རེད།	*A strange horse has eaten our hay.*
གཙང་པོའི་འགྲམ་ལ་བསྡད་ཀྱི་ཡོད།	*I live near a large river.*

4. Annexed to approximate numerals, it signifies collectiveness. Thus :—

མི་གསུམ་བཞི་ཞིག། *A group of three or four men.*

དམག་སྨར་སྟོང་ཕྲག་གཅིག་གཉིས་ཤིག། *A force of one or two thousand soldiers.*

5. Used with the adverb ཙམ་ TSAM, *About*, it signifies SOME. Thus :—

ལུག་བདུན་ཅུ་དགུ་བཅུ་ཙམ་ཞིག། *Some seventy or ninety sheep.*

Another expression for SOME is ཁ་ཤས་ K'A-SHĂ, and another is ཏོག་ཙེ་ TOǴ-TSE.

The Literary form of ཁ་ཤས་ is འགའ་ཞིག་ ĞA-ŹHYI'.

A few, *Solely*, *Only*, *Alone*, may be rendered in Colloquial by ཏོག་ཙེ་ TOǴ-TSE, ཤ་སྟག་ SHA-ṪA', and གཅིག་པོ་ CHIǴ-PO ; and in Literature by འབའ་ཞིག་ B̆A-ŹHYI'.

6. Affixed to Interrogative Pronouns, the Article signifies (in Literary Tibetan) *Whoever*, *Whatever*, *Whichever*, *Anyone*, *Anything*. Thus :—

སུ་ཞིག་བྱམས་པའི་མིག་གིས་བལྟ་ན་ཡང་ etc. *Whoever with loving eyes shoul even regard*, etc. (S.C.D.), i.e *anyone who*, etc.

དེའི་ནང་ལ་གང་ཞིག་ (or. ཅི་ཞིག་) མི་འདུག། *There is nothing* (*anything*, wit negative) *in it.*

The Article is also used thus in Literature :—

གང་ཞིག་ཁ་མཆུ་རྐྱེན་གྱིས། *On account of some law-suit.*

ཅི་ཞིག་ཏུ་དགོས། *What* (*is it*) *wanted for ?*

ཅི་ཞིག་ན། *Once, on some occasion, some tim*

ཅི་ཞིག་ནས། *After a little, some time afterward*

7. Affixed in any of its appropriate forms to a verbal root, it imports in Literature the Imperative Mood as addressed to servants and inferiors, and also the Hortative and Optative Moods. Thus :—

བྱས་ཤིག། *Do ; Let do.*

བྱོས་ཤིག། ⎫ *Let . . do ; may . . do ;*

བྱེད་པར་གྱུར་ཅིག། ⎭ *May . . be done.*

In the Colloquial also it is frequently used to express an emphatic order, and commonly takes the form ཤིག་ SHI', though it would be more correct to say ཤིག་ SHI', ཞིག་ ŻHYI', or ཅིག་ CHI', according to rule. Ex. :—

མགྱོགས་པོར་རྒྱུགས་ཤིག། *Run quickly.*

སྒོ་རྒྱབས་ཤིག། *Shut the door.*

ཁ་བཙུམས་ཤིག། *Be quiet.*

8. Here may also be mentioned གང་ཡང་ ANY. Ex. :—

དེ་རིང་སྐད་ཆ་གསར་པ་གང་ཡང་ཡོད་དམ། *Is there any fresh news to-day?*

§ 29.—THE NOUN.

A.—*Structure.*

1. The Tibetan Noun ends in either a consonant or a vowel, and is either :—

(*a*) A MONOSYLLABLE WITHOUT ANY AFFIXED PARTICLE, and either without or with any vowel-sign, head-letter, subjunct or prefix. Ex. :—

ཉ་ *Fish* ; མཐ་ *End* ; ལ་ *Mountain-pass* ; ཤ་ *Flesh* ; ས་ *Earth, soil, ground, place* ; མི་ *Man* ; མེ་ *Fire* ; ཆུ་ *Water* ; བྱ་ *Bird, fowl* ; མགོ་ *Head* ; སྒོ་ *Door* ; ཤྭ་ *Deer* ; རྨ་ *Wound* ;

ལོ་ *Year*; ལྟོ་ *Food, provisions*; དབུ་ *Head* (Honorific); སྐྲ་ *Hair* (Human, on head).

(*b*) A MONOSYLLABLE, SIMPLE OR COMPLEX, WITH AN AFFIXED PARTICLE, such as པ་, པོ་, ཕོ་, བ་, བོ་, མ་, མོ་, ཀ་, ཁ་, ག་, ཙ་, ཙེ་, ཚ་, ཀུ་, གུ་, ཁུ་, བུ་, ཅུ་, ལུ་, ཙུ་, ཡུ་, and which particle sometimes indicates the gender. Ex.:— ཝ་ཕོ་ *Fox*; ཝ་མོ་ *Vixen*; ཨ་ཕ་ *Father*; ཨ་མ་ *Mother*; ཁྱི་མོ་ *Bitch*; བྱ་ཕོ་ *Cock-bird*; བྱ་མོ་ *Hen-bird*; གྲྭ་པ་ or ཆོས་པ་ *Monk*; ཆོས་མ་ *Nun*; རྒོད་མ་ *Mare*; སྲས་པོ་ *Son*; སྲས་མོ་ *daughter*; ལུག་ཕོ་ *Ram.*

Sometimes, however, the particle does not indicate gender. Ex.:— སྟུ་མ་ *A mountain-shrub*; ཉི་མ་ *Day, sun*; དགོང་མོ་ *Evening*; བླ་མ་ *Monk, priest*; རོལ་མོ་ *Music*; གླང་མ་ *A kind of tree*; ལྦ་བ་ BA-WA, *Goitre*; གཏའ་མ་ *Pledge*; ཤུ་མ་ *Envelope, wrapper.*

Sometimes the particle serves merely to differentiate the meanings of roots otherwise similarly or somewhat similarly spelt. Ex.:—

སྟོན་པ་ *To show, to teach*; but སྟོན་ཁ་ *Autumn*; རྐང་ *Marrow, pith, descent, origin*; but རྐང་པ་ *Foot*; གདེང་ *Confidence*; but གདེངས་ཀ་ *The expanded hood of a snake.*

If the particle is either པ་, བ་, པོ་, or བོ་, it may be and often is dropped (especially when followed by an adjective), without affecting the meaning of the word. Ex.:—

གླང་པོ་ཆེན་པོ། གླང་ཆེན	*The* or *a great elephant.*
རྒྱལ་པོ་ཆེན་པོ་བཞི། རྒྱལ་ཆེན་བཞི་	*The four great kings.*

Some of such particles perform the functions of DIMINUTIVES Thus, in the case of ཙུ་, the inherent ཨ་, or ཨོ་, of the final or the only consonant of the noun, is turned into ཨི་, and is followed by the particle. Ex. :—

ཉ་ *Fish* ; ཉེའུ་ *Little fish* ; བ་ *Cow* ; བེའུ་ *Calf.*

In other cases the final consonant, if a ག་, is cut off the noun, and turned into a second syllable, to which *Żhyab-kyu* is added. Ex. :—

ཕྱག་ *Hand* ; ཕྱ་གུ་ *Little hand* ; ཕྲུག་ *Child* ; ཕྲུ་གུ་ *Little child* ; ལུག་ *Sheep* ; ལུ་གུ་ *Lamb.*

In other cases the Diminutive particle is simply added to the primitive noun as it stands. Ex. :— མི་ *Man* ; མིའུ་ *Mannikin* ; ཕད་ *Sack* ; ཕད་བུ་ *Sacklet.*

Another way of expressing the Diminutive is to qualify the noun by the adjective ཆུང་ *Small.* Ex. :—

མགྲོན་ཁང་ཆུང་ *A little inn.*

བློ་ཆུང་ *A little mind, narrow mind.*

Or lastly—

(*c*) A DISSYLLABLE, OR EVEN A POLYSYLLABLE, either without or with a particle. Those nouns, and especially the polysyllabic nouns, which are mostly proper names, and sometimes even amount to phrases, are often comparatively modern words which have either gradually developed or been deliberately compounded out of originally simple elements. Ex. :—

རྐུབ་ཀྱག་ *Chair* ; ཞི་མི་ *Cat* ; མི་སྐྱ་ *Layman* ; ཆད་ཡིག་ *Contract* ; བརྩོན་འགྲུས་ *Diligence, industry, zeal* ; གྲོང་ཁྱེར་ *City* ; ཞུ་དོན་པ་ or བར་མི་བྱེད་མཁན་ *Advocate* or *pleader* ; ཞུ་བ་པོ་ *Petitioner* ; སྙན་ཞུ་ NYE-ŻHYU, *Petition* ; ཐ་སྙད་པ *Gamester, juggler with words* ; ཐ་མ་ཁ *Tobacco* ; ཕྱེ་མ་ལེབ་ or ཕྱེ་འདྲེན་མ་ CH'EN-DEM-MA, (Colloquial), or ཕྱེམ་ཕྱེམ་མ་ (Literary), *Butterfly.*

N.B.—Words with the definite particles པ་, པོ་, etc., are generally used without the article འདི་, or དེ་, unless the latter is intended to express *This* or *That*.

2. Besides the particles above referred to, mention may be made of མཁན་ K'ÄN, which, annexed to substantives or verbal roots, is extensively used in the Colloquial to signify a person who, in some capacity or character, is connected with some particular act, state, or thing. Ex. :—

སྲུང་མཁན་ *Guard* ; ཧམ་པ་བཤད་མཁན་ *Liar* ; མིག་འཕྲུལ་སྟོན་མཁན་ *Magician* ; རྩོམ་མཁན་ *Author* ; མགོ་སྐོར་གཏོང་མཁན་ *Deceiver* : མི་བསད་མཁན་ *Murderer* ; ལན་སྒྲོད་མཁན་ *Informant.*

In book-language the following may be found :—

གར་མཁན་ *Dancer* ; ལམ་མཁན་ *Guide* ; གླིང་བུ་མཁན་ *Flutist* ; པི་ཝང་མཁན་ *Violinist, harpist* ; ཤིང་མཁན་ *Joiner, carpenter* ; གཞུ་མཁན་ *Bow-maker* ; བཟོ་མཁན་ *Artisan, worker* ; ས་མཁན་ *Peasant, agriculturist, raïat.*

Such compounds in མཁན་ (at least in the Literary language) may take the indicative particles པ་, པོ་, མ་, or མོ་, as expressive not only of the definite or indefinite article but also of gender. Ex. :—

འགྲོ་མཁན་པ་	(Masculine)	*A Walker, The Walker.*
འགྲོ་མཁན་མ་	(Feminine)	
འགྲོ་མཁན་པོ་	Masculine)	Ditto.
འགྲོ་མཁན་མོ་	(Feminine)	

3. Instead of མཁན་ use is sometimes made of the verb བྱེད་པ་ *To do.*

Ex. :—

བྱེད་པ་པ་ བྱེད་པ་ བྱེད་པ་པོ་ བྱེད་པོ་	(Masculine)	*A doer, The doer.*
བྱེད་པ་མ་ བྱེད་མ་ བྱེད་པ་མོ་ བྱེད་མོ་	(Feminine)	

Sometimes, even in the Colloquial, both བྱེད་ and མཁན་ are used together, either with or without the Indicative Particles པ་, པོ་, མ་, མོ་, though in the Colloquial these are commonly discarded. Ex. :—

Literary.

འགྲོ་བྱེད་མཁན་	(Common)	*A walker, The walker.*
འགྲོ་བྱེད་མཁན་པ་ འགྲོ་བྱེད་མཁན་པོ་	(Masculine)	
འགྲོ་བྱེད་མཁན་མ་ འགྲོ་བྱེད་མཁན་མོ་	(Feminine)	

N.B.—When འདི་, or དེ་ or the indefinite article ཅིག་ is used with any of the above, the indicative particle is discarded, e.g. :—

འགྲོ་བྱེད་མཁན་དེ་ *The walker, That walker.*

འགྲོ་བྱེད་མཁན་ཅིག་ *A walker.*

COLLOQUIAL.

སོ་ནམས་བྱེད་མཁན་ *Agriculturist, Farmer.*

ལམ་རྒྱུད་བྱེད་མཁན་ *Guide.*

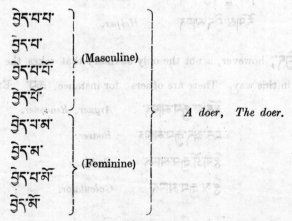

ཁས་ཁྲུག་བྱེད་མཁན་ *Guarantor.*

རོགས་བྱེད་མཁན་ *Helper.*

4. བྱེད་, however, is not the only auxiliary that takes the affix མཁན in this way. There are others; for instance, རྒྱབ་ Ex. :—

རྩོད་པ་རྒྱབ་མཁན་ *Arguer, Reasoner.*

ངར་སྐད་རྒྱབ་མཁན་ *Roarer.*

རྩིག་སྒོ་རྒྱབ་མཁན་ *Briber.*

རྩིས་རྒྱབ་མཁན་ *Calculator.*

In fact, the functions of མཁན་, བྱེད་, and རྒྱབ་ in this respect, are very similar to those of the Urdu word والا, *wālā*, or the Persian words بان *bān*, گر *gar*, گار *gār*, کار *kār*, etc., or even the Tibetan particle པ་ in words like གྲྭ་པ་ *Scholar, Monk, Disciple, Novice*; ཆུ་པ་ *Water-carrier, Bhīsti*; རྟ་པ་ *Horseman*, etc.

5. Another common affix of a similar nature annexed to noun-substantives is བཟོ་བ་, or བཟོ་ *Maker, Manufacturer*, etc. Ex. :—

ལྷམ་བཟོ་བ་ }
དྲོ་བཟོ་ } *Boot-maker.*

ཤིང་བཟོ་བ་ *Carpenter.*

གསེར་བཟོ་བ་ *Goldsmith.*

དངུལ་བཟོ་བ་ *Silversmith.*

ཟངས་བཟོ་བ་ *Coppersmith.*

6. *Abstract Nouns.*

In the Colloquial these are seldom used, resort being generally had to an adjective phrase. Thus, instead of saying རྒྱལ་བ་རིན་པོ་ཆེའི་བཟང་

ངན་དེ་ཆེ་གི་རེད་ *The goodness of the Dalai Lama is great*, a Tibetan would probably say རྒྱལ་བ་རིན་པོ་ཆེ་ད་ཅང་བཟང་པོ་རེད་ *The Dalai Lama is very good*. When, however, an abstract noun is used, it can be formed in two ways. First, by placing in juxtaposition the roots of two adjectives with opposite meanings, e.g. མང་ཉུང་ *Quantity*, from མང་པོ་ *Much*, and ཉུང་བ་ *Little*; ཉེ་རིང་ *Distance*, from ཉེ་བ་ *Near*, and རིང་བ་ *Far*; བཟང་ངན་ *Goodness*, from བཟང་པོ་ *Good*, and ངན་པ་ *Bad*; and so on. Secondly, by affixing ཡོས་ Lö, to the root of any adjective, e.g. གསལ་ཡོས་ *Brightness*, *Clearness*, from གསལ་པོ་ *Bright*, *Clear*; ངན་ཡོས་ *Badness*, from ངན་པ་ *Bad*; བདེ་ཡོས་ *Goodness*, from བདེ་པོ་ *Good*.

In Literary Tibetan abstract nouns are formed by adding ཉིད་ Nyi', to the adjective in its full form, that is, not the mere root, but the root plus one of the indicative particles. Ex.:—

སླ	*Easy*, but	སླ་བ་ཉིད་	*Easiness, facility.*
དཀའ་	*Difficult*, but	དཀའ་བ་ཉིད་	*Difficulty.*
ཐར་	*Free*, but	ཐར་པ་ཉིད་	*Freedom.*
ངེས་	*True*, but	ངེས་པ་ཉིད་	*Truth.*
གཞོན་	*Young*, but	གཞོན་པ་ཉིད་	*Youth.*
ནག་	*Black*, but	ནག་པ་ཉིད་	*Blackness.*
སྨྱོན་	*Mad*, but	སྨྱོན་པ་ཉིད་	*Madness, Lunacy.*
སྐྱུན་	*Tedious*, but	སྐྱུན་པ་ཉིད་	*Tedium.*

B.—*Inflexion.*

The Tibetan Noun-Substantive is inflected in relation to:—

1.—Gender.

The names of all males, females and inanimate objects are naturally masculine, feminine, and common respectively, e.g., མི་ *Man* (m.); སྐྱེས་དམན་ *Woman* (f.); རྡོ་ *Stone* (c.).

Nouns ending in པ་ or པོ་ or བ་ or བོ་ or with ཕ་ or ཕོ་ prefixed or affixed, are generally (in the last two cases always) masculine. Ex.:—

གྲྭ་པ་ *Pupil or novice in a monastery.*	ཕོ་རྟ་ *Stallion.*
རྒྱལ་པོ་ *King, Regent, Temporal Ruler, Rajah.*	ཕོ་ཕག་ *Boar.*
རྟ་ཕོ་ or ཕོ་རྟ་ *Horse.*	ཨ་ཕ་ *Father.*
ཕག་ཕོ་ or ཕོ་ཕག་ *Hog.*	ཨ་ཕོ་ང་ *This old chap; I myself.*
ཕོ་གླང་ *Bull.*	གཙོ་བོ་ *Official chief.*
ཕོ་གཡག་ *Bull-yak.*	ཚ་བོ་ *Grandson.*

But sometimes nouns in པ་ or པོ་ or བ་ or བོ་ are common. Ex.:—

གཅེས་པོ་, བྱམས་པ་, འདྲིས་པ་ } *Beloved, Sweetheart, Lover.*	འགྲུལ་པ་ *Traveller.*
	གསང་བ་ *Secret.*
	གཡོག་པོ་ *Servant.*
ཚོལ་པོ་, སླེ་པོ་ } *Basket.*	ཁུ་བ་ *Liquid.*
	ཀོ་བ་ *Leather.*
ལྷན་པ་ *Patch.*	བྲ་བོ་ *Bitter buck-wheat.*

Nouns with མ་ affixed, or with མོ་ affixed or prefixed are generally feminine. Ex.:—

རྒོད་མ་ *Mare.*	བུ་མོ་ *Daughter, girl.*
ཨ་མ་ *Mother.*	ཁྱི་མོ་, མོ་ཁྱི་ } *Bitch.*
ཞལ་ཏ་མ་ *Maidservant.*	
སྟག་མོ་ *Tigress.*	ཚ་མོ་ *Niece.*

But མ་ and མོ་ do not always denote the feminine gender. Ex. :—

ལོ་མ་ *Leaf.*	རྩེད་མོ་ *Sport, game, play.*
པད་མ་ *Lotus.*	གྲོ་མོ་ *Chūmbi.*
གདུང་མ་ *Beam of wood.*	གྲོགས་མོ་ *Friend.*
སྲན་མ་ *Bean.*	དགོང་མོ་ *Evening.*
དོར་མ་ *Breeches, pants.*	རོལ་མོ་ *Music, cymbals.*
ཐུར་མ་ *Spoon.*	སྐྱིད་མོ་ *Fun.*
འཇག་མ་ *Shovel, spade.*	སྲེ་བྱ་གོང་མོ་ *Grouse.*
གྲོག་མ་ *Ant.*	གཟིག་མོ་ *Hedgehog.*
ཡིང་ཀྲུ་མ་ *Hawk, kite.*	པུས་མོ་ *Knee.*

Masculine nouns may be turned into feminine nouns by substituting a feminine affix for a masculine one. Ex. :—

ལྷ་ས་པ་ *A man of Lhasa.*	ལྷ་ས་མོ་ *A woman of Lhasa.*
རྒྱ་གར་པ་ *An Indian.*	རྒྱ་གར་མོ་ *A woman of India.*
བོད་པ་ *A Tibetan.*	བོད་མོ་ *A woman of Tibet.*
རྒྱ་ནག་པ་ or རྒྱ་མི་ *A Chinaman.*	རྒྱ་ནག་མོ་ or རྒྱ་མོ་ *A woman of China.*
བལ་པོ་ *A Nepāli.*	བལ་མོ་ *A Nepāli woman.*

2.—Number

(*a*) There are several signs in Tibetan denoting the plural number, e.g.—

ཚོ་ T'so. This is the sign commonly used now in the Colloquial with any kind of noun or adjective.

(*b*) རྣམས་ Ñam. This is Literary, and is seldom if ever heard in the Colloquial. It is largely used, for instance, in the Tibetan translation of the New Testament. རྣམ་པ་ is used when things or persons are referred to separately from others, e.g. ང་རྣམ་པ་ལྔ་ *We five.*

(*c*) དག་ D́A'. This is an elegant substitute for རྣམས།

(*d*) ཅག་ CHA'. Another book term. Used also in Sikhim and Būtān with personal pronouns, e.g. ང་ཅག་ *We*, etc.

(*e*) No plural sign at all need be used when, from the context, it is clear that the plural number is implied. In such cases the noun remains in the singular number. Ex. :—

ལྷ་ས་ལ་བླ་མ་མང་པོ་ཡོད་པ་རེད། *There are (I understand) many lamas in Lhasa.* Or, *Lhasa (I believe) has many lamas.*

(*f*) When, however, the plural sign is expressly used, it, and not the noun, nor the adjective, if any, takes the case-sign. Ex. :—

མི་བཟང་པོ་ཚོས་ཁོ་ལ་ཐོབ་བྱུང་། *The virtuous men received him.*

(*g*) When expressly used, the plural sign comes after the noun if there is no adjective and no article, definite or indefinite. Ex. :—

དུས་རྒྱུན་མི་ཚོ་མགོ་སྐོར་གཏོང་མཁན་རེད། *Men were deceivers ever.*

(*h*) When there is only an adjective after the noun, the plural sign is annexed to the adjective, not to the noun. Ex. :—

མི་བཟང་པོ་ཚོ། *Good men.*

(*i*) If, however, the adjective be used as an attribute predicated of the noun, then the plural sign is annexed to the noun, not to the adjective. Ex. :—

མི་ཚོ་བཟང་པོ་རེད། *The men are good.*

(*k*) If the noun be distinguished by an article, or distinguished by an article and also qualified by an adjective, the plural sign is annexed to the article.

Ex.:—

མི་འདི་ཚོ།	*The* or *these men.*
མི་དེ་ཚོ།	*The* or *those men.*
མི་བཟང་པོ་འདི་ཚོ།	*The* or *these good men.*
མི་བཟང་པོ་དེ་ཚོ།	*The* or *those good men.*
མི་དེ་ཚོ་བཟང་པོ་འདུག།	*Those men are good.*

3.—Case.

By way of supplementing what has already been said on this subject in § 25, examples are now given of the Declension of Nouns ending in (1) a vowel, (2) final consonants ག་ or ང་; ད་, བ་ or ས་; and ན་, མ་, ར་ or ལ།

The particular postpositions given are, of course, only examples out of many that might be used.

I.—Noun ending in a Vowel.

(*i*) *Singular.*

ཟླ་བ་ *Month*, or *Moon*.

Nom. Voc. Acc.	ཟླ་བ་	*Month.*
Gen.	ཟླ་བའི་ or བ་ཡི་	*Of month.*
Agent.	ཟླ་བས་ or བ་ཡིས་	*By month.*
Dat.	ཟླ་བ་ལ་	*To month*, or *moon.*
Loc.	ཟླ་བ་ན་	*On moon.*
Per.	ཟླ་བ་ལ་	*In* or *during month.*
Mod.	ཟླ་བའི་རྐྱེན་གྱིས་	*On account of moon* or *month.*
Abl.	ཟླ་བ་ལས་	*Than month* or *moon.*
Term.	ཟླ་བའི་བར་དུ་	*Until month* : *as far as moon.*

Plural.

ཟླ་བ་ཚོ་ *Months, Moons.*

Nom. Voc. Acc.	ཟླ་བ་ཚོ་	*Months, Moons.*
Gen.	ཟླ་བ་ཚོའི་ or ཚོ་ཡི་	*Of months, Of moons.*
Agent.	ཟླ་བ་ཚོ་ས་ or ཚོ་ཡིས་	*By months, By moons.*
Dat.	ཟླ་བ་ཚོ་ལ་	*To months, To moons.*
Loc.	ཟླ་བ་ཚོ་ན་	*On moons.*
Per.	ཟླ་བ་ཚོ་ལ་	*In* or *during months.*
Mod.	ཟླ་བ་ཚོའི་རྐྱེན་གྱིས་	*On account of moons* or *months.*
Abl.	ཟླ་བ་ཚོ་ལས་	*Than months* or *moons.*
Term.	ཟླ་བ་ཚོའི་བར་དུ་	*Until months: as far as moons.*

(ii) *Similar with Definite Article.*

Singular.

ཉི་མ་ *Sun* or *Day.*

Nom. Voc. Acc.	ཉི་མ་འདི་	*The sun* or *the day.*
Gen.	ཉི་མ་འདིའི་	*Of the sun* or *day.*
Agent.	ཉི་མ་འདིས་	*By the sun* or *day.*
Dat.	ཉི་མ་འདི་ལ་	*To the sun* or *day.*
Loc.	ཉི་མ་འདི་ན་	*On the sun.*
Per.	ཉི་མ་འདི་ན་	*During the day.*
Mod.	ཉི་མ་འདི་དང་	*With the sun* or *day.*
Abl.	ཉི་མ་འདི་ལས་	*Than the sun* or *day.*
Term.	ཉི་མ་འདིའི་ཕྱོགས་ས་ལ་	*Towards the sun.*

N.B.—In Colloquial the Definite Article is as a matter of fact seldom used.

PLURAL.

ཉི་མ་འདི་ཚོ་ *The suns* or *days.*

Nom. Voc. Acc.	ཉི་མ་འདི་ཚོ་	*The suns* or *days.*
Gen.	ཉི་མ་འདི་ཚོའི་	*Of the suns* or *days.*
Agent.	ཉི་མ་འདི་ཚོས་	*By the suns* or *days.*
Dat.	ཉི་མ་འདི་ཚོ་ལ་	*To the suns* or *days.*
Loc.	ཉི་མ་འདི་ཚོ་ན་	*On the suns* or *days.*
Per.	ཉི་མ་འདི་ཚོ་ལ་	*In* or *during the days.*
Mod.	ཉི་མ་འདི་ཚོ་དང་	*With the suns* or *days.*
Abl.	ཉི་མ་འདི་ཚོ་ལས་	*Than the suns* or *days.*
Term.	ཉི་མ་འདི་ཚོ་ནས་	*From the suns* or *days.*

(iii)—*Similar with Indefinite Article.*

དགོན་པ་ཞིག་ *A monastery.*

Nom. Voc. Acc.	དགོན་པ་ཞིག	*A monastery.*
Gen.	དགོན་པ་ཞིག་གི་	*Of a monastery.*
Agent.	དགོན་པ་ཞིག་གིས་	*By a monastery.*
Dat.	དགོན་པ་ཞིག་ལ་	*To a monastery.*
Loc.	དགོན་པ་ཞིག་ལ་	*In a monastery.*
Per.	(Not used).	(Not used).
Mod.	དགོན་པ་ཞིག་དང་	*With a monastery.*
Abl.	དགོན་པ་ཞིག་ལས་	*Than a monastery.*
Term.	དགོན་པ་ཞིག་ནས་	*From a monastery.*

N.B.—In conversation ཅིག་, ཞིག་, and ཤིག་, in this sense is usually dropped in all cases except the Nominative, or Agentive.

(iv)—*Similar with a higher Numeral.*

Nom. Voc. Acc.	ཕོ་ཉ་བདུན་	*Seven angels.*
Gen.	ཕོ་ཉ་བདུན་གྱི་	*Of seven angels.*
Agent.	ཕོ་ཉ་བདུན་གྱིས་	*By seven angels.*
Dat.	ཕོ་ཉ་བདུན་ལ་	*To seven angels.*

etc., etc.

(v)—*The same with a Definite Particle.*

Nom. Voc. Acc.	ཕོ་ཉ་བདུན་པོ་	*The seven angels.*
Gen.	ཕོ་ཉ་བདུན་པོའི་	*Of the seven angels.*
Agent.	ཕོ་ཉ་བདུན་པོས་	*By the seven angels.*
Dat.	ཕོ་ཉ་བདུན་པོ་ལ་	*To the seven angels.*

etc., etc.

(vi) *The same in the Singular with Cardinal.*

Nom. Voc. Acc.	ཕོ་ཉ་བདུན་པ་	*The seventh angel.*
Gen.	ཕོ་ཉ་བདུན་པའི་	*Of the seventh angel.*
Agent.	ཕོ་ཉ་བདུན་པས་	*By the seventh angel.*
Dat.	ཕོ་ཉ་བདུན་པ་ལ་	*To the seventh angel*

etc., etc.

(vii) *Similar with Definite Article.*

Nom. Voc. Acc.	ཕོ་ཉ་དང་པོ་འདི་	*The first angel.*
Gen.	ཕོ་ཉ་དང་པོ་འདིའི་	*Of the first angel.*

Agent.	ཕོ་ཉ་དང་པོ་འདིས་	*By the first angel.*
Dat.	ཕོ་ཉ་དང་པོ་ལ་	*To the first angel.*
	etc.,	etc.

(viii) When, as is sometimes the case, the adjective precedes the noun, the former must be put in the genitive case, and the case-sign must be attached to the noun, or to the definite or indefinite article, if any, or to the plural sign, if any. Ex. :—

ཡག་པོའི་བྱེད་སྟངས་	*Good behaviour.*
ཡག་པོའི་བྱེད་སྟངས་ནས་	*From good behaviour.*
ཡག་པོའི་བྱེད་སྟངས་འདིས་	*By this good behaviour.*
ཡག་པོའི་ལས་ཀ་ཞིག་གིས་	*By a good deed.*
ཡག་པོའི་ལས་ཀ་ཚོ་ལ་	*To good deeds.*
ཡག་པོའི་ལས་ཀ་དེ་ཚོ་ལ་	*To those good deeds.*

II.—Noun ending in ག, or ང།

ལུག་ *Sheep.*

Nom. Voc. Acc.	ལུག་	*Sheep.*
Gen.	ལུག་གི་	*Of the sheep.*
Agent.	ལུག་གིས་	*By the sheep.*
Dat.	ལུག་ལ་	*To the sheep.*
	etc.,	etc.

ཤིང་ *Tree.*

Nom. Voc. Acc.	ཤིང་	*Tree.*
Gen.	ཤིང་གི་	*Of the tree.*
Agent.	ཤིང་གིས་	*By the tree.*
Dat.	ཤིང་ལ་	*To the tree.*
	etc.,	etc.

III.—Noun ending in ད, བ or ས།

བོད་ *Tibet ;* ཚབ་ *Delegate ;* ཆས་ *Costume.*

Declined like any other noun, save that the genitive sign is ཀྱི་ and the agentive sign is ཀྱིས།

IV.—Noun ending in ན, མ, ར or ལ།

ཉོ་མཁན་ *Buyer ;* ལྷམ་ *Boot ;* གྲོང་ཁྱེར་ *City ;* རྡོ་སོལ་ *Coal.*

Declined like any other noun, save that the genitive sign is གྱི་, and the agentive sign is གྱིས་ It must be remembered, however, that in Colloquial it is allowable to pronounce all these signs གི་ and གིས།

§ 30.—The Adjective.

I.—*Form and Place.*

(i) There is little or no structural difference between the noun and the adjective. In fact, the latter may, for the most part, be regarded merely as a noun performing qualifying functions with respect to some other noun or verbal substantive.

As a rule the adjective follows the noun, and then it is the adjective and not the noun which takes the case-sign. If the adjective is distinguished by a following article, definite or indefinite, or a demonstrative pronoun, it is the article or the pronoun and not the adjective which takes the case-sign. So, the adjective, and not the noun, takes the sign of the plural, if there is no article or demonstrative pronoun If there is, the article or pronoun takes the sign.

If, as is sometimes the case, the adjective precedes the noun, the adjective is put in the genitive case, and the case-sign is annexed to the noun, or to the article, if any, or to the plural sign, if any.

Examples :—

ཞི་མི་ནག་པོ་དེས་ཙི་ཙི་དཀར་པོ་ (ཞིག་) མཐོང་འདུག། — *That black cat saw a white mouse.*

ཞི་མི་ནག་པོས་ཙི་ཙི་ཟིན་པ་རེད། — *The black cat has caught the mouse.*

གཟིག་དཀར་པོ་ཆོ་འཞིལ་པོ་མ་རེད། *White leopards are uncommon.*

གཟིག་དཀར་པོ་འདི་ཆོ་རྩ་ཆེན་པོ་རེད། *These white leopards are valuable.*

གཅན་གཟན་མཛེས་པོ་དཀར་པོ་འདི་ཆོས་
རི་དྭགས་གཞན་པ་གསོད་ཀྱི་འདུག། *These beautiful white beasts of prey kill other wild animals.*

དམར་པོ་འི་སྤྲིན་པ་དེ་ཆོ་ཧ་ཅང་མཛེས་
པོ་རེད། *Those crimson clouds are very beautiful.*

(ii) A very common practice in Colloquial is to turn what we would call a relative clause into an adjectival phrase. Ex. :—

སྤྱང་ཀུ་བསད་མཁན་གྱི་མི་དེ་ or སྤྱང་ཀུ་
བསད་མཁན་མི་དེ། *The man who killed the wolf.* Literally, *the wolf-killing man.*

མི་བསད་མཁན་གྱི་སྤྱང་ཀུ་དེ་ or མི་བསད་
མཁན་སྤྱང་ཀུ་དེ། *The wolf that killed the man.*

(iii) The idiomatic use of this affix མཁན་ is undoubtedly most difficult to understand, for Colloquially it may express the passive as well as the active voice. For instance, བསད་མཁན་གྱི་མི་ signifies, not only *The man who kills or killed*, but also *the man who was or has been killed.* Probably the difficulty arose with the alleged Colloquial custom of using the perfect root of most verbs even in the present tense. If only that custom were not in vogue, it would be possible to use present roots in present tenses, and perfect roots in past tenses, and confine the use of མཁན་ to the active voice, and use the past participle of the verb for the passive voice alone. Ex. :—

གསོད་མཁན་གྱི་མི་དེ་, or མི་གསོད་
མཁན་དེ། *The man who kills.*

བསད་མཁན་གྱི་མི་དེ་, or མི་བསད་
མཁན་དེ། *The man who killed.*

བསད་པའི་མི་དེ་, or མི་བསད་པ་དེ། *The man who was killed.*

This can be done, of course, even as things are; nevertheless it remains a fact that, in Colloquial, བསད་མཁན་གྱི་མི་དེ་, and མི་བསད་མཁན་དེ་ may also signify *The man who is*, or *was*, or *has been*, *killed*. Under these circumstances the context alone can decide what the intended meaning really is.

See § 31, IX, A, on the use of the different roots of the auxiliary verb བྱེད་པ་ *To do*, for the purpose of distinguishing the Active from the Passive Voice.

(iv) The Relative Idea is also frequently expressed by turning a participial clause into an adjectival phrase. Ex. :—

ཆེར་སྐྱེ་བའི་ཕྲུ་གུས་གང་བྱུང་བྱུང་ཟས་ཡོང་ or ཟ་གི་རེད། — *A growing child (a child that is growing) will eat anything it gets.*

ཁས་ས་ (or Literary ཁ་སང་) ཁྱོད་ཀྱིས་བཏང་བའི་མི་དེ་ཤི་སོང་འདུག། — *The man whom you sent yesterday is dead.* Literally, *The yesterday-by-you-sent man is dead.*

The participle, being here an adjective, may also follow the noun. Thus :—

ཁ་སང་ཁྱོད་ཀྱིས་མི་བཏང་བ་དེ་ཤི་སོང་། — *The man*, etc.

Now, let another adjective be inserted, thus :—

ཁ་སང་ཁྱོད་ཀྱིས་བཏང་བའི་མི་བཟང་པོ་དེ་ཤི་སོང་། — *The good man whom you sent yesterday is dead.*

Or thus :—

ཁ་སང་ཁྱོད་ཀྱིས་མི་བཏང་བ་བཟང་པོ་དེ་ཤི་སོང་། — *The good man*, etc.

The negative is inserted thus :—

ཁ་སང་ཁྱོད་ཀྱིས་མ་བཏང་བའི་མི་བཟང་པོ་དེ་ཤི་སོང་འདུག། — *The good man whom you did not send yesterday is dead.*

(v) Use of the Particles པ, པོ, མ, མོ, བ, བོ།

If we desired to be very correct as regards the particles annexed to adjectival roots, we would use པོ, or པ, with a masculine noun, and མོ, with a feminine noun; པ, being more properly employed with the Indefinite Article, and པོ, with the Definite Article, when masculine nouns are concerned; while མོ, may be used with either the Indefinite or the Definite Article when the noun is feminine. In common parlance པོ is often pronounced *pu.*

Ex. :—

ཁྱི་ནག་པོ	*A black dog*	ཁྱི་མོ་ནག་མོ	*A* or *the black bitch.*
རྟ་ཕོ་དཀར་པོ	*The white horse*	རྒོད་མ་དཀར་མོ	*A* or *the white mare.*

But, as a matter of fact, these distinctions are not observed Colloquially, and a Tibetan would express himself thus :—

ཁྱི་ནག་པོ་ཞིག།	*A black dog.*
རྟ་ཕོ་དཀར་པོ། རྟ་ཕོ་དཀར་པོ་དེ།	*The white horse.*
ཁྱི་མོ་ནག་པོ་ཞིག།	*A black bitch.*
རྒོད་མ་དཀར་པོ། རྒོད་མ་དཀར་པོ་དེ།	*The white mare.*

However, there are many adjectives which, even in Colloquial, are seen in པ and མ without reference to gender. Ex. :—

སྨྱོན་པ	*Mad, insane.*	རློན་པ	*Wet.*
དགོས་པ	*Necessary, needful.*	མ་དག་པ	*Wrong, incorrect.*
གསར་པ	*New.*	ཚང་མ	*All.*
རྙིང་པ	*Old.*	དཀྱུས་མ	*Ordinary, vulgar.*
གཞོན་པ	*Young.*	རྫུས་མ	*Sham.*

གཞན་པ་ / ཡན་པ་	Other.	སྔོན་མ་	*Previous, former.*
		གཙང་མ་	*Clean.*

There are also one or two seen in མོ་ without reference to gender. Ex. :—

མངར་མོ་	*Sweet.*
གྲང་མོ་	*Cold, chilly.*
དགའ་མོ་	*Joyous.*

In the Literary language the adjective, in its root form alone, is often seen immediately preceding the noun. Ex. :—

ནག་ཁྱི་	*Black dog.*
ནག་ཁྱི་མོ་	*Black bitch.*

So, when the adjective has a particle and precedes the noun, Literary Tibetan follows the same rule as obtains in the Colloquial, of putting the adjective in the genitive case. Ex. :—

ནག་པའི་ཁྱི་	*A black dog.*
ནག་པོའི་ཁྱི་	*The black dog.*
ནག་མོའི་ཁྱི་མོ་	*A or the black bitch.*

But even in the Colloquial it is allowable, for brevity's sake, to form adjectival expressions by placing before a noun an adjective minus its particle. Ex. :—

ངའི་སེམས་ལ་རྒྱ་མཚོ་ལས་སྐམ་ས་ཡག་གི་རེད། — *To my mind the dry land is better than the ocean.*

Instead of :—

ངའི་སེམས་ལ་རྒྱ་མཚོ་ལས་ས་སྐམ་པོ་ (or སྐམ་པོའི་ས་) ཡག་གི་རེད། — *To my mind*, etc.

So also :—

སྔོན་ལ་བོད་ཡུལ་ནི་སྦས་ཡུལ་ཞིག་རེད། — *Formerly Tibet was a secret (or hidden) country.*

Instead of :—

སྔོན་ལ་བོད་ཡུལ་ནི་ལུང་པ་སྦམས་པ་ (or སྦམས་པའི་ལུང་པ་) ཞིག་རེད། — *Formerly Tibet*, etc.

(vi) Adjectives are also sometimes formed from nouns and post-positions, the latter being put in the genitive case, and the whole expression made to precede the noun that it qualifies. Ex. :—

སྔར་ཕྱི་གླིང་གི་དམག་མི་ཞིག་བོད་ཡུལ་ལ་སྡོད་ཀྱི་ཡོད་པ་རེད། — *Some time ago a European soldier was living in Tibet.*

ད་རུང་སྔོན་གྱི་རྒྱལ་ཁམས་ཆེན་པོ་མང་པོ་འི་དཀྱིལ་ནས་ཁ་ཤས་དྲན་གསོས་འདུག། — *Some of the many great ancient empires are still remembered.*

ཞི་མི་འདིས་རྡོ་གི་ (or རྡོ་འི་) ཆུ་སྣོད་བཅག་ག་རེད། — *The cat has broken the stone jug.*

ང་ཁང་པ་དེའི་ or ཡ་གིའི་སྟེང་ཐོག་གི་ཁང་མིག་ཅིག་གི་ནང་ལ་སྡོད་ཀྱི་ཡོད། — *I live* (or *have a dwelling place*) *in an upper room of that house.*

The adjectives to which attention is drawn in the foregoing illustrations are, in the first ཕྱི་གླིང་གི་ *European ;* in the second, སྔོན་གྱི་ *Ancient ;* in the third རྡོ་གི་ or རྡོ་འི་ *Stone ;* and, in the fourth, སྟེང་ཐོག་གི་ *Upper.*

(vii) Some adjectives consist merely of a primitive repeated. Ex. :—

ཆག་ཆག་	*Broken.*	ཀོར་ཀོར་	*Circular, round.*
ཀོང་ཀོང་	*Concave.*	ཀྱིར་ཀྱིར་	*Circular, round.*
ཀྱང་ཀྱང་	*Straight.*	ཀྱར་ཀྱར་	*Flat.*

ཀྱོག་ཀྱོག་ / ཀུག་ཀུག་	Bent, curved.	ལེབ་ལེབ་ / ལྡེང་ལྡེང་	Flat.
ཀྱོམ་ཀྱོམ་	*Pliant, flexible.*	གུལ་གུལ་	*Quaking, trembling.*

(viii) Others consist of two primitives, similar as regards their consonantal form, but with different vowels. Ex. :—

སམ་སུམ་	*Soft, low.*
ཁྲག་ཁྲུག	*Promiscuous, disorderly.*
གཙང་གཙོང་	*Steep, rugged.*
ཀྱར་ཀྱོར་	*Weak, feeble.*
ཀུག་ཀྱོག	*Curved, crooked.*

(ix) Or of a repeated dissyllable with a difference in the vowels. Ex. :—

མལ་ལ་མུལ་ལེ་ / བལ་ལ་བུལ་ལེ་	*Lukewarm.*
ཚ་ལེ་ཚོ་ལེ་	*Irregular.*
ཚག་ག་ཚོག་གེ་ / ཙུག་ག་ཙོག་གེ་	*Mixed up, jumbled.*

(x) Or of two different dissyllables in juxtaposition. Ex. :—

ཙ་ར་མ་ར *Raving.*

(xi) Or of two different monosyllables in juxtaposition. Ex. :—

ཐག་རིང་	*Far, distant, remote.*
དཔག་བྲལ་	*Measureless, immeasurable.*
དཔག་ཡས་	*Immense.*

(xii) As to the formation of Abstract Nouns from adjectives, *see* § 29, A. 6.

(xiii) English adjectives ending in *able* and *ible* are usually rendered in Colloquial Tibetan by ཉན་, **Nyän**, or ཆོག་ Ch'o', or ཆོག་ཆོག་ Ch'oǵ ch'o', added to the root of the verb. Ex. :—

ལམ་ཀ་འདི་ཐར་ཆོག་གས་ or ཐར་ཆོག་གི་རེད་པས།	*Is this road passable?*
ལགས་ལམ་ཀ་དེ་ཐར་མི་ཆོག་ or ཐར་ཆོག་མི་འདུག།	*No, the road is not passable.*
རྒྱུག་ཆུ་འདི་རྒལ་ཆོག་གས།	*Is this stream fordable?*
ལགས་རྒྱུག་ཆུ་དེ་རྒལ་ཆོག་མ་རེད།	*No, the stream is not fordable.*
ཁོ་འགྲོ་ཆོག་ཆོག་ཡོད།	*He is ready to go.*
ཇ་འདི་ཧ་ཅང་འཐུང་ཉན་འདུག།	*This tea is very drinkable.*
མོག་མོག་དེ་ཟ་ཉན་མི་འདུག།	*That pastry is not eatable.*
ཅ་ལག་འདི་ཚོ་འཚོང་ཆོག་མི་འདུག།	*These goods are not saleable.*
དཀོན་མཆོག་ནི་མཐོང་ཐུབ་པ་མི་འདུག།	*God is invisible.*
དཀོན་མཆོག་ནི་ཀུན་མཁྱེན་ཡིན།	*God is knowable.*

(xiv) The Literary equivalent of ཆོག་, or ཉན་, is རུང་བ་ Rung-wa, or རུང་ Rung. Ex. :—

ལྟད་མོ་འདི་འཇིགས་སུ་རུང་ངོ་, or རུང་གི་རེད།	*This spectacle is terrible*, or *calculated to terrify.*
ཇ་དེ་འཐུང་དུ་མི་རུང་ངོ་, or ཐུང་གི་མ་རེད།	*This tea is not drinkable, or fit to drink.*
ཟས་འདི་ཟར་མི་རུང་ངོ་, or རུང་གི་མ་རེད།	*This food is not eatable*, or *fit to eat.*

Sometimes, however, the supinal particle སུ་, དུ་, or ར་, attached to the verbal root, is omitted, and the particle བ་ after རུང་ is also dropped. Ex. :—

ལྟད་མོ་འདི་འཇིགས་རྩང་ངེ་། — *This sight is terrible.*

ཇ་དེ་འཐུང་རྩང་གི་མ་རེད་ or འཐུང་མི་རྩང་བ་རེད། — *That tea is undrinkable.*

ཟས་འདི་ཟ་རྩང་གི་མ་རེད་ or ཟ་མི་རྩང་བ་རེད། — *This food is uneatable.*

(xv) Where a noun is qualified by two or more adjectives joined by the conjunction *and*, or *or*, the construction is as follows:—

སྒོ་ང་ཡག་པོ་དང་སྡུག་པོ་ (or ཉོག་པོ་)
སྒོ་ང་ཡག་པོ་དང་སྡུག་པོ་ (or ཉོག་པོ་) ཚོ། } *Good and bad (addled) eggs.*

མི་གསུམ་བཞི། — *Three or four men.*

(xvi) Negative Adjectives corresponding to such as begin in English with *Un*, *In*, *Il*, *Im*, *Ir*, or *Dis*, or end in *less*, are not very much used, Tibetans preferring to use an affirmative adjective and to put the verb in the negative. Ex. :—

Instead of saying :—

ཁོ་མི་ཆོས་སེམས་མེད་མཁན་རེད། — *He is an irreligious man.*

A Tibetan would prefer to say :—

ཁོ་མི་ཆོས་སེམས་ཅན་མ་རེད། — *He is not a religious man.*

However, when such negative adjectives are employed, they are formed with the aid of the Colloquial negative expressions མི་, མ་, and མེད་, and the Literary expressions མི་ལྡན་, མི་མངའ་, བྲལ་, and ཡས། Ex. :—

དགོས་པ་མེད་ མི་དགོས་པ་	} *Unnecessary.*	མི་ཐུབ་པ་ མི་སྲིད་པ་	} *Impossible.*
ཁྲུག་བྲོ་པོ་མེད་ མི་གནོད་པ་	} *Innocuous.*	སྐྱོན་མི་མངའ་	*Without fault.*

མི་འོས་པ་ / འོས་མེད་ — *Unbecoming.*

སེམས་དགའ་མེད་ — *Cheerless.*

ཤི་རྒྱུ་མེད་ — *Immortal.*

གཡོ་རྒྱུ་མེད་ — *Immovable.*

དད་མེད་ / མ་དད་པ་ — *Unbelieving.*

སྙིང་རྗེ་མེད་ — *Merciless.*

རེ་བ་མེད་ — *Hopeless.*

མཐའ་ཡས་ — *Infinite.*

དཔག་ཡས་ — *Immeasurable.*

དབུ་མེད་ / མགོ་མེད་ — *Headless, Unsurmounted.*

ནོར་མེད་ / ནོར་མི་ལྡན་ — *Without riches.*

བསྙེན་བཀུར་མེད་ / མ་གུས་པ་ — *Disrespectful.*

མ་དག་པ་ — *Incorrect, wrong.*

མ་ཁོམ་པ་ — *Having no leisure.*

མ་ཐོས་པ་ — *Unheard of.*

མ་སྨིན་པ་ — *Immature, raw, callow.*

ངོ་ཚ་མེད་ — *Immodest.*

ཡོན་ཏན་མེད་ — *Illiterate.*

མོས་མེད་ / མི་མོས་པ་ — *Without faith.*

ལུས་བྲལ་ — *Incorporeal.*

འདོད་བྲལ་ — *Passionless.*

སྡིག་བྲལ་ — *Sinless.*

ཁྲིམས་མེད་ — *Lawless, Illicit.*

(xvii) Sometimes, in the Colloquial, the Active Participles ཡོད་པ་ for inanimate objects, and ཡོད་མཁན་ for animate objects, meaning *which is, or are, who is, or are,* are used adjectivally. Ex. :—

བླ་མ་དེ་གཅང་ཡོད་མཁན་ཞིག་རེད། — *That lama is a wily one.*

ཡུལ་འདི་ལོ་ཕྱུག་འཛོམ་ཡོད་པ་ཞིག་རེད། — *This country is a fertile one.*

(xviii) In Literary Tibetan adjectives are frequently formed by adding to a noun, or to its root, or to a whole phrase, one of the expressions ཅན་ CHĂN, ལྡན་ DĂN, ལྡན་ཅན་ DĂN-CHĂN, བཅས་ CHĂ, མངའ་ NGĀ, and ཡོད་ YÖ', and so representing that class of English adjectives which end in *ful, y, ous, eous, ious, ate, ent, ic, ish, ed, ly, ive,* etc.

Ex. :—

བློ་ཅན་	*Intelligent, Sagacious.*
ཚོད་ཅན་	*Punctilious, moderate.*
ཕན་ཅན་	*Beneficial, useful.*
གྲགས་ཅན་	*Renowned, famous*
རིན་ཅན་	*Costly, expensive.*
འདོད་ལྡན་	*Passionate, amorous.*
བྲག་ལྡན་	*Rocky.*
དགའ་ལྡན་	*Blissful, joyous.*
ཡོན་ཏན་མངའ་	*Talented, literate, accomplished.*
དོན་ཡོད་	*Intelligent.*
ནོར་ལྡན་ཅན་	*Wealthy, opulent.*
ག་ཞེར་ལྡན་ཅན་	*Full of moisture.*
ཤུགས་ལྡན་ཅན་	*Full of energy.*
སྡིག་བཅས་	*Sinful.*
མཁས་པོ་མཚན་ལྡན	*A perfectly accomplished scholar.*
གདོང་མཚེར་པོ་ཅན་	*Having a pretty face.*
ཁ་མི་སྡུག་པ་ཅན་	*Having an ugly mouth.*

ཅན་ is also said to be sometimes used thus :—
བླ་མ་མ་ཎི་འཁོར་ལོ་ཅན་ instead of བླ་མའི་མ་ཎི་འཁོར་ལོ་ *The Lama's prayer-wheel:* but བླ་མ་མ་ཎི་འཁོར་ལོ་ཅན་ would seem to be the more correct. *See*, however, § 31, V, (*b*).

Instead of constructing an adjective out of the root, the particle, and the affix ཅན་, resort is often had to the root alone plus the affix ཅ་ J'A, or CHA. Ex. :—

From དགའ་བ་ཅན་ may be formed དགའ་བུ་ *Cheerful.*

From འཆི་བ་ཅན་ may be formed འཆི་བུ་ *Mortal.*

From ཤེས་པ་ཅན་ may be formed ཤེས་བུ་ཆེན་པོ་ *Very learned.*

II.—*Augmenting of adjectives.*

This can be done in several ways :—

(*a*) By simply repeating the adjective, either in the shape of the primitive root, or of the root with the particle. Ex. :—

ཀྱོག་ཀྱོག་ *Very crooked.*

ལྐུགས་ལྐུགས་ *Very silly.*

སྐྱུར་སྐྱུར་ *Very sour.*

མངར་མངར་ *Very sweet.*

བཙོག་པ་བཙོག་པ་ *Very dirty.*

གཙང་མ་གཙང་མ་ *Very clean.*

སྔ་པོ་སྔ་པོ་ *Very early in the morning.*

ཕྱི་པོ་ཕྱི་པོ་ *Very late.*

(*b*) By repeating the adjective, in any of its forms, with ཡང་ Yang, inserted between them. In the Colloquial ཡང་ becomes འང་ 'ang, after consonants other than ག, ད, བ, and ས། Ex. :—

མཛེས་ཡང་མཛེས། *Very beautiful.*

སྦོམ་ཡང་སྦོམ། *Very thick.*

ཡོན་ཏན་འང་ཡོན་ཏན། *Very learned.*

ཡང་ also becomes འང་ after vowels, both in the Literary language and in Colloquial. Ex. :—

ལྕི་བ་འང་ལྕི་བ། *Very heavy* (Lit.).

ཡང་པོ་འང་ཡང་པོ། *Very light* (Coll.).

In the Literary language ཡང་ becomesཀྱང་ KYANG, after final consonants ག, ད, བ, and ས་ Ex. :—

ངེས་ཀྱང་ངེས།	*Very true.*
སྒྲིབ་ཀྱང་སྒྲིབ།	*Very obscure*
སྙུག་ཀྱང་སྙུག།	*Very neat.*
ཐལ་མེད་ཀྱང་ཐལ་མེད།	*Very narrow.*

(*c*) By use of the affix ཆེ་ CH'E signifying emphasis generally. Ex. :—

སྡིག་པོ་ཆེ་	*Extremely sinful.*
གཟི་ར་པོ་ཆེ་	*Exceedingly brilliant.*
རིན་པོ་ཆེ་	*Very precious.*

The above, however, is more Literary than Colloquial. In the Colloquial ཆེན་པོ་, added to the root, is more common, but it is often used merely to form the adjective, and not so much to augment its force. Ex. :—

རྩ་ཆེན་པོ་	*Precious.*
འོད་ཆེན་པོ་	*Brilliant.*
བློ་གྲོས་ཆེན་པོ་	*Intellectual.*
སྡིག་ཆེན་པོ་	*Sinful.*

(*d*) By inserting ན་ཅང་ *Very*, immediately before the adjective, or by adding ཐག་ཆོད་ *Very*, to the adjectival root :—

བོད་སྐད་ན་ཅང་དཀའ་ལས་ཁག་པོ་རེད།	*Tibetan is very difficult.*
ད་ལྟ་གནམ་ཚ་ཐག་ཆོད་རེད།	*The weather just now is very hot.*

Certain other adverbs may be inserted in the same way when the sentence is a negative one. Ex. :—

འདི་ནད་དེ་འོས་པོ་མ་རེད།	*This is quite* (or ***absolutely*** *improper.*
ཁོ་རྩ་ནས་འགྲིག་པ་ (or འགྲིག་གི་) མི་འདུག།	*He is not right at all.*
སྐད་ཆ་དེ་མ་ནས་དངོས་ནས་མ་རེད།	*That statement is not at all true.*

III.—The Comparative Degree.

(*a*) To express this Tibetans make use of the postpositions ལས་ LĂ, in the Colloquial, and ལས་ or པས་ PĂ (བས་ WĂ, after vowels, or final ང་, ར་, or ལ་) in Literature, signifying *Than*, or *More than*, but they so manipulate the sentence as to place first the object with which the subject is being compared, then the postposition, next the subject, then the adjective in its positive degree, and lastly the verb. Ex. :—

ཁང་པ་དེ་ལས་འདི་མཐོ་པོ་རེད།	*This house is higher than that one.* Literally, *Than that house this high is.*
འབྲས་ལྗོངས་ (pronounced *Den-jong*) པས་ (or ལས་) བོད་ཡུལ་གྲང་མོ་ཡིན།	*Tibet is colder than Sikhim.*
འཇིག་རྟེན་པ་ལས་ཆོས་སེམས་ཅན་དགའ་ང་རེད།	*A religious man is happier than a worldling.*
ཟ་ཆོས་མཁན་ཚོ་བས་ནང་དོན་ཅན་ཚོ་དགའ་གི་རེད།	*Philosophers are happier than ritualists.*
མཁན་པོ་ཚོ་ལས་སྒོམ་ཆེན་པ་ཚོ་དགའ་བ་འདུག།	*Ascetics* (*meditators*) *are happier than professors.*

(*b*) When there is no expressed object with which to compare the subject, an object may be supplied by means of འདི་ THIS or དེ་ THAT. Ex. :—

འདི་ལས་མཐོ་བོ་འི་ཁང་པ་ཞིག།	*A higher house than this.*
དེ་ལས་མགྱོགས་པོའི་རྟ་ཞིག།	*A fleeter horse than that.*
འདི་ལས་གྲོས་ལྷག་པ་ཞིག།	*A counsel exceeding this.*

(*c*) In the Colloquial the comparative degree of certain common adjectives has a special form. For instance, the comparative of ཡག་པོ་ *Good*, is ཡག་ག་ *Better ;* of མང་པོ་ *Much*, it is མང་ང་ *More ;* of སྦོམ་པོ་ *Thick*, it is སྦོམ་པ་ *Thicker ;* of ཆེན་པོ་ *Large, big, great*, it is ཆེ་བ་ *Larger, bigger, greater*. Even with them the same construction in ལས་ is employed. Ex. :—

ཁང་པ་དེ་ལས་འདི་ཆེ་བ་རེད།	*This house is larger than that one.*
ཁྱོད་ཀྱི་དཔེ་ཆ་ལས་ངའི་དཔེ་ཆ་ཡག་ག་རེད།	*My book is better than yours.*

(*d*) The particle belonging to an adjective is sometimes vulgarly conjugated, *i.e.* transmuted into གི་, གྱི་, or ཀྱི་, according to the rule with reference to the last letter of the root. It is better, however, to avoid this. Ex. :—

སྐྱེ་དམན་འདི་དེན་དེན་མཛེས་པོ་རེད་ may be rendered མཛེས་ཀྱི་རེད།	*This woman is indeed pretty.*
ཆང་འདི་ཡག་པོ་མ་རེད་ may be rendered ཡག་གི་མ་རེད།	*This wine is not good.*
ཁང་པ་དེ་ལས་འདི་ཆེན་པོ་རེད་ may be rendered ཆེ་གི་རེད།	*This house is larger than that one.*

But not where ཡོད་པ་, etc., has the sense of *To have.* Ex. :—

མི་དེ་ལས་འདི་ལ་གྲོགས་པོ་མཁས་པ་འདུག not མཁས་ཀྱི་འདུག།	*This man has wiser friends than that one.*

IV.—The Superlative Degree.

(*a*) To express this a universal comparison is resorted to, the subject being placed, at option, either before or after the expression used for the universal comparison. This latter may take numerous forms such as :—

ཚང་མ་ལས་ ཐམས་ཅད་ལས་ གང་ག་ལས་ སྒང་ཁ་ལས་ ཀུན་ལས་ (Literary)	*Than all.*
ཚང་མའི་ནང་ནས་ ཐམས་ཅད་ཀྱི་ནང་ནས་ གང་གའི་ནང་ནས་ སྒང་ཁའི་ནང་ནས་ ཀུན་གྱི་ནང་ནས་ (Literary)	*From among all.*
ཚང་མའི་དཀྱིལ་ནས་ ཐམས་ཅད་ཀྱི་དཀྱིལ་ནས་ གང་གའི་དཀྱིལ་ནས་ སྒང་ཁའི་དཀྱིལ་ནས་ ཀུན་གྱི་དཀྱིལ་ནས་ (Literary)	*From among all.*

Ex. :—

བླ་མ་དེ་ཐམས་ཅད་ལས་མཁས་པ་རེད། or :— ཐམས་ཅད་ལས་བླ་མ་དེ་མཁས་པ་རེད།	*That lama is the most learned (of all).*

སྐང་ཁ་ལས་རྟ་འདི་མགྱོགས་ཀྱི་རེད། *This is the swiftest horse.*

སྲུད་ཡག་ཚང་མའི་དཀྱིལ་ནས་རྡོ་འདི་རིན་ཐང་ཆེ་བ་རེད་ or ཆེ་གི་རེད་ (or ཆེ་ཤོས་རེད་)། *This stone is the most valuable of all well secured things.*

རིན་པོ་ཆེ་ or ཞུ་བའི་ཁམས་སྐང་ཁའི་དཀྱིལ་ནས་གསེར་ནི་རྩ་ཆེན་པོ་ (or ཆེ་གྱི་) རེད། *Gold is the most precious of all metals (meltable things).*

N.B.—Note that ཆེན་པོ་ in its conjugated form becomes ཆེ།

(*b*) Another equally common method of expressing the superlative degree is to affix ཤོས་ Shö to the root of the adjective. The order in which the sentence is constructed does not much matter, and even the use of ལས་ (in Literature ལས་, པས་, or བས་) is optional. Ex. :—

རྟ་འདི་མགྱོགས་ཤོས་རེད། *This horse is the fleetest.*

རིན་པོ་ཆེའི་ནང་ནས་ (or དཀྱིལ་ནས་) གསེར་རིན་ཐང་ཆེ་ཤོས་རེད། *Gold is the dearest of metals.*

If the speaker likes he may insert དེ་ The, after ཤོས་, thus :—

རྟ་འདི་མགྱོགས་ཤོས་དེ་རེད། *This horse is the fleetest.*

རྡོ་འདི་རྩ་ཆེ་ཤོས་ (དེ་) རེད། *This stone is the most valuable.*

N.B.—རིན་པོ་ཆེ་འི་, like many other words in *MS.*, is often abbreviated into རིནྣོའི།

ལྷ་ས་གྲོང་ཁྱེར་ཚང་མའི་དཀྱིལ་ནས་ཁྱད་པར་དུ་འཕགས་ཤོས་ (དེ་) རེད། *Lhasa is the most transcendent of cities.*

N.B.—ཐམས་ཅད་ is often abbreviated into ཐོད་, and འཕགས་ into འཕང་།

(*c*) Yet another expression used to indicate the superlative idea is མཆོག་ CH'O', signifying *The best*, *The most*, etc. It is a Literary word, and only rarely comes into the Colloquial. It may be either prefixed or affixed to the word that it qualifies, and when prefixed should be put in the genitive case. Ex.:—

མཆོག་གི་བདག།	*The chief noble or lord.*
མཆོག་གི་མ།	*The chief mother: the goddess Ḋölma.*
མཆོག་གི་ལྕུག་མ།	*The principal woman in a family.*
མཆོག་གི་མཆོག།	*The best of the best.*

In Literary Tibetan the substantive is put in the genitive case when མཆོག་ is affixed. Ex.:—

བཟང་པོའི་མཆོག།	*The best among the good or noble.*
དམ་པའི་མཆོག།	*The holiest.*
དཀོན་པའི་མཆོག།	*The Chief of Rarities; the rarest Being or Object; the Supreme Being.*
འཕགས་པའི་མཆོག།	*The sublimest, most excellent.*
མིའི་མཆོག།	*The best or greatest of men.*
མཁས་པའི་མཆོག་ཆེ།	*The wisest or most learned.*

In the Colloquial མཆོག་, if used at all, is sometimes prefixed and sometimes affixed, but neither it nor the substantive is put in the genitive case. Ex.:—

མཆོག་སྐྱོང་།	*The Chief Protector.*
དཀོན་མཆོག།	*Anything excellent of its kind;* also an abbreviation of དཀོན་པའི་མཆོག།
མཆོག་དགའ།	*The highest joy, rapture, bliss.*
འཕགས་མཆོག།	*The noblest, sublimest.*
རོ་མཆོག།	*The most excellent taste, delicious.*
མཁས་མཆོག་ཆེ།	*The wisest, most learned.*
གཞུང་མཆོག་ཆེན་པོ།	*The very utmost attention.*
སྐྱེ་བུ་མཆོག་ or སྐྱེ་མཆོག།	*The Chief of Beings, Buddha.*
མི་མཆོག་ཁྱོད།	*Thou best of men!*

མཆོག་ is also used thus in Literary Tibetan :—

མཆོག་དང་ཐུན་མོང་།	*Nobles and commonalty.*
མཆོག་དང་ཕལ་པ།	*The great and the vulgar.*
མཆོག་དམན།	*Great and small.*
ཤིན་ཏུ་མཆོག།	*The very excellent or superior.*

V.—Other Methods of Comparison.

The Tibetan rendering of English phrases constructed with As..as, may be illustrated thus :—

ང་ལ་དེ་ནས་གང་མང་ཞིག་ (or ག་རེ་མང་ཞིག་, or གང་ཉིད་ཅིག་, or གང་ཞེ་ཞིག་, or ག་རེ་ཞེ་ཞིག་) གནང་རོགས་གནང་།	*Please give me as much* (or *many*) *of that as possible.*

or :—

ཁྱོད་ཀྱིས་ང་ལ་དེ་ནས་ག་རེ་གནང་ཐུབ་པ་དེ་ ད་ག་རང་གནང་རོགས་གནང་། — *Please give*, etc.

or :—

ང་ལ་དེ་ནས་གནང་ཐུབ་པ་དེ་ད་ག་རང་ གནང་རོགས་གནང་། — *Please give*, etc.

ཁྱོད་ཕ་གི་ཁང་པ་ཐུག་ (or ཐུག་ལ་, or བར་དུ་) ཡོང་གི་ཡིན་པས་ or Literary ཡིན་ནམ། — *Will you come as far as to yonder house?*

ལམ་ཀ་འདི་ཕ་གི་ཁང་པ་དག་ག་ཙ་ཞིག ལ་འགྲོ་གི་འདུག། — *This road goes about as far as to that house.*

ཕ་གི་ཤིང་སྡོང་མཐོ་པོ་ཡོད་པ་ཙམ་ད་ག་ རང་འདི་ཡང་ཡོད། — *As high as that tree-trunk is (may be) this one also is.*

ངས་རྒྱུས་ཡོད་པ་བཞིན་ (or ཤང་བཞིན་, or འདྲ་པོ་) ཡིན་ན་དེ་ད་ག་རང་ཡིན། — *As far as I know, that is so:* Literary, *If it be according to the knowledge I possess, it is just like that.*

ཁོ་ལངས་མ་ཐག་ (or མ་ཐག་ཏུ་, or མ་ཁད་ or མ་ཁད་དུ་) ངས་མེ་མདའ་ བརྒྱབ་སོང་། — *As soon as he rose I fired.*

ངའི་དཔེ་ཆ་ (དེ་) ཁྱོད་ཀྱི་དཔེ་ཆ་དང་ ལེགས་ཉེས་གཅིག་གི་རེད། — *My book is as good as yours:* Literally, *My book is equally good-bad with yours.*

§ 31.—The Pronoun.

I.—Personal Pronouns.

(*a*) I.

ང་ } Commonest forms in Colloquial.
ང་རང་ }

བདག་ Expressive of humility. Chiefly used in Tsang. Like Persian بنده *Bandeh.*

ང་ང་རང་ / ང་རང་རང་ — Emphatic forms.

ཨ་ཕོ་ང་ *This old fellow* or *chap.* Used by the speaker in reference to himself, but only in a comic way.

The following are Book-terms :—

བདག་ / ཕྲན་ / ཕྲན་རང་ / བདག་རང་ / བདག་ཉིད་ / བདག་ནི་ — Expressive of humility.

ང་ཉིད་ / ང་ནི་ — *I myself.*

ཁོ་བོ་ (masc.) / ཁོ་མོ་ (fem.) — *This one, This person, This individual.* Used by the speaker with reference to himself or herself.

ང་ཁོ་ན་ *I myself, I alone.*

བདག་ཁོ་ན་ Humble form of foregoing.

The following are Colloquially used by the Kyrong-pas, or Nipāl Frontier Tibetans :—

ངེད་རང་ Pronounced almost like ཡི་རང་ *I myself.*

ངྦ་རང་ *We ourselves*

(*b*) THOU.

ཁྱོད་ / ཁྱོད་རང་ — Common Colloquial forms.

The genitive of ཁྱོད་ is either ཁྱོད་ཀྱི་, or ཁྱོད་རེའི་ *Thy, Thine:* and the Agentive is either ཁྱོད་ཀྱིས་ or ཁྱོད་རེས་ *By thee.*

ཁྱེད་ }
ཁྱེད་རང་ } Colloquial honorifics.

ཉིད་ Used in official correspondence.

ཉིད་རང་ (pl. ཉིད་ཚག་) met with in dialects.

ཁྱེད་ }
ཁྱེད་ཉིད་ } Polite Literary forms.
ཁྱེད་ཁོ་ན་ }

ཁྱེད་ཉིཾ་པ་ Literary honorific

ཁྱོད་ཉིད་ }
ཁྱོད་ཁོ་ན་ } Other Literary forms.

(*c*) He, or She.

ཁོ་ }
ཁོ་རང་ } Common Colloquial forms.

The genitive of ཁོ་ is either ཁོའི་, or ཁོ་རེའི་ *His*, and the agentive is either ཁོས་, or ཁོ་རེས།

ཁོང་ }
ཁོང་རང་ } Polite forms, Literary and Colloquial.

ཁོང་ཉིཾ་པ་ Honorific form, Literary and Colloquial.

ཁོ་པ་ }
ཁོ་བ་ }
ཁོ་མ་ } Literary forms.
ཁོ་ཉིད་ }
ཁོང་ཉིད་ }
ཉིད་ }

Other forms for SHE :—

མོ་ } Colloquial.
མོ་རང་ }

The genitive of མོ་ is either མོའི་ or མོ་རེའི་, and the Agentive is either མོས་, or མོ་རེས།

(*d*) IT.

There is no special term for this pronoun. It is often not rendered at all. Ex. :—

རྟ་འདི་ངའི་རེད་པས། ལགས་རེད།	*Is this my horse? Yes, it is.*
ངའི་སྨྱུ་གུ་ག་པ་ཡོད་ or འདུག། བཅག་ག་རེད།	*Where is my pen? It is broken.*

If used at all it is generally rendered by དེ་, or དེ་རང་ Ex. :—

ཁྱོད་རེའི་སྨྱུ་གུ་འདིར་ or འདི་ཙ་འདུག་ དེའི་རྩེ་བཅག་ག་རེད།	*Here is your pen: its point is broken.*

Usually Pronouns are not repeated in ordinary conversation after the first reference.

(*e*) REFLEXIVES.

རང་ *Self*, *One's self*, is the commonest expression, both in the Colloquial and in Book-language. Other Book-terms with the same meaning are :— བདག་, ཉིད་, རང་ཉིད་, and བདག་ཉིད།

II.—DECLENSION OF PERSONAL PRONOUNS.

This follows the same rules as apply in the case of Substantives. Ex. :—

	Singular.		*Plural.*	
Nom. Voc. Acc.	ང་	*I.*	ང་ཚོ་	*We.*
Gen.	ངའི་	*Of me.*	ང་ཚོའི་	*Of us.*
Agent.	ངས་	*By me.*	ང་ཚོས་	*By us.*
Dat.	ང་ལ་	*To me.*	ང་ཚོ་ལ་	*To us.*
Loc.	ང་ན་	*On me.*	ང་ཚོ་ན་	*On us*
Per.	———		———	
Mod.	ང་དང་	*Against me.*	ང་ཚོ་དང་	*Against us.*
Abl.	ང་ལས་	*Than me.*	ང་ཚོ་ལས་	*Than us.*
Term.	ངའི་ཕྱོགས་ལ་	*Towards me.*	ང་ཚོའི་ཕྱོགས་ལ་	*Towards us.*
	ང་ནས་	*From me.*	ང་ཚོ་ནས་	*From us.*
Nom. Voc. Acc.	ང་རང་	*I.*	ང་རང་ཚོ་	*We.*
Gen.	ང་རང་གི་	*Of me.*	ང་རང་ཚོའི་	*Of us.*
Agent.	ང་རང་གིས་	*By me.*	ང་རང་ཚོས་	*By us.*
Dat.	ང་རང་ལ་	*To me.*	ང་རང་ཚོ་ལ་	*To us.*

And so forth.

Nom. Voc. Acc.	ཁྱོད་	*Thou.*	ཁྱོད་ཚོ་	*You.*
Gen.	ཁྱོད་ཀྱི་	*Of thee, Thy.*	ཁྱོད་ཚོའི་	*Of you, yours.*
Agent.	ཁྱོད་ཀྱིས་	*By thee.*	ཁྱོད་ཚོས་	*By you.*

And so forth.

Or:—

Gen.	ཁྱོད་རེའི་	*Of thee, Thy.*	ཁྱོད་ཚོའི་	*Of you, yours.*
Agent	ཁྱོད་རེས་	*By thee.*	ཁྱོད་ཚོས་	*By you.*

ཁྱོད་རང་ *Thou*, is declined like ང་རང་ *I.*

	Singular		Plural	
Nom. Voc. Acc.	ཁོ	*He.*	ཁོ་ཚོ་	*They.*
Gen.	ཁོའི་ / ཁོ་རའི་	*Of him, His.*	ཁོ་ཚོའི་	*Of them, Their.*
Agent.	ཁོས་ / ཁོ་རས་	*By him.*	ཁོ་ཚོས་	*By them.*

And so forth.

ཁོང་ *He*, is declined like ང་རང་ *I.*

མོ་ *She*, is declined like ཁོ *He.*

ཕྲན་ *This humble one*, has for genitive གྱི་, and for Agentive གྱིས།

བདག་ *This humble one*, has for genitive གི་, and for Agentive གིས།

All those ending in པ་, བ་, མ་, ན་, and ང་ are declined like ང་ *I.*

Those ending in ད་ are declined like ཁྱོད་ *Thou*, save as regards the forms in རེ།

N.B.—Plural Nouns do not take the plural sign ཚོ་ if from the context it is clear that plurality is intended [*See* § 29 B, 2 (*e*)], but plural Pronouns always take the sign, except when they are qualified by Numeral Adjectives.

EXAMPLE :—

ང་བཞི་ *We four.*

ང་རང་ལྔ་ *We five.*

III. THE REFLEXIVE PRONOUN.

The following are examples of རང་ SELF, ONE'S SELF, used reflexively :—

ངས་རང་དགེ་སེམས་ཆེན་པོར་ངོ་ཤེས་ན་ དཀོན་མཆོག་ལ་མཐོང་གི་ཡིན།	*If I know myself spiritually I shall see God.*
ངས་དཀོན་མཆོག་ལ་དགེ་སེམས་ཆེན་པོར་ མཐོང་ན་རང་ངོ་ཤེས་ཀྱི་ཡིན།	*If I see God spiritually I shall know myself.*
ཀྱེ་མི་རང་ངོ་ཤེས་ཤིག།	*Man, know thyself.*
མི་བསད་མཁན་དེས་རང་བསད་པ་རེད།	*The murderer has killed himself.*
ཁྱོད་རེས་དངུལ་རང་ལ་བཞག་ག་ཡིན་པས་ or ཡིན་ནམ།	*Did you keep the money for yourself?*
དོན་དེ་རང་ནས་བྱུང་།	*The idea originated from myself.*
ཁྱིས་རུས་ཁོག་རང་གི་ཕྱོགས་ལ་འཐེན་ སོང་།	*The dog pulled the bone towards itself.*
སེམས་ཉིད་ (or དྭངས་པ་) གཅིག་པོ་རང་ ངེས་པར་ངོ་ཤེས་ཀྱིན་འདུག།	*The soul alone really knows itself.*
མི་གཞན་པ་ཚོ་རང་ཚོའི་གནས་ཚུལ་གཞན་ པ་ཚོའི་ནང་ལ་སྤྲུལ་ཀྱི་འདུག།	*Other men are ourselves incarnate under other conditions.*

(*ii*) The following are Literary :—

སུས་ཀྱང་རང་གི་ནང་ (or better, བློ་འདོད་) ནས་གཏམ་བྱེད་པ་དེས་རང་ གི་གྲགས་པ་འདོད་པ་རེད་ or འདོད་ ཀྱི་འདུག, or འདོད་དོ།	*He that speaketh of* (*from*) *himself, seeketh his own glory* (John vii. 18).
ང་ནི་རང་བཞིན་ནས་མ་བྱུང་།	*I am not come of myself* (John vii. 28).

Or better :—

ང་ནི་རང་གི་ཆེད་དུ་ (or དོན་དུ་) ཡོང་བ་མིན། — *I am not, etc.*

ངས་ནི་རང་བཞིན་ནས་ཅི་ཡང་བྱེད་མི་ཐུབ། — *I can of mine own self do nothin* (John v. 30).

Or better :—

ངས་ང་རང་གི་མཐུས་ནི་ཅི་ཡང་བྱེད་པར་མི་ནུས་སོ། — *I can, etc.*

ངས་ཀྱང་རང་གི་ཁྲིམས་མི་གཅོད་དོ། — *I judge not mine own self* (1 Co iv. 3).

Or better :—

ངས་ང་རང་རང་གི་སྟེང་ལ་ཁྲིམས་མི་གཅོད་དོ, or ཁྲིམས་གཅོད་མི་བྱའོ་ or གཅོད་ཀྱི་མེད། — *I judge not, etc.*

—

ཁྱེད་རང་གི་དོན་དུ་ཅི་ཟེར། — *What sayest thou of thyself* (Joh i. 22).

Or better :—

ཁྱེད་རང་གི་སྐོར་ལ་ལབ་རྒྱུ་ཅི་ཡོད། — *What sayest, etc.*

འདི་ཁྱེད་རང་གིས་འདྲི་འམ། — *Askest thou this of thyself?* (Joh xviii. 34).

Or better :—

ཁྱོད་ཀྱིས་འདི་ཁྱོད་རང་གི་བློ་འདོད་ལས་དྲི་བ་ཡིན་ནམ། — *Askest thou this, etc.*

སུ་ཡང་རང་གིས་རང་མཐོ་བར་བྱེད་ན་དམའ་བར་བྱེད་པར་འགྱུར། སུ་ཡང་རང་གི་རང་དམའ་བར་བྱེད་ན་མཐོ་བར་བྱེད་པར་འགྱུར་རོ། — *Whosoever shall exalt himself sh be humbled ; and whosoever sh humble himself shall be exalt* (Matt. xxiii. 12).

IV.—Compounds in རང་ Rang.

(*a*) རང་ frequently forms the first part of a compound. Ex. :—

རང་ཉིད།	*Self ; One's self.*
རང་སེམས།	*One's own soul.*
རང་རེ།	*Each ; each respectively ;* Hon. for *you.*
རང་རེའི་སྣ་ཐག།	*Each has hold of his own leading-string* (D).
རང་རེས་བཟུང་།	
རང་རེའི་སྒོ་དྲུང་ན།	*Each at his own door.*
རང་ཤུགས་ལ།	*Spontaneous ; of itself.*
རང་ཤུགས་ཀྱིས།	*Spontaneously.*
རང་བྱུང་།	*Self-sprung.*
མ་རིག་པའི་དབང་གིས་ཕྱུགས་ནི་རང་ཁོ་ན་འཕྱུང་བར་གྱུར་སོ།	*By ignorance one's future was of its own self destroyed.*
བྱམས་པ་རང་དོན་མི་བྱེད།	*Love seeketh not its own* (N. T.). *Bringeth not about its own ends.*

Or better :—

བྱམས་པ་རང་དོན་བྱེད་ཀྱི་མི་འདུག།	*Love, etc.*
ང་རང་འབྱུང་ཁང་ལ་འགྲོ་གི་ཡིན།	*I shall go to the house of my own accord.*
རང་གཉིས་སྐྱེབ་ལ་འདི་ནས་འགྲོ་འོ།	*Let us (the two of us) go hence together.*
རང་རིག་རང་གསལ་རང་བདེ་གསུམ།	*One's own perception, intelligence, and happiness, three things* (D).
རང་སྲོག་རང་གིས་གཅོད་ཀྱི་རེད།	*You will take your own life* (D).

(*b*) རང་ also often forms the second part of a compound. Ex. :—

ཕོ་རང་།	*An unmarried man.*
མོ་རང་།	*A spinster ; a woman by herself.*
དེ་རང་།	*The very same, exactly, quite so.*
དེ་ག་རང་ཡིན་ དེ་རང་ཡིན་	*It is just so ; it is precisely so.*
སྔ་མོ་རང་།	*Quite early in the morning.*
ཞེན་པོ་རང་ ཞེ་པོ་རང་ མང་པོ་རང་	With negative—*Not much, Not many.*
ང་དང་ཕྲད་པ་རང་གིས།	*By the mere (just by) meeting with me.*
མི་རང་།	*A man all by himself ; just a man.*

V.—Possessive Pronouns.

1.—Ordinary Personal Pronouns.

(*a*) Possessive Pronouns are formed by putting the Personal Pronouns in the Genitive case. They may either precede or follow the noun or object in respect of which possession is predicated. Ex. :—

དེ་ངའི་འབྲུག་སྐད་རེད།	*That is my thunder.*

Or :—

འབྲུག་སྐད་དེ་ངའི་རེད།	*That thunder is mine.*
འདི་ཁྱེད་རེའི་ཚིག་མཛོད་རེད།	*This is your dictionary.*

Or :—

ཚིག་མཛོད་འདི་ཁྱེད་རེའི་རེད།	*This dictionary is yours.*

(*b*) In some works it is stated that the Possessive case may also be formed by affixing ཅན་ to the shorter forms of the Personal Pronouns. Thus, ང་ཅན་ *My, mine, of me* ; ཁོ་ཅན་ *His, of him,* and so forth. If this be so, it must be a very obscure Literary usage. If an Ü-pa heard or saw the expression ང་ཅན་, it would probably raise in his mind the idea of *egoism*, *selfishness*, etc., and not that of the Possessive case as associated with the first person. Compare the phrase ང་རྒྱལ་ཅན་, *I the chief*, i.e., *possessed of pride*, i.e., *proud.*

So, also, the expression བླ་མ་མ་ཎི་འཁོར་ལོ་ཅན་, said to be the the equivalent of བླ་མའི་མ་ཎི་འཁོར་ལོ་ *The Lama's prayer-wheel*, probably means *The Lama with*, or *possessed of*, *the prayer-wheel.*

2.—Reflexive Possessive Pronouns.

These are merely the Reflexive Pronouns put in the Genitive case. They then signify One's, One's own, My own, Thy own, Thine own, His own, Her own, Its own, Our own, Your own, Their own, according to the pronoun, either expressed or implied, to which, in the same sentence, they respectively refer back.

Colloquial Examples :—

ངས་རང་གི་རྟ་ལ་ཞོན་གྱི་ཡིན།	*I shall ride my own horse.*
ང་ཚོས་རང་ཚོའི་ཁ་ལག་བཙོ་དགོས་ཀྱི་ཡོད།	*We shall have to cook our own food.*
ཁྱེད་རེས་རང་གི་གཡོག་པོ་འཁྲིད་ཡོང་གི་ཡིན་པས་ or Literary ཡིན་ནམ།	*Will you bring your own servant?*
ཁྱེད་ཐཾད་ཀྱིས་རང་ཚོའི་གྲི་ཚོ་དང་ཤ་འཛེན་ཚོ་དང་ཐུར་མ་ཚོ་འཁྱེར་དགོས་ཀྱི་རེད།	*You must all bring your own knives, forks and spoons.*
Or :—	
ཁྱེད་སོ་སོས་རང་གི་གྲི་དང་ཤ་འཛེན་དང་ཐུར་མ་འཁྱེར་དགོས་ཀྱི་རེད།	*Each of you must bring his own knife, fork and spoon.*
ཁོས།རང་གི་བསོད་བདེ་ཧ་གོ་བ་མ་རེད།	*He did not realize his own good luck.*
ཁོ་ཚོས་རང་ཚོའི་མིང་ཚོ་བཤད་ཐུབ་ཀྱི་མ་རེད།	*They cannot tell their own names.*

མི་རེ་རེས་ (or མི་སོ་སོས་) རང་གི་ཆུ་ཚོད་འཁོར་ལོ་བརྟན་ཤོས་ཡིད་ཆེས་ཀྱི་འདུག།

Every man believes his own watch is the most accurate.

ཁོ་ཐམས་ཅད་རང་ཚོ་འི་གྲོང་གསེབ་ནས་ཐོན་སོང་།

They have all cleared out of their own village.

ཁང་པ་རེ་རེ་ལ་རང་གི་གླིང་དགའ་ཡོད།

Every house has its own park (compound).

ང་རང་གི་ཨ་མས་ང་ (ལ་) ཡི་གེ་བསླབས་བྱུང་།

My own mother educated me.

In honorific form:—

ང་རང་གི་ཡུམ་སྐུ་གཞོགས་ཀྱིས་ང་ཕྱུག་ཁྲིས་བསླབ་པ་གནང་ཡོད།

My own mother, etc.

ཁོ་རང་གི་བསོད་བདེའི་བཟོ་མཁན་དེ་ཡིན་པ་རེད།

He was the architect of his own good fortune.

གནས་མོ་རེ་རེས་རང་གི་ཕྱག་མ་ཡག་ཤོས་ཡིན་བསམ་གྱི་འདུག།

Every housewife thinks her own broom is the best.

ཁོ་རང་གི་སྙིང་རུས་ཀྱི་རྐྱེན་གྱིས་མགོ་ཐོན་བྱུང་།

He succeeded because of his own diligence.

The following are Literary:—

ཁོང་རང་གིས་ངེད་ཚོ་འི་སྡིག་པ་ཚོ་རང་གི་སྐུ་ལུས་ལ་ཤིང་གི་ཁར་འཁུར་ཏེ།

He himself bearing our sins in his own body upon the tree (1 Peter ii. 24).

སུ་ཡང་ཁོ་རང་གི་སློ་འདོད་ནས་བྱེད་པ་དེས་རང་གི་གྲགས་པ་འདོད་ཀྱི་འདུག།

He who speaks of himself seeks his own glory (John vii. 18).

ཁོང་ནི་རང་གི་རྒྱལ་ཁམས་སུ་བྱོན་ཀྱང་། ཁོང་རང་གི་འབངས་རྣམས་ཀྱིས་མ་བཀུར་རོ།	*He came to his own kingdom, but his own subjects received him not* (John i. 11).
བྱམས་པ་རང་དོན་བྱེད་ཀྱི་མི་འདུག།	*Love seeketh not her own* (1 Cor. xiii. 5).
རང་སྲོག་རང་གིས་གཅོད་ཀྱི་རེད།	*You will take your own life* (D).
རང་ལ་བུ་མེད་ན།	*If one have no son of his own* (D).

VI.—Demonstrative Pronouns.

These may also be called Distinguishing Adjectives. The commonest are འདི་ THIS, and དེ་ THAT, as to which see § 27.

The following are also common :—

འདི་རང་	*This very, This same.*
དེ་རང་	*That very, That same.*
འདི་ཀ་རང་	*This particular.*
དེ་ཀ་རང་	*That particular.*
ད་ག་རང་ དག་ག་རང་ དག་ག	*That very ; that precisely ; just so ; like that, thus ; so ; just that.*

Also the following :—

ཕ་གི་	*That over there, Yonder* (far off).
ད་གི་	*That just there* (nearer).
ཡ་གི་	*That up there.*
མ་གི་	*That down there.*

These latter may be used just as they stand, or they may be put in the genitive case. Whichever method is adopted, they precede the noun that they distinguish, and they may be used with or without དེ་

Also the following: —

འདི་ད་ དེ་ད་	*Such, such as.*

EXAMPLES :—

འདི་སུ་ཡིན།	*Who is this?*
དེ་སུ་ཡིན།	*Who is that?*
འདི་ངའི་སྤུན་ (ཀུག་) ཡིན།	*This is my brother, or sister.*
དེ་ངའི་སྦྱིན་བདག་ཡིན།	*That is my master.*
སྐུ་དྲག་དེ་རང་གིས་ཁྱོད་སྐོ་བ་གནང་གི་རེད།	*That same gentleman will employ you.*
ང་ལ་དེ་ནས་གནང་ཐུབ་པ་དེ་ད་ག་རང་ གནང་རོགས་གནང་།	*Please give me what you can of that:* literally, *what you can from that, just that please give.*
ལམ་ཀ་འདི་ཕ་གི་ཁང་པ་དག་ག་ཙམ་ཞིག ལ་འགྲོ་གི།	*This road goes* **as far as** *to that house:* literally, *this road to that house,* **about** *just that goes.*
ལའི་ལམ་ཀ་ག་འདྲས་ཡོད་པས།	*What is the road like to the pass?*
ལགས་གཟར་གཟར་དང་ཀྱོག་ཀྱོག་དག་ག རེད།	*Very steep and crooked, just like* **that.**
དག་ག་ཙ་ནས་ (or མ་ནས་) མི་ཡོང་།	*That won't do at all:* literally *like that will not come at all.*
ད་ག་རང་ཡིན།	*That is so.*
ཕ་གི་རིའི་མིང་ལ་ག་རེ་ཟེར་གྱི་ཡོད།	*What is the name of that hill away yonder?*

Or :—

ཕ་གི་ (or ཕ་གིའི་) རི་དེའི་མིང་ལ་ག རེ་ཟེར་གྱི་ཡོད།	*What is the name,* etc.

མ་གི་རོང་ཆེན་པོ་དི་མིང་ལ་གྲོ་མོ་ཟེར་གྱི་འདུག།	*The name of that big valley down there is Ḍo-mo* (Chŭmbi).
ཁྱོད་རེས་མིང་འདི་ད་སྔོན་ལ་ཐོས་མྱོང་ངམ།	*Have you ever heard such a name before?*

The Literary equivalents for most of the above are :—

འདི་	*This.*	འདི་རྣམས་	*These.*	
དེ་	*That.*	དེ་རྣམས་	*Those.*	
འདི་ནི་ འདི་ཉིད་ འདི་རང་ འདི་ཁོ་ན་ འདི་ཁོ་ན་ཉིད་	*This very ; This same.*	དེ་ནི་ དེ་ཉིད་ དེ་རང་ དེ་ཁོ་ན་ དེ་ཁོ་ན་ཉིད་	*That very ; That same.*	
འདི་ཀ་ འདི་ག་ འདི་ཀ་རང་	*This particular.*	དེ་ཀ་ དེ་ག། དེ་ཀ་རང་	*That particular.*	
ཚུ་ཁ ཚུ་བི་ མ་གི་ བུ་ནི་	*This here.*	ཕ་བི་ ཕ་གི་ ཊོ་ནི་	*That there.*	Save མ་གི་ and ཕ་གི་ these are not used in Ü, or Tsang.
		ཊོ་	*That.*	
འདི་འདྲ་བ་ དེ་འདྲ་བ་ འདི་ལྟར་	*Such, Such as.*			
ཞེས་བྱ་བ་ བྱ་བ་	*So named, Named.*			

EXAMPLES :—

ང་དང་མིང་ (or མཚན་) འདི་ཞེས་བྱ་བ།	*I and one so named ; I and so and so.*
ཀི་རེ་ནེ་པ་སི་མོན་བྱ་བ་ཞིག་ཞིང་ནས་ཡོངས་པ་ལས་དེ་བཟུང་ནས།	*They laid hold upon one Simon of Cyrene, coming from the country* (Luke xxiii. 26).
ཡང་ལྟོས་ཤིག། གྲོས་མི་ཆོས་ལྡན་ཞིང་བཟང་པོ་ཡ་ཧུ་དཱ་པའི་གྲོང་ཁྱེར་ཨ་རི་མ་ཐཱ་ཡཱ་པ་ཡོ་སེབ་བྱ་བ།	*And behold, a man named Joseph, who was a councillor, a good man and a rightcous, of Arimathœa, a city of the Jews* (Luke xxiii. 50).
ང་འདི་ལྟར་ཡིན།	*Such as this am I* (D).

VII.—THE RECIPROCAL PRONOUN.

གཅིག་གཅིག། ONE ANOTHER ; EACH OTHER.

EXAMPLES :—

ཁོ་ཚོ་གཅིག་གིས་གཅིག་བྱམས་པོ་བྱས་སོང་།	*They loved each other*
ལྕམ་ལྕམ་སྐུ་གཞོགས་ཚོ་གཅིག་ལ་གཅིག་དགའ་ཚོར་ཆེན་པོར་གཟིགས་སོང་།	*The ladies looked at one another mirthfully.*
ཁོ་ཚོ་གཅིག་གི་རྩ་ལ་གཅིག་ཕྱིན་པ་རེད།	*They have gone up to each other.*
ཁོ་ཚོ་གཅིག་གིས་གཅིག་གི་དུག་ལོག་ཞིབ་དཔྱོད་བྱས་པ་རེད།	*They have scrutinized each other's garments.*
བླ་མ་ཚོ་གཅིག་ནས་གཅིག་གིས་ཁ་བཏགས་ཐོབ་བྱུང་།	*The Lamas received ceremonial scarfs from one another.*
ཁོ་ཚོ་གཅིག་དང་མཉམ་དུ་གཅིག་ཕྱིན་པ་རེད།	*They have gone in company with one another.*

ཁོ་ཚོ་གཅིག་ལ་གཅིག་ཁ་ལས་བཤད་ཀྱི་འདུག། — *They are conversing with each other.*

ཁྱོད་ཚོ་ཡང་གཅིག་གིས་གཅིག་གི་རྐང་པ་འཁྲུད་དགོས་ཀྱི་རེད། — *Ye also ought to wash one another's feet* (John xiii. 14).

ཁོང་གི་ཉེ་གནས་ཚོའི་ནང་ནས་ཁ་ཤས་གཅིག་ལ་གཅིག་ལབ་སོང་། — *Some of his disciples said one to another.*

VIII.—Interrogative Pronouns.

In the Colloquial these are :—

སུ་,	plural form	སུ་སུ་	Who ?
ག་རེ་,	,,	ག་རེ་ག་རེ་	What ? which ?
གང་,	,,	གང་གང་	What ? which ?
ག་གི་,	,,	ག་གི་ག་གི་	Which ?

ག་རེ་ is more commonly used than གང་

All the above are declinable like nouns.

The Literary equivalents are :—

སུ་, གང་	Who ?	These are also declinable like nouns.
ཅི་, གང་	What ?	
གང་	Which ?	

In simple questions the Interrogative Pronoun is usually placed immediately before the verb. Ex. :—

ཁྱོད་སུ་ཡིན། — *Who are you ?* (singular).

ཁྱོད་སུ་སུ་ཡིན། — *Who are you ?* (plural).

འདི་ཙ་སུ་ཡོད།	*Who is present?*
བླ་མ་འདི་ཚོ་སུ་སུ་རེད།	*Who are these Lamas?*
དེ་ཙ་བླ་མ་སུ་སུ་འདུག།	*What Lamas were there?*
ཁྱོད་ཀྱི་མིང་ལ་ག་རེ་ཟེར་གྱི་རེད།	*What is your name?*
སྒམ་དེ་ག་རེས་བཟོས་པ་རེད།	*What is that box made of* (by)*?*
ཁ་ལ་འདི་ཚོ་ག་རེ་ག་རེ་རེད།	*What are these loads?*
དེ་ཙ་རྟ་ག་རེ་ག་རེ་འདུག།	*What horses were there?*
དཔེ་ཆ་འདི་སུས་བཏང་ང་རེད།	*Who sent this book?*
དཔེ་ཆ་འདི་ཚོའི་དཀྱིལ་ནས་ཁྱོད་ཀྱིས་ག་གི་འདོད་ཀྱི་འདུག།	*Which of these books do you want?*

If, however, the Interrogative is in the genitive case, it may come either before the verb or before its noun. Ex. :—

པ་གི་ཁང་པ་སུའི་རེད་ or པ་གི་སུའི་ཁང་པ་རེད།	*Whose house is that?*

When, too, the sentence is more complex, the pronoun, though it precedes, need not immediately precede the verb. Ex. :—

ཁྱོད་ཚོའི་ནང་ནས་སུས་ང་ལ་སྒོར་མོ་སྤྲེར་ཐུབ་ཀྱི་འདུག།	*Which of you can give me a rupee?*
དཀོན་མཆོག་གི་རྒྱལ་སྲིད་ནི་དཔེ་གང་དང་སྡུར་བར་བྱའམ།	*With what is the Kingdom of God to be compared?* (Mark iv. 30).
ཁྱེད་ཚོའི་ནང་ནས་སུས་ང་ལ་སྡིག་པ་གཅིག་འགེལ་བར་ནུས་ཀྱི་འདུག།	*Who among you can charge me with any sin?*

When the sentence contains an Interrogative Pronoun the Interrogative particle is not usually added to the verb. However, there is no harm in adding it. Ex. :—

ཁྱོད་ཀྱིས་ག་རེ་བཟོས་ཀྱི་ཡོད་དམ། — *What are you building?*

ཁང་པ་དེ་སུས་བཟོས་ཡོང་ or ཡོང་ང་, or ཡོང་ངས་ or ཡོང་ངམ། — *Who is going to build that house?*

ཕ་གི་མཁན་པོ་འདི་མཚན་ལ་ག་རེ་ཞུ་གི་ཡོད། — *What is that abbot's name?*

Here may also be mentioned ག་ཚོད་ WHAT MEASURE? It is often used as an adverb, signifying *How much?* but it may also be regarded as an Interrogative Pronoun signifying WHAT? Ex.:—

ཆུ་ཚོད་ག་ཚོད་རེད། — *What o'clock is it? What is the time,* or *hour?* Literally *What water-measure is it.*

Also ག་འདྲས་, or གང་འདྲ་ LIKE WHAT, WHAT SORT, WHAT KIND? This is really the adverb *how*, but it is often used as an Interrogative Pronoun in the sense now given. Ex.:—

མ་གི་རོང་ཆེན་པོ་འདི་ནང་ལ་རི་དྭགས་ག་འདྲས་འདུག། — *What sort of sport (wild animals, game) is there in that big valley down there?*

ལྷ་ས་ནས་བཀྲ་ཤིས་ལྷུན་པོ་ (or གཞི་ག་རྩེ་) བར་ལམ་ཀ་བདེ་ཡོས་ག་འདྲས་ཡོད། — *What is the road like from Lhasa to Ṭa-shī-lhüm-po (Shi-ġa-tse)?*

The Literary equivalent of ག་འདྲས་ is ཇི་ལྟར་, or ཅི་ལྟར་ or ཇི་ལྟ་བུ, or ཅི་ལྟ་བུ or Ex.:—

ད་ཅི་ལྟར་བྱས་ན་ལེགས། — *What is best to be done now? How best to act now?*

སངས་རྒྱས་ཞེས་བྱ་བ་ཅི་ལྟ་བུ་ཡིན། — *What sort of Being is the so-called Buddha?*

N.B.—ཅི་ is more correct, but ཇི་ is also used interrogatively.

IX.—RELATIVE AND CORRELATIVE PRONOUNS.

A.—*Relative Pronouns*.

In the Colloquial there is no pronoun corresponding to our Relative Pronoun WHO, the force and effect of which are expressed by turning what we call the relative clause in the sentence into a kind of adjectiva or noun phrase. This is done by adding to the root of the verb th affix མཁན་, which, it will be remembered, may take the Article, Definit or Indefinite. Ex. :—

ལུག་ཚོ་གསོད་མཁན་དེ་ངས་མཐོང་བྱུང་།
Or :—
ལུག་ཚོ་གསོད་མཁན་མི་དེ་ངས་མཐོང་བྱུང་།
} *I have seen the man who kills th sheep.*

Or :—

ལུག་ཚོ་གསོད་མཁན་གྱི་མི་དེ་ཁོས་མཐོང་འདུག། — *He has seen the man who kills th sheep.*

མི་བསད་མཁན་དེ་བྲོས་ཕྱིན་སོང་། — *He who killed the man* (i.e., *th man-killer, or murderer*) *ha run away.*

སྤྱང་ཀུ་བསད་མཁན་དེ་ངས་མཐོང་བྱུང་།
སྤྱང་ཀུ་བསད་མཁན་མི་དེ་ངས་མཐོང་བྱུང་།
སྤྱང་ཀུ་བསད་མཁན་གྱི་མི་དེ་ངས་མཐོང་བྱུང་།
} *I have seen the man who killed th wolf*, i.e., *the wolf-killer*, or *wol killing man.*

སྤྱང་ཀུ་བསད་མཁན་མི་དེའི་སྤུན་ཆ་ངས་ངོ་ཤེས་ཀྱི་ཡོད། — *I know the brother of the man wh killed the wolf.*

སྤྱང་ཀུ་བསད་མཁན་མི་དེས་སྤྱང་ཀུའི་པགས་པ་ང་ལ་སྟེར་སོང་། — *The man who killed the wolf h given me its skin.*

སྤྱང་ཀུ་བསད་མཁན་གྱི་མི་དང་མཉམ་དུ་ང་ཕྱིན་སོང་། — *I went mith the man who killed t wolf.*

གྲོང་པ་ཐམས་ཅད་སྤྱང་ཀུ་བསད་མཁན་མིའི་རྩ་ལ་བརྒྱུགས་སོང་། — *All the villagers ran to the man w killed the wolf.*

སྤྱང་ཀུ་བསད་མཁན་གྱི་མི་ལ་མཁན་པོས་
སྒོར་མོ་གཅིག་སྤྲད་སོང་ or སྤྲད་ར་
(བ) རེད།

The abbot gave the man who killed the wolf a rupee.

ཞབས་པད་དང་མཉམ་དུ་ཡོང་མཁན་གྱི་མི་
ཞིག་ཁང་པ་ཕ་གི་ལ་སྡོད་ཀྱི་འདུག།

A man who came with the Sha-pé is staying in that house.

མི་དེ་ཞབས་པད་དང་མཉམ་དུ་ཡོང་མཁན་
གྱི་དཔོན་པོ་འདི་གཡོག་པོ་རེད།

That man is the servant of an official who came with the Sha-pé.

འཆིང་ཡིག་རྟགས་རྒྱབ་མཁན་གྱི་མིའི་མིང་
ལ་ག་རེ་ཟེར་གྱི་འདུག།

What is the name of the man who signed the Treaty?

ཞབས་པད་དང་མཉམ་དུ་ཡོང་མཁན་གྱི་
འཁོར་གཡོག་གིས་ཀལ་ཀཏ་ད་ལ་ཅ་
ལག་ཁྱད་མཚར་པོ་མང་པོ་ཉིས་སོང་།

The attendants who came with the Sha-pé bought many quaint things in Calcutta.

ཁྱོད་རེས་རྒྱ་ནག་ནས་ཡོང་མཁན་གྱི་ཨམ་
བན་ལ་སྐད་ཆ་བྱས་པ་ཡིན་ནམ།

Did you converse with the Amban who came from China?

ལྷ་ས་ལ་སྡོད་མཁན་མི་ཅིག་གི་རྩ་ནས་ང་ལ་
རལ་གྲི་གཉིས་ཁ་ཐོབ་བྱུང་།

I have got two two-edged bāns (swords) from a man who used to live in Lhasa.

The above are all in the Active Voice, but a difficulty occurs when there is nothing in the context to show whether the Active or the Passive Voice is meant. In the following examples, for instance, either voice may be implied :—

ངས་མི་བསད་མཁན་དེ་མཐོང་བྱུང་།
ངས་བསད་མཁན་མི་དེ་མཐོང་བྱུང་།
ངས་བསད་མཁན་གྱི་མི་དེ་མཐོང་བྱུང་།

I have seen the man who killed, i.e., *the murderer*, or *killing-man*; or *I have seen the man who was killed.*

In such cases the general drift of the conversation is the sole guide to what the meaning really is. In fact, the last three examples are susceptible of a third rendering, namely, *The man who was killed by me has been seen*; and, if this is not the meaning intended by the speaker, the Personal Pronoun ངས་ should be inserted immediately before the verb. Thus :—

མི་བསད་མཁན་དེ་ངས་མཐོང་བྱུང་། བསད་མཁན་མི་དེ་ངས་མཐོང་བྱུང་། བསད་མཁན་གྱི་མི་དེ་ངས་མཐོང་བྱུང་།	*I have seen the man who killed;* or *I have seen the man who was killed.*

The difficulty as regards Voice is, however, removable by avoiding the construction in མཁན་ for the Passive Voice, and using instead the simple Participle as an adjective either preceding or following its noun. Ex. :—

བསད་པའི་མི་དེ་ངས་མཐོང་བྱུང་། མི་བསད་པ་དེ་ངས་མཐོང་བྱུང་།	*I have seen the man who was killed.*

Or the construction in མཁན་ may be retained and something introduced to indicate by whom or by what the man was killed. Ex. :—

དམག་མིས་བསད་མཁན་མི་དེ་ཁོས་མཐོང་འདུག།	*He has seen the man who was killed by the soldier.*
དམག་མིས་མི་བསད་མཁན་དེ་ངས་མཐོང་བྱུང་། དམག་མིས་བསད་མཁན་གྱི་མི་དེ་ངས་མཐོང་བྱུང་།	*I have seen the man who was killed by the soldiers.*

The best way of differentiating between the voices in cases of this sort is to make use of the different roots of the auxiliary verb བྱེད་པ་ *To do*. Thus :—

ངས་མི་བསད་ (or གསོད་) བྱེད་པ་ མཐོང་བྱུང་།	*I have seen the man who killed* or *kills.*

ངས་མི་བསད་ (or གསོད་) བྱས་པ་མཐོང་བྱུང་། — *I have seen the man who was killed.*

ངས་མི་བསད་ (or གསོད་) བྱ་བ་མཐོང་བྱུང་། — *I have seen the man who is to be killed.*

The Relative Pronouns THAT and WHICH may refer either to Animates or to Inanimates. When Animates are concerned, the construction for the Active Voice should be in མཁན, as above exemplified. Ex. :—

ཁྱི་བསད་མཁན་དེ་ངས་མཐོང་བྱུང་།
བསད་མཁན་གྱི་ཁྱི་དེ་ངས་མཐོང་བྱུང་།
— *I have seen the dog that killed.*

ཁྱི་བསད་མཁན་དེའི་མགོ་བཅད་པ་རེད།
བསད་མཁན་གྱི་ཁྱི་དེའི་མགོ་བཅད་པ་རེད།
— *The head of the dog that killed has been chopped off.*

མི་བསད་མཁན་གྱི་ཁྱི་དེ་ཟིན་མི་འདུག།
མི་ཁྱི་བསད་མཁན་དེ་ཟིན་མི་འདུག།
— *The dog that killed the man has not been caught.*

When Animates are concerned, the construction for the Passive Voice is also in མཁན, when the Agent is indicated; and in a simple Participle used as an adjective, either preceding or following its noun, when the Agent is not indicated. Ex. :—

ཁྱིས་ཞི་མི་བསད་མཁན་དེ་ངས་མཐོང་བྱུང་།
ཁྱིས་བསད་མཁན་ཞི་མི་དེ་ངས་མཐོང་བྱུང་།
ཁྱིས་བསད་མཁན་གྱི་ཞི་མི་དེ་ངས་མཐོང་བྱུང་།
— *I have seen the cat that was killed by the dog.*

བསད་པའི་ཞི་མི་དེ་ངས་མཐོང་བྱུང་།
ཞི་མི་བསད་པ་དེ་ངས་མཐོང་བྱུང་།
— *I have seen the cat that was killed.*

This construction may also be used when the agent is indicated. Ex. :—

ཁྱིས་བསད་པའི་ཞི་མི་དེ་ངས་མཐོང་བྱུང་།

ཁྱིས་ཞི་མི་བསད་པ་དེ་ངས་མཐོང་བྱུང་།

} *I have seen the cat that was killed by the dog.*

When Inanimates are concerned the Participial construction should be adopted. This construction, like the one in མཁན་, is also in itself incapable of differentiating between the Active and the Passive Voice. Thus :—

ལྕགས་ཆག་པ་དེ་འདི་རེད།

or འདི་ལྕགས་ཆག་པ་དེ་རེད།

} *This is the iron that broke (something)* ; or, *This is the iron that was broken.*

The following, however, illustrate the Active Voice, as an object is mentioned, and the sense is therefore clear. Ex. :—

རྡོ་བཅག་པའི་ལྕགས་དེ་འདི་རེད། — *This is the iron that broke the stone*, i.e., *the stone-breaking iron.*

ལྕགས་བཅག་པའི་རྡོ་དེ་འདི་རེད།

Or :—

ལྕགས་རྡོ་བཅག་པ་དེ་འདི་རེད།

} *This is the stone that broke the iron.*

བྲག་ལ་འཕོག་པའི་མདའ་དེ་འདི་ཙུ་

(འདུས་ in Colloquial) འདུག།

Or :—

བྲག་མདའ་འཕོག་པ་དེ་འདི་ཙུ་འདུག།

} *Here is the arrow that struck the rock.*

The following illustrate the Passive Voice :—

རྡོས་བཅག་པའི་ལྕགས་དེ་འདི་རེད་ or

རྡོ་འདིས་ལྕགས་བཅག་པ་དེ་རེད།

} *This is the iron that was broken by the stone.*

ལྕགས་ཀྱིས་བཅག་པའི་རྡོ་འདི་རེད་ or

ལྕགས་ཀྱིས་རྡོ་བཅག་པ་དེ་འདི་རེད།

} *This is the stone that was broken by the iron.*

མདས་འཕོག་པའི་བྲག་དེ་འདི་རུ་འདུག།	*Here is the rock that was struck by the arrow.*
ཁྱོད་རེས་ང་ལ་བསླབ་པའི་དཔེ་ཆ་དེ་ངས་ ཁྱོད་ལ་སྟེར་གྱི་ཡིན་ or ཁྱོད་རེས་ང་ལ་དཔེ་ཆ་བསླབ་པ་དེ་ངས་ ཁྱོད་ལ་སྟེར་ཡོང་།	*I will give you the book that you read to me.*

The Active Participles ཡོད་མཁན་, for Animates, and ཡོད་པ་, for Inanimates, may also be used for the construction of Relative clauses, the former being put in the Genitive case, and the latter also, if it precedes its noun, but in the Nominative case if it follows its noun.

EXAMPLES :—

ད་ལྟ་ལྷ་ས་ལ་ཡོད་མཁན་གྱི་མི་ཞིག་ཡོང་ གི་རེད།	*A man who is now in Lhasa will come.*
ཤིང་ནགས་ལ་ཡོད་པའི་བྲག་ཕུག་དེ་ འཚོལ་དགོས་ཀྱི་འདུག།	*The cave that is in the forest must be searched.*
བྲག་ཕུག་ཤིང་ནགས་ལ་ཡོད་པ་དེ་འཚོལ་ དགོས་ཀྱི་འདུག།	*The cave that is in the forest must be searched.*

In this last case the Pronoun ག་རེ་ (or གང་), WHICH, may be used thus :—

བྲག་ཕུག་ག་རེ་ (or གང་) ཤིང་ནགས་ ལ་ཡོད་པ་དེ་འཚོལ་དགོས་ཀྱི་འདུག།	*The cave that is in the forest must be searched.*
ལྷ་ས་ལ་རྟགས་བརྒྱབ་པའི་འཆིང་ཡིག་དེ་ ཁྱོད་རེས་མཐོང་བྱུང་ངམ། Or :— འཆིང་ཡིག་ (ག་རེ་) ལྷ་ས་ལ་རྟགས་ བརྒྱབ་པ་དེ་ཁྱོད་རེས་མཐོང་བྱུང་ངམ།	*Have you seen the Treaty that was signed at Lhasa?*

B.—*Correlative Pronouns.*

The English Personal Correlative Pronouns, the rendering of which into Tibetan has now to be considered, are :—

I or We Thou or You } Who. He or They	Anybody Anyone Nobody } Who. No one
Whoso.	
Whoever.	
Whosoever.	

The Impersonal Correlative Pronouns may refer either to Animates or to Inanimates, and are :—

What, or That which.	Whatsoever.
What so.	Whichsoever.
Whatever.	Anything that.
Whichever.	Nothing that.

1.—*Personal Pronouns.*

When the Pronoun is in the first or second person, singular or plural, one construction is to use the Pronoun itself, in its ordinary non-relative form (ང་, ཁྱོད་, ཁོ་, ང་ཚོ་, etc.), and to turn what we call the Relative part of the sentence into a sort of Noun-phrase, with the aid of the affix མཁན་. Ex. :—

ང་ཁྱོད་ལ་སྐད་ཆ་བྱེད་མཁན་དེ་ཁྱོད་རེའི་ རྒྱལ་པོ་ཡིན།	*I who am conversing with you* (i.e., *I the converser with you*) *am your king.*
ང་ཚོ་ཁྱེད་ (ལ་) ཕྱག་འབུལ་ཞུ་མཁན་ དེ་ཚོ་ཁྱེད་ཀྱི་འབངས་ (or མི་སེར་) ཡིན།	*We who salute you* (i.e., *we your saluters*) *are your subjects.*
ཁྱེད་སུ་རྒྱལ་མཁན་དེ་ལ་ང་ཚོས་མགོ་ དགུར་གྱི་ཡོད།	*We submit to thee who hast subdued us*, i.e., *to thee our subduer.*

Sometimes, however, the sentence has to be wholly recast and a participial construction adopted instead. Ex. :—

ཁྱེད་ཀྱི་སྲས་ང་ཚོ་དང་མཉམ་དུ་བསྡད་ཙང་ ཁྱེད་ང་ཚོའི་རྒྱལ་པོ་དགོས་ཀྱི་རེད།	*Thou whose son is with us* (i.e., *thy son being with us, thou*) *must be our king.*

When the Pronoun is in the third person, the construction may be either in སུ་ཡང་ WHOEVER, ANYONE WHO, HE WHO, etc., or in མཁན་ Ex. :—

སུ་བྲོས་ (or བོས་) ཕྱིན་ན་ (or ཕྱིན་ནས་) ཡང་སྙིང་ཆུང་ཆུང་རེད་ or ཡོང་།	*He who* (or *whoever*, or *anyone who*) *runs away is* (or *will be*) *a coward.*
སུ་ཡོང་ན་ (or ཡོང་ནས་) ཡང་ནམ་ ཡང་ལོག་གི་མ་རེད།	*Nobody* (or *no-one*) *who comes will ever return :* or, *he who* (or *whoever*, or *anyone who*) *comes will never return.*
སུའི་སྡིག་པ་ཁྱོད་ཀྱིས་བསལ་ན་ཡང་དེ་ ཚོའི་སྡིག་པ་བསལ་ར་ (for བ་) རེད།	*Whose-soever sins ye remit they are remitted.*
སུ་བྲོས་ཕྱིན་ནས་ཡང་བརྒྱབ་ཡོང་།	*He who* (or *whoever*, or *anyone who*) *runs away will be shot.*
དེ་རུ་སུ་གཉིད་ཁུག་ན་ཡང་རྩ་ནས་གཉིད་ སད་མི་ཡོང་ (or ནམ་ཡང་གཉིད་ སད་ཀྱི་མ་རེད།	*Anybody who* (or *he who*, or *whoever*) *goes to sleep there will never wake up.*
ཆུ་འདི་སུས་འཐུངས་ན་ཡང་ཡང་སྐྱར་ཁ་ སྐོམ་ཡོང་།	*Whoever* (or *anyone who*, or *he who*) *drinks this water will be thirsty again.*
སུ་ཡོང་ན་ཡང་ལས་ཀ་བྱེད་དགོས་ཀྱི་རེད།	*He who* (or *whoever*, or *anyone who*) *comes must work.*
སུས་ལས་ཀ་བྱས་ན་ཡང་དེ་ (ལ་) ཕོགས་ སྤྲོད་ཀྱི་རེད།	*Whoever* (or *he who*, or *whosoever* or *anyone who*) *works will be paid.*
སུ་ལ་ཡོད་པ་དེ་ལ་སྟེར་ན་ཧ་ཅང་མང་པོ་ ཡོང་གི་རེད། སུ་ལ་མེད་པ་དེ་ལས་	*Whosoever hath, to him having been given, he shall have abundance ; but whosoever hath not,*

ཀྱང་ཡོད་པ་དེ་འཕྲོག་ཡོང་ or འཕྲོག་པར་འགྱུར་རོ།

from him even that which he hath shall be taken away.

སུའི་ཕྱོགས་ལ་གླང་དེ་བརྒྱུགས་ནས་ཡོང་གི་ཡོད་ན་དེ་རང་བཞིན་གྱིས་ (or རང་ཤུགས་ཀྱིས་) བྲོས་ཕྱིན་ཡོང་།

Anyone towards whom the bull rushes will naturally run away.

བླ་མ་ ཕ་ གིས་ སུ་ དང་ རྒྱབ་ འདྲེ་ བརྒྱབ་ ན་ (or རྒྱག་རེ་གཏོང་ན་) ཡང་དེ་སེམས་སྐྱོ་གི་རེད།

Anyone with whom that Lama over there quarrels will regret it.

Sometimes both སུ་ཡང་ and མཁན་ are used together. Ex. :—

སུ་ཡི་གེ་འདི་འཁྱེར་ མཁན་དེ་ལ་ ཡང་ངས་སྒོར་མོ་སྤྲེར་ཡོང་།

I will give a rupee to anyone who will carry this letter.

N.B.—It will be noticed that སུ་ is usually separated from ཡང་ Moreover, it is the སུ་ and not the ཡང་ which takes whatever case-signs are necessary, and the ཡང་ comes in at the end of the relative clause.

2.—*Impersonal Pronouns.*

In the case of WHAT (in the sense of THAT WHICH) which is really a Correlative Pronoun, the participial construction is adopted, and the Pronoun ག་རེ་ (or གང་) THAT WHICH may be used or not at pleasure. Ex. :—

ཁྱོད་རེས་ག་རེ་ (or གང་) ཀློག་པ་དེའི་དོན་ (དག་) ཧ་གོ་གི་རེད་དམ།

Or simply :—

ཁྱོད་རེས་ ཀློག་ པ་ དེའི་དོན་ དག་ ཧ་ གོ་གི་འདུག་གས།

Do you understand what you are reading?

ངས་ཁྱོད་ལ་ (ག་རེ་ or གང་) བཤད་པ་ དེ་ཁྱོད་རེས་བྱེད་དགོས་ཀྱི་རེད། — *You must do what I tell you.*

ཁྱོད་ལ་ (ག་རེ་ or གང་) དགོས་པ་དེ་ ངས་ཉོས་ཡོང་། — *I will buy what you want.*

རིན་ (ག་རེ་ or གང་) ཡོད་པ་དེ་ངས་རྩ་ ནས་ཤེས་ཀྱི་མེད། — *I do not know exactly what they cost.*

ཁྱོད་རེས་ (ག་རེ་ or གང་) འདོད་པ་བྱེད་ པ་དེ་ངས་ཁོ་ལ་སྟེར་ཡོང་། — *I will give him what you like.*

The other Impersonal Correlative Pronouns, which are more forcible than ག་རེ་ and གང་ WHAT, THAT WHICH, namely, ག་རེ་ཡང་, གང་ཡང་, and གང་གང་, WHAT SO, WHATEVER, WHATSOEVER, ANYTHING THAT, and, with a negative, NOTHING THAT, may be illustrated thus:—

Whatever, or anything that, she does is good.

མོ་རེས་ག་རེ་བྱེད་ན་ཡང་ཡག་པོ་འདུག།

Or:—

མོ་རེས་ག་རེ་བྱེད་པ་དེ་ཡང་ཡག་པོ་འདུག།

Or:—

མོ་རེས་གང་བྱེད་པ་དེ་ཡང་ཡག་པོ་འདུག།

Or:—

མོ་རེ་ གང་ གང་ བྱེད་ པ་ དེ་ ཡང་ ཡག་པོ་ འདུག།

ཁྱོད་རེའི་ཁང་པའི་ནང་ལ་ག་རེ་ཡོད་པ་དེའི་ རིན་གོང་ཡང་ཁོས་བཤད་ཐུབ་ཀྱི་རེད། — *He can tell the price of anything that, or whatever, is in your house.*

Whatsoever is in a man's heart will influence his whole life.

མིའི་སྙིང་གི་ནང་ལ་ག་རེ་ཡོད་པ་དེས་ཡང་ ཁོའི་སྲོག་ཚང་མ་དབང་བྱེད་ཡོང་།

Or:—

མིའི་སྙིང་གི་ནང་ལ་གང་གང་ཡོད་པ་དེས་
ཁོ་འི་སྲོག་སྐྱང་ཁ་བསྒྱུལ་ཡོང་།

Whatsoever is in a man's heart will influence his whole life.

ངའི་དབང་ལ་ག་རེ་ཡོད་པ་ཡང་ངས་ཁྱེད་ལ་
སྟེར་གྱི་ཡིན།

Or:—

ངའི་དབང་ལ་གང་འདུག་པ་ཡང་ངས་ཁྱོད་
ལ་སྟེར་ཡོང་།

Or:—

ངའི་དབང་ལ་གང་ཡོད་པ་དེ་ངས་ཁྱོད་ལ་
སྟེར་ཡོང་།

I will give you anything that, or *whatever, is in my power.*

དགྲས་གང་བྱེད་ནའང་རྫོང་སྐྱབས་བྱེད་མི་
ཡོང་།

Or:—

དགྲས་གང་བྱེད་པ་དེས་རྫོང་སྐྱབས་བྱེད་ཀྱི་
མ་རེད།

Nothing that the enemy does will save the fortress.

ཁྱོད་རེས་གང་ལབ་པ་དེ་ལ་མ་ནས་འགྲིག་གི་
མ་རེད།

You are right in absolutely nothing that you have said.

ངས་གང་བྲིས་པ་དེ་ནས་ལོག་གི་མེད།

I recede from nothing that I have written.

ངས་ག་གས་མཐོང་མ་སོང་ (or མ་བྱུང་)

I have not seen anything.

3.—*Literary Constructions.*

(*a*) The following examples illustrate the Literary method of rendering relative clauses:—

ཤིང་སྡོང་འབྲས་བུ་བཟང་པོ་མི་སྐྱེད་པ་
ཐམས་ཅད་བཅད་ནས་མེ་ལ་སྒྲིག་པར་
བྱེད་དོ།

Every tree that bringeth not forth good fruit is hewn down and cast into the fire (Matt. vii. 19).

ཁྱོད་ཀྱིས་ རང་གི་ སྤུན་ གྱི་ མིག་ ལ་ཡོད་ པའི་
སྤུར་མ་ཞིག་མཐོང་ཡང་། རང་གི་མིག་ལ་
ཡོད་པའི་གདུང་མ་དེ་ཅི་ལ་མི་མཐོང་།

And why beholdest thou the mote that is in thy brother's eye, but considerest not the beam that is in thine own eye? (Matt. vii. 3).

རྡིག་བཟོ་པ་ རྣམས་ཀྱིས་ དབྱུག་ བཞག་ པའི་
རྡོ། དེ་རང་ཟུར་གྱི་རྨང་རྫོར་གྱུར་པ་ཡིན།

The stone that the builders rejected the same was made the head of the corner (Matt. xxi. 42)

དེ་བས་ན་ཅི་ རྒྱལ་པོ་འི་ཡིན་ པ་དེ་ རྒྱལ་པོ་ལ་
ཕུལ། ཅི་དཀོན་མཆོག་གི་ཡིན་པ་དེ་
དཀོན་ མཆོག་ གི་ཡིན་ པ་དེ་དཀོན་ མཆོག་
ལ་ཕུལ་ཞིག།

Render therefore unto Cæsar the things that are Cæsar's and unto God the things that are God's (Matt. xxii. 21).

ཡང་ ཁྱེད་ ཀྱིས་ ང་ལ་ གནང་བའི་གཟི་བརྗིད་
དེ་ཉི་དེ་དག་ལ་ཡང་སྟེར་རོ།

And the glory which thou hast given me I have given also unto them (John xvii. 22).

ངའི་ ཡབ་ ཀྱིས་ ང་ལ་ གནང་བའི་མཆོད་ཞལ་
དེ་ནས་ངས་མ་འཐུང་བར་བཞག་ཡོད་དཾ།

The cup which my father hath given me, shall I not drink it? (John xviii. 11).

ངས་ ཡབ་ ཀྱི་ མཚན་ བརྗོད་ ནས་ བྱས་ པའི་
ལས་རྣམས་ཀྱིས་ང་ལ་དཔང་པོ་བྱེད་དོ།

The works that I do in my father's name, they testify of me (John x. 25).

མི་གྲུམ་ནད་ན་མཁན་ཅལ་ཁྲི་ལ་ཉལ་བ་ཞིག།

A man sick of the palsy, lying on a bed (Luke v. 18).

གསོད་པར་བྱ་བའི་བ་སྤྲུག།
Or :—
གསོད་བྱའི་བ་སྤྲུག།

The calf that is to be killed.

ཕི་ལིབ་ དེའི་ ཙར་ བརྒྱུགས་ ནས་ ཁྱོད་ཀྱིས་
གང་ ཀློག་པ་ དེའི་ དོན་ ཧ་ གོའམ་ ཞེས་
དྲིས་སོ།

And Philip ran to him and said, understandest thou what thou readest? (Acts viii. 30).

(*b*) The Literary Correlative Pronouns are :—

སུ་ སུ་ཞིག་ གང་སུ་ གང་ཡང་	WHOEVER, WHOSOEVER, ANYONE WHO, HE WHO, etc.
ཇི་ or in certain cases ཅི་ གང་ གང་ཞིག་ གང་ཅི་ གང་ཉིད་ གང་དག་ཉིད་ གང་ཡང་ ཅི་ཡང་ ཅི་འང་	WHATEVER, WHATSOEVER, WHICHEVER, ANYTHING THAT, THAT WHICH, WHAT, etc.

The following examples will serve to illustrate the Literary rendering of the Correlative :—

སུས་ང་ཅག་ལ་དགྲ་མི་བྱེད་པ་དེས་ངེད་ཀྱི་ཕྱོགས་བྱེད་དོ།	*He that is not against us is for us* (Mark ix. 40).
ང་ལ་གཙོ་བོ་ལགས་གཙོ་བོ་ལགས་ཞེས་ཞུས་པའི་མི་ཐམས་ཅད་ནམ་མཁའི་རྒྱལ་སྲིད་དུ་འཛུག་མི་ཡོང་།	*Not everyone that saith unto me Lord, Lord, shall enter into the Kingdom of Heaven* (Matt. vii. 21).
བུད་མེད་རྣམས་ལ་སྐྱེས་པ་ཐམས་ཅད་ཀྱི་ནང་ནས་ཁྲུས་གསོལ་མཁན་ཡོ་ཧ་ནན་ལས་ཆེན་པོ་ཞིག་མ་བྱུང་། འོན་ཀྱང་ནས་	*Among them that are born of women there hath not arisen a greater than John the Baptist ; yet he that is but little in the*

མཁའི་རྒྱལ་སྲིད་དུ་ཆུང་བ་ཡིན་པ་དེ་ཡོ་
ཧ་ནན་ལས་ཆེ་བ་ཡིན་ནོ། — *kingdom of heaven is greater than John* (Matt. v. 11).

ཁྱོད་ཀྱིས་མི་ངན་པ་ལ་མ་རྒོལ་ཞིག། — *Resist not him that is evil* (Matt. v. 38).

ཇི་བཞིན་དུ་ཁྱོད་ཚོས་ཞལ་ཆེ་གཅོད་པ། དེ་བཞིན་དུ་ཁྱོད་རྣམས་ཀྱི་ཞལ་ཆེ་ཡང་གཅོད་པར་འགྱུར་རོ། — *With what judgment ye judge, ye shall be judged* (Matt. vii. 2).

ཡང་སུ་ཞིག་གིས་ཁྱོད་དཔག་ཚད་གཅིག་ཏུ་ལག་བསྐུལ་ན། དེ་དང་དཔག་ཚད་གཉིས་སོང་ཞིག། — *And whosoever shall compel thee to go one mile, go with him twain* (Matt. v. 41).

ཁྱོད་ལ་ཞུས་པ་དེ་ལ་སྟེར་ཞིག། ཁྱོད་ནས་ནོར་ཀྱི་བར་འདོད་པ་དེ་ལ་རྒྱབ་མ་སྟོན་ཅིག། — *Give to him that asketh thee, and from him that would borrow of thee turn not thou away* (Matt. v. 42).

སུ་ཡང་རྡོ་འདི་ལ་འགྲིལ་བ་དེ་དུམ་བུར་འཆག། སུ་ལ་རྡོ་དེ་འཐོག་ན་རྡུལ་ལྟར་བརྫི་བར་འགྱུར། — *And he that falleth on this stone shall be broken to pieces, but on whomsoever it shall fall it will scatter him as dust* (Matt. xxi. 44).

སུས་ཀྱང་རང་གི་སྲོག་སྐྱོབ་པར་བརྩོན་པ་དེས་བརླག་པར་འགྱུར། སུས་ཀྱང་རང་གི་སྲོག་བརླག་པ་དེས་སྐྱོབ་པར་འགྱུར་རོ། — *Whosoever shall seek to gain his life shall lose it, but whosoever shall lose his life shall preserve it* (Luke xvii. 33).

སུས་ཀྱང་ཆུ་འདི་ལས་འཐུང་ན་ཡང་སྐོམ་པར་འགྱུར། སུས་ཀྱང་ངས་སྟེར་བའི་ཆུ་དེ་ལས་འཐུང་ན་ནམ་ཡང་མི་སྐོམ་སྟེ། — *Everyone that drinketh of this water shall thirst again, but whosoever drinketh of the water that I shall give him shall never thirst* (John iv. 13).

etc.

སྟེང་ནས་བྱོན་ པ་དེ་ཐམས་ ཅད་ལས་ གོང་མ་ ཡིན། གང་ས་ནས་བྱུང་བ་ནི་ས་ནས་ཡིན་ དེ་སའི་གཏམ་བྱེད་ཀྱི།

He that cometh from above is above all : he that is of the earth is of the earth, and of the earth he speaketh (John iii. 31).

ཁོང་གིས་ གང་ མཐོང་ བ་ དང་ཐོས་ པ་དེ་ ལ་ དཔང་པོ་མཛད།

What he hath seen and heard, of that he beareth witness (John iii. 32).

དཀོན་མཆོག་ནི་ཐུགས་ཉིད་ཡིན་པས། ཁོང་ ལ་བསྙེན་ བཀུར་ བྱེད་ མཁན་ རྣམས་ཀྱིས་ སེམས་ ཉིད་ དང་ བདེན་ པ་ ཉིད་ཀྱི་ ངང་ནས་ བསྙེན་བཀུར་བྱེད་དགོས་སོ།

God is spirit : and they that worship him must worship in spirit and in truth (John iv. 24).

གང་ཤ་ནས་སྐྱེས་པ་ནི་ཤ་ཡིན། གང་ཐུགས་ ཉིད་ནས་སྐྱེས་པ་ནི་སེམས་ཉིད་ཡིན་ནོ།

That which is born of the flesh is flesh ; and that which is born of spirit is spirit (John iii. 6).

ཡེ་ཤུས་དེ་ལ་གསུངས་པ། ང་རང་ཁྱོད་དང་ གླེང་མོ་བྱེད་མཁན་ནི་མ་ཤི་ཀ་དེ་ཡིན་ནོ།

Jesus said unto her, I that speak unto thee am the Christ (John iv. 26).

སུའི་སྡིག་པ་ཁྱེད་ རྣམས་ཀྱིས་སེལ་ན་དེ་དག་ གི་སྡིག་པ་སེལ་ཚར།

Whosesoever's sins ye remit they are remitted (John xx. 23).

སུ་ ལ་ཡོད་ པ་དེ་ ལ་ གནང་ སྟེ་ ལྷག་ པ་ཡོད་ པར་འགྱུར། འོན་ཀྱང་སུ་ལ་མེད་པ་དེ་ ལས་ཇི་ཡོད་པ་དེ་ཡང་ལེན་པར་འགྱུར་རོ།

Unto everyone that hath shall be given, and he shall have abundance ; but from him that hath not, even that which he hath shall be taken away (Matt. xxv. 29).

སུས་ ཀྱང་ ང་བོར་ དེ་ངས་སྨྲས་ པ་མི་ གླང་བ་ དེའི་ཁྲིམས་གཅོད་མཁན་ཞིག་ཡོད་དོ།

He that rejecteth me and receiveth not my sayings hath one that judgeth him (John xii. 48).

ཁྱེད་ རྣམས་ སེམས་ འཁྲུག་ཏུ་ བཙུག་མཁན་ སུ་ ཡིན་ ཀྱང་ དེ་ ལ་ ཆད་ པ་ འཐོབ་ པར་ འགྱུར་རོ།

But he that troubleth you shall bear his judgment, whosoever he be (Gal. v. 10).

སུས་ཀྱང་རང་བཏང་མཁན་གྱི་གྲགས་པ་ འདོད་པ་དེ་ནི་བདེན་པ་ཡིན་ནོ། *But he hath seeketh the glory of him that sent him, the same is true* (John vii. 18).

ང་བཏང་མཁན་དེའི་བསྟན་པ་ཡིན་ནོ། *It is his teaching who sent me* (John vii. 16).

དངོས་པོ་ཐམས་ཅད་བཀོད་མཁན་ནི་དཀོན་མཆོག་ལགས་སོ། *He who built all things is God* (Heb. iii. 4).

གང་ཐོག་མ་ནས་ཡོད་པ་དང་། གང་ངེད་རང་གིས་ཐོས། གང་མིག་གིས་མཐོང་། གང་ལ་བལྟས་དེ་ལག་པ་ཡང་རེག་པ་ཡིན་པ་... དེ་ནི་ཁྱེད་ཚག་ལ་སྒྲོག་གོ། *That which was from the beginning, that which we have heard, that which we have seen with our eyes, that which we beheld and our hands handled..declare we unto you* (I John i. 1).

ཇི་བདེན་པ། ཇི་བཙུན་པ། ཇི་ཁྲིམས་དང་མཐུན་པ། ཇི་དག་པ། ཇི་ཡིད་དུ་འོང་བ། ཇི་སྙན་པ། ཇི་དགེ་བ། ཇི་སྟོད་དུ་རུང་བ་ ཡོད་པ་དེ་ལ་བསམ་བློ་ཐོངས་ཤིག། *Whatsoever things are true, whatsoever things are honourable, whatsoever things are just, whatsoever things are pure, whatsoever things are lovely, whatsoever things are of good report; if there be any virtue and any praise, think on these things* (Phil. iv. 8).

X.—Indefinite Pronouns or Pronominal Adjectives.

1. In the Colloquial the following are the most common :—

སུ་ཞིག *Some one ; a certain* (person).

གང་ཞིག *Something ; a certain* (thing).

ག་རེ་ཡིན་ན
ག་རེ་ཡིན་ན་ཡང (or ཡིན་ནས་) } *Something.*
ག་རེ་ཞིག

སུ་ཡང *Anyone, Anybody, Whoever ;* or, with a negative, *No one, Nobody, None.*

གང་ཡང་ *Any.*

གཱ་རེ་ཡང་
གང་ཡང་
གང་གང་
ག་གས་
} *Anything;* or, with a negative, *Nothing*, *None;* *Whatever*, *Whichever*.

གང་ག་ or གང་
ཧྲང་ཁ་ or ཧྲང་
ཐམས་ཅད་
ཚང་མ་
} *All, Whole, Entire, Every, Complete, Full.*

འགའ་ཆེན་ *Several.*

མང་ཤོས་ *Most.*

གཞན་པ་
ཡན་པ་
} *Other.*

གཞན་པ་ཞིག་
ཡན་པ་ཞིག་
ད་རུང་
} *Another.*

རེ་
རེ་རེ་
སོ་སོ་
} *Each, Every.*

གཉིས་ཀ་ *Both.*

གཅིག་གཅིག་ *One another, Each other.*

ཁ་ཤས་ *Some.*

ཉོག་ཙོ་ *A few, Few, A little, Little.*

གཅིག་པོ་ *Sole, Only, Mere.*

གཅིག་པ་ }
ཁྱད་མེད་ } *Same* ; but དེ་རང་ *That same.*

མི་གཅིག་པ་ *Various, Sundry, Divers.*

རང་ *Self, One's self.*

གཅིག་ཡང་ *Even one, Either.* With a negative, *None, Neither.*

འདི་འདྲ་ *Such.*

EXAMPLES :—

དུས་ཞིག (or དུས་རེ་ཞིག་གི་ཚེ་) ལ་བླ་མ་ཞིག་ལྷ་ས་ནས་ཕེབས་སོང་། — *Once upon a time a certain Lama came from Lhasa.*

བླ་མ་དེ་རང་གྲོང་གསེབ་ཞིག་ལ་ཕྱིན་སོང་། — *That same Lama went to a certain village.*

ངའི་སེམས་ལ་ཁོ་ག་རེ་ཞིག་ཐོབ་པའི་ཕྱིར་ཕྱིན་སོང་། — *I think he went to get something.*

ཁ་སང་ཁྲིམས་ཁང་ལ་སུ་ཡང་ཕྱིན་མ་སོང་། — *No one went to Court yesterday.*

སུ་ལ་ཡང་དྲིན་སྟེར་མི་ཡོང་། — *No favour will be accorded to anybody.*

ལས་ཀ་འདི་སུ་ཡང་བྱེད་ཐུབ་ཀྱི་རེད། — *Anybody can do this work.*

མི་འདིས་ག་རེ་བྱེད་པ་དེ་གསེར་ལ་འགྱུར་གྱི་འདུག། — *Anything that this man does turns into gold.*

ཁོས་འགོ་བཙུགས་པ་དེ་ནམ་ཡང་ཚར་གི་མ་རེད། — *Nothing that he begins is ever finished.*

དམག་དཔུང་སྒང་ཁའི་ནང་ནས་མི་གཅིག་ཀྱང་ཐར་མ་སོང་། — *Out of the whole army not one man (nobody) was saved.*

སྐུ་དྲག་འདི་ལ་གསོལ་ཇ་ཞལ་དཀར་གང་དགོས་ཀྱི་འདུག།	*This gentleman desires a cup of tea.*
དེའི་རྗེས་ལ་ཁྲུ་ཐམས་ཅད་མགྱོགས་པོར་ཡལ་སོང་།	*Soon afterwards the entire herd of cattle vanished.*
དེ་རིང་ཁྱོད་ལ་ཚ་ལུམ་པ་ཡག་པོ་ག་རེ་ཡོད་དམ།	*Have you any good oranges to-day?*
ལས་ཀ་དེ་ལ་དོས་པ་འགའ་ཆེན་དགོས་ཀྱི་རེད།	*Several coolies will be needed for the work.*
རྒྱ་གར་ལ་མི་མང་ཤོས་ཧ་ཅང་ཆོས་སེམས་ཅན་འདུག།	*In India most people are very religious.*
བོད་ཀྱི་སྐུ་དྲག་པོ་ཁ་ཤས་གུམ་པ་རི་ལ་བཞུགས་ཀྱི་འདུག།	*Some Tibetan officials are staying at Gúm (Ghoom).*
གཞན་པ་ (or ཡན་པ་) ཐམས་ཅད་ལྷ་ས་ལ་ལོག་ཕེབས་འདུག།	*All the others have returned to Lhasa.*
དེའི་ནང་ནས་གཞན་ཁ་ཤས་རྡོ་རྗེ་གླིང་ལ་བཞུགས་ཀྱི་འདུག།	*Some of the others are staying in Darjeeling.*
ང་ལ་ད་རུང་ཇ་ (or གསོལ་ཇ་) དཀར་ཡོལ་གང་གནང་རོགས་གནང་།	*Kindly give me another cup of tea.*
མི་རེས་ཤ་བོ་རེ་ལ་མེ་མདའ་བརྒྱབས་ནས་བསད་སོང་།	*Each man shot one stag.*

མི་རེ་རེས་བླ་མ་ལ་ཁ་བཏགས་རེ་རེ་ཕྱུལ་སོང་། Or :— མི་སོ་སོས་བླ་མ་ལ་ཁ་བཏགས་རེ་རེ་ཕྱུལ་སོང་།	*Each man presented a complimentary scarf to the lama.*
རྟ་རེ་རེ་ལ་ཆུ་ཟོམ་རེ་རེ་སྟེར་ཞིག།	*Give each horse a pail of water.*
མི་རེ་རེས་སྒམ་ཆེན་པོ་གསུམ་གསུམ་འཁྱེར་ཁྱིན་སོང་།	*Each man carried three big boxes.*
འདི་བུ་གུ་གཉིས་ཀའི་ཨ་ཕ་ཡིན།	*This is the father of both the boys.*
ང་གཉིས་ཀས་དོམ་ལ་མེ་མདའ་བརྒྱབས་ནས་བསད་སོང་།	*Both of us shot the bear.*
བུ་མོ་མཛེས་པོ་གཉིས་ཀ་སླེབས་སོང་།	*Both the pretty girls have come.*
འདི་དང་དེ་གཉིས་ཀ་འོས་ཀྱི་རེད།	*Both this and that will be suitable.*
ཚིག་འདི་གཉིས་ཀྱི་དོན་དག་གཅིག་པ་རེད་དམ།	*Do these two words mean the same?*
ལགས། དེ་གཉིས་ཀའི་དོན་དག་གཅིག་པ་ཡིན་པ་འདུག།	*Yes, both their meanings appear to be the same.*
ཚིག་འདིའི་དོན་དག་དང་དེའི་དོན་དག་དང་གཅིག་པ་རེད་དམ།	*Is the meaning of this word exactly the same as the meaning of that word?*
ལགས། དེ་གཉིས་ཀའི་དོན་དག་ཐད་གཅིག་པ་མ་རེད།	*No, both their meanings are not absolutely the same.*
རྒུན་འབྲུམ་ཏོག་ཙོང་དགོས་ཀྱི་ཡོད།	*I want a few grapes.*

རྒུན་འབྲུམ་ དེ་ཚོའི་ ནང་ ནས་ཏོག་ཙོ་ང་ ལ་ དགོས། — *I want a few of those grapes.*

ང་ལ་དངུལ་ཏོག་ཙོ་ ཅིག་གི་ཡོང་། — *A very little money will do for me.*

མི་གཅིག་པའི་དུས་ (or དུས་མི་གཅིག་པ་) ལ་ང་ཚོའི་ འཛམ་བུ་ གླིང་ འདི་ལ་ སངས་རྒྱས་མང་པོ་བྱུང་བ་རེད། — *At sundry (various, or divers) times many Buddhas have appeared in this world of ours.*

དེ་ཚོ་འི་དཀྱིལ་ལ་བླ་མ་དེ་གཅིག་པོ་མི་རེད། — *The lama was the only man among them.*

ཚིག་པ་ག་རེ་དོན་ལ་ཟ་གི་འདུག། མོ་ཕྲུ་གུ་ གཅིག་པོ་རེད། — *Why be angry? She is a mere child?*

འདི་གཉིས་ ཀྱི་ནང་ ནས་གཅིག་ གིས་ཡོང་གི་ རེད། — *Either of these two will do.*

འདི་གཉིས་ ཀྱི་ནང་ ནས་གཅིག་ ཡང་འོས་མི་ ཡོང་། — *Neither of these two will suit.*

མི་སྟོང་ཕྲག་མང་པོའི་ནང་ནས་གཅིག་ཡང་ ཐོར་མ་སོང་། — *Of the entire thousand men not even one escaped*

Examples of རང་ SELF, ONE'S SELF, will be found at § 31, iii, IV.

Examples of གཅིག་གཅིག་ ONE ANOTHER, EACH OTHER, will be found at § 31, vii.

སྐད་དཀའ་ལས་ཁག་པོ་འདི་འདྲ་ངས་མཐོང་ མ་མྱོང་། (pron. *nyúng*). — *I have never seen such a difficult language.*

2. The following are the Literary equivalents of the above :—

གཅིག་ཅིག་	*Someone, Somebody, A certain* (person).
ཅི་ཞིག་	*Something, A certain* (thing.)

ཁ་ཤས་ འགའ་ཆེན་ འགའ་ཞིག་ འགའ་ཡང་ ལ་ལ་ ལ་ལ་ཞིག་	*Some, Several, A good many, A good deal.*
སུ་ཞིག་ གང་ཞིག་	*Anyone, Anybody, Whoever ;* or, with negative, *No one, Nobody.*
སུ་ཡང་ གང་ཡང་	*Everyone, Either, Each ;* or, with negative, *No one, Neither.*
ཅི་ཡང་ ཅི་ཞིག་	*Anything, Whatever, Everything, Either, Each* ; or, with negative, *Nothing, None, Neither.*
ཐམས་ཅད་ ཀུན་ ཚང་མ་	*All, The whole, Every, Entire, Complete, All.*
འབའ་ཞིག་	*Mere, Sole, Only.*
གཞན་	*Other.*
གཞན་ཞིག་	*Another.*
གཅིག་གཅིག་	*Each other, One another.*
རེ་ རེ་རེ་	*Each, Every.*
སོ་སོ་ མི་གཅིག་པ་ མི་འདྲ་བ་	*Various, Sundry, Divers.*

ཀུན་ལས་ལྷག་ མང་པོ་	*Most.*
གཉིས་ཀ་	*Both.*
ཉུང་ངུ་	*Few, Little.*
ཉུང་ངུ་ཞིག་ འགའ་ འགའ་ཙམ་ ཅིག་	*A few, A little.*
བདག་ ཉིད་ རང་ ང་	*Self, One's self.*
ཉིད་ གཅིག་པ་	*Same.*
དེ་ཁོ་ན་ དེ་ཀ་ དེ་རང་ དེ་ཀ་རང་ འདི་རང་	*The very same.*
འདི་འདྲ་བ་ དེ་ལྟ་བུ་	*Such.*
ཕན་ཚུན་	*Either, Each of two. Ex. :—*

མ་ཕམ་གྱི་འགྲམ་ཕན་ཚུན་དུ། *On each side of the two shor of (lake) Mapham (Jäschke).*

ཕན་ཚུན་གཉིས། *Either, Both.* Ex. :—

ཡང་གཙང་པོའི་འགྲམ་ཕན་ཚུན་གཉིས་ན། *And on either side* (i.e. *both sides*) *of the river* (*Jäschke*).

§ 32. Adverbs.

These are both primitive and derivative. Of Derivatives, some are formed from Pronouns, others from Nouns, and others from Adjectives or Participles. There are also Adverbs of Time, Place, and Manner, Interrogative, Negative, and (added to verbal roots) Relative adverbs.

Those derived from adjectives are formed either by putting the adjective in the terminative case, or by adding to the adjective the expression བྱས་ནས་ It is a common habit, however, in the Colloquial to use an adjective adverbially without changing its form.

Adverbs are always placed somewhere before the verb. Interrogative adverbs come immediately before the verb. Others may be inserted at any convenient place in the sentence, so long as the rule is observed that they precede the verb.

The following are some of the commonest adverbs and adverbial phrases used in the Colloquial :—

Adverbs of Time.

ག་དུས་ / ནམ་	*When?*
གང་	(Added to verbal infinitive) *When, At the time of..ing.*
ག་དུས་ ··· ཡང་	*Whenever.*
དུས་	(Added to verbal root) *When*, used relatively; *While.*
ད་ལྟ་	*Now* (at this time); ད་ལྟ་རང་ *Just now, At present.*
ད་བར་དུ་	*Hitherto, Up to now.*
དེ་དུས་	*Then* (at that time).

དེ་ནས་	*Then* (after that).
ད་ནས་ཕྱིན་ཆད་	*Hereafter*, *Henceforth.*
ནམ་ཡང་	*Ever*, *Always.* With negative, *Never.*
ནམ་རྒྱུན་ དུས་རྒྱུན་ རྟག་པ་རེ་བཞིན་	*Ever*, *Always*, *Constantly*, *Incessantly*, etc.
ཚམ་ན་ ཙ་ན་	*When*, *Just when*, *About*, *At the time.*
ད་དུང་ཡང་ ད་དུང་ ད་གདོས་	*Moreover*, *Furthermore.*
སྐྱོང་	(Added to root of verb) *Ever*, with negative *Never.*
དེ་རིང་སང་ དེང་སང་	*Now-a-days.*
མཚམས་མཚམས་ རེ་འགའ་	*Now and then*, *Often*, *Sometimes*, *Occasionally*, with negative, *Seldom.*
ཡང་སྐྱར་	*Again*, *Afresh*, *Anew.*
ཚར་གཅིག་ ཐེངས་གཅིག་	*Once.*
ལམ་སང་	*At once*, *Immediately*, *Hurriedly*, *Hastily*, *Directly.*
ད་འདོ་ཚར་གཅིག་ ད་དུང་ཚར་གཅིག་	*Once more.*
རྩ་ནས་ མ་ནས་	(With negative) *Not at all*, *Never*, *In no case.*

སྔོན་ལ་ *A short time ago*
སྔར་ *A long time ago* } *Formerly, Previously,*

མགྱོགས་པོར་ or མགྱོགས་པོ་
རྩ་པོར་ or རྩ་བོ་
ཆ་དྲག་
ཧྲིབ་ཙམ་གཅིག་
} *Quickly, Soon, Presently, Directly, In a little while, In a few minutes.*

གཞུག་ལ་
རྗེས་ལ་
} *After, Subsequently, Afterwards, Next, Last, In future, At last, At length.*

ད་གི་ནས་ *Already.*

སྔོན་ལ་
སྔོན་དུས་
} *Anciently.*

ད་རུང་
ཡང་
ད་འདོ་ (Vulg.)
} *Still, Yet.*

ཁ་སང་ *Lately, Recently.*

ཕྱི་པོ་ *Late.*

སྔ་པོ་ནས་ *Early.*

འགོར་པོ་མ་བྱེད་པར་ *Without delay.*

ག་ལེ་ག་ལེ་ *Slowly, Gradually, Gently, Softly.*

མདངས་དགོངས་ *Last night, Last evening.*

ཁྲ་སྙིང་
ན་ནིང་
} *Last year.*

ཕར་ཕར་ *Eventually, Later on, Indirectly.*

འགྲོ་ (Added to verbal root) *Just, Just about, On the point of, Going to.*

ད་རེ་ *Some time ago.*

ད་ལོ་, or འདི་ལོ་, or ལོ་འདི་ *This year.*

ཞི་སྙིང་ *Year before last.*

ཕྱི་ལོ་ }
ད་གསོས་ } *Next year.*
སང་ཕོད་ }

ན་ཉིན་ }
ན་སྙིང་ } *Last year.*
ཐོ་ལོ་ }

ལོ་རེ་རེ་ *Yearly, Annually.*

ཉི་མ་དགུ་པ་རེ་བཞིན་ *Daily.*

སང་ཉིན་ *To-morrow.*

དེ་རིང་ *To-day.*

ཁ་སང་ *Yesterday.*

ཞག་མ་རེ་རེ་ *Every day.*

ཉི་མ་ཅིག *Some day.*

ADVERBS OF PLACE

ག་པ་ }
ག་ཙ་ } *Where? Whither?* (Also relatively.)
ག་ན་ }

ག་པ་...ཡང་ *Wherever, Anywhere.*

ག་པ་…མ་ }
ག་རེ་…མ་ } *Nowhere.*

འདི་ རུ་, or འདིར་ }
འདི་ལ་ } *Here, Hither.*
འདི་ན་ }

དེ་རུ་ }
དེར་ }
དེ་ལ་ } *There, Thither.*
དེ་ན་ }

NOTE.—In Lhassa འདིར་ ḌIR, *Here, Hither,* is loosely pronounced as if it were spelt འདས་ ḌÄ, i.e. something like the English word *They*, as pronounced by a Eurasian, with a slight dental *d* sound to the *Th*. Hence one sometimes sees the Colloquial form of *Here, Hither*, spelt འདད་, which is not quite a correct form of the loose Lhassa pronunciation. Similarly one sometimes sees the Colloquial form of དེར་ *There* spelt དད་ DÁ'.

Both འདད་ and དད་ are incorrect. For the former the student should always use འདི་རུ་, or འདིར་, when writing; and, if he chooses to affect the Lhassa pronunciation when speaking, he should say འདས་, not འདད་ For དད་ he should always write དེ་རུ་, or དེར།

ཕ་གི་ *Over there, Yonder.*

ཡ་གི་ *Up there.*

མ་གི་ *Down there.*

ཡར་ *Upwards.*

མར་ *Downwards.*

གྱེན་ གྱེན་དམ་པོ་	*Uphill.*
ཐུར་	*Downhill.*
མགོ་མཇུག་ལོག་པ་ མགོ་གཞུག་ལོག་པ་ ཨ་ལོག་	*Upside down.*
འདི་ནས་	*Hence.*
དེ་ནས་	*Thence.*
མདུན་ལ་	*Before.*
གདོང་ལ་ སྔོན་ལ་	*Ahead, In front, Onwards, Forwards.*
རྒྱབ་ལ་ གཞུག་ལ་	*Behind.*
ཐག་རིང་པོ་	*Afar.*
ཁ་ཐུག་ལ་	*Opposite, Over against.*
ཚབ་ལ་	*Instead of.*
རྩ་ལ་	*Just by, Close by.*
ནས་	*Off.*
རྒྱབ་ཕྱོགས་ལ་	*Backwards.*
ཕྱི་ལོགས་ལ་	*Outside, Without.*
ནང་ལ་	*Within, Inside, At home.*
ནང་ནས་	*From within, From home.*
ཕྱི་ལོག་ནས་	*From without.*
གཡོན་ལ་	*To the left.*

གཡས་ལ་ *To the right.*

མཉམ་འབྲེ་ *Together, Jointly.*

ག་ས་ག་ལ་ *Everywhere.*

འཁོར་ལ་
ཕན་ཚུན་ལ་
> *Around, Round about, All round.*

གཞན་དུ་ *Elsewhere.*

ཟུར་དུ་ *Aside.*

སོ་སོར་ *Asunder, Apart.*

Adverbs of Manner.

འགྲོ་ or འདྲ་ (The first added to root and the second to infinitive of auxiliary verb) *Probably, Likely, Perhaps.*

ག་འདྲས་
གང་འདྲ་
> *How?*

འདི་འདྲ་ (pronounced Ďin-ḍa)
འདི་ནང་བཞིན་
ཅེས་
ཞེས་
ཤེས་
ད་ག་ཟེར་
ད་ག་རང་
> *Thus, So.*

ད་ག་རེད་ *Quite so, Just so, Precisely, Exactly.*

རིམ་བཞིན་ *By degrees, Gradually.*

ཐད་དེ་ (Used with negative.) ***Quite, Completely, Absolutely, Thoroughly.***

དེའི་རྐྱེན་བྱས་ནས་ *Consequently.*

གཅིག་པོ་ *Simply, Merely, Only, Solely.*

རང་ *Simply, Merely, Just, Only.*

རེ་མོས་བྱས་ནས་ *Alternately.*

ཧ་ལམ་ *Almost, Nearly.*

མཉམ་འབྲེལ་ }
མཉམ་བྲེ } *Together, Jointly, Unitedly.*

ཁ་ཁ་བྱས་ནས་ *Separately, Individually.*

སོ་སོ་བྱས་ནས་ *Severally.*

རེ་རེ་བྱས་ནས་ *Singly.*

ལུགས་སྲོལ་ནང་བཞིན་ *Formally.*

ཤ་སྟག་ *Merely, Only, Solely, Entirely.*

མ་ནས་ }
རྩ་བ་ཉིད་ནས་ } (Used with negative.) *At all, On any account.*
རྩ་ནས་ }

ཡག་པོར་ or ཡག་པོ་ *Well*, with negative, *Ill, Badly.*

ཡག་ག་ *Better.*

ཡག་ཤོས་ *Best.*

ཡང་ *Even, Likewise.*

དྲང་པོ་བྱས་ནས་ *Fairly, Honestly.*

ཅག་བྱས་ནས་ *Carefully.*

ཏེན་ཏེན་བྱས་ནས་ *Definitely, Punctually, Steadily*

ཁྲིམས་ནང་བཞིན་ *Justly, Legally.*

ཏེན་ལྡན་ }
ང་ཐོག་ } *Certainly.*

ཁ་ནས་ *Orally.*

རང་ *Personally, Precisely, Exactly.*

གསང་བ་བྱས་ནས་ *Privately.*

ངེས་པར་
དངོས་གནས་བྱས་ནས་ } *Really, Sincerely, Surely.*
དྲང་པོ་བྱས་ནས་

མགྱོགས་པོ་བྱས་ནས་ *Promptly.*

མ་འཕྱུག་པ་བྱས་ནས་ *Punctually.*

ཁྱད་པར་དུ་ *Especially, Particularly.*

རྟག་པར་
ཕལ་ཆེར་ } *Ordinarily, Usually, Generally, Universally, Chiefly, Principally.*

ཐག་ཆོད་ *Decidedly, Exceedingly.*

སྒྲ་དག་པོ་ *Clearly, Distinctly, Lucidly, Intelligibly.*

ནམ་རྒྱུན་ *As a rule, Usually.*

པར་པར་ *Indirectly.*

རྒྱབ་ལོགས་ལ་ *Aback.*

སྙིང་རུས་བྱས་ནས་ *Diligently, Zealously, Earnestly, Heartily, Genuinely.*

འདི་དང་མཉམ་དུ་ *Herewith.*

ལས་སླ་པོ་ *Easily.*

ག་ལེ་ག་ལེ་ *Gradually, Gently, Slowly, Softly.*

ད་ **(Between a duplicated adjective or adverb, with** རེ་ **at end of sentence)** ***Of course.***

Adverbs of Quantity and Comparison.

ག་ཚོད་ *How much? How many?*

ཕལ་ཆེར་ *Chiefly, Generally.*

ཡང་ *Even, Likewise.*

ཟད་དེ་ (Used with negative.) *Quite, Completely, Absolutely, For the most part, Mostly.*

ཧ་ལམ་
འགའ་ཆེན་ } *Almost, Nearly.* With negative, *Scarcely.*

ཙམ་, or in Coll. ཙེ་ *About, Approximately.*

མང་བ་
ལྷག་པ་ } *More.*

མང་ཤོས་ *Most.*

ཉུང་ཤོས་ *Least.*

ཧ་ཅང་ *Too;* or add སོང་ to any root; or add དྲག་པ་ as a verb to any root.

དཀོན་པོར་ *Scarcely.*

ལྡང་བ་
འགྲིག་པ་ } *Enough.*

ཤ་སྟག་ *Only, Entirely, All.*

ཏོག་ཙེ་ *Partly.*

མང་པོ་
ཞེད་པོ་
ཞེ་པོ་ } *Much.* With རང་ added, and followed by a negative, *Not much.*

ཁ་གྲངས་མང་པོ་ *Many.*

གཡོ་མ་སྲུ་
མང་ཐག་ཚོད་ } *Very many.*

མང་སོང་ *Too much, Too many.*

ཅུང་ཟད་ *Few.*

ཉུང་ *Little.*

ཏོག་ཙོ་ *A little, A few, Some.*

ཡང་
ད་རུང་
ད་རུང་ཡང་ } *Besides, More yet.*

ཉུང་སོང་ *Too little.*

Interrogative Adverbs.

ག་རེ་དོན་ལ་
ག་གི་དོན་དག་
གང་ལ་
དོན་གང་ལ་
ཅི་ལ་ } *Why?*

ཅི་
ག་འདྲས་
ཇི་ལྟར་, or ཅི་ལྟར་
གང་འདྲ་ } *How?*

ག་དུས་
ནམ་ } *When?*

ག་པ་
ག་རུ་
ག་ན་ } *Where? Whither?*

ག་ནས་
གང་ནས་ } *Whence?*

ག་ཚོད་ ཇི་ཙམ་	*How much? How many?*

Adverbs of Affirmation, Doubt and Negation.

ཡགས་ ཡ་ལགས་ ཡགས་སོ་ ལ་ཡོང་ ལ་འོང་ ལགས་རེད་ ལགས་ཡོད་	*Yes.*
ལགས་མིན་ ལགས་མེད་	*No.*
ལས་ . . . . དགའ་	*Rather* (i.e. *Than*. . . .) *pleases.*
གཅིག་བྱེད་ན་ ཡིན་པ་འདྲ་ ཡིན་འགྲོ་	*Perhaps, Probably.*
གང་ཡིན་ཀྱང་ ག་རེ་ཡིན་རུང་	*At all events, In any case.*
ཐེ་ཚོམ་མེད་པར་	*Without doubt, Unhesitatingly.*
ཆ་ལམ་ ད་ལམ་	*Rather, For the most part, Somewhat, Almost, Nearly,* with negative, *Scarcely.*
རྩ་ནས་ མ་ནས་	*At all, Ever.* (With negative) *Not at all, Never.*

ངེས་པར་ }
གང་གིས་ཀྱང་ } *Surely, Certainly, By all means.*
ཅིས་ཀྱང་ }

རེ་སྐན་ — *By no means, Never.*

ཧེན་ཧེན་ }
ངོ་ཐོག་ } *Indeed.*

མྱོང་ — (Added to root of verb), *Ever*. With negative, *Never*.

མ་ }
མི་ } *Not.*

མེད་པ་ }
མེད་ } *Not possessed of, Devoid of.*

མིན་ — Abbreviation of མ་ཡིན་ *Is not, Are not.*

མེད་ — Abbreviation of མི་ཡོད་ *Is not, Are not.*

As regards the Adverbs and Adverbial phrases used in the Literary language, it is hardly worth while giving a list of them, as the student can easily find them for himself in Jäschke's or Rai Sarat Chandra Das's Dictionary, or in Csoma de Körös's Grammar, where he will see how and to what extent they differ from the Colloquial expressions.

Examples of the use of Adverbs and Adverbial expressions in the Colloquial :—

པཎ་ཆེན་རིན་པོ་ཆེ་བཀྲ་ཤིས་ལྷུན་པོ་ (or གཞི་ག་རྩེ་) ནས་ག་དུས་འཆིབ་རྒྱུ་གནང་ང་རེད།	*When did the Pāṇ-ch'en-rin-po-ch'e* (or *Ṭa-shī Lama*) *come from Ṭā-shī-lhūm-po* (or *Zhyi-ġa-tse*) ?
བཀའ་བློན་གྱི་སྲས་ཀྱིས་མནའ་མ་བཞེས་དུས་མགྲོན་ཆེན་པོ་བྱུང་བ་ (or ཡོད་པ་) རེད།	*When the minister's son got married there were great festivities.*
ཤ་ཏ་ལས་ཚོས་ཚར་བ་དང་།	*When the meat is nearly boiled.*

ཁྱོད་ཀྱིས་ག་དུས་ཐུབ་ན་ཡང་མནའ་མ་ (or མག་པ་) ལོངས་ (or ལེན)།	*Whenever you can, get married.*
ཁྱོད་ག་པ་སྡོད་ཀྱི་ཡོད།	*Where are you living?*
གྲྭ་པ་ག་པ་འགྲོ་གི་འདུག།	*Whither is the monk going?*
ཁོ་ག་ནས་ཡོང་གི་འདུག།	*Whence comes he?*
ཁྱོད་ཀྱི་ཡུམ་གྱི་སྐུ་གཟུགས་ག་འདྲས་ཡོད།	*How is your mother's health?*
རྟ་དེའི་རིན་ག་ཚོད་རེད།	*What is the price of that horse?*
ད་ལྟ་ཆུ་ཚོད་ག་ཚོད་རེད།	*What o'clock is it now?*
ཁྱོད་རེས་ཁང་པ་ཕ་གི་བཟོས་ནས་དོན་དག་ག་རེ་རེད།	*What have you built yonder house for?*
ཁྱོད་འདི་རུ་ག་རེ་དོན་ལ་ཡོང་བ་རེད།	*Why have you come here?*
ཁང་པ་བཟོ་དུས་འགྱེལ་སོང་།	*While the house was being built, it collapsed.*
སྲོད་ཙམ་ན་ཁོ་ཤི་སོང་།	*He died about dusk.*
ཁང་པ་ལ་ཕྱིན་ཙམ་ན་ཁོས་དགོང་མོའི་ཁ་ལག་བཟས་སོང་།	*When he went home he ate his dinner.*
ཟ་གི་ཡོད་ཙ་ཁོ་འགྱེལ་སོང་།	*When he was eating, he fell.*
ཁོ་བཞུགས་ནས་ཆུ་ཚོད་ག་ཚོད་སོང་།	*How long (how many hours) is it since he died?* i.e. *was alive.*
ཁྱོད་ལྷ་ས་ལ་ཕྱིན་མྱོང་ངམ།	*Have you ever been to Lhasa?*
ལགས། ང་ལྷ་ས་ལ་ (ནམ་ཡང་) ཕྱིན་མ་མྱོང་། (pron. *nyúng.*)	*No, I have never been to Lhasa.*
ཁྱོད་དེར་ནམ་ཡང་ཕྱིན་ཡོང་ངམ།	*Will you ever go there?*

...མ་ཅིག་ང་ལྷ་ས་ལ་འགྲོ་གི་ཡིན་པ་འདྲ or ཡིན་གྲོ།	*Some day I may go to Lhasa.*
...ཀྱི་མོ་ལ་ཡང་ཕྱིན་མ་མྱོང་། (pron. ...*yúng.*)	*I have never even been to Chūmbi.*
...མང་པོ་རི་ཚོ་ལ་རྒྱ་ནས་ (or མ་ནས་) ...ཕྱིན་མ་སོང་།	*Many people have never been to the hills at all.*
...ཚོ་ཐག་རིང་ཐག་ཆོད་འདུག།	*The hills are very far away.*
...ས་ཧ་ཅང་ཐག་རིང་པོ་ལ་ (or ཐག་རིང་ ...ག་ཆོད་) འདུག།	*Lhasa is too far away.*
...ང་ལྷ་ས་ཧ་ཅང་གྲང་ཐག་ཆོད་འདུག།	*Moreover, Lhasa is too cold.*
...མས་ཅན་མེད། ད་རུང་མང་པོ་ཡོད།	*That is not all. There is much more yet.*
...ང་ལྷ་ས་ལ་བྱེད་རྒྱུ་ཞིག་པོ་རང་མི་ཡོང་།	*Furthermore, there would not be much to do in Lhasa.*
...ས་ལ་འགྲོ་བ་ལས་ རྡོ་རྗེ་གླིང་ལ་སྡོད་པ ...དགའ་གི་རེད།	*I would rather stay in Darjeeling than go to Lhasa.*
...་གཅིག་ང་ཚོ་འི་དམག་དཔུང་ཚོ་ལྷ་ས་ལ ...ཕྱིན་སོང་།	*Our troops once went to Lhasa.*
...ང་ (or Vulgar Coll. ད་འདྲོ་) ཚར་ ...གཅིག་དེར་འགྲོ་དགོས་གི་ཡིན་པ་འདྲ།	*They may have to go there again;* or, *Perhaps they will have, etc.*
...ཕྱི་གླིང་གི་ཡུལ་ལ་ཕྱིན་ནས་ལོ་བཅུ་གཉིས་ ...སོང་།	*Twelve years ago I went to Europe.*
...ང་པ་གི་ལོ་ག་ཚོད་རེད།	*How old is that tree?*
...ད་ལོ་ག་ཚོད་ཡིན།	*How old are you?*

དཔེ་ཆ་དེ་ངས་སློགས་ (or བཀླགས་) ནས་ དུས་ (མང་པོ་) སོང་འདུག།	*I read that book some time ago.*
སྔོན་ལ་སྔོན་འཇུག་ལྔ་བརྗོད་པ་རེད།	*Anciently (of yore) the five fixes were pronounced.*
དེང་སང་བརྗོད་ཀྱི་མི་འདུག།	*Now-a-days they are not nounced.*
ངས་དཔེ་ཆ་དེ་ག་པ་ཡང་རྙེད་ཐུབ་ཀྱི་མི་འདུག།	*I cannot find the book anywher*
གང་ཡིན་ཀྱང་ངས་དེ་ད་ལྟ་མཐོང་གི་མི་འདུག།	*At all events I do not see it no*
འདི་རུ་ཤོག།	*Come here.*
འདི་རུ་མ་ཡོང་།	*Do not come here.*
ཁ་སང་ཁོ་ཚོ་ཕར་ཕྱིན་སོང་།	*They went away yesterday.*
ལམ་སང་ཕར་རྒྱུག།	*Go away immediately.*
ངའི་སློབ་དཔོན་གྱིས་ད་ཅང་གསལ་པོ་གསུང་གི་འདུག།	*My teacher speaks very distinct*
དུས་རྒྱུན་ཁོས་ད་ཅང་མགྱོགས་པོ་ཟེར་གྱི་འདུག།	*He always speaks very fast.*
ཁོས་ལབ་པ་དེ་ངས་ལས་སླ་པོར་ཧ་གོ་གི་མི་འདུག།	*I do not understand him easil*
ཅུར་སྒྲ་འདི་འདྲ་མ་རྒྱབ།	*Do not make so much noise.*
ཁྱོད་རེས་སྐད་ཆེན་པོ་འདི་འདྲ་རྒྱབ་ནས་དོན་དག་ག་རེ་རེད།	*Why are you talking so loudly*

་འདི་ཁྱོད་ལ་སྐད་ཆ་དྲང་པོ་ཤ་སྟག་ཤོད་ཀྱི་འདུག།	*This lama is only telling you the truth.*
་ཁྲིམས་དཔོན་ཁྲིམས་ཁང་ལ་ཧ་ཅང་སྔ་ནས་ཕེབས་སོང་།	*The judge came to court very early to-day.*
ཉིན་ཁོང་ཕྱི་པོ་བྱེད་ཀྱི་ཡིན་འགྲོ་ or བྱེད་ང་ངས།	*Probably he will be late to-morrow.*
རང་ཀ་ལ་ཀ་ཏ་ལ་ཞེད་སྣག་ཚད་པ་ཆེ་འདུག།	*Just now it is terribly hot in Calcutta.*
རང་གིས་དངུལ་ཁྲིམས་ཁང་ལ་འཁྱེར་ག།	*Take the money to court personally.*
ཆུང་ཆུང་འདི་ཤན་གཞོན་ག་འདུས་ད།	*How old is this little child?*
འདྲི་གནམ་སྐྱག་པ་ལ།	*What pleasant weather!*
འདྲི་ལྷག་མ་པ་གསིལ་པ་ལ།	*What a cutting breeze!*
འདྲི་ལམ་ཀ་ལག་ག་ལ།	*What an excellent road!*
འདྲི་ཁྱི་ཆེ་བ་ལ།	*What an enormous dog!*
འདྲི་ཡལ་ག་སྦོམ་པ་ལ།	*What a thick branch!*
འདྲི་བུ་མོ་མཛེས་པ་ལ།	*What a beautiful girl!*
སྐུག་སྡོད། ཁྱོད་བཟོད་པ་མི་སྒོམ་དོན་དག་ག་རེ་རེད།	*Wait a little: why are you so impatient?*
ཁྱིམ་ཁང་པ་འདི་བཟོ་བའི་དོན་དག་ག་རེད།	*Why are you building this house?*

ཕྲུ་གུ་འདི་འདྲ་གང་ལ་ངུ་གི་འདུག། — *Why is the child crying like tha*

གཡོག་པོ་ཐམས་ཅད་གདོང་ལ་ཕྱིན་སོང་ངམ་ (or Coll. ངས)། — *Have all the servants gone ahead?*

དང་པོ་ གཡས་ ཕྱོགས་ ལ་ དེ་ ནས་ གཡོན་ ཕྱོགས་ལ་ཕྱིན་ནས་དོག་ཙོ་ཁ་ཐུག་ལ་གོམ་པ་བཅུ་གཉིས་ཙ་འགྲོ་དགོས་ཀྱི་རེད། — *First you must turn to the ri then to the left, and then straight on for a distance about twelve paces.*

ཁྱོད་ལམ་ཀའི་མཐའ་ལ་སླེབས་པ་དང་ང་ལ་སྐད་གཏོང་། — *When you reach the road shout to me.*

ཁང་པ་འདི་ལ་ཙི་ཙི་ག་ས་ག་ལ་ཡོད། — *There are rats everywhere in house.*

ཀ་ལ་ཀ་ཏ་ནས་རྡོ་རྗེ་གླིང་ལ་ཐག་རིང་ཐུང་ག་ཚོད་རེད། — *How far is it from Calcutta Darjeeling?*

བཀའ་བློན་སྤུང་རྫོང་རྡོ་རྗེ་གླིང་ནས་ཐག་ཉེ་པོ་རེད་དམ། ཐག་རིང་པོ་རེད། — *Is Kalimpong close to or far a from Darjeeling?*

གསོལ་ བ་ བཏབ་ པ་ དེ་ ཡག་པོ་ ད་ ཡག་པོ་རེད་དེ། — *To pray is of course very excell*

§ 33. Postpositions.

What we call Prepositions, such as *Of*, *To*, *In*, *On*, *By*, *W* *From*, *About*, *Concerning*, etc., and certain Prepositional phrases *By reason of*, *For the sake of*, *With respect to*, *According to*, *In of*, etc., are rendered in Tibetan by Postpositions, some of which simple, and others compound.

The Simple Postpositions consist of the primitive part which are used in the formation of the Cases. (*See* § 25.)

As regards the *Nominative Case*, no such particles are (*See* § 25, I.)

As regards the *Vocative Case*. (*See* § 25, II.)

As regards the *Accusative Case*, no particle is necessary, but if desired the Postposition ལ་ may be inserted. Ex. :—

ཁོས་བུ་མོ་བྱམས་པོ་བྱེད་ཀྱི་འདུག། }
Or :— } *He loves the girl.*
ཁོས་བུ་མོ་ལ་བྱམས་པོ་བྱེད་ཀྱི་འདུག། }

With this case the postpositions ཐུག་, བར་, and ཏུ་, *As far as*, *Up to*, *To*, *Till*, are used.

N.B.—The following verbs may be used either with the bare accusative or with that and the postposition ལ།

སྦེར་བ་, གཏང་བ་, འབུལ་བ་, སྤྲོད་པ་, *To give, to deliver.*

སྟོན་པ་, སློབ་པ་, *To teach.*

འཆད་པ་, བཤད་པ་, *To tell, To explain.*

སྟོན་པ་, སྤྱན་འབེབས་ཞུ་བ་, སྤྱན་བདར་ཞུ་བ་, *To show.*

ཞུ་བ་, *To petition, To beg, To offer.*

ཞེད་པ་, *To fear, To be afraid of.*

འཕོག་པ་, *To strike against.*

རོགས་བྱེད་པ་ *To help, To aid.*

འཁྱེར་ཡོང་བ་ *To bring.*

As regards the *Genitive Case*, the particles are གི་, ཀྱི་, གྱི་, འི་, ཡི་ (*see* § 25, IV). Ex. :—

ལུག་གི་མགོ། *The sheep's head*, or *the head of the sheep.*

གླང་གི་ར་ཅོ། *The bull's horn*, or *the horn of the bull.*

ཕལ་སྐད་ཀྱི་སྐད་ལུགས་ཞིག། *A dialect of the Colloquial.*

བག་ལེབ་ཀྱི་གོང་། *Price of bread.*

ཉམས་ཀྱི་གླེན་པ། *The foolishness of pride.*

ཁང་པ་འདིའི་མཐོ་དམན། *The height of this house.*

སྐྱེས་དམན་གྱི་མིང་།	*The woman's name.*
ཐེ་ཚོམ་གྱི་ཉེན།	*The danger of uncertainty.*
ཤར་གྱི་མཁས་པ་ or རིག་པ།	*The wisdom of the East.*
ལུགས་སྲོལ་གྱི་ཁྲིམས།	*The law of custom.*
ཁང་པ་དེའི་མཐོ་དམན།	*The height of that house.*
ལེའུའི་རྫོགས་མཚམས།	*The end of a chapter.*
སྟ་རེའི་ཡུ་བ།	*The handle of an axe.*
གཡུའི་མདོག།	*The colour of a turquoise.*

As regards the *Dative Case*, the particle used is ལ་ (*see* § 25, V).

As regards the *Agentive Case*, the particles used are ས་, གིས་, ཀྱིས་, གྱིས་, འིས་, and ཡིས་ (*see* § 25, VI). Ex.:—

ཁོས་བུ་མོ་བྱམས་པོ་བྱེད་ཀྱི་འདུག།	*He loves the girl.*
ཁྲས་ཕུག་རོན་བསད་སོང་།	*The hawk killed the pigeon.*
འབྲུག་གིས་ཟླ་བ་ཟ་གི་འདུག།	*The dragon is eating the moon.*
ང་རང་གིས་དཔེ་ཆ་དེ་ཀློགས་ཡོད།	*I have read that book.*
ཁྱོད་ཀྱིས་མཛུབ་གུ་ལ་རྨ་བཟོས་སོང་ངམ།	*Have you hurt your finger?*
ཁོའི་ཨ་ཕས་ (or ཕས་) ཁོ་ཁ་བསླབ་སོང་།	*His father taught him.*
ཁོའི་གྲོགས་པོས་ལས་ཀ་བྱས་སོང་།	*His companion did the work.*
རྩྭ་ངན་གྱིས་ལོ་ཏོག་སུབ་ཀྱི་འདུག།	*Weeds are choking the corn.*
སྒྲིག་ལམ་གྱིས་མི་ཐམས་ཅད་བཟོ་སྐྱོར་བྱེད་ཀྱི་འདུག།	*Discipline improves all men.*

དགའ་ ཚོར་གྱིས་ མཚམས་ མཚམས་ ལ་ མི་ བསད་ཡོང་།	*Joy will sometimes kill people.*
དངུལ་གྱིས་ཁོ་མེད་པ་བཟོས་འདུག།	*Money ruined him.*
མི་འདིས་ཁོ་ལ་རོགས་བྱས་སོང་།	*This man helped him.*
ཚད་པ་ཡིས་ངའི་རྟ་བསད་སོང་ or ཚད་པས་ངའི་རྟ་བསད་སོང་།	*The heat killed my horse.*

As regards the *Locative Case* the particles used are :—

ལ་ }
ན་ } *In, On, At, By*, etc.

བརྒྱུད་ནས་ *Through.*

ཏུ་ }
དུ་ }
རུ་ } *In, On, At, By*, etc.
ར་ }
སུ་ }

(See § 25, vii.)

As regards the *Periodal* or *Durational Case*, the particles used are ན་ and ལ་ *At, In, During*, etc.

(See § 25, viii.)

As regards the Modal Case, the particles used are :—

ནས་ *By, Through, By way of, Via.*

དང་ *Against, With*, e.g., with verbs of meeting, fighting, payin; respect to, visiting, etc.

ས་ (Silent) *With, Because, Since*, etc.

ཕྱིར་ (Rather literary) *By, Through, On account of, For, By reason of* etc.

(See § 25, ix.)

As regards the *Ablative Case*, in the limited sense in which it is used in this Manual, the particles used are :—

ལས་ *Than*, *Except*, *Save*, *But*, *But for*, *Besides*, etc.

ནས་ }
ན་ } *Unless.*

(See § 25, x.)

As regards the *Terminative Case*, which in this Manual includes certain aspects of what is usually called the Ablative Case, the particles used are :—

ཏུ་, དུ་, ར་, རུ་, སུ་, and ལ་, signifying *Direction towards*, and དང་, ནས་, and ལས་, signifying *Direction from*. (*See* § 25, xi.)

Of the COMPOUND POSTPOSITIONS, most are used with the Genitive Case. The following are a few of them :—

དོན་ལ་ }
སྐོར་ལ་ } *About*, *Concerning*, *Regarding*, *With respect to.*

དོན་ལ་ *On behalf of*, *For the sake of*, *With the object of*, *For the purpose of*, *In order to.*

རྐྱེན་གྱིས་ *On account of*, *By reason of*, *In consequence of*, *Through*, *By*, *Because of.*

སྟེང་ལ་ }
སྒང་ལ་ } *Above* (on top of), *Upon.*

ཡ་ལ་ }
ཡར་ or ཡར་རུ་ } *Above* (Higher up).

ནང་བཞིན་ }
ནང་ལྟར་ } *According to*, *As*, *Like.*

དཀྱིལ་ལ་ *Amidst*, *Among*, *In the middle of.*

རྒྱབ་ལ་ རྗེས་ལ་ གཞུག་ལ་	*Behind*, *Back*, *Afterwards*, *Next*.
མདུན་ལ་ གདོང་ལ་	*Before* (place), *In front of*.
དྲུང་དུ་	*Into the presence of*.
ཚབ་ལ་	*Instead of*, *In place of*.
ནང་ནས་	*From within*.
ནང་ལ་	*Inside*, *Within*, *In*.
རྩ་ལ་	*Just by*, *At the side of*.
རྩ་ ཐག་ཉེ་པོ་ (used with ནས་)	*Close to*.
དུས་ལ་	*During*.
རྩར་ or རྩ་ལ་ འགྲམ་ལ་ ཟུར་ལ་	*On the edge of*.
ལན་ལ་	*In reply or answer to*, *In return for*.
འོག་ལ་ གཤམ་ལ་	*Below*, *Under*, *Beneath*, *After*.
ཕྱོགས་ལ་ ངོས་ལ་	*Towards*.

The following are used with the *Accusative*.

དང་མཉམ་དུ་ དང་ལྷན་ཅིག་ དང་བཅས་པ་	*With*, i.e., *Along with*, *Together with*, *In company with*.

དང་འདྲ་པོ་ or དང་འདྲ་བ་ *Equal to.*

དང་ཉེ་པོ་ *Near to.*

དང་རིང་པོ་ *Far from.*

ཐུག་ *Until, For* (time), *As far as, For* (space).

མ་གཏོགས་ }
མིན་པ་ } *Save, Except.*

Examples.

ངས་དེའི་དོན་ལ་ཚང་མ་ཤེས་ཀྱི་ཡོད།	*I know all about that.*
ཁོ་ལ་ཁོའི་བོད་ཡུལ་ལ་ཕྱིན་པའི་ལམ་གྱི་སྐོར་ཐམས་ཅད་དྲིས་དང་།	*Ask him all about his journey to Tibet.*
འདི་དོན་དག་གི་ནང་བཞིན་མི་འདུག།	*This is not according to reason.*
མི་ཚོ་མུ་གེའི་རྐྱེན་གྱིས་ཤི་སོང་།	*The people died in consequence of the famine.*
ཁོ་གླེན་པའི་ནང་བཞིན་བྱས་པ་རེད།	*He behaved like a fool.*
དམག་མི་ཚོ་ཨམ་བན་གྱི་རྗེས་ལ་འགྲོ་གི་འགྲོ་གི་བྱས་པ་རེད།	*The soldiers used to march after the Amban.*
རིའི་ཕ་གི་སྟེང་ལ་གངས་ཉེད་པོ་རང་མི་འདུག།	*There is not much snow on that hill.*
ངའི་མདུན་ལ་མ་འགྲོ།	*Do not walk before me.*
ཁོ་ཚོ་རྒྱལ་བ་རིན་པོ་ཆེའི་དྲུང་དུ་ཡོངས་པ་རེད།	*They came into the presence of the Dalai Lama.*
ཡི་གེ་དེའི་ལན་ང་ལ་བྲིས་བཙུག་ཨ།	*Let me write in reply to that letter.*
ཁྱོད་ཀྱི་གཡོག་པོ་དོས་པ་ཚོ་དང་མཉམ་དུ་ཕྱིན་ཆོག་གི་རེད།	*Your servant may go with the coolies.*

ཕ་གི་ཁང་པ་ཐུག (or བར་དུ་) ང་དང་མཉམ་དུ་ཤོག། *Come with me as far as that house.*

§ 34. Conjunctions.

1. In Tibetan the use, as in English, of Conjunctions like *And* and *But* is generally avoided, and the sentence is reconstructed, so as to begin with a subordinate participial clause, of which clauses there is often a long string before the principal verb is reached.

Example :—

ཁང་པ་ཕ་གི་ངའི་མིན་པ་ལ་ངས་དེ་ཁྱོད་ལ་ སྟེར་ཐུབ་ཀྱི་མེད་ or སྟེར་མི་ཐུབ་ or སྟེར་ཐུབ་ཀྱི་མ་རེད། *That house is not mine, and I cannot give it to you.*

Here the sentence is turned into: *That house not being mine, I cannot give it to you.*

Not being, the negative form of the participle present of the verb *To be*, is rendered མིན་པ་ལ་ The affirmative form *Being*, would be ཡོད་པ་ལ་, or ཡིན་པ་ལ།

2. But where the Disjunctive idea is sought to be expressed the form ན་ཡང་ is used thus :—

ཁང་པ་ཕ་གི་ངའི་ཡིན་ན་ཡང་དེ་ངས་ཁྱོད་ལ་སྟེར་ཐུབ་ཀྱི་མེད། *That house is mine, but I cannot give it to you.*

Here the sentence is turned into: *Though that house is mine, (yet) I cannot give it to you.*

3. It would be quite allowable, however, to avoid using the Conjunctions altogether, and simply say :—

ཁང་པ་ཕ་གི་ངའི་མིན། དེ་ངས་ཁྱོད་ལ་སྟེར་ཐུབ་ཀྱི་མེད་, or སྟེར་མི་ཐུབ། *That house is not mine. I cannot give it to you.*

4. Instead of ན་ཡང་, as above, ཡང་ alone, or ཀྱང་ according to the final of the preceding word, or the gerundial particles ཏེ་ (after final ད་), དེ་ (after final ན་, ར་, ལ་, and ས་) or སྟེ་ (after final ག་, ང་, བ་, མ་ and all vowels) may be used. Thus :—

ཁང་པ་ཕ་གི་ངའི་ཡིན་ཡང་ (or ཡོད་དེ་) དེ་ངས་ཁྱོད་ལ་སྟེར་ཐུབ་ཀྱི་མེད། — *Though that house is mine, I cannot give it to you.*

5. Another way of expressing the same idea is the following :—

ཁང་པ་ཕ་གི་ངའི་མིན་པས་ (or མིན་ཙང་) དེ་ངས་ཁྱོད་ལ་སྟེར་ཐུབ་ཀྱི་མེད། — *As, since,* or *because the house is not mine, I cannot give it to you.*

6. As illustrative of similar formations in connection with verbs other than ཡོད་པ་ and ཡིན་པ་, note the following :—

གངས་མང་པོ་བབས་ན་ཡང་ང་རྡོ་རྗེ་གླིང་ལ་ཐོན་སོང་། — *Though it was snowing hard I set out for Darjeeling.*

གངས་མང་པོ་བབས་ཀྱང་ང་རྡོ་རྗེ་གླིང་ལ་ཐོན་པ་ཡིན། — *Ditto.*

ཆར་པ་མ་བབས་པས་ (or བབས་ཙང་) ང་རྡོ་རྗེ་གླིང་ལ་ཐོན་སོང་། — *As, since,* or *because it was not raining I set out for Darjeeling.*

ཆར་པ་མ་བབས་ནས་ཐོན་སོང་། — *As it was not raining he set out.*

ཆར་པ་མི་འབབ་ཙང་ (or འབབ་པ་ལ་) ང་འཐོན་གྱི་ཡིན། — *As it is not raining I shall set out.*

ཆར་པ་མི་འབབ་ན་ཡང་ང་འཐོན་གྱི་མིན། — *It is not raining, but I shall not set out.*

7. The expression *Either....or*, is rendered by ཡང་ན་, or by འམ་, ནམ་, etc., or by ཡང་མིན་ན་ Thus :—

ཡང་ན་ཆར་པ་གངས་རྒྱབ་འགྲོ་རེད།

Or :—

ཆར་པའམ་གངས་འབབ་འགྲོ་རེད།

Or :—

ཆར་པ་ཡང་ན་གངས་འབབ་འགྲོ་རེད།

Either it is about to rain or about to snow.

ཀྱེ་ གཙོ་བོ་ ཡང་ མིན་ ན་ ཁྱོད་འགྲོ་ གི་རེད་ ཡང་ མིན་ ན་ ཁྱོད་ སྐེ་ ལ་ ཐག་ པ་ བསྡམས་ནས་བསད་ཡོང་། — *Either, lord, you will go or you will hang.*

ང་ཡང་ན་ དག་པ་ ཡིན་ ཡང་ མིན་ན་ དག་པ་ མིན།

Or :—

ང་དག་པ་ཡིན་ནམ་མིན་ནམ།

Either I am right or wrong.

རྟ་རྟ་ར་ལ་འདུག་གམ་མི་འདུག། — *Is the horse in the stable or not?*

8. If is rendered by the expression གལ་ཏེ་ or གལ་སྲིད་ . . . ན་ or, as is more usual, by ན་ alone. Thus :—

གལ་སྲིད་ང་དག་པ་ཡོད་ན་ (or འདུག་ན་) — *If I am right, or if I were right.*

Or simply :—

ང་དག་པ་ཡོད་ན་ (or འདུག་ན་)། — *Ditto.*

The second and third persons also take this ཡོད་ན་ or འདུག་ན། Thus :—

ཁྱོད་དག་པ་ཡོད་ན་ (or འདུག་ན་)། — *If thou art, or wert, right.*

ཁོ་དག་པ་ཡོད་ན་ (or འདུག་ན་)། — *If he is, or were, right.*

So with the verb *To have* :—

ང་ལ་བསོད་བདེ་ཡོད་ན་ (or འདུག་ན་)། — *If I have, or had, good fortune.*

And similarly for the other two persons.

With verbs other than ཡོད་ and འདུག་ (*To be*, or *To have*), the conditional sign ན་ is simply added to the verbal root, Present, or Perfect, for all persons. Thus :—

ངས་སྟེར་ཐུབ་ན།	*If I can, or could, give.*
ཁྱོད་ཀྱིས་སྟེར་ཐུབ་ན།	*If thou canst, or couldst, give.*
ཁོས་སྟེར་ཐུབ་ན།	*If he can, or could, give.*
ངས་ཁོ་ལ་ཞུ་ན་ or ཞུས་ན།	*If I ask, or asked, him.*
ཁྱོད་ཀྱིས་ཁོ་ལ་ཞུ་ན་ or ཞུས་ན།	*If thou askest, or askedst, him.*
ཁོས་ཁོ་ལ་ཞུ་ན་ or ཞུས་ན།	*If he asks, or asked, him.*

ཅི་སྟེ་ . . . ན་ *But if*, is confined to Literary Tibetan.

9. Expressions like *Ago*, and *Since*, in the sense of *From the time that*, are rendered thus :—

ངས་ཤ་བཟས་ནས་ལོ་གསུམ་སོང་།

Or :—

ངས་ཤ་མ་བཟས་ནས་ལོ་གསུམ་སོང་།

Three years ago I ate meat ; or, *It is three years since I ate meat ;* or, *I have not eaten meat for three years.*

10. Our common conjunction *And* is expressed by དང་ meaning *with*, used as an enclitic, but only the first two nouns in a series are connected by it, however numerous the series may be. Thus :—

དུས་ཚོད་དང་དུས་རླབས་དང་འཆི་བས་སུ་ལ་ཡང་སྒུག་གི་མི་འདུག། *Time and tide and death tarry for nobody.*

Between two Imperatives, especially in Literary Tibetan, *And* is rendered by ལ་. Thus :—

ཤོག་ལ་ལྟོས་ཤིག། *Come and see.*

In Literary Tibetan, moreover, in addition to དང་ and ལ་, *And* and *But* are rendered by ཡང་ and ཀྱང་, and by the gerundial particles

ཅིང་, ཤིང་, or ཞིང་, and དེ་, ཏེ་ or སྟེ་, especially in sentences in which *And* occurs frequently, and it is desired to vary the particle. Thus :—

ཤ་ལ་ཟ་ཞིང་ཁྲག་ལ་འཐུང་བ།	*Eating flesh and drinking blood* (*Das*).
ཆེ་ཞིང་ལེགས་པ།	*Tall and well made.* (*D.*)
དྲོད་གནོད་ཅིང་བསིལ་བ་ཕན།	*Heat is hurtful* (*but*) *cold is beneficial.* (*D.*)
ཁྱོད་རིགས་ཆེ་ཞིང་མཐོ་བ་སྟེ།	*As you are of high and noble birth.* (*D.*)
གལ་ཏེ་ང་མངོན་ཤེས་དང་ལྡན་ཞིང་གསང་བ་ ཐམས་ཅད་ཤེས་ཏེ་རྟོགས་པ་ཀུན་དང་རི་ སྤོ་བ་ཙམ་དུ་དད་པ་ཐམས་ཅད་ཡོད་ཀྱང་། བྱམས་པ་མེད་ན། ང་ཅི་ཡང་མ་ཡིན་ནོ།	*If I have prophecy and know all mysteries and all knowledge, and if I have all faith, so as to remove mountains, but have not love, I am nothing.* (1 Corinthians xiii. 2.)
ཁྱེད་ཅག་དེ་དག་གི་དཀྱིལ་ནས་ཐོན་ལ། འབྲལ་བར་གྱུར་ཅིག་ཅེས་བཀའ་སྩལ་ཏོ། ཡང་མི་གཙང་བ་ཞིག་ལ་མ་རེག་ཅིག། ངས་ཁྱེད་རྣམས་ལ་ནང་དུ་ཤོག་ཟེར་ཏེ། ཁྱེད་ཀྱི་ཕ་ལྟར་འགྱུར། ཁྱེད་ངའི་བུ་ དང་བུ་མོ་ལྟར་འགྱུར་བར་འགྱུར་རོ། ཞེས་གཙོ་བོ་ཀུན་དབང་གིས་བཀའ སྩལ་ཏོ།	*Come ye out from among them, and be ye separate, saith the Lord. And touch no unclean thing; and I will receive you, and will be to you a Father, and ye shall be to me sons and daughters, saith the Almighty.* (2 Corinthians vi. 17, 18.)

11. In the Colloquial ཡང་ or, after final ག་, ད་, བ་, or ས་, ཀྱང་ may signify *And*, *Either*, *Neither*, or *Nor*, according to the context. At the beginning of sentences the following are common: འོ་ན་ *However, But, Well;* ཡིན་ཀྱང་ *However, But, Moreover;* དེ་ནས་ *Then;* དེའི་རྐྱེན་བྱས་ནས་ *Then, In that case, Consequently*

EXAMPLES :—

ཡང་ལྟོས་ཞིག།	*And behold.*
བྱེ་མ་ཀ་ར་ཡང་ཡོད་པ་མ་རེད།	*There is no sugar either.*
འོ་མ་ཡང་མེད།	*Nor milk.*
འོ་སྣོད་ཀྱང་མེད།	*Nor milk-jug.*
ཡིན་ཀྱང་ཁྱོད་ལ་དགོས་ན།	*However, if you want them.*
དེ་ནས་ཁྲིམས་དཔོན་གྱིས་བཙོན་པ་ལ་གསུང་བ་རེད།	*Then the judge said to the prisoner.*
དེའི་རྐྱེན་བྱས་ནས་ངས་ཁྱོད་ལ་བཏང་ བཞག་གི་ཡིན།	*In that case I shall acquit you.*
འོ་ན་དགོངས་པ་མ་མཚུངས།	*Well, don't be angry.*

The Literary equivalent of ཡིན་ཀྱང་ *But, However*, is འོན་ཀྱང་།

12. *Whether* is expressed by using the interrogative duplicative suffix. Thus :—

ང་དག་པོ་ཡོད་ དམ་མེད་ དམ་སུས་ ཤེས་ཀྱི་ འདུག།	*Whether I am right or not, who knows?*
དེ་ཁྲིག་ཁྲིག་ཡིན་ ནམ་མིན་ནམ་ ངས་ ཤེས་ཀྱི་ མེད།	*Whether it is correct or not, I do not know.*
ཆར་པ་འབབ་ཡོང་ངམ་མི་ཡོང་ སུས་ཟེར་ཐུབ་ ཀྱི་རེད།	*Whether it will rain or not, who can say?*
ཁོ་ཐོན་སོང་ངམ་མ་སོང་ཁྱོད་རང་གིས་ཤེས་ ཀྱི་འདུག།	*Whether he set out or not, you know.*

13. OR may be expressed either as explained in clause 7 of this §, or thus :—

ཁོ་ལྟོགས་ཀྱི་འདུག་གམ་ཁ་སྐོམ་གྱི་འདུག།	*Is he hungry or thirsty?*

14. As to the use of Conjunctions with Numerals, see § 26, II, *Note* 3.

§ 35. The Substantive Verb ཡོད་པ་ *To be.*

The primary meaning of this verb is *To exist, To be present,* but it is often used attributively, i.e., as a mere copula to connect subject and attribute, and also as an auxiliary to other verbs.

As a substantive verb and when used attributively it may be conjugated thus :—

Present Indicative.

Affirmative.

ང་འདི་རུ་ཡོད།	*I am here.*	ང་ཚོ་འདི་རུ་ཡོད།	*We are here.*
ཁྱོད་འདི་རུ་ཡོད་, or འདུག།	*Thou art here.*	ཁྱོད་ཚོ་འདི་རུ་ཡོད་, or འདུག།	*You are here.*
ཁོ་འདི་རུ་ཡོད་, or འདུག་, or ཡོད་པ་རེད། (pronounced *yo'-a-re'*).	*He is here.*	ཁོ་ཚོ་འདི་རུ་ཡོད་, or འདུག་, or ཡོད་པ་རེད།	*They are here.*

There being no difference between the singular and plural constructions, only the singular will henceforth be given.

ཡོད་ and འདུག་, connected as above with the third person, may also be used for phrases like *There is, There was, There are, There were,* etc. Thus :—

གྲོང་གསེབ་འདིའི་ནང་ལ་ཁང་ཆུང་སུམ་ཅུ་ ཡོད། *There are thirty huts in this village.*

ཡོད་པ་རེད་ also may apparently be so used when the speaker expresses knowledge derived from information. Thus :—

རིའི་ཕ་གི་སྟེང་ལ་གངས་ཡོད་པ་རེད་དམ་ ཡོད་པ་མ་རེད། *Is there snow on that hill or not?*

ལགས། ཡོད་པ་མ་རེད། *No, there is not.*

According, however, to Mr. C. A. Bell, ཡོད་པ་རེད་ implies uncertainty.

The future root ཡོང་, for all persons, is sometimes used for the present tense, when vagueness or indefiniteness is implied. Thus :—

རོང་མ་གིའི་ནང་ལ་སེམས་ཅན་རི་དྭགས་ཆེ་ ཡོང་།	*There are wild animals down in that valley.*

An Intensive form of ཡོད་པ་ is མོད་པ་, similarly conjugated, but not now in use.

An elegant Literary form, not much used however, is :—

མཆིས་	*I am.*
གདའ་	*Thou art.*
མཆིས་, or གདའ་, or མཆིས་པ་ཡིན།	*He is.*

And the Respectful form is :—

བཞུགས་	*I am.*
མངའ་	*Thou art.*
བཞུགས, or མངའ་, or བཞུགས་པ་ཡིན།	*He is.*

Negative of ཡོད་པ།

ང་དེ་རུ་མེད།	*I am not there.*
ཁྱོད་འདི་རུ་མེད་, or མི་འདུག།	*Thou art not here.*
ཁོ་འདི་རུ་མེད་, or མི་འདུག་, or ཡོད་ པ་མ་རེད།	*He is not here.*

Interrogative Form.

ང་འདི་རུ་ཡོད་དམ་, ཡོད་ད་, or ཡོད་ པས་ or ཡོད་པ་, or ཨ་ཡོད།	*Am I here?*

ཁྱོད་འདི་རུ་འདུག་གམ་ (or ག་), or འདུག་གས།	*Art thou here?*
ཁོ་འདི་རུ་འདུག་གམ་, or འདུག་གས་, or ཡོད་པ་རེད་དམ་, or ཡོད་པ་རེད་པས་, or ཡོད་པ་རེད་པ།	*Is he here?*
ང་འདི་རུ་མེད་དམ་, or མེད་པས་, or མེད་པ།	*Am I not here?*
ཁྱོད་འདི་རུ་མི་འདུག་ག་ or མི་འདུག་གམ།	*Art thou not here?*
ཁོ་འདི་རུ་མེད་ད་ (or པས་), or མི་འདུག་ག་ (or གས་), or ཡོད་པ་མ་རེད་ད་, or རེད་པས་, or རེད་པ།	*Is he not here?*

Attributive.

ང་ཡག་པོ་ཡོད།	*I am good.*
ཁྱོད་ཡག་པོ་ཡོད་, or འདུག།	*Thou art good.*
ཁོ་ཡག་པོ་ཡོད་, or འདུག་, or ཡོད་པ་རེད།	*He is good.*

Colloquially, ཡག་པོ་ is sometimes pronounced *Ya'-pu*, instead of *Ya'-po.*

In some phrases, like the following, འདུག་ and not ཡོད་ is used with the first person; probably because there is really no nominative "I," but the construction is "There is to me."

Moreover, the phrase is conjugated with གི, etc. Thus :—

ང་གྲང་གི་འདུག།	*I am cold.*
ང་ན་གི་འདུག།	*I am ill.*

ང་ལྟོགས་ཀྱི་འདུག། *I am hungry.*

ང་ཁ་སྐོམ་གྱི་འདུག། *I am thirsty.*

Imperfect Indicative.

This may be formed just like the Present Indicative, the context generally sufficing to show what the tense is. Thus :—

Affirmative.

ཁ་སང་ང་འདི་རུ་ཡོད། *I was here yesterday.*

ཁ་སང་ཁྱོད་འདི་རུ་ཡོད་, or འདུག། *Thou wast here yesterday.*

ཁ་སང་ཁོ་འདི་རུ་ཡོད་, or འདུག་ or ཡོད་པ་རེད། *He was here yesterday.*

སྔོན་ལ་ང་ཕྱུག་པོ་ཡོད། *I was rich once.*

སྔོན་ལ་ཁྱོད་ཕྱུག་པོ་ཡོད་, or འདུག། *Thou wast rich once.*

སྔོན་ལ་ཁོ་ཕྱུག་པོ་ཡོད་, or འདུག་, or ཡོད་པ་རེད། *He was rich once.*

Apart from contextual indications as above, this tense may also be formed with the aid of the auxiliary verbs ཡིན་པ་ and རེད་པ་. Thus :—

Affirmative.

ང་འདི་རུ་ཡོད་པ་ཡིན། *I was here.*

ཁྱོད་འདི་རུ་ཡོད་པ་འདུག་, or occasionally ཡོད་པ་རེད། *Thou wast here.*

ཁོ་འདི་རུ་ཡོད་པ་རེད་, or occasionally ཡོད་པ་འདུག། *He was here.*

Negative.

ང་འདི་རུ་ཡོད་པ་མིན་ (vulgarly མན་)། *I was not here.*

ཁྱོད་འདི་རུ་ཡོད་པ་མ་རེད། *Thou wast not here.*

ཁོ་འདི་རུ་ཡོད་པ་མ་རེད། *He was not here.*

Attributive.

ང་ཕྱུག་པོ་ཡོད་པ་ཡིན། *I was rich.*

ཁྱོད་ཕྱུག་པོ་ཡོད་པ་རེད། *Thou wast rich.*

ཁོ་ཕྱུག་པོ་ཡོད་པ་རེད། *He was rich.*

Interrogative.

ང་འདི་རུ་ཡོད་པ་ཡིན་ནམ་ or ཡིན་པས་, or ཡིན་པ། *Was I here?*

ཁྱོད་འདི་རུ་ཡོད་པ་རེད་དམ་ (or པས་ or པ་), or ཡོད་པ་ཡིན་ནམ་ (or པས་, or པ)། *Wast thou here?*

ཁོ་འདི་རུ་ཡོད་པ་རེད་དམ་ (or པས་, or པ་)། *Was he here?*

And so forth.

PERFECT AND PLUPERFECT INDICATIVE.

Same as the Imperfect Indicative. Thus :—

སྔོན་ལ་ང་འདི་རུ་ཡོད། *I have*, or *had*, *been here before.*

And so forth, throughout all constructions.

FUTURE.

The Future Simple is expressed Colloquially by ཡོང་ for all persons. Thus :—

Affirmative.

ང་	འདི་རུ་ཡོང་	*I shall be here.*
ཁྱོད་		*Thou wilt be here.*
ཁོ་		*He will be here.*

Attributive.

ང་ཡག་པོ་ཡོང་, or, in Literature, བཟང་པོར་འགྱུར་རོ། — *I shall be good.*

ཁྱེད་ཡག་པོ་ཡོང་, or, in Literature, བཟང་པོར་འགྱུར་རོ། — *Thou wilt be good.*

ཁོ་ཡག་པོ་ཡོང་, or, in Literature, བཟང་པོར་འགྱུར་རོ། — *He will be good.*

N.B.—རྒྱུ་ or རྒྱུའོ་ in Literary Tibetan should not be used as a mere copula to connect subject and attribute, nor should it be used substantively, but only as an auxiliary to verbs.

Negative (Col.).

ང་འདི་རུ་མི་ཡོང་། — *I shall not be here.*

ང་ཡག་པོ་མི་ཡོང་། — *I shall not be good.*

And so throughout, inserting མི་ before ཡོང་།

Interrogative (Col.).

ང་འདི་རུ་ཡོང་ངམ་ — *Shall I be here?*

ང་ཡག་པོ་ཡོང་ངམ་ — *Shall I be good?*

ང་འདི་རུ་མི་ཡོང་ངམ་ — *Shall I not be here?*

ང་ཡག་པོ་མི་ཡོང་ངམ་ — *Shall I not be good?*

(or ཡོང་ངས། in each of the above)

And so throughout. Also with ཨ་, or ཨེ་ Thus :—

ང་ཡག་པོ་ཨ་ཡོང་། — *Shall I be good?*

The other tenses (which really represent the Conditional) are as follows :—

ང་འདི་རུ་ཡོད་པ་ཡིན།	*I would be here.*
ཁྱོད་འདི་རུ་ཡོད་པ་འདུག, or ཡོད་པ་རེད།	*Thou wouldst be here.*
ཁོ་འདི་རུ་ཡོད་པ་རེད, or ཡོད་པ་འདུག།	*He would be here.*

ང་འདི་རུ་	ཡོད, or བྱུང, or འདུག	*I would have been here.*
ཁྱོད་འདི་རུ་		*Thou wouldst have been here.*
ཁོ་འདི་རུ་		*He would have been here.*

Literary.

ང་འདི་རུ་ཡོད་པར་འགྱུར་རོ།	*I shall be here.*

And so for all persons.

ང་འདི་རུ་ཡོད་པར་གྱུར་པ་ཡིན་ནོ།	*I would be here.*
ཁྱོད་འདི་རུ་ཡོད་པར་གྱུར་པ་འདུག་གོ, or རེད་དོ།	*Thou wouldst be here.*
ཁོང་འདི་རུ་ཡོད་པར་གྱུར་པ་རེད་དོ, or འདུག་གོ།	*He would be here.*
ང་འདི་རུ་ཡོད་པར་གྱུར་པ་ཡོད་དོ།	*I would have been here.*
ཁྱོད་འདི་རུ་ཡོད་པར་གྱུར་པ་འདུག་གོ།	*Thou wouldst have been here.*
ཁོང་འདི་རུ་ཡོད་པར་གྱུར་པ་ཡོད་དོ, or འདུག་གོ, or ཡོད་པ་རེད་དོ།	*He would have been here.*

SUBJUNCTIVE.

Phrases like *If I am, If I be, Should I be....then....I will or would be;* or, *If I were....then....I would be,* or *would have been,* are formed, for the present tense, by using the expression གལ་སྲིད་....ཡོད་ན, or འདུག་ན, or གལ་ཏེ་....ཡོད་ན, or འདུག་ན, or simply ....ཡོད་ན, or འདུག་ན for all persons, and then using the future root ཡོང་ Thus:—

Attributive Present.

གལ་ཏེ་ང་ཕྱུག་པོ་ཡོད་ན་སྐྱིད་པོ་ཡོང་། Or :— ང་ཕྱུག་པོ་ཡོད་ན་སྐྱིད་པོ་ཡོང་། Or ང་ཕྱུག་པོ་འདུག་ན་སྐྱིད་པོ་ཡོང་།	*If I am*, or *If I be*, or *should I be, rich, I will be happy* or *comfortable.*
ཁྱོད་ཕྱུག་པོ་ཡོད་ན་ (or འདུག་ན་) སྐྱིད་པོ་ཡོང་།	*If thou art*, etc., *thou wilt be happy.*
ཁོ་ཕྱུག་པོ་ཡོད་ན་ (or འདུག་ན་) སྐྱིད་པོ་ཡོང་།	*If he is*, etc., *he will be happy.*

For the past tense the construction is similar, save that ཡོད་པ་ཡིན་, etc., for *Would be*, and ཡོད་, or འདུག་, or བྱུང་ for *Would have been*, are used instead of ཡོང་, though for *Would be* ཡོང་ may also be used.

ང་ཕྱུག་པོ་ཡོད་ན་ (or འདུག་ན་) སྐྱིད་པོ་ཡོད་པ་ཡིན་, or སྐྱིད་པོ་ཡོད་, or འདུག་, or བྱུང་།	*If I were*, or *had I been, rich, I would be*, or *would have been, comfortable.*
ཁྱོད་ཕྱུག་པོ་ཡོད་ན་ (or འདུག་ན་) སྐྱིད་པོ་ཡོད་པ་འདུག་, or ཡོད་པ་རེད་, or སྐྱིད་པོ་ཡོད་, འདུག་, or བྱུང་།	*If thou*, etc., *thou wouldst be*, or *wouldst have been, comfortable.*
ཁོ་ཕྱུག་པོ་ཡོད་ན་ (or འདུག་ན་) སྐྱིད་པོ་ཡོད་པ་རེད་, or ཡོད་པ་འདུག་, or སྐྱིད་པོ་ཡོད་, or འདུག་, or བྱུང་།	*If he*, etc., *he would be*, or *would have been, comfortable.*

Substantively (Col.).

The construction is just the same as when used attributively.

Negative.

Same construction, but with མེད་ན་ instead of ཡོད་ན་, or འདུག་ན Thus :—

ང་ཕྱུག་པོ་མེད་ན་སྐྱིད་པོ་མི་ཡོང་།	*If I am not*, etc., *I will not be comfortable.*

The Literary attributive construction is :—

ང་ཕྱུག་པོ་ཡོད་ན་བདེ་བར་འགྱུར་རོ།	*If I am rich I shall be happy.*
ང་ཕྱུག་པོ་ཡོད་ན་བདེ་བར་གྱུར་པ་ཡིན་ནོ།	*If I were rich I would be happy.*
ང་ཕྱུག་པོ་ཡོད་ན་བདེ་བར་གྱུར་པ་ཡོད་དོ།	*Had I been rich I would have been happy.*

POTENTIAL.

Phrases expressive of *ability to be present*, or *ability to be anything* (e.g. good), are rendered with the aid of ཐུབ་པ་ *To be able*, or by that and other auxiliaries, added to the root of ཡོད་པ་ Thus :—

Present.

ང་འདི་རུ་ཡོད་ཐུབ་ or ཐུབ་ཡོང་, or ཐུབ་ཀྱི་ཡིན།	*I can be here.*
ང་ཡག་པོ་ཡོད་ཐུབ་ or ཐུབ་ཡོང་ or ཐུབ་ཀྱི་ཡིན།	*I can be good.*
ཁྱོད་འདི་རུ་ཡོད་ཐུབ་, or ཐུབ་ཡོང་, or ཐུབ་ཀྱི་རེད།	*Thou canst be here.*
ཁོ་ཡག་པོ་ཡོད་ཐུབ་, or ཐུབ་ཡོང་, or ཐུབ་ཀྱི་རེད།	*He can be good.*

Past.

ང་འདི་རུ་ཡོད་ཐུབ་པ་ཨིན་		*I could be here.*
ང་ཡག་པོ་ཡོད་ཐུབ་པ་ཨིན་	or ཐུབ་སོང་ །	*I could be good.*
ཁྱོད་འདི་རུ་ཡོད་ཐུབ་པ་རེད་		*Thou couldst be here.*
ཁོ་ཡག་པོ་ཡོད་ཐུབ་པ་རེད་		*He could be good.*

PROBABILITY.

Phrases expressive of *likelihood or probability of being present*, or of *being anything* (e.g., good), are rendered by means of གཅིག་བྱེད་ན with ཡོང་, or by means of ཡིན་པ་འདྲ་, or ཡིན་གྲོ་ Thus, Colloquially :—

Present.

གཅིག་བྱེད་ནང་འདི་རུ་ཡོང་ །	
ང་འདི་རུ་ཡོང་གི་ཡིན་པ་འདྲ།	*I may be here. Perhaps I shall be here. It is likely that I shall be here.*
ང་འདི་རུ་ཡོང་གི་ཡིན་གྲོ །	
ཁྱོད་འདི་རུ་ཡོང་གི་ཡིན་པ་འདྲ་ or ཡོང་ *Thou mayest be here.*	
གི་ཡིན་གྲོ །	
གཅིག་བྱེད་ནང་ཡག་པོ་ཡོང་ །	
ང་ཡག་པོ་ཡོང་གི་ཡིན་པ་འདྲ་ or ཡོང་གི་	*I may be good.*
ཡིན་གྲོ །	
ཁོ་ཡག་པོ་ཡོང་གི་ཡིན་པ་འདྲ་ or ཡོང་ *He may be good.*	
གི་ཡིན་གྲོ །	

N.B.—ཡིན་གྲོ, ཡོང་གྲོ, and similar expressions are sometimes written ཡིན་འགྲོ ཡོང་འགྲོ, etc. The correct form is probably གྲོ, but this is not quite clear.

Past.

གཅིག་བྱེད་ན་ང་འདི་རུ་ཡོད་, or འདུག། *I might be here.*

ཁྱོད་འདི་རུ་ཡོད་པ་ (or འདུག་པ་) ཡིན་ *Thou mightest be here.*
པ་འདྲ་, or ཡིན་གྲོ།

ཁོ་འདི་རུ་ཡོད་པ་ (or འདུག་པ་) ཡིན་ *He might be here.*
པ་འདྲ་, or ཡིན་གྲོ།

Similarly with ཡག་པོ་ *Good*, instead of འདི་རུ་ *Here.*

Negative.

As regards the phrases in which ཡིན་པ་འདྲ་ and ཡིན་གྲོ་ occur, the negative construction is to change these into མིན་པ་འདྲ་ or མིན་གྲོ, or མན་པ་འདྲ, or མན་གྲོ། Ex. :—

ང་འདི་རུ་ཡོང་གི་མིན་པ་འདྲ། *Perhaps I shall not be here.*

Literary.

This construction is in སྲིད་པ་ *To be possible*, combined, sometimes with the Verbal Root, but usually with the Infinitive in the Terminative case. Thus :—

ང་དེ་རུ་ཡོད་པར་ (or ཡོད་) སྲིད་དོ། *I may be there.*

ང་དེ་རུ་ཡོད་པར་ (or ཡོད་) མི་སྲིད་དོ། *I may not be there.*

ང་དེ་རུ་ཡོད་པར་ (or ཡོད་) སྲིད་པ་ *I might be there.*
ཡིན་ནོ།

ང་དེ་རུ་ཡོད་པར་ (or ཡོད་) སྲིད་པ་ *I might not be there.*
མིན་ནོ།

ང་དེ་རུ་ཡོད་པར་ (or ཡོད་) སྲིད་པ་ཡོད་དོ། *I might have been there.*

ང་དེ་རུ་ཡོད་པར་ (or ཡོད་) སྲིད་པ་མེད། *I might not have been there.*

There is also another construction in བགྲང་བ་ *To calculate, reckon*, used thus :—

དེ་ལྟར་ཡིན་བགྲང་།	*It may be so ; I reckon*, or *guess it is so.*

HORTATIVE.

Phrases like *Must*, *Ought*, *Should* (in these senses), *Need*, *Want*, etc., *to be*, are rendered by means of དགོས་པ་, or perhaps more Colloquially དགོ་བ་, or by that and other auxiliaries, added to the root of ཡོད་པ་ Thus :—

Present.

ང་འདི་ཙུ་ཡོད་དགོས། ང་འདི་ཙུ་ཡོད་དགོས་ཀྱི་ཡིན་, or དགོས་ཡོང་།	*I must be here. To me it is necessary to be here.*
ཁྱོད་འདི་ཙུ་ཡོད་དགོས་ཀྱི་རེད་, or དགོས་ཡོང་། ཁྱོད་འདི་ཙུ་ཡོད་དགོས།	*Thou must be here.*
ཁོ་འདི་ཙུ་ཡོད་དགོས་ཀྱི་རེད་, or དགོས་ཡོང་། ཁོ་འདི་ཙུ་ཡོད་དགོས།	*He must be here.*

Past.

ང་འདི་ཙུ་ཡོད་དགོས་པ་ཡིན་, or དགོས་ བྱུང་།	*I should have been here. To me it was necessary to be here.*
ཁྱོད་འདི་ཙུ་ཡོད་དགོས་པ་རེད་, or དགོས་ བྱུང་།	*Thou shouldst have been here.*
ཁོ་འདི་ཙུ་ཡོད་དགོས་པ་རེད་, or དགོས་ བྱུང་།	*He should have been here.*

Or (instead of བྱུང་) ཡོད་, or འདུག་ for all persons.

N.B.—If there is an adverb to show the tense, the Past may be constructed like the Present.

PURPOSIVE.

Phrases like *That....may* or *might be ; In order that....may* or *might be ; So that....may* or *might be ; In order to be*, etc., are expressed by means of the Infinitive put in the Genitive Case and followed by དོན་ལ་ or, in Literary Tibetan, ཕྱིར་དུ་, or དོན་དུ་ Thus :—

ང་འདི་རུ་ཡོད་པའི་དོན་ལ།	*That I may* (or *might*) *be here.*
ཁོ་བཙན་པོ་ཡོད་པའི་དོན་ལ།	*So that he may* (or *might*) *be safe.*

The Literary construction is to put ཡོད་པ་ in the Terminative Case followed by བྱ་ or བྱ་བ་ in the Genitive Case, and winding up with ཕྱིར་ Thus :—

ང་ཡོད་པར་བྱ་ (or བྱ་བ) འི་ཕྱིར། *That I may* or *might exist.*

Or the construction may be in འགྱུར་བ་ put in the Genitive Case and followed by ཕྱིར་ Thus :—

དེ་དག་ཐམས་ཅད་གཅིག་ཏུ་འགྱུར་བའི་ཕྱིར་རོ། *That they may all be one* (John xvii. 21).

IMPERATIVE.

ཡོད་པ་ does not seem to possess any Imperative Root of its own.

Regarded as a substantive verb, its Imperative would perhaps best be expressed, as in Literary Tibetan, by ཡོད་པར་གྱུར་, or, more emphatically, ཡོད་པར་གྱུར་ཅིག་, literally *Become being*, or *Begin to exist.* Thus :—

ཉིན་དགུང་ལ་འདི་རུ་ཡོད་པར་གྱུར་, or གྱུར་ཅིག། *Be here at midday.*

Such an expression, however, would probably never be used in fact. A Tibetan would ordinarily say :—

ཉིན་དགུང་ལ་འདི་རུ་ཤོག། *Come here at midday.*

If the idea of *origination*, or *becoming*, be implied, the proper Imperative would probably be བྱུང་ Negative མ་འབྱུང་།

Colloquially the Imperative of བྱེད་པ་, or, more elegantly, བགྱིད་པ་ or respectfully མཛད་པ་ *To make*, *To do*, *To act*, might be brought into requisition. Thus :—

ཉིན་དགུང་ལ་འདི་རུ་ཡོད་པ་བྱེས་(or better བྱས་ཤོག) *Be here at midday* ; i.e., *Make to be here, etc.*

(*N.B.*—བྱེས་ is vulgar Colloquial. བྱེད་ is sometimes used instead of བྱས་, but བྱས་ seems more correct.)

Negative :—

ཉིན་དགུང་ལ་འདི་རུ་མེད་པ་བྱེད་, or མེད་པ་བགྱིད་, or མེད་པ་མཛོད། *Do not be here at midday.*

Note that in *prohibitions* the Imperative takes the Present Root of the verb.

When used attributively the Imperative of ཡོད་པ་ is, in the Colloquial, formed with the auxiliary verbs བྱེད་པ་, བགྱིད་པ་ and མཛད་པ་ just mentioned. Thus :—

མགྱོགས་པ་བྱེད་, or བྱས་, or གྱིས་, or མཛོད། *Be quick.*

Negatively :—

མ་ཕྱི་པོ་བྱེད་ (or བགྱིད་, or མཛད་)།

Or :—

ཕྱི་པོ་མ་བྱེད་ (or བགྱིད་, or མཛད་)།

} *Do not be late.*

Another way, which, however, is rather Hortative than Imperative, is to use the auxiliary verb དགོས་པ་ In this case, there being no real

Imperative root, and what is said being only a statement of fact and not a command, the negative མི་, instead of མ་, is used. Thus :—

ཞེད་མི་དགོས། — *Do not be afraid.* Literally, *Fearing, or fear, is not necessary.*

This also, however, may be expressed in the usual way. Thus :—

ཞེད་པ་མ་བྱེད་ (or མ་བགྱིད་ or མ་མཛད་) or མ་ཞེད་པ་བྱེད། — *Do not fear ;* i.e., *Do not make fear.*

The enclitic particles ཅིག་ (after final ག་, ད་ or བ་, and after anything in the Colloquial), ཞིག་ (after all vowels, or after final ང་, ན་, མ་, ར་, or ལ་), and ཤིག་ (after final ས་), are only used for peremptory orders and stern commands. Ordinarily they are omitted. Even then the order is softened in various ways, e.g. by using the polite expression རོགས་བྱེད་, or the still politer one རོགས་གནང་ *Please.* Thus :—

བརྟན་བརྟན་གནང་རོགས་གནང་། — *Please be careful.*

སྙིང་རྗེ་མེད་པ་མ་བྱེད་རོགས་བྱེད། — *Please do not be cruel.*

When addressing equals or inferiors familiarly, the following constructions may be adopted :—

མགྱོགས་པོ་བྱེད་དང་ or བྱས་ཤིག་དང་། — *Now then, be quick ;* or *Do be quick.*

དེན་དེན་བྱེད་ཨ། — *Do be punctual.*

A more Literary form would be :—

སེམས་གསོ་བར་གྱུར་ཅིག་ཨང་། — *Now, do be comforted.*

PRECATIVE.

This is formed with the aid of Literary ཆུག་ or Colloquial བཅུག་ (the Perfect Root), Imperatives of the verb འཇུག་པ་ *To allow*, added in Colloquial to the Root, or, in Literature, to the Terminative case of the Infinitive.

Thus :—

ང་དང་པོ་ཡོད་བཅུག།
ང་དང་པོ་ཡོད་བཅུག་ཅིག།
ང་དང་པོ་ཡོད་བཅུག (ཅིག) རོགས་གནང་
or རོགས་བྱེད།
ང་དང་པོ་ཡོད་བཅུག (ཅིག) དང་།
ང་དང་པོ་ཡོད་བཅུག་ཨ། — *Let me be first.*

ཁོ་དང་པོ་ཡོད་བཅུག — *Let him be first.*

ངས་ཁྱོད་དང་པོ་ཡོད་བཅུག་མི་ཡོང་ — *I shall not let thee be first.*

ཁོས་ང་དང་པོ་ཡོད་བཅུག་གི་རེད་པས, — *Will he let me be first?*
or བཅུག་ཡོང་ངས།

Literary.

ང་དང་པོ་ཡོད་པར་ཚུག་ཅིག།
ང་དང་པོར་ཚུག་ཅིག། — *Let me be first.*

Or :—The root of the verb ཡོད་པ་ may be put in the terminativ case, and the auxiliary verb གསོལ་བ་ used. Thus :—

ང་དང་པོ་ཡོད་དུ་གསོལ་ལོ། — *Pray let me be first; I beg you t let me be first.*

PERMISSIVE.

This is formed with the aid of ཆོག་པ་ *To be allowed*. Thus :—

ང་འདི་རུ་ཡོད་ཆོག་ or ཆོག་གི་ཡོད། — *I may be here. I am allowed t be here.*

ཁྱོད་འདི་རུ་ཡོད་ཆོག་ or ཆོག་གི་འདུག། — *Thou art allowed to be here.*

ཁོ་འདི་རུ་ཡོད་ཆོག་ or ཆོག་གི་འདུག། — *He is allowed to be here.*

ང་འདི་རུ་ཡོད་ཆོག་པ་ཡིན་ or ཆོག་སོང་། — *I was allowed to be here.*

Negatively :—

ང་འདི་རུ་ཡོད་མི་ཆོག །
ང་འདི་རུ་ཡོད་ཆོག་གི་མེད། } *I may not be here. I am not allowed to be here.*

ང་འདི་རུ་ཡོད་ཆོག་པ་མིན་ or ཆོག་མ་སོང་། *I was not allowed*, etc.

Interrogatively :—

ང་འདི་རུ་ཡོད་ཆོག་གམ།
ང་འདི་རུ་ཡོད་ཆོག་གི་ཡོད་དམ། } *May I be here? Am I allowed to be here?*

ང་འདི་རུ་ཡོད་མི་ཆོག་གམ།
ང་འདི་རུ་ཡོད་ཆོག་གི་མེད་དམ། } *Am I not allowed to be here?*

ང་འདི་རུ་ཡོད་ཆོག་པ་ཡིན་ནམ་ or ཆོག་ སོང་ངམ། *Was I not allowed to be here?*

Optative.

This is formed with the aid of ཤོག, the Imperative of ཡོང་བ་ *To come.* Thus :—

ང་ (ལ་) དེ་རུ་ཡོད་ (པ་) ཤོག། *Oh, or Would, that I were there.*

The construction is the same for all persons.

In Literary Tibetan :—

ང་ (ལ་) དེ་རུ་ཡོད་པར་གྱུར། *Would I were there.*

And so for all persons.

Infinitive.

ཡོད་པ། *To be present, To exist.* Or, attributively, *To be anything* (e.g., *good*).

ཡོད་པ་ཡིན་པ། *To have been*, etc.

ཡོང་གྲོ་ (or ཡོང་རྒྱུ་) ཡིན་པ། *To be about to be.*

In Literary Tibetan the Infinitive is also ཡོད་པ་, but it is often seen in the terminative case, as ཡོད་པར་ Thus :—

ཁྱེད་ནི་ ··· སྟོན་པ་ཞིག་ཡོད་པར་ (or ཡིན་པར་) ངེད་རྣམས་ཀྱིས་ཤེས་སོ། — *We know that thou art a teacher.* That is, *We know thee* TO BE *a teacher.*

Again:—

ཁྱེད་ཀྱིས་རང་སུ་ཡོད་པར་ (or ཡིན་པར་) བསམས། — *Whom makest thou thyself?* Literally, *Who thinkest thou that thou art?* That is, *Who thinkest thou thyself* TO BE?

Colloquially these would be:—

ཁྱོད་ ··· སློབ་དཔོན་ཞིག་ཡོད་པ་ (or ཡིན་པ་) ང་ཚོས་ཤེས་ཀྱི་ཡོད། — *We know thee* TO BE *a teacher.*

ཁྱོད་ཀྱིས་རང་སུ་ཡོད་པ་ (or ཡིན་པ་) བསམ་གྱི་འདུག། — *Who thinkest thou thyself* TO BE?

Sometimes the plain root is found in Literary Tibetan used in an Infinitive sense. Thus:—

དེ་དག་གིས་ཁོང་ལམ་གྲོགས་ཚོའི་ནང་ན་ཡོད་བསམས་སྟེ། — *They supposing him to be (have been,* or *that he was) in the company* (Luke ii. 44).

Where mandatory Imperative verbs like *Tell*, or *Order*, govern (in English) an Infinitive, the proper way of rendering the phrase in Tibetan is to turn the Infinitive into an Imperative. Thus:—

ཁོ་ལ་ཕྱི་པོ་མ་བྱེད་ལབ། — *Tell him not to be late.*

ཁོ་ཚོ་ལ་ནམ་ལངས་ལ་འདི་རུ་ཤོག་ཅིག་ལབ། — *Order them to be here at dawn.*

Participles.

ཡོད་པ་ having only one root, the Present and Past Participles are the same and exactly like the Infinitive. Thus:—

ཡོད་པ་ *Being;* ཡོད་པ་ *Been.*

The Compound Perfect Participle is ཡོད་པ་ཡིན་པ་ *Having been.*

In Colloquial the Future Participle is ཡོང་རྒྱུ་ or ཡོང་གྲོ་ *About to be.*

Periphrastic Participle :—

In the Colloquial this is ཡོད་མཁན་ for animates, and ཡོད་པ for inanimates, the former meaning *who is*, or *was*, or *which is* or *was*, and the latter *which is*, or *was*. It is really used as a kind of adjective.

Examples :—

ང་ལ་ གཡོག་པོ་ དྲང་པོ་ཡོད་ མཁན་ ཞིག་ དགོས། — *I want a servant who is honest*

རྟ་འདི་རྒྱོལ་ཡོད་མཁན་ཞིག་རེད། — *This horse is a fleet one (one that is fleet).*

ཁྱོད་ཀྱི་གྲི་རྣོ་པོ་མེད་པ་ཞིག་རེད། — *Your knife is a blunt one.*

The Past is similarly constructed. Thus :—

ང་ལ་གཡོག་པོ་སྔོན་ལ་དྲང་པོ་ཡོད་མཁན་དེ་ དགོས། — *I want the servant who was honest.*

The Future may be constructed like the Present. Thus :—

ང་ལ་ གཡོག་པོ་ དྲང་ པོ་ཡོད་ མཁན་ ཞིག་ དགོས། — *I want a servant who will be honest.*

Or thus :—

ང་ལ་ གཡོག་པོ་ དྲང་ པོ་བྱེད་ མཁན་ ཞིག་ དགོས། — *Ditto.*

Or :—

ང་ལ་དྲང་པོ་ཡོང་རྒྱུའི་ (or ཡོང་གྲུའི་) གཡོག་པོ་ཞིག་དགོས། — *Ditto.*

In Literary Tibetan the Present Participle is also ཡོད་པ་ or other variant of the verb *To be*.

Examples :—

ཁྱེད་ ཁང་ མིག་ འདི་ནང་ ན་ཡོད་པ་ རྣམས་ལ་ གཏམ་ བྱེད་དོ། — *I speak to you who are in this room.*

དེ་ལས་ལྷག་པ་ཇི་ཡོད་པ་དེ་ངན་པ་ལས་འབྱུང་ངོ་།	*And whatsoever is (that which is) more than this is of the evil one* (Matt v. 37).
དམ་པ། དམ་པ། དམ་པ་ལགས་པའི་གཙོ་བོ་དཀོན་མཆོག་ཀུན་དབང་སྔར་ཡོད་པ་དང་། ད་ལྟ་ཡོད་པ་དང་།	*Holy, holy, holy, Lord God, Almighty, which was and which is* (Rev. iv. 8).
ང་ནི་…ད་ལྟ་མཆིས་པ་དང་སྔར་མཆིས་པ་དང་འོང་བར་འགྱུར་བ་ཡིན་ནོ།	*I am....which is, and which was, and which is to come.*

As the above examples show, the Past construction is similar, the context giving the tense.

The Literary Future for the Periphrastic Participle follows the lines of the Colloquial.

Other Literary Participial Expressions.

Present.

ཡོད་དེ་ / ཡོད་ཅིང་ } *Being ; as, since, when, after, while...is, are.*

ཡོད་པའི་ཚེ་ལ་ *At the time of being: when, while...is, are.*

ཡོད་ན་ *In* or *by being ; if, when...is, are.*

ཡོད་ལ་ *Being.*

ཡོད་ཀྱིས་ *Though, since, because...is, are.*

ཡོད་པའི་ཕྱིར་དུ་ or དོན་དུ་ *For being.*

Past.

ཡོད་དེ་ / ཡོད་ནས་ } *Having been ; as, since, when, after...was, were.*

ཡོད་པས་ *Because, since, when...was, were ; Having been.*

ཡོད་པ་ལས་ *After, since, because, when...was, were.*

ཡོད་ན་ *In* or *by having been ; if, when...was, were.*

ཡོད་པ་དང་ *Having been ; as, since, when, after...was, were.*

OTHER COLLOQUIAL PARTICIPIAL EXPRESSIONS.

Present.

ཡོད་ཙང་ *As, since, because,* etc., ...*is, are.*

ཡོད་དུས་ } *At the time of being ; when, while...is, are.*
ཡོད་པའི་དུས་ལ་ }

ཡོད་ན་ *In* or *by being ; if, when...is, are.*

ཡོད་ལ་ *Being.*

ཡོད་པའི་དོན་ལ་ } *For being.*
ཡོད་ལ་ }

Past.

ཡོད་པས་ }
ཡོད་པ་དང་ } *Because, since, when, after, as...was, were.*
ཡོད་པ་ལས་ }

SUPINE.

This is formed in Literature by putting the Infinitive in the Terminative case. Thus, ཡོད་པར་ *To be.* Or it may be formed by putting the Root in the same case. Thus ཡོད་དུ་ *To be.*

In Colloquial the supines are ཡོད་པ་, and ཡོད་རྒྱུ།

Verbal Noun.

In Literary Tibetan ཡོད་པ་ *To be,* is often seen turned into a Gerund, or Verbal Noun, by the addition of the Definite Article དེ་, or ནི་, or sometimes both. Thus ཡོད་པ་དེ་, ཡོད་པ་ནི་, ཡོད་པ་དེ་ནི་ *The being.*

EXAMPLE :—

གཙོ་བོ། ང་ཅག་འདི་རུ་ཡོད་པ་ནི་ཡག་པོ་འདུག།	*Master, it is good for us to be here.* Literally, *The being here is good* (Matt. xvii. 4).

The Colloquial Verbal Noun is simply the Infinitive with or without དེ་

EXAMPLE :—

དཔོན་པོ། ང་ཚོ་འདི་རུ་ཡོད་པ་ (དེ་) ཡག་པོ་རེད།	*Lord, the being here is good for us.*

§ 36. THE VERB 'TO HAVE.'

Like the Latin MIHI EST, or the Russian U MENYA YEST, *There is to me*, this verb in Tibetan is merely an adaptation of the Substantive Verb ཡོད་པ་ *To be*, with the subject put in the dative. But whereas, in Latin and Russian, this construction is only an alternative one, in Tibetan it is the only idiom used.

EXAMPLES :—

ང་ལ་ཨ་མ་ཡོད།	*I have a mother.*
ང་ལ་ཨ་ཕ་མེད།	*I have not a father.*
སྔོན་ལ་ང་ལ་མེ་མདའ་ཡོད།	*Once I had a gun.*
ལུང་པ་དེ་ལ་རྒྱལ་པོ་མི་ཡོང་།	*That country will not have a king.*

And so throughout the conjugation.

PERIPHRASTIC PARTICIPLE.

EXAMPLES :—

ཁྱོད་ལ་ཡོད་པའི་དད་པ་དེ།	*The faith which thou hast.*
ཁྱོད་ལ་སྔོན་ལ་ཡོད་པའི་དད་པ་དེ།	*The faith which thou hadst.*
ཁྱོད་ལ་ཡོད་རྒྱུའི་དད་པ་དེ།	*The faith which thou wilt have.*
སུ་ལ་ཡོད་པ་དེ།	*He that hath.* } (Matt. xxv. 29.)
སུ་ལ་མེད་པ་དེ།	*He that hath not.* }
ཇི་ཡོད་པ་དེ་ཡང་།	*Even that which he hath (ib.).*

§ 37. ཡིན་པ་ To Be.

Like ཡོད་པ་ this verb is used to express direct affirmation, or, with a negative particle, direct negation, and also to connect any subject with its attribute. It cannot, however, like ཡོད་པ་, be used to express *presence*, or *existence*, or the idea of *possession*. In other words, though ཡོད་པ་ may be employed in every case in which ཡིན་པ་ is used, yet ཡིན་པ་ never takes the place of ཡོད་པ།

It may be conjugated thus:—

Present Indicative.

Affirmative.

ང་ཡག་པོ་ཡིན།	*I am good.*
ཁྱེད་ཡག་པོ་འདུག, or occasionally རེད་ Very rarely ཡིན་	*Thou art good.*
ཁོ་ཡག་པོ་རེད། Or, occasionally:— ཁོ་ཡག་པོ་འདུག or very rarely ཡིན།	*He is good.*

Literary Tibetan.

ང་བཟང་པོ་ཡིན་ནོ།	*I am good.*
ཁྱེད་བཟང་པོ་འདུག་གོ། Or occasionally:— ཁྱེད་བཟང་པོ་ཡིན་ནོ།	*Thou art good.*
ཁོང་བཟང་པོ་ཡིན་ནོ།	*He is good.*

The plural being the same as the singular, it is omitted.

Honorific construction in Literary Tibetan :—

(Not used).	*I am good.*
ཁྱེད་བཟང་པོ་གདའོ།	*Thou art good.*
ཁོང་བཟང་པོ་ལགས་སོ, or གདའོ, or ལགས་པ་ཡིན།	*He is good.*

Colloquial Negative.

ང་ཡག་པོ་མིན་ (or vulgarly མན་)། — *I am not good.*

ཁྱོད་ཡག་པོ་མི་འདུག, or མ་རེད། — *Thou art not good.*

ཁོ་ཡག་པོ་མ་རེད།
Or occasionally :—
ཁོ་ཡག་པོ་མི་འདུག། — *He is not good.*

མིན་ is Literary, and both མིན་ and མན་ Colloquial. Whether Literary or Colloquial it is best to use མིན།

Interrogative.

ང་ཡག་པོ་ཡིན་ནམ་, or ཡིན་པས་, or ཡིན་པ། — *Am I good?*

ཁྱོད་ཡག་པོ་འདུག་གམ་, or འདུག་གས། — *Art thou good?*

ཁོ་ཡག་པོ་རེད་དམ་, or རེད་པས་, or རེད་པ།
Or occasionally :—
ཁོ་ཡག་པོ་འདུག་གམ་, or འདུག་གམ། — *Is he good?*

Literary.

ང་བཟང་པོ་ཡིན་ནམ། — *Am I good?*

ཁྱོད་བཟང་པོ་ཡིན་ནམ་, or འདུག་གམ། — *Art thou good?*

ཁོང་བཟང་པོ་ཡིན་ནམ། — *Is he good?*

N.B.—If and when, in the Colloquial, ཡིན་ is used with the 2nd person, it is generally when a question is being asked. It is hardly ever used in the Colloquial with the 3rd person, though it is not absolutely wrong so to use it.

IMPERFECT INDICATIVE.

Same as Present Indicative, the context generally showing what that tense is. Thus :—

ཁ་སང་ང་ཡག་པོ་ཡིན། *Yesterday I was good.*

ཁ་སང་ཁྱོད་ཡག་པོ་འདུག, or རེད། ,, *thou wast good.*

ཁ་སང་ཁོ་ཡག་པོ་རེད་, or occasionally འདུག། ,, *he was good.*

In Literary Tibetan the construction is similar, but of course the *Literary* forms of the verb must be used.

Another method is similarly to rely on the context for the tense, and to use ཡོད་པ་ཡིན་ for all persons, or to vary the last syllable according to the rule of the Present Indicative. Thus :—

སྔོན་ (Coll. སྔན་) ལ་ང་ཡག་པོ་ཡོད་པ་ཡིན། *Formerly I was good.*

སྔོན་ (Co སྔན་) ལ་ཁྱོད་ཡག་པོ་འདུག, or ཡོད་པ་རེད། ,, *thou wast good.*

སྔོན་ (Coll. སྔན་) ལ་ཁོ་ཡག་པོ་ཡོད་པ་རེད་, or ཡོད་པ་འདུག། ,, *he was good.*

The Literary form of this construction would be ཡོད་པ་ཡིན་ for all persons, preceded by སྔོན་, or other indication of tense; and བཟང་པོ་ would replace ཡག་པོ།

PERFECT AND PLUPERFECT INDICATIVE.

Same as Imperfect. Thus :—

སྔོན་ལ་ང་ཡག་པོ་ཡིན། *I have, or had, been good.*

And so forth, throughout all constructions.

FUTURE.

Same as in ཡོད་པ་, i.e. expressed by ཡོང་ for all persons.

The Literarv construction is :—

ང་རྫི་བོར་འགྱུར་རོ།	*I shall be a shepherd.*
ཁྱེད་རྫི་བོར་འགྱུར་རོ།	*Thou wilt be a shepherd.*
ཁོང་རྫི་བོར་འགྱུར་རོ།	*He will be a shepherd.*
ང་····པར་གྱུར་པ་ཡིན་ནོ།	*I shall have been.............*
ཁྱེད་··པར་གྱུར་པ་འདུག་གོ།	*Thou wilt have been. ....*
ཁོང་··པར་གྱུར་པ་ཡིན་ནོ།	*He will have been. ....*

When ཡིན་པ་ is used as an auxiliary to other verbs, we shall find that in the Colloquial there is another Future construction, namely, ···གི་ཡིན་ for the 1st person, and ···གི་རེད་ for the 2nd and 3rd persons.

Subjunctive or Conditional.

Same as in ཡོད་པ་, substituting ཡིན་ for ཡོད་ or འདུག་ wherever they occur, and, in the negative forms, མིན་ or མན་ for མེད་, in the first part of the sentence, but keeping the second part as it stands there. Thus :—

Present.

ང་ཕྱུག་པོ་ཡིན་ན་སྐྱིད་པོ་ཡོང་།	*If I be rich, I shall be happy.*

Past.

ང་ཕྱུག་པོ་ཡིན་ན་སྐྱིད་པོ་ཡོད།	*If I were rich*, or *had been rich, I would be* or *would have been happy.*

The Literary construction is :—

ང་ཕྱུག་པོ་ཡིན་ན་བདེ་བར་འགྱུར་རོ།	*If I am rich I shall be happy.*
ང་ཕྱུག་པོ་ཡིན་ན་བདེ་བར་གྱུར་པ་ཡིན།	*If I were rich I would be happy.*
ང་ཕྱུག་པོ་ཡིན་ན་བདེ་བར་གྱུར་པ་ཡོད།	*Had I been rich I would have been happy.*

Potential

Same as in ཡོད་པ་, substituting ཡིན་ for the ཡོད་ to which ཐུབ་ is annexed. Thus :—

Present.

ང་ཡག་པོ་ཡིན་ཐུབ་, or ཐུབ་ཡོང་, or ཐུབ་ཀྱི་ཡིན། — *I can be good.*

Past.

ང་ཡག་པོ་ཡིན་ཐུབ་པ་ཡིན། — *I could be good.*

Perfect.

ང་ཡག་པོ་ཡིན་ཐུབ་པ་ཡོད། — *I could have been good.*

Or :—

ཡག་པོ་ཡིན་ཐུབ་སོང་། (for all persons).

LIKELIHOOD.

The construction is the same as in ཡོད་པ་ Thus :—

གཅིག་བྱེད་ན་ང་ཕྱུག་པོ་ཡོང་, or ང་ཕྱུག་པོ་ཡོང་གི་ཡིན་པ་འདྲ་ or ཡིན་གྱི། — *I may possibly be rich.*

HORTATIVE.

Same construction as in ཡོད་པ, changing ཡོད་ into ཡིན་ Thus :—

Present.

ང་ཡག་པོ་ཡིན་དགོས། — *I must be good.*

Past.

ང་ཡག་པོ་ཡིན་དགོས་བྱུང་། — *I ought to have been good.*

PURPOSIVE.

Same as in ཡོད་པ, changing ཡོད་ into ཡིན་ Thus :—

ང་བཙན་པོ་ཡིན་པའི་དོན་ལ། — *In order that I may be, or might be, safe.*

The Literary construction is in འགྱུར་བ་ or ཡོད་པ་ or ཡིན་པ་ put in the genitive case and followed by ཕྱིར།

EXAMPLE :—

དེ་དག་ཐམས་ཅད་གཅིག་ཏུ་འགྱུར་བའི་ཕྱིར་རོ་ or ཡོད་པའི་ཕྱིར་རོ་ or ཡིན་པའི་ཕྱིར་རོ།	*That they may all be one.* (John xvii. 21.)

IMPERATIVE.

Literary.

བཟང་པོར་གྱུར་ (ཞིག)།	*Be good.*
མི་ཡིན་པར་གྱུར་ (ཞིག)།	*Be a man*

Colloquially.

As stated under ཡོད་པ།

PRECATIVE.

Same construction as in ཡོད་པ་, changing ཡོད་ into ཡིན་. Thus :—

ང་བླ་མ་ཡིན་བཅུག་ ང་བླ་མ་ཡིན་པར་ཆུག་ཅིག།	*Let me be a lama*

PERMISSIVE

Same as in ཡོད་པ་, changing ཡོད་ into ཡིན་ Thus :—

ང་བླ་མ་ཡིན་ཆོག་, or ཆོག་གི་ཡོད།	*I am allowed to be a lama.*
ང་བླ་མ་ཡིན་ཆོག་པ་ཡིན་, or ཆོག་སོང་།	*I was allowed to be a lama.*

OPTATIVE.

Same as in ཡོད་པ་, changing ཡོད་ into ཡིན་ Thus :—

ང་རང་ཕྱུག་པོ་ཡིན་ (པ་) ཤོག།	*Would I were rich.*

Literary.

ང་ཕྱུག་པོ་ཡིན་པར་གྱུར།	*Would I were rich.*

INFINITIVE.

ཡིན་པ་ *To be.* In Literary Tibetan it is the same.

ཡོད་པ་ཡིན་པ།	*To have been.*
ཡོང་གྱི་ (or ཡོང་རྒྱུ་) ཡིན་པ།	*To be about to be* (Coll.).
ཡིན་པར་འགྱུར་བ། ཡོང་རྒྱུ་ (or ཡོང་གྱི་) ཡིན་པ།	*To be about to be* (Lit.).

EXAMPLES :—

ད་མི་འདི་ག་འདྲས་ཆེན་པོ་ཡིན་པ་ལྟོས།	*Now, consider (see) how great this man was (to be).*

In Literary Tibetan :—

ད་མི་འདི་ཇི་ཙམ་ཆེན་པོ་ཡིན་པར་ལྟོས་ཤིག།	*Ditto.*
མི་འདི་ལུང་སྟོན་པ་ཞིག་ཡིན་ན་ཁོ་ལ་རིག་པའི་བུད་མེད་འདི་སུ་དང་ཅི་ལྟ་བུ་ཞིག་ཡིན་པ་དང་། སྡིག་ཅན་ཞིག་ཡིན་པ་ངོ་ཤེས་ཡོང་ཞེས་བསམས་སོ།	*This man, if he were a prophet, would have perceived who and what manner of woman this is which toucheth him, that she is (to be) a sinner.* (Luke vii. 39.)
ཁོང་གི་གནང་བའི་བཀའ་དེ་ནི་ཚེ་མཐའ་མེད་པ་ཡིན་པ་ཤེས་སོ།	*I know that his commandment is (to be) life eternal.*
ཁྱོད་ཀྱིས་རང་སུ་ཡིན་པ་བསམ། Or, in Literary Tibetan :— ཁྱེད་ཀྱིས་རང་སུ་ཡིན་པར་བསམ།	*Who thinkest thou that thou art, or thyself to be?*

Participles.

Present:	ཡིན་པ་	*Being*	(both in Coll. and Lit.).
Past:	ཡིན་པ་	*Been*	
Compound Perfect:	ཡོད་པ་ཡིན་པ་	*Having been*	
Future:	ཡོང་རྒྱུ་ ཡོང་གྲོ་	*About to be*	

Periphrastic.

Both in Colloquial and Literary Tibetan, Present and Past Tenses, this is:—

ཡིན་པ་, or ཡིན་པ་དེ། — *Who* or *which am, is* or *was.*

Examples:—

ལྷག་མ་ཡིན་པ་དེ་ཐར་བར་འགྱུར། — *A remnant (that which is a remnant) shall be saved.* (Rom. ix. 27.)

ཁྱོད་རང་གི་ཡིན་པ་དེ་བཞེས་ཤིག། — *Take that which is thine own.* (Matt. xxv. 25.)

ད་ང་པའུ་ལུ་ཁྱོད་རྣམས་ཀྱི་རྩར་ཡོད་པའི་དུས་སུ་དམའ་བ་ཡིན་པ་དང་། ང་མེད་པའི་དུས་སུ་ཁྱེད་ཀྱི་ཕྱོགས་སུ་སྤོབས་པ་ཅན་ཡིན་པ་དེ་རང་གིས། — *Now, I, Paul, myself, who in your presence am lowly among you, but being absent am of good courage toward you.* (2 Cor. x. 1.)

ཁྱེད་ཕྱི་པ་ཡིན་པ་རྣམས་ལ་གདམ་བྱེད་དེ། — *I speak to you that are gentiles.* (Rom. xi. 13.)

ངའི་འབངས་མ་ཡིན་པ་དེ་ལ་ངའི་འབངས་དང་གཅེས་པ་མ་ཡིན་པ་དེ་ལ་གཅེས་པ་ཟེར་བར་འགྱུར། — *I will call them my people which were not my people; and her my beloved which was not beloved.* (Rom. ix. 25.)

The Future Periphrastic Participle both in Colloquial and Literary Tibetan, follows the lines of ཡོད་པ།

Other Participial Expressions.

Literary.

Present.

ཡིན་དེ་ / ཡིན་ཞིང་ — *Being; as, since, when, after, while . . . am, is, are.*

ཡིན་པའི་ཚེ་ལ་ / ཡིན་པའི་དུས་ལ་ — *At the time of being; when, while . . . am, is, are.*

ཡིན་ན་ — *In or by being; If, when . . . am, is, are.*

ཡིན་ལ་ — *Being.*

ཡིན་གྱིས་ — *Though, since, because . . . am, is, are.*

ཡིན་པའི་ — *Of or for being.*

Past.

ཡིན་ཏེ / ཡིན་ནས་ — *Having been; As, since, when, after . . . was, were.*

ཡིན་པས་ / ཡིན་པ་ལས་ — *Because, since, when . . . was, were; Having been.*

ཡིན་པ་དང་ — *As, when . . . was, were.*

ཡིན་ན་ — *In or by being; If, when . . . was, were.*

Colloquial.

Present.

ཡིན་དུས་ / ཡིན་པའི་དུས་ལ་ — *At the time of being; When, while . . . am, is, are.*

ཙང་, or ཡིན་ཙང་ — *Being; because, since, as, when . . . am, is, are.*

ཡིན་ན་ — *In or by being; If, when . . . am, is, are.*

ཡིན་པའི་ — *Of or for being.*

ཡིན་ལ་ — *Being.*

Past.

ཡིན་པས་	*Because, since, when, after, as . . . was, were; having been.*
ཡིན་ནས་	*Having been; as, since, when, after . . . was, were.*
ཡིན་པའི་	*Of* or *for having been.*
ཡིན་པ་ལས་	*As, since, when, after . . . was, were.*
ཡིན་པ་དང་	*As, when . . . was, were.*
ཡིན་ན་	*In* or *by having been; If, when . . . was, were.*

Supine.

Literary: ཡིན་པར་, and ཡིན་དུ་ *To be.*

Colloquial: ཡིན་པ་, and ཡིན་གྱུ་ *To be.*

Verbal Noun.

Either ཡིན་པ *Being, To be,* or the Infinitive of the verb, which in itself includes the idea of *To be.* It may either be used alone, or, in the Colloquial, with དེ་, or in Literary Tibetan དེ་, or ནི་, or དེ་ནི།

EXAMPLES:—

རྒྱལ་པོ་ཞིག་ཡིན་པ་ (དེ་) མཚམས་ མཚམས་ཧ་ཅང་སྐྱིད་པོ་མ་རེད།	*Sometimes it is not very pleasant to be a king.*
ར་བཟི་བ་ (དེ་) ངོ་ཚ་པོ་རེད།	*It is shameful to be drunk.*
ཉེ་གནས་རང་གི་སློབ་དཔོན་དང་གཡོག་པོ་ རང་གི་དཔོན་པོ་དང་འདྲ་བ་ཡིན་པ་ (དེ་) ལྡང་གི་འདུག།	*It suffices for the disciple that he be as (to be as) his master, and the servant as his lord.*

N.B.—It must always be remembered that ཡིན་པ་ is never used substantively, but always in connection with some noun, adjective, or verb, into which its forms have to be moulded.

§ 38. The Verb.

I.—Preliminary. The Tibetan Verb denotes only a sort of indefinite happening or state, and this not of itself, but rather by means of certain auxiliaries, including the verb *To be*, which alone really constitutes the verb in a Tibetan sentence.

Thus:—

སོན་རྒྱབ་མཁན་གྱིས་སོན་རྒྱབ་ཀྱི་འདུག། Or ཞིང་པས་ (or སོན་བཏབ་མཁན་གྱིས་) བོན་འདེབས་ཀྱིན་འདུག་གོ།	*The sower is sowing the seed.*

Literally, this is: *By the sower, as regards the seed, a sowing is.*

In fact the so-called Verb is rather a kind of Noun, modified in its significations by the verb *To be*, according to the mood or tense of the latter. It possesses in itself no means whereby to distinguish between the active and passive voices; the singular and plural numbers are alike in construction; and, except as regards the auxiliary *To be*, all its forms can be used with any of the persons indiscriminately.

The changes or inflections undergone by the Tibetan Verb are effected in three ways:—

1. By structural alterations in the *Root*;
2. By making use of *Auxiliary Verbs*;
3. By resorting to divers monosyllabic *Particles* for the formation of Infinitives, Participles, Supines, etc.

II.—Roots.

These in Literary Tibetan are four:—1. Present; 2. Perfect; 3. Future; and 4. Imperative.

Thus:—

བྱེད་པ་ *To do, To make, To act.*

Present Root:	བྱེད་	*Do, Does, Doing.*
Perfect Root:	བྱས་	*Have* or *has done.*
Future Root:	བྱ་	*Will do.*
Imperative Root:	བྱོས་	*Do.*

However, every Tibetan Verb does not possess all four roots. Some only possess three. Thus :—

འཛག་པ་ *To drop, drip, trickle, leak.*

Present Root : འཛག་ *Drop, Drops, Dropping.*

Perfect Root : གཟགས་, or ཟགས་ *Have* or *has dropped.*

Future Root : གཟག་ *Will drop.*

Some possess only two roots. Thus :—

འགྲོ་བ་ *To go, To walk.*

Present and Future Root : འགྲོ་ *Goes, Will go.*

Perfect and Imperative Root : སོང་ *Have* or *has gone, Go.*

A Colloquial Imperative is རྒྱུག་ *Go.*

Many possess only one root for all tenses. Thus :—

མཐོང་བ་ *To see.*

གཟོ་བ་ *To remember.*

ཐུབ་པ་ *To be able.*

ཐོབ་པ་ *To receive, get, obtain.*

འགྲིག་པ་ *To suit, to agree, to be satisfied.*

Where, in Literary Tibetan, a verb possesses a special root for each or any of the different tenses, and for the Imperative Mood, that special root must be used for those tenses and that mood, save that when the Future construction is in འགྱུར་རོ་ or བྱའོ་ or བྱ་, the Present Root is retained instead of the Future Root. Where there is no special Future root or Imperative root, the Present root is used for the Future and Imperative. It is impossible, of course, to learn the root-forms of all the verbs, but there is no reason why those of the commoner verbs should not be memorized to some extent.

As regards the Colloquial, though it is quite allowable to use the roots that are assigned to particular moods and tenses for those moods and tenses, yet it is said that as a matter of fact, at least in vulgar Colloquial, this is seldom or never done, and the root generally used is the Perfect root. When, however, the Present root of a verb ends in an inherent ཨ་ (for instance, ལྟ་བ་ *To look*), or in an inherent འ་ (e.g., བཙའ་བ་ *To bear, or bring forth*), or in ུ (e.g., ཞུ་བ་ *To request, ask*), or in ོ (e.g., ཚོ་བ་ *To live, feed, nourish*), it is said that that Present root is generally used for the Present Indicative, the Future Indicative in གི་ཡིན་, or གི་རེད་, the Present Participle, Active Present Participle, Present Infinitive, Supine and Verbal Noun. If, in these verbs, the Future is formed with ཡོང་ instead of གི་ཡིན་ etc., the Perfect root (or perhaps more correctly the Future Root) must be used. Thus :—

ངས་ལྟ་གི་ཡིན།	*I shall see.*
ཁྱོད་ཀྱིས་བཙའ་གི་རེད།	*Thou wilt bear.*

But :—

ངས་བལྟ་ (ས་) ཡོང་།	*I shall see.*
ཁྱོད་ཀྱིས་བཙས་ཡོང་། (no Future Root)	*Thou wilt bear.*

In Literary Tibetan :—

ངས་ལྟ་བར་འགྱུར་, or བལྟ་རྒྱུ་ཡིན་, or ལྟ་བར་བྱ་, or བལྟའོ།	*I shall see.*
ཁྱེད་ཀྱིས་བཙའ་བར་འགྱུར།	*Thou wilt bear.*

The above idea that the Perfect Root should be used in the Colloquial probably arises from the fact that it sometimes has the same sound as the Future root. For instance, in the verb གཏོང་བ་ *To send*, the Perfect Root བཏང་ and the Future Root གཏང་ sound nearly alike.

Of course it must be remembered that the Colloquial, as such, pays no regard to *spelling*, but only to *its own phonetics*. Hence, if one writes Tibetan, one should spell properly. Therefore, also, if one attempts to *write* Colloquial, as such, it must always look wrong, as regards spelling.

In Compound Honorific verbs the first retains the Present root throughout, e.g., སྐྱབ་པ་གནང་བ་ *To provide.*

EXAMPLE :—

ཁྱོད་ཀྱིས་ང་ལ་སྐྱབ་པ་གནང་བ་རེད་ (pronounced གནང་ང་རེད་)།	*Thou providest for me.*

With all other verbs the vulgar Colloquial, it is said, usually adopts the Perfect root, if any, *or at least the sound of it*, as above explained, for all moods and tenses. Thus, for གཏོང་བ་ *To send, let go, dismiss*, the roots are :—

Present Root :	གཏོང་	*Send, Sends, Sending.*
Perfect Root :	བཏང་	*Have* or *has sent.*
Future Root :	གཏང་	*Will send.*
Imperative Root :	ཐོང་	*Send.*

In Literary Tibetan the Present Indicative is :—

ངས་གཏོང་ངོ་།	*I send.*
ངས་གཏོང་བར་བྱེད་ (or བྱེད་དོ་)།	*I do send.*
ངས་གཏོང་གིན་ཡོད། ངས་གཏོང་གི་ཡོད་	*I am sending.*

But in the vulgar Colloquial it is :— ངས་བཏང་, or གཏང་ *I send,* and ངས་བཏང་ (or གཏང་) གི་ཡོད་ *I am sending.*

In Literary Tibetan the Future Indicative is expressible in several ways with different roots. Thus :—

ངས་གཏང་ངོ་། ⎫
ངས་གཏང་རྒྱུ་ཡིན་ (or ཡིན་ནོ་)། ⎪
ངས་གཏོང་བར་བྱའོ་། ⎬ *I shall send.*
ངས་གཏོང་བར་འགྱུར་ (or འགྱུར་རོ་)། ⎪
ངས་གཏང་ཡོང་། ⎭

But in Colloquial it is :—

ངས་གཏོང་གི་ཡིན། ⎫
Or :— ⎬ *I shall send.*
ངས་བཏང་ (or གཏང་) ཡོང་། ⎭

There seems also to be an emphatic form in which ཡ་ is affixed to the Future root, and is followed by རེད་ for all persons. Thus :—

ངས་གཏང་ཡ་རེད། *I shall send; I am to send*, i.e., *by me a sending is to be.*

So, in Literary Tibetan the Present Participle is གཏོང་སྟེ་ *Sending;* the Active Participle གཏོང་མཁན་ or གཏོང་བ་ *He who*, or *It that, sends;* the Terminative Infinitive གཏོང་བ ་ར *To send ;* and the Supine གཏོང་དུ་ *For sending*, etc. ; but in Colloquial the Present Participle is བཏང་བ་དང་, the Active Participle བཏང་མཁན་, or བཏང་པ་; the Infinitive བཏང་བ་; and the Verbal Noun or Gerund and Supine བཏང་ཡ་, བཏང་རྒྱུ་, or བཏང་ལ་ The Literary Imperative is ཐོང་, or ཐོང་ཞིག་, but the Colloquial is གཏོང་, or གཏོང་ཅིག་, though ཐོང་ would be understood quite well. Vulgar Colloquial would be བཏང་ཅིག།

III.—Auxiliary Verbs.

These are ཡོད་པ་, ཡིན་པ་, འདུག་པ་, རེད་པ་ and other forms of the verb *To be*, which it is not necessary to specify here; བྱ་བ་, འགྱུར་བ་,

and འབྱུང་བ་ *To become, To happen, To take place, To occur;* འཚར་བ་ *To be finished, completed, terminated;* འགྲུབ་པ་ *To be made ready, finished, accomplished;* ཟིན་པ་ *To be ended, concluded, exhausted;* ཐུབ་པ་ and ནུས་པ་ *To be able;* འགྲོ་བ་ *To go*, but used idiomatically; དགོས་པ་ and བྱ་བ་ *To be necessary*, or *expedient* or expressive of the idea of *obligation* or *duty;* འཇུག་པ་ *To allow, suffer, permit;* ཆོག་པ་ *To be allowed* or *permitted;* བྱེད་པ་ *To make, do, act, perform;* བགྱིད་པ་ and མཛད་པ་ elegant and respectful forms of བྱེད་པ་; ཡོང་བ་ or འོང་བ་ *To come*, but used idiomatically; སྲིད་པ་, ཡིན་པ་འདྲ་, ཡིན་གྲོ་ *To be possible, probable, likely*, etc., etc.

IV.—Auxiliary Particles.

(1)—གི་, ཀྱི་, གྱི་, ཡི་, འི་ annexed to the Verbal Root according to rule, with reference to the final letter of the root (see § 25, iv). Used to connect the root with ཡོད་, ཡིན་, འདུག་ or རེད་ they form a periphrastical Present Tense. For example, in the Colloquial, which loosely uses the sound of the Perfect Root —

ངས་བཏང་། *I send.*

But:—

ངས་བཏང་གི་ཡོད། *I am sending*, or *I send.*

Sometimes, in the vulgar Colloquial, they are annexed to the roots of adjectives, taking the place of the adjectival particle པོ་, པ་, or བ་ Thus:—

ལམ་ཀ་རྩུབ་ཀྱི་རེད་ instead of ལམ་ཀ་རྩུབ་པོ་རེད་ *The road is rough.*

ཕྲུ་གུ་ཡག་གི་རེད་ instead of ཕྲུ་གུ་ཡག་པོ་རེད་ *The child is good.*

It is better, however, to use the adjective in full, and not to employ the construction in གི་, ཀྱི་ etc.

These Particles are sometimes used at the end of a sentence in the sense of a finite verb, and more particularly in the 1st Person Future.

EXAMPLES:—

ངས་བཙུག་གི། *I shall put in.*

ངས་རོགས་བྱེད་ཀྱི་, or བྱ་ཡི། *I shall help.*

(2)—གིས་, གྱིས་, ཀྱིས་, ཡིས་ These are annexed to the root as Gerunds, and signify *By* (doing something), or *Because*, *Since*, etc., but more usually antithetically as *But*, *Though*.

EXAMPLES:—

ངས་ཁོ་ལ་སྐད་བཏང་གིས་ཁོ་ སོང་པ་རེད། *I called him, but he has gone; or, Though I called him he has gone.*

ང་ཚོས་ འདི་ རུ་ ལངས་ ནས་ བསྡད་ ཀྱིས་ བལྟད་མོ་མཐོང་གི་ཡིན། *By standing here we shall see the tamasha.*

It may even be annexed to the root of the verb *To be.* Thus:—

ལོ་ རྒྱུས་ལེགས་པ་ཡིན་གྱིས། *Though it is a good story, or It is a good story but . . .*

When used antithetically a pleonastic འོན་ཀྱང་ sometimes follows—:

ཐོང་གིས་ ང་ ལ་ བསད་ ཀྱིས་ འོན་ ཀྱང་ ངས་ ཁོང་ལ་རྟོན་པར་འགྱུར། *Though he slay me, yet will I trust in him.*

When annexed to the root of an adjective it includes the verb *To be*. Thus:—

མོ་ གཟུགས་ བཟང་ གྱིས་ = མོ་གཟུགས་ བཟང་པོ་ཡིན་གྱིས། *Since, Because, or Though (she was, or is) of fine stature.*

(3)—གིན་, གྱིན་ ཀྱིན་, and ཡིན། Annexed to the root. These are Literary forms, and denote the Participle Present.

EXAMPLES :—

ཁོང་སྨོན་ལམ་འདེབས་ཀྱིན་ཕྱིན་པ་རེད། *He went on his way praying.*

Used to connect the root with ཡོད་, ཡིན་, འདུག་ or རེད་ they form a periphrastical Present Tense, just as གི་, གྱི་, etc., do in the Colloquial.

EXAMPLES :—

ཀྱེ་ཧོ་ང་ནི་འོང་གིན་ཡོད། *Lo, I come (am coming).* (Heb. x. 7.)

ཁོང་གླུ་ལེན་གྱིན་འདུག། *He is singing.*

When connecting the root with དང་ *Together with*, they are often used gerundially.

EXAMPLES :—

གཏོང་གིན་དང་། *In, when,* or *while sending.*

གླུ་ལེན་གྱིན་དང་། *In,* etc., *singing.*

བྱེད་ཀྱིན་དང་། *In,* etc., *doing.*

འགྲོ་ཡིན་དང་། *In,* etc., *going.*

Thus :—

གླུ་ལེན་གྱིན་དང་ལངས་ནས་སྡོད་པ་ནི་ཡག་ ཤོས་རེད། *In,* or *when, singing it is best to stand up.*

In the Colloquial this may be rendered :—

གླུ་ལེན་དུས་ (or ལེན་པའི་དུས་ལ་, or ལེན་པ་དང་) ལངས་ནས་སྡོད་ཡ་དེ་ཡག་ ཤོས་རེད།

(4).—ཏེ་ after final ད་

དེ་ after final ན་, ར་, ལ་, ས་

སྟེ་ after final ག་, ང་, བ་, མ་ and all vowels.

These are a sort of Continuative Particles or Suspensives, and may be annexed to all Present and Perfect roots, but according to rule, with reference to the final letter of the root. Annexed to Present roots they form a Present Participle, or Gerund, and, annexed to Perfect roots, a Past Participle, or Gerund. Thus, they may be rendered.... *ing*, or... *ing been*, or....*ing*....*ed*, or *As*, *when*, *after*, etc. They are Literary rather than Colloquial, though not altogether absent from the latter, and are largely met with in those subordinate clauses a longer or shorter string of which generally goes to the construction of a Tibetan sentence.

EXAMPLES :—

པི་ལ་ཏོ་དང་ཧེ་རོ་དེ་སྔར་གཅིག་དང་གཅིག་ཁ་མི་འཆམ་པ་ཡོད་དེ།	*Pilate and Herod were formerly (formerly having been) at enmity with each other.* (Luke (xxiii. 12.)
དེ་ནས་ཁོང་གིས་མི་ཚོགས་རྣམས་གཟིགས་ཏེ།	*And seeing the multitudes he*, etc. (Matt. v. 1.)
དེ་ནས་དགོངས་མོ་འི་དུས་སུ་ཉེ་གནས་རྣམས་མཚོ་འི་འགྲམ་དུ་སོང་སྟེ།	*And when even was come his disciples went (having gone) down to the sea*, etc. (John vi. 16.)

(5)— ཅིང་ after final ག, ད, བ, or the vowel ཨོ་

ཞིང་ after final ང, ན, མ, ར, ལ, and all vowels except ཨོ་

ཤིང་ after final ས་

This Suspensive, which is Literary rather than Colloquial, is annexed to the Root, and expresses in one or other of its forms the Present Participle, but sometimes also the Past Participle. It is also sometimes used instead of the conjunction *And*. Lastly, it often expresses a causal relationship. It is generally met with at the end of minor interpolations within subordinate clauses.

EXAMPLES :—

མགྱོགས་པོ་འགྲོ་ཞིང་དམག་དཔུང་སླེབས་སོང་།	*(By) Marching quickly the army arrived.*

དེ་ནས་ཡེ་ཤུ་གྲོང་ཁྱེར་དང་ཡུལ་ཚོ་ཀུན་དུ་རྒྱུ་ཞིང་།	*And Jesus went (having gone) about all the cities and villages.* (Matt. ix. 35.)
འཇིགས་ཤིང་འབོད་དེ།	*Being afraid and calling out.*
འོད་མེད་ཅིང་རླུང་མེད།	*Light not being, air is not;* or *Light is not and air is not;* or *Light and air not being;* or *Without light or air.* (*Das.*)
ཉལ་ཞིང་གཉིད་དུ་འགྲོ་བ།	*Lying down, to go to sleep;* or *To lie down and go to sleep.*
ནམ་མཁའ་ཕྱེས་ (perfect of འབྱེད་པ་) ཤིང་།	*The heavens having parted,* or *rent asunder.* (Mark i. 10.)

(6)— པས་ and བས།

These are merely the particles པ་ and བ་ of the Infinitive, or simple Participle, put in the Instrumental or Modal case. Practically they are equivalent to དེ་, ཏེ་, and སྟེ་ and the next noted Suspensive ནས་ They are often used as a variant of these, when the latter have already occurred in the same sentence. This is merely a matter of taste, to avoid repetition. Primarily they mean *Because*, *Since*, *Seeing that*, etc., but they also carry the sense of *When*, and of the Participle, both Present and Past. Both Literary and Colloquial Tibetan make use of them :—

Examples :—

ང་རང་གིས་བལྟས་པས།	*When I looked;* i.e., *I having looked.*
ཤིན་ཏུ་དཀའ་བ་ཡིན་པས།	*As, since, because it is very difficult;* or *It being very difficult.*
ང་ཡིན་པས་མ་འཇིགས་ཤིག།	*Since it is I,* or *It being I,* or *It is I, be not afraid.* (Matt. xiv. 27.)
དེར་སི་མོན་གྱི་སྒྱུག་མོ་ཚད་པའི་ནད་ཀྱིས་བཏབ་ (perfect of འདེབས་པ་) སྟེ་ཉལ་ནས་ཡོད་པས།	*Then Simon's mother-in-law having been seized by a fever-illness and having lain down.* (Mark i. 30.)

ད་ཁྱེད་ཀྱིས། ང་ཚོས་མཐོང་ངོ་ཞེས་ཟེར་བས།	*Now, since* (or *because*) *ye say, we see.* (John ix. 41).

(7)—ནས་. This Suspensive, both in Literary and Colloquial Tibetan, is annexed to the Perfect root, and expresses a Past signification. Otherwise it has practically the same functions as དེ་, ཏེ་, སྟེ་, པས་, and བས་. It means *After*, or *When*, and conveys also the idea of the Past Participle.

EXAMPLES :—

ཁོང་གིས་དེ་དག་ལ། ངའི་མ་དང་ངའི་སྤུན་སུ་ཡིན། ཞེས་གསུངས་ནས།	*He to them, my mother and my brother who is? Thus having said.* (Matt. xii. 48, and elsewhere).
ཁྱེད་ཀྱི་ལས་ཀ་ཚར་ནས་ཁྱེད་ཁང་པ་ལ་འགྲོ་ཆོག།	*When your work is finished you may go home.*
ཁྱེད་ཞོགས་གེའི་ཁ་ལག་བཟས་ནས་འཐོན་དགོས།	*After eating* (*having eaten*) *chhoti hāzirī you must set out.*
ང་ལོ་གཞོན་གཞོན་ཡིན་ནས།	*I have been* (*having been*) *young.*
སྔོན་ལ་ང་རྡོ་རྗེ་གླིང་ལ་ཡོད་ནས།	*I was formerly* (*having formerly been*) *in Darjeeling.*

Annexed thus to the Verbal Root, and followed by ཡོད་ or འདུག, it indicates either the Pluperfect (active), or the Perfect (passive). Thus :—

སྟག་གིས་ཤྭ་ལ་བཟས་ནས་ཡོད་, or འདུག།	*The tiger had eaten the deer.*
ཤྭ་ལ་བཟས་ནས་ཡོད་, or འདུག།	*The deer has been eaten.*
ང་ཁང་པ་ལ་ཕྱིན་ནས་ཡོད།	*I had gone home.*
ང་ (ལ་) དྲིས་ནས་ཡོད།	*I had been asked.*
ཤོག་སྒྲིལ་ནང་ན་ངའི་ཕྱིར་བྲིས་ནས་འདུག།	*In the roll-book it is* (*has been*) *written of me.* (Heb. x. 7).

(8)—ལས་. This particle has (perhaps) sometimes a Present but more often a Past signification, and is always found attached to the simple Participle in པ་ or བ་. It means *From;* or *When . . . . ed;*

or *Being . . . ed* ; or *Having been:* or *As* or *While*, followed by a Past tense ; or *As* or *While*, followed by a Present Participle (in which case the root of the verb is often repeated, the particle པ་ or བ་ coming next, and then the ལས་) ; or *When on the point of; When about to; When going to; Being about to*, or *on the point of*, when used with འགྲོ་བ་ or གཟམས་པ།

EXAMPLES :—

དེ་དག་གིས་ཁོང་ལ་ཡང་ནས་ཡང་དུ་བཀའ་འདྲི་ཞུས་པ་ལས།	*When they continued asking*, i.e., *again and again asked, him.* (John viii. 7).
དེ་ནས་ཁོང་ཕར་ཕེབས་པ་ལས།	*Thereupon as he passed by.* (John ix. 1).
དེ་ནས་ཁོ་སོང་ནས་ཡུལ་དེའི་ཁྱིམ་བདག་ཅིག་དང་འགྲོགས་ནས་བསྡད་པ་ལས།	*And he, having gone, and having associated with a householder of that country, after having settled.* (Luke xv. 15).
དེ་ནས་ཡི་ཤུས་ཡང་མཚོའི་འགྲམ་ལ་ཆོས་སྟོན་པ་ལས།	*Then Jesus, having begun again to teach by the seaside.* (Mark iv. 1).
ཁོང་གིས་ད་རུང་བཀའ་གསུངས་པ་ལས།	*And while he yet spake.* (Matt. xxvi. 47).
དེ་དག་སོང་བ་ལས།	*When they were going* (*As they went*). (Matt. xxviii. 11).
ཉེ་གནས་རྣམས་ཀྱང་སོང་བ་ལས།	*And the disciples as they went.* (Mark ii. 23).
དེའི་ཚེ་མི་གཉིས་ཞིང་ལ་ཡོད་པ་ལས།	*There shall two men be in the field*, i.e. *while being.* (Matt. xxiv. 40).
ཡང་དེ་དག་གིས་སྟེ་ཕན་རྡོ་རྒྱབ་ལ་བརྡུང་བ་ལས།	*And they stoned Stephen* ; or *As* or *while they stoned*, or *were stoning Stephen.* (Acts vii. 59).
དེའི་རྗེས་སུ་ཉེ་གནས་རྣམས་ཀྱི་ནང་ནས་གཉིས་ལམ་དུ་ཞུགས་ནས་ཡུལ་ཞིག་ཏུ་འགྲོ་བ་ལས།	*After that, two of his disciples, having set out on a journey, as they were going to a country.* (Mark xvi. 12).

ཡང་དེ་དག་ལམ་ལ་སོང་སོང་བ་ལས། *And as they went on their way.* (Acts viii. 36).

ཡང་དེ་དག་དེ་ལྟར་གཏམ་བྱེད་ཅིང་གཅིག་ལ་གཅིག་གིས་དྲི་བ་དྲིས་པ་ལས། *And while they, thus conversing, questioned each other.* (Acts xxiv. 15).

དེའི་ཚེ་ཤ་ཡུལ་ད་རུང་གཙོ་བོ་འི་གནས་རྣམས་ལ་དགྲར་སྣང་ཞིང་སྲོག་གཅོད་པ་ལ་རྔམས་ (Present root) པ་ལས། *And Saul, yet breathing out threatenings and slaughter against the Lord's disciples.* (Acts ix. 1).

པའུ་ལུ་ཞལ་འབྱེད་འགྲོ་ཡོད་པ་ལས། *And when Paul was now about to open his mouth.* (Acts xviii. 14).

བསད་པར་གཟམས་པ་ལས། *And should have been killed*, i.e., *being about to be*, or *on the point of being killed.* (Acts xxiii. 27).

(9)—ན་. This is expressive of *condition*, *hypothesis*, *contingency* and even *doubt*, and may be rendered by *If*, *When*, *On*, *Since*, *As*, *Should*, *Had*, *Were*, etc. It is generally added to the Root, but sometimes (though not often) to the Infinitive, and is much used at the end of verbal phrases both in the Colloquial and in the written language. Sometimes the phrase which it concludes is introduced by the expression གལ་ཏེ་ or གལ་སྲིད་, but the subjunctive idea is in no way affected even if this expression be omitted.

Examples of its use with the Root are given under ཡོད་པ་ (§ 35), and ཡིན་པ། (§ 37).

ན་ is also used in Literary Tibetan, adversatively, to express *Though*, *Although*. Thus:—

འདི་སྔོན་དུ་སྡིག་པ་སྤྱོད་པ་ཞིག་ཡིན་ན། *Although he was formerly a transgressor.* (Das.)

It also expresses the idea of *Reason for*, or *Causality*. Thus:—

འདི་ཡོད་ན་འདི་བྱུང་། *Since this existed, thát arose.* (Das.)

མེ་ཡོད་ན་དུ་བ་བྱུང་། — *Since fire existed, smoke arose.* (Das.)

ང་ལ་མཐོང་ན་ཀུ་མ་དེ་བྲོས། — *(On) seeing me the thief fled.*

Used with ནས་ it expresses *When*, or *If and when*. Thus:—

ནམ་ང་འགྲོ་ན། — *If and when*, or *when*, *I go.* (Das.)

ནམ་དུས་ལ་འབབ་ན། — *If and when*, or *when the time comes*, i.e., *it comes down to the time.* (Das.)

(10)—ལ་. Annexed to the Participle, this Suspensive may mean *To*, *At*, *In*; *With respect*, *regard*, or *reference to*; *Concerning*; *Relative to*; *In consequence of*.

Examples:—

གསོད་པ་ལ་དགའ་བ། — *To rejoice in killing.* (Jäschke.)

སྡིག་པ་ལ་འཛེམས་པ། — *To shrink from*, or *be afraid of* (i.e., *with respect to*) *sinning.* (Das.)

Annexed to the Root, it may be used for the Present Participle in a minor phrase, much like ཅིང་ and its variants. Thus:—

བདག་འཛིན་སྒྲོས་ཐོང་ལ་རང་གི་བརྒྱངས་ཞིང་ཁུར་ནས། — *Denying himself and taking up his cross.*

It is also often used like དེ་, ཏེ་, སྟེ་, but annexed to the Participle, and meaning *As*.

Examples:—

ལྷ་རྟེན་ཞིག་ཡོད་པ་ལ། — *As there is (was) an idol shrine.* (Das.)

རྒྱལ་པོ་ཉིན་རེ་བཞིན་དུ་དེར་ཁྲུས་བྱེད་དུ་འགྲོ་བ་ལ། — *As the king goes there daily to bathe.*

འཇིག་རྟེན་གྱི་ནང་ན་མི་འོང་བ་ལ། — *As it does not occur in the world.* (Jäschke.)

Annexed to the Root, it is used adversatively for *Though, Although.*

EXAMPLE :—

ཁོས་ལྟ་ལ་མ་མཐོང་བྱུང་། *Though looking, he did not see.*

Annexed to the Repeated Root, it expresses *While, Whilst.*

EXAMPLE :—

ངས་དཔེ་ཆ་འདི་ཀློག་ཀློག་ལ་ (གང་) ཟེར་ བ་དེ་བྲིས་ཞིག། *Whilst I am reading this book note down what I say.*

When annexed to adjectives, ལ་ includes the idea of the verb *To be*, being indeed an abbreviation of ཡིན་པ་ལ་ *Being*, and seems to have the force of *And*, or *But*, according to circumstances.

EXAMPLES :—

སྐྲ་དང་ཁ་སྤུ་སེར་ལ་རིང་བ། *Hair and beard being yellow and long.* (Das.)

ལུས་མི་སྡུག་ཅིང་ཐུང་ལ་དབྱངས་སྙན་པ། *Being ugly as to his body and of small stature and* (or *but*) *having a fine voice.* (Das.)

མི་སྡུག་ལ་ཐུང་ངུ་ཡིན་དེ། *Being ugly and short.* (Jäschke.)

དབྱིབས་ལེགས་ཤིང་ལྟ་ན་སྡུག་ལ་མཛེས་པ། *Being of good figure, nice to look at, and pretty.*

In double Imperative or Precative expressions, ལ་ has the force of the Present Participle, or of *And*, and is annexed to the root of the first verb.

EXAMPLES :—

ཤོག་ལ་ལྟོས་ཞིག། *Come and see (coming, see).*

ད་ལོང་ལ་ཚུར་ཤོག།
ད་ལྟ་ལངས་ལ་འདི་རུ་ཤོག། } *Now, rise and come hither (rising, come hither).*

སོང་ལ་ལྟོས་ཞིག།
རྒྱུག་ལ་ལྟོས། } *Go and look (going, look).*

In sentences like the following, where our Supine means *In order to*, or *For the purpose of*, ལ་, annexed to the verbal Root, is used Supinally both in Literary Tibetan and in the Colloquial.

EXAMPLES :—

འོ་ན་ང་ཟ་ལ་འགྲོ་གྱུ་ཡིན།	*Well, I am going to dine.*
བུ་གུ་ཁྱོད་རང་གི་ཡི་གེ་འཁྱེར་ལ་སླེབས་སོང་།	*The boy has come to get your letter.*

(11)—གྱུ་

When connecting a verbal root with the auxiliary verb ཡིན་པ་, or རེད་པ་, this particle forms, in modern Literary Tibetan, a Future tense which is practically a kind of periphrastic conjugation of གྱུ་ (as a Future Participle, *About to . . . .*) with the auxiliary verb.

EXAMPLES :—

ང་འོང་གྱུ་ཡིན།	*I shall come ; I am about to come.*
ཁོང་གསུང་གྱུ་མ་རེད།	*He will not speak ; He is not about to speak.*

It is also used in older Literary Tibetan to express *necessity*, *obligation*, *expediency*.

EXAMPLES :—

ང་འོང་གྱུ་ཡིན་ནམ།	*Am I to come ? Must I come ?*
ཁོང་གིས་རྟ་ལ་རྡུང་གྱུ་མིན།	*He ought not to beat the horse.*
ང་ལ་འབྲི་གྱུ་མང་པོ་ཡོད།	*I have many things to write.*

In the Colloquial གྱུ་, annexed to the verbal Root, is extensively used for the Infinitive.

EXAMPLES :—

ང་དེ་རུ་འགྲོ་གྱུ་མི་འདོད།	*I do not wish to go there.*
ཁང་པ་སླེབ་པ་ལ་འགྲོ་གྱུ་ག་ཚོད་ཡོད།	*How far have we to walk to reach home ?*

ཁྱོད་གང་ལབ་རྒྱུ་ཡོད།	*What have you to say?*
ཙ་ནས་ལབ་རྒྱུ་མི་འདུག།	*There is nothing at all to say.*
མར་འཆིབ་རྒྱུ་གནང་།	*Be pleased to rise.*
འདི་ཙ་རི་དྭགས་གང་ཡང་ཐོབ་རྒྱུ་ཡོད་ངས།	*Is there any sport (game) to be got here?*
ང་དེ་ཙ་ཡོད་རྒྱུ་མི་འདོད།	*I do not wish to be there.*

(12)— ལ་···· འདི་ (དི་)

In the Colloquial this particle, with or without the འདི་, is also xtensively used, annexed to the Verbal Root, to express what corres-pond to our Verbal Nouns in *ing*, i.e. the Latin Gerund.

EXAMPLES :—

ཆོས་སྐད་ཀློག་ལ་ (འདི་) ན་ཙང་མགོ་ འཐོམ་པོ་རེད།	*It is very confusing to read the Literary language : The reading of the Literary language*, etc.
རྫུན་པ་བཤད་ལ་ (འདི་) ན་ཙང་ངན་པ་ རེད།	*It is very wrong to tell lies : The telling lies*, etc.
ཟླ་བ་གཉིས་པ་སྐལ་བ་འཚོང་ཡའི་དུས་རེད།	*The second month (March) is the time for selling (of selling) shares.*
་མང་པོ་སྐད་ཁད་མཚར་པོ་འདི་སློབ་ དགོས་ཡའི་དོན་དག་ཡོད་པ་མ་རེད།	*Few people need learn this extra-ordinary language ; There is no meaning of many people having to learn this*, etc.

(13)—དང་

Both in Literary Tibetan and in the Colloquial this enclitic, used fter the Infinitive or Participle in པ་ or བ་, may be rendered *As*, *Vhen* (carrying a Past signification), and it also has the force of the 'ast Participle.

EXAMPLES :—

་དང་བཀའ་དེ་ནི་ཤ་ཙ་གྱུར་པ་དང་།	*And the Word became (having become) flesh.* (John i. 14).

ས་མར་ཡཱ་ཡུལ་གྱི་བུད་མེད་ཅིག་ཆུ་ལེན་ལ་ འོངས་པ་དང་། — *There cometh a woman of Samaria (a woman of Samaria having come) to draw water.* (John iv. 7).

ཐོག་མར་བཀའ་ཡོད་ལགས་པ་དང་། — *In the beginning was the Word (the Word having been).* (John i. 1).

ཁྱོད་རྣམས་ཀྱིས་ནམ་མཁའ་ཕྱེས་པ་དང་ ... མཐོང་བར་འགྱུར་རོ། — *Ye shall see the heavens opened and*, etc. (*The heavens having opened, ye shall see*, etc.). (John i. 51).

དེ་ནས་རྩིས་པའི་རྩིས་ལ་ལོ་ཁམས་མཐུན་པོ་ ཡོད་པ་དང་། — *Then, in the calculator's computations the year omens having been harmonious.*

ཁོ་མི་ཚང་དེའི་ཁང་པ་ལ་སླེབས་པ་དང་། — *When he has arrived (He having arrived) at the house of the family.*

ཡང་ལོ་གཅིག་ཙམ་སོང་བ་དང་། — *When about a year had elapsed.*

དེ་ནས་གཞུག་ལ་ཆང་ས་དེ་ཚར་ར་དང་། — *When at last the wedding was over.*

དྲིལ་ཆེན་དེ་དཀྲོལ་བ་དང་། — *As the big bell was tolled.*

In Literary Tibetan, especially in Western Tibet, དང་ is often used gerundially with the Present Participle in གིན་, གྱིན་, etc., and means *In*, *When*, *While*, etc.

EXAMPLE :—

གླུ་ལེན་གྱིན་དང་ལངས་ནས་སྡོད་པ་ནི་ཡག་ ཤེས་རེད། — *When singing, it is best to stand up.*

In Literary Tibetan, and especially of late in the Colloquial, it is used as a familiar form of the Imperative, and implies *advice*, *exhortation* and *entreaty*.

EXAMPLES :

འོ་ན་ཁྱོད་ཀྱི་ཁ་ལག་ཟོས་ (ཤིག་) དང་། — *Oh, do eat your food.*

ཁྱོད་རང་གི་ཡིག་རྒྱུགས་སློབ་ (ཅིག་) དང་། — *Do learn your lesson.*

(14)—དུ་ after ང་, ད་, ན་, མ་, ར་, ལ་

ཏུ་ after ག་, བ་, དདྲག་

ར་ }
རུ་ } after vowels.

སུ་ after ས་

ལ་ after anything.

These particles, as Verbal Auxiliaries, are extensively used in Literary Tibetan to express the Infinitive Future and the Supine. They are seldom, if at all, used in the Colloquial, save by those who affect Literary forms.

EXAMPLES :—

སུ་རྒྱལ་བ་དེ་ལ་ངས་སྲོག་གི་ཤིང་ལས་ཟ་རུ་
འཇུག་པར་འགྱུར་རོ། — *To him that overcometh will I give* TO EAT *of the tree of life.* (Rev. ii. 7).

སུ་རྒྱལ་ བ་དེ་ལ་ ངས་ང་ རང་ དང་ མཉམ་དུ་
ངའི་ཁྲི་ལ་སྡོད་དུ་འཇུག་པར་འགྱུར་རོ། — *To him that overcometh will I grant* TO SIT *with me in my throne.* (Rev. iii. 21).

ཡིག་སྐྲིལ་ དེ་ འབྱེད་ ཅིང་ དེའི་ ཐུག་ དམ་
རྣམས་གཅོག་པར་འོས་པ་སུ་ཡིན། — *Who is worthy to open (opening) the book and* TO LOOSE *the seals thereof?* (Rev. v. 2).

་དག་ ལ་མི་ རྣམས་ མི་ གསོད་ པར་ ཟླ་ བ་
ལྔའི་ བར་ དུ་ སྡུག་ བསྔལ་ གཏོང་ དུ་ འཇུག་
པའི་དབང་བསྐུར་བར་གྱུར་ཏོ། — *And to them it was given that they should not kill them (not* TO KILL *them) but that they should be tormented (but* TO BE TORMENTED*) five months.* (Rev. ix. 5).

ོད་ཚོའི་ནང་ན་འཇིགས་ པ་ མེད་ པར་ ཁྱེད་
དང་མཉམ་དུ་འདུག་པར་ལྟོས་ཤིག། — *See that he* BE *with you without fear.* (1 Cor. xvi. 10).

ན་ཀྱང་ངའི་ གཡས་ སམ་གཡོན་ལ་སྡོད་དུ་
འཇུག་པ་ནི་ངའི་དབང་ལ་མེད། — *But* TO SIT *on my right hand or on my left hand is not mine to give.* (Mark x. 40).

ཡང་གཙོ་བོ་འི་གཡོག་པོ་མི་ལ་ཆོས་སློབ་ཏུ་རུང་སྟེ། — *And the Lord's servant being apt* TO TEACH. (2 Tim. ii. 24).

སྔ་དྲོ་ལ་བླ་མས་ཁྱེད་ལ་དགོན་པ་ལ་སྨོན་ལམ་འདེབས་སུ་འཇུག་པར་འགྱུར་རོ། — *The Lama will allow you* TO OFFEF *prayers to-morrow in the monastery.*

དེ་དག་གིས་ཁོང་ལ་ཁྱིམ་རྩིག་ཏུ་བཅུག་སོང་། — *They have allowed him* TO BUILI *the house.*

The last of these particles, namely ལ་, is not much used in this connection in Literary Tibetan. It may, however, be so used insteac of any of the others.

EXAMPLE :—

ང་ལྟ་ལ་འགྲོ་འོ། — *I go to see.*

(15)—བཞིན་ and བཞིན་དུ་. Annexed to verbal Roots, བཞིན་ has, i Literary Tibetan, the force of the Present Participle, and, with པ added, may be used as an adjective; while བཞིན་དུ་ serves as a Gerund meaning *As*, *While*, or *Whilst*, and also *Though*, and *Because*, or *Since* according to circumstances.

EXAMPLES :—

ང་འགྲོ་བཞིན་མཆིས། — *I am going.* (Elegant form).

ང་ལ་ཆགས་བཞིན་པའི་ལྟ་སྟངས་ཞིག་དང་བལྟས་སོ། — *He glanced at me with a lovi look.*

བླ་མ་རྣམས་ཀྱིས་དགོན་པ་ལ་འཇུག་བཞིན་དུ་གླུ་བླངས་སོ། — *As the Lamas entered the monaste (while entering the monaster they chanted hymns.*

ཁོང་ལ་གསོལ་ཇ་ཡོད་བཞིན་དུ་མ་བཞེས་སོ། — *Though he had tea he did not dri*

ཆང་ཁོང་གི་སྔོན་དུ་ཡོད་བཞིན་དུ་འཐུངས་སོ། — *Since the beer was in front of h he drank.*

(16)—ཙང་.

This is a Colloquial Suspensive. Added to the verbal Root, it means *As*, *Since*, *Because*, and implies either Present or Past.

EXAMPLES :—

འོ་ན་ཁྱོད་འགྲོ་ཙང་ངའི་རྟ་ལ་ཞོན་དང་། *Well, as you are going, ride my horse, do.*

ཁྱོད་ཀྱིས་དཔེ་ཆ་བཏང་ཙང་ངས་དེ་ཀློག་གི་ཡིན། *As you have sent the book, I will read it*

(17)— དུས་ and དུས་ལ།

These also are much used Colloquially. Annexed to the verbal Root དུས་ acts as a Gerund, meaning *As*, *When*, *While*, *At the time of*, etc.

EXAMPLES :—

ཁྱོད་ཀྱིས་འབྲི་དུས་ག་རེ་ཟེར་ར་ (བ་) དེ་ལ་བརྟན་བརྟན་གྱིས། *When writing take care what you say.*

ཁོ་ཐོན་དུས་ཁ་ཚོག་ཚོག་བྱས་པ་རེད། *As he went off, he smiled.*

དུས་ལ་ has the same meaning, but is annexed to the simple Infinitive, or Participial form of the verb, put into the genitive case.

EXAMPLES :—

ཁྱོད་ཀྱིས་འབྲི་བའི་དུས་ལ་ཟེར་ར་ (བ་) དེ་ལ་བརྟན་བརྟན་གྱིས། *When writing take care what you say.*

ཁོ་འཐོན་པའི་དུས་ལ་ཁ་ཚོག་ཚོག་བྱས་པ་རེད། *As he went off, he smiled.*

A Literary equivalent of དུས་ལ is ཚེ་ལ།

V.—MOODS AND TENSES.

A.—*Infinitive Mood.*

The Infinitive, both in Literature and in the Colloquial, is the simple form of the verb as given in dictionaries, i.e. the Root, with པ་ or བ་

annexed, according to the rule regarding the final letter of the root. It is the same as the Participial form, and also as the form of the verb regarded as a substantive. Thus བྱེད་པ་ may mean *To do*, or *Doing*, or *A, or the, doing*.

Each root can be regarded as the basis of a special Infinitive. Thus:—

Present:	གཏོང་བ་	*To send.*
Perfect:	བཏང་བ་ བཏང་ཚར་བ་ བཏང་བ་ཡིན་པ་ བཏང་ཡོད་པ་	*To have sent.*
Future:	གཏང་བ་ གཏང་རྒྱུ་ཡིན་པ་ གཏང་གྲོ་ཡོད་པ་ གཏོང་རྒྱུ་ཡིན་པ་	*To be about to send*, or *To be sent.*

In Tibetan the latter of two related English verbs takes precedence of the other, and may be put in the Infinitive, or in the Genitive form of the Infinitive. Thus:—

ང་ཁང་པ་ལ་འགྲོ་བ་འདོད།
ང་ཁང་པ་ལ་འགྲོ་བའི་འདོད་པ་ཡོད། } *I wish to go home.*

At the same time the Colloquial construction by which རྒྱུ་ is added to the verbal Root has largely taken the place of the Infinitive. Thus:—

ང་ཁང་པ་ལ་འགྲོ་རྒྱུ་འདོད། *I wish to go home.*

ད་ལྟ་འཚོང་བའི་ (or འཚོང་རྒྱུའི་) དུས་
འདི་རེད། } *Now is the time to sell.*

In conversation, however, it is quite allowable and common to omit the པ or བ་ of the verb that is governed by the other. Thus :—

ང་ཁང་པ་ལ་འགྲོ་འདོད། — *I wish to go home.*

ང་སྣག་ཚ་དང་སྨྱུ་གུས་འབྲི་མི་འདོད། — *I am unwilling to write with ink and pen.*

This is particularly the case where the governing verb is ཐུབ་པ་ *To be able*, ཆོག་པ་ *To be allowed*, འཇུག་པ་ *To allow*, དགོས་པ་ *To be necessary*; *must*, *ought*, and the like.

EXAMPLES :—

ངས་རིའི་སྟེང་ལ་ཡོད་པའི་གངས་མཐོང་མི་ཐུབ། — *I cannot see the snow on the hill.*

ང་ཚོས་ཁང་མིག་འདིའི་ནང་ལ་ཐ་མག་འཐེན་ཆོག་གི་རེད་དམ་ or ཆོག་གམ། — *Are we allowed to smoke in the room?*

ང་ཚོ་འཐོན་བཅུག། — *Let us go away.*

ངས་ཁྱེད་ལ་འཐོན་འཇུག། — *I allow you to depart.*

གསོན་པའི་དོན་ལ་ཟ་དགོས། — *In order to live it is necessary to eat.*

ཁྱེད་བསླབ་གྲྭ་ལ་འགྲོ་དགོས། — *You must go to school.*

ཁྱེད་ཀྱིས་ཕྲུ་གུ་དེ་རྡུང་མི་དགོས། — *You ought not to beat that child.*

Where the governing verb is one of *Knowing*, *Saying*, *Hearing*, *Thinking*, or the like, the governed verb, in sentences like the following, is put in the Infinitive, or else the verbal Root, with ཀྱི་ annexed, is used.

EXAMPLES :—

ཁྱེད་འདི་རུ་ཡོད་པ་ངས་མ་ཤེས། — *I did not know that you were here (you to be here).*

ཁྱོད་ག་པ་འགྲོ་བ་ (or འགྲོ་རྒྱུ་) ངས་མི་ཤེས། — *I do not know where you are going (you to be going).*

ལོ་རྒྱུས་ཀྱིས་ སངས་ རྒྱས་ སྔར་ རྒྱལ་པོ་ ཡིན་པ་ (or ཡིན་རྒྱུ་) བཤད། — *History relates that Buddha was (Buddha to have been) at first a king.*

ཁྱོད་རྡོ་རྗེ་གླིང་ལ་འགྲོ་བ་ (or འགྲོ་རྒྱུ་) ངས་གོ་བ་ཡིན། — *I heard you were going (you to be going) to Darjeeling.*

ཁྱོད་རྡོ་རྗེ་གླིང་ལ་ཐོན་པ་ཡིན་པ་ངས་གོ་བ་ཡིན། — *I heard you had left (you to have left) for Darjeeling.*

ངས་ཁྱོད་ཀྱིས་རྟ་ཉོས་པ་ཡིན་པ་བསམས། — *I thought you had bought (to have bought) the horse.*

ཁོ་ཚོས་ང་ལ་ལས་ཀ་དེ་བཅོལ་བ་ཡིན་པ་མཐོང་ནས། — *When they saw that the work had been entrusted to me (the work to have been entrusted to me).*

The same construction is also used in connection with phrases like *It were better that, It is evident that.*

ཁོའི་སྐེ་ལ་རྡོ་ཆེན་པོ་ཞིག་བསྡམས་ནས་ཁོ་རྒྱ་མཚོའི་ནང་ལ་དབྱུག་རྒྱུ་ཡག་པོ་རེད། — *It were better that a large stone were bound on his neck and he were (he to be) cast into the sea.* (Mark ix. 42).

བཀའ་ཁྲིམས་ཀྱི་སྒོ་ནས་སུ་ཡང་དཀོན་མཆོག་གི་སྤྱན་སྔར་དྲང་དེ་དག་པ་ཡིན་པ་ངེས་ཀྱི་རེད། — *It is evident that no one is justified by the law in God's sight.* (Gal. iii. 11).

In phrases containing *That, So that, In order that, With the object of, To the end that, For the purpose of,* the verb is put in the genitive case of the Infinitive, and is followed by དོན་ལ་ in the Colloquial, and by ཕྱིར་ or ཕྱིར་དུ་ or དོན་དུ་ in Literary Tibetan.

EXAMPLES :—

ང་འདི་རུ་ཡོད་པའི་དོན་ལ།
ང་འདི་རུ་ཡོད་པའི་ཕྱིར། } *In order that I may, or might, be here.*

ཁོ་ནང་ལ་འགྲོ་བའི་དོན་ལ། ཁོང་ནང་ལ་འགྲོ་བའི་ཕྱིར་དུ།	*So that he may*, or *might, go home.*
ལ་ཡི་ཐུག་ལ་འཛེག་པའི་དོན་ལ།	*With the object of climbing to the pass.*
ཁྱོད་ཀྱིས་ཁོ་ངོ་ཤེས་པའི་དོན་ལ། ཁྱེད་ཀྱིས་ཁོང་ངོ་ཤེས་པའི་ཕྱིར་དུ།	*To the end that you should know him.*
ཁང་པ་འདི་རྩིག་པའི་དོན་ལ་ or ཕྱིར་དུ་ or དོན་དུ།	*For the purpose of building the house.*

Where, in English, a mandatory Imperative governs a verb in the Infinitive, e.g. *Order him to come*, *Tell him not to go*, the Tibetan construction puts the governed verb also in the Imperative, not the Infinitive, mood.

EXAMPLES :—

ཁོ་ལ་ཤོག་ (ཅིག་) ལབ།	*Tell him, come (to come).*
ཁོ་ལ་མ་འགྲོ་ (ཞིག་) བཀའ་གནང་།	*Order him, do not go (not to go).*
བརྟན་བརྟན་བྱིས། སུས་ཀྱང་ཁྱོད་སླུ་བ་ས་འཛུག།	*Take care that no man lead you astray.*

Whenever it is possible to turn a verb into a Verbal Noun, or what is called in Latin a Gerund, it should be done.

EXAMPLES :—

ཀ་ལི་ཀ་ཏ་ལ་སྡོད་པ་ (འདི་) ལས་རྡོ་རྗེ་གླིང་ལ་ཡོད་པ་ (འདི་) (or ཡོད་ས་ or ཡོད་རྒྱུ་) ཡག་ག་རེད།	*It is better to be in Darjeeling than in Calcutta*, i.e. *the being in Darjeeling is better than the staying in Calcutta.*
ང་རང་ལ་འཚོ་བ་ (ནི་) མ་ཤི་ཀ་ཡིན། འཆི་བ་ (ནི་) ཡང་ཕན་པའི་དོན་ཡིན་ནོ།	*For to me to live is Christ and to die is gain.* (Philipp. i. 21).

B.—The Supine.

The genius of the Tibetan language is so different from that of other languages, both Eastern and Western, ancient or modern, that to speak of Supines, Gerunds, and the like, in connection with it, is at least to strain the limits of analogy, if not to indulge in the illegitimate. But, so long as this is remembered, the Supine of Literary Tibetan may be said to be susceptible of several constructions. First, it may appear in the shape of the Infinitive put in the Terminative case with ར་

EXAMPLES:—

ཐུས་ཀྱང་ཉན་གོ་བར་ནུས་པ་དེ་ཉན་གོ་བར་བྱོས་ཤིག། — *He that is able to receive (hear) it let him receive (hear) it.* (Matt. xix. 12).

མི་རིགས་པ་དེ་བཟོད་པར་ཞུ། — *I ask to be forgiven this wrong.* (2 Cor. xii. 13).

ཁྱོད་ནི་གཟི་བརྗིད་བཞེས་པར་འོས་པ་ལགས་སོ། — *Worthy art thou to receive glory.* (Rev. iv. 11).

ངས་འབྲི་བར་གཟས་པ་ལས། — *I was about to write.* (Rev. x. 4).

འགྲོན་པོ་རྣམས་ལ་གནས་ཚང་སྦྱིན་པར་མ་རྗེད་ཅིག། — *Forget not to show love unto (bestow love on) strangers.* (Heb. xiii. 2).

Secondly, it may take the form of the Verbal Root, with རུ་, དུ་, ཏུ་, སུ་, or, less frequently, ལ་, annexed.

EXAMPLES:—

ང་ནི་ཆོས་དྲང་པོ་འི་མི་རྣམས་འབོད་དུ་མ་འོངས་ཀྱིས། སྡིག་ཅན་རྣམས་འབོད་དུ་འོངས་སོ། — *I came not to call the righteous but sinners.* (Mark ii. 17).

འདི་དག་གི་མགོ་ལ་ཕྱག་བཞག་སྟེ་སྨོན་ལམ་གདབ་ཏུ། — *That he should lay his hands on their heads and pray.* (Matt. xix. 13).

ངས་ཁོང་ལ་སྲོག་གི་ཤིང་ལས་ཟ་རུ་འཇུག་པར་འགྱུར་རོ། — *I will give him to eat of the tree of life.*

ཤུམ་པ་འདི་འགས་སུ་འདུག། — *This bottle is (likely) to crack.*

ཁོང་ཆིབས་པ་ཞིག་གཟིགས་ལ་ཕེབས་སོ། — *He has gone to buy a horse.*

Thirdly, it may appear as the Infinitive, put in the genitive case and followed by ཕྱིར་ or ཕྱིར་དུ།

EXAMPLES :—

ལྷོ་ཕྱོགས་ཀྱི་རྒྱལ་མོ་སོ་ལོ་མོན་གྱི་རིག་པ་ ལ་ཉན་པའི་ཕྱིར་སའི་མཐའ་ནས་འོངས་སོ།	*The Queen of the South came from the ends of the Earth to hear the wisdom of Solomon.* (Luke xi. 31).
ཁོང་རྒྱལ་ཞིང་རྒྱལ་བའི་ཕྱིར་དུ་ཐོན་ནོ།	*He came forth conquering and to conquer.* (Rev. vi. 2).

The Colloquial has no Infinitive in the Terminative case with ར་ That is only found in Literary Tibetan. In the Colloquial, therefore, the Supine never appears in that form. It expresses itself either through the Infinitive alone, or through the Infinitive put in the genitive case and followed by དོན་ལ་ (and generally means "In order to," or "For the purpose of"), or through the particles རྒྱུ་ (when *necessity* or *obligation* is implied), or ལ་ (*object* or *purpose*) annexed to Verbal Roots.

EXAMPLES :—

ཤིང་བཟོ་བ་ཀུབ་ཀྱག་དེ་སྒྲིག་པ་སླེབས་སོང་།	*A carpenter has come to mend the chair.*
ང་ཁྲིམས་ཁང་ལ་ཞིབ་དཔྱོད་དེ་བལྟ་བའི་དོན་ ལ་འགྲོ་གི་ཡོད།	*I am on my way (going) to Court, to see the trial.*
ང་དང་མཉམ་དུ་རོལ་མོ་ཉན་པའི་དོན་ལ་ ཤོག།	*Come with me to hear the music.*
ང་ཀ་ལི་ཀ་ཏ་ལ་ངའི་ཁང་པ་འཚོང་ལ་ཕྱིན་ པ་ཡིན།	*I went to Calcutta to sell my house.*
རྡོ་རྗེ་གླིང་ལ་འགྲོ་རྒྱུ་ཐག་རིང་ཐུང་ག་ཚོད།	*How far is it (to go) to Darjeeling.*

C.—*The Verbal Noun.*

What this is may be seen in the sentence, *For to me to live is Christ, and to die is gain.* Here, the Infinitives, *To live*, and *To die*, may be turned into Nouns, *The living*, and *The dying*.

In Literary Tibetan the Verbal Noun appears either in the guise of the Infinitive (which, as already explained, is formally the same as the Noun and the Participle) or in the guise of the Infinitive followed by the Definite Article ནི་ Thus, in Literary Tibetan, either of the following contsructions is right :—

ང་རང་ལ་འཚོ་བ་ཡང་མ་ཤི་ཀ་ཡིན། འཆི་
བ་ཡང་ཕན་པའི་དོན་ཡིན་ནོ།

Or :—

ང་རང་ལ་འཚོ་བ་ནི་མ་ཤི་ཀ་ཡིན། འཆི་བ་
ཡང་ཕན་པའི་དོན་ཡིན་ནོ།

For to me to live is Christ, and to die is gain. (Philip. i. 21).

So also :—

བཟའ་མི་བྱེད་པ་ (ནི་) ལེགས་པ་མ་ཡིན། *It is not expedient to marry.* (Matt. xix. 10).

མི་ཕྱུག་པོ་ཞིག་ནམ་མཁའི་རྒྱལ་སྲིད་དུ་
འཛུག་པ་ (ནི་) དཀའོ། *It is hard for a rich man to enter into the kingdom of heaven.* (Matt. xix. 23).

སྟོན་པ། ངེད་རྣམས་འདིར་ཡོད་པ་ (ནི་)
ཡག་པོ་ཡིན། *Master, it is good for us to be here.* (Luke ix. 33).

Colloquially the Verbal Noun may be expressed either through the Infinitive followed by འདི་, or དེ་, or through the Verbal Root followed by ཀྱུ་, or ཡ་, with or without དེ།

EXAMPLES :—

འགྱེལ་བའི་མི་ལ་རྡུང་ཡ་སེམས་ཆུང་ཆུང་
རེད། *The hitting,* i.e. *To hit a man when he is down, is cowardly.*

འདི་རུ་ཡོད་པ་འདི་ལས་དེར་ཡོད་པ་འདི་
ཡག་ག་རེད། *It is better to be here than there, The being here is better*, etc.

འདི་ or དེ་ may be annexed to ཡ་ if desired, but its omission makes no difference.

EXAMPLES :—

འདི་རུ་འགྲོ་ཡ་སྐྱིད་པོ་རེད། } *It is pleasant to walk here.*

Or :—

འདི་རུ་འགྲོ་ཡ་འདི་སྐྱིད་པོ་རེད། }

In fact, the Verbal Noun, just like any other noun, is subject to declension.

EXAMPLES :—

མི་ཀུན་ནི་ཉན་པ་ལ་མགྱོགས་ཤིང་ལབ་པ་ལ་དལ། ཁོང་ཁྲོ་ཟ་བ་ལ་ཡང་དལ་པོ་ཡིན་པར་དགོས། — *Let every man be swift to hear, slow to speak, slow to wrath. (Every man should be swift as regards hearing, slow as regards speaking, slow as regards being angry).* (James i. 19).

The Verbal Noun may be formed out of any of the Infinitives, Present, Past, or Future.

D.—Participles.

The Present Participle of every verb is, in its simplest form, the Present Root with པ་ annexed after final ག་, ད་, ན་, བ་, མ་ and ས་, as འཛེག་པ *Climbing*; ཡོད་པ་ *Being*; འཐོན་པ་ *Leaving*; ཐོབ་པ་ *Receiving*; འཛོམས་པ་ *Crowding*; ཐོས་པ་ *Hearing*; or with བ་ annexed after final ང་, ར་, ལ་, འ་, and all vowels, as རྡུང་བ་ *Beating*; སྨུར་བ་ *Gnawing*; འགྲིལ་བ་ *Falling*; དགའ་བ་ *Rejoicing*; འགྲོ་བ་ *Going*; and the Past Participle in its simplest form is the Perfect Root with པ་ annexed, as གསུངས་པ་ *Spoken*, or with བ་ annexed, as ཕྱུང་བ་ *Pulled out*; or, where there is no Perfect Root, then the Present Root, with པ་ or བ་, as the case may be, added to the completive auxiliary as ཐོབ་ཟིན་པ་ or ཚར་བ་, and མཐོང་བྱུང་བ།

From either of these Participles may be formed the Active Participle, by taking the Present or Perfect Root and adding to it the word བྱེད་པ་, or བྱེད་པ་པོ་, or མཁན་, or བྱེད་མཁན་, signifying the *Doer*,

Agent, or *Instrument*. The phrase thus formed can be used either as an adjective or as noun.

EXAMPLES :—

ལུག་གསོད་ (or བསད་) མཁན་དེ། *The sheep-killer.*

ལུག་གསོད་ (or བསད་) མཁན་གྱི་མི་དེ། *The sheep-killing man.*

These, it is obvious, can also be rendered periphrastically, thus: *He who kills*, or *killed*, *the sheep.*

But the simple Participles, Present or Past, can also themselves be used periphrastically, by regarding either as an adjective and putting it in the genitive case if it precedes its noun, or in the nominative if it follows its noun.

EXAMPLES :—

ངས་བྱེད་པའི་ལས་དེ་རང་གིས་ང་ཡབ་ཀྱིས་བཏང་བ་ཡིན་པར་དཔང་པོ་བྱེད་དོ། *The work that I do (the by me doing work) itself bears witness that the Father hath sent me (to have sent me).* (John v. 36).

ཡང་ང་བཏང་བའི་ཡབ་ཉིད་ཀྱིས་ཀྱང་ང་ལ་དཔང་པོ་མཛད་པ་ཡིན། *And the Father which sent me (the me having sent Father) hath also borne witness of me.* (John v. 37).

The above illustrate the adjective phrase preceding its noun. The following are examples of the Participial Adjective following its noun :—

མི་འོང་བ་དེ་, instead of འོང་བའི་མི་དེ། — *The man who is coming: The coming man.*

དཔེ་ཆ་བཏང་བ་དེ་, instead of བཏང་བའི་དཔེ་ཆ་དེ། — *The book that was sent: The sent book.*

In the Colloquial the construction of these Active Participles and Periphrastic Participial phrases is in མཁན་ for *animates*, human or otherwise, and in པ་ or བ་ for *inanimates*, in both cases annexed to the root. Here, too, the expression or phrase may be treated either as a noun or as an adjective, and in the latter case it may precede or follow its noun.

EXAMPLES :—

ཡོང་མཁན་གྱི་མི་དེ།
Or :—
མི་ཡོང་མཁན་དེ། — *The coming man ; the man who is coming ; the comer.*

སྐད་རྒྱབ་མཁན་གྱི་ཕག་པ།
Or :—
ཕག་པ་སྐད་རྒྱབ་མཁན་དེ། — *The grunting pig ; the pig that is grunting ; the grunter.*

ཡོངས་མཁན་གྱི་མི་དེ།
Or :—
མི་ཡོངས་མཁན་དེ། — *The man who came.*

སྐད་བརྒྱབ་མཁན་གྱི་ཕག་པ།
Or :—
ཕག་པ་སྐད་བརྒྱབ་མཁན་དེ། — *The pig that grunted.*

ཆེ་རུ་ཆེ་རུ་འགྲོ་བའི་ཤིང་སྡོང་དེ།
Or :—
ཤིང་སྡོང་ཆེ་རུ་ཆེ་རུ་འགྲོ་བ་དེ། — *The growing tree ; the tree that grows.*

ཆེ་རུ་ཆེ་རུ་སོང་བའི་ཤིང་སྡོང་དེ།
Or :—
ཤིང་སྡོང་ཆེ་རུ་ཆེ་རུ་སོང་བ་དེ། — *The grown tree : the tree that grew.*

In the case of verbs with no Future root, the Literary Future Active Participle is formed thus :—

ཆེ་རུ་ཆེ་རུ་འགྲོ་མཁན་གྱི་ཤིང་སྡོང་དེ། or perhaps འགྲོ་རྒྱུ་ཡིན་པའི་ཤིང་སྡོང་དེ། — *The tree that is to grow, or will grow.*

མཐོང་མཁན་གྱི་མི་དེ། or perhaps མཐོང་རྒྱུ་ཡིན་པའི་མི་དེ། — *The man who is to see, or who will see.*

In the Colloquial རྒྱུ་ is used thus :—

ཆེ་རུ་ཆེ་རུ་འགྲོ་རྒྱུའི་ཤིང་སྡོང་དེ། — *The tree that is to grow, or that will grow.*

As regards the rendering of the Passive Voice, see § 31, ix. A. *Relative Pronouns.*

The Future Participle, in Literary Tibetan, is expressed by the Present Participle put in the terminative case with ར་, and followed by བྱ་བ་, signifying *About to...., or To be....ed.* In fact, formally, it is the same as the Present Infinitive of the Passive Verb.

Also by the Future Root with བྱ་ annexed, signifying *For ing* or by the Present or Future Root with ཀྱུ་ annexed.

EXAMPLES :—

ངེད་ རྣམས་ གསོད་ པར་ བྱ་ བའི་ ལུག་ ལྟར་ རྩིས་པ་ཡིན། — *We were accounted as sheep for the slaughter (To be slaughtered sheep).* (Rom. viii. 36).

སྔར་ བྲིས་པ་ ཐམས་ཅད་ང་ཚོ་ འི་ བསླབ་ བྱའི་ དོན་དུ་ བྲིས་པ་ཡིན། — *Whatsoever things were written aforetime were written for our learning.* (Rom. xv. 4).

The Colloquial is the Root with ཀྱུའི་ or པའི, or བའི་ annexed :

ང་ཚོ་ གསོད་ ཀྱུའི་ ལུག་ ནང་ བཞིན་ བསམས་ པ་ཡིན་ (or གསོད་པའི་ལུག)། — *We were regarded as sheep for the slaughter.*

སྔར་ བྲིས་ པ་ ཐམས་ ཅད་ང་ ཚོའི་སློབ་པའི་ (or ཀྱུའི་) དོན་ལ་བྲིས་པ་ཡིན། — *Whatever was formerly written was written for our learning.*

Many Participial expressions with a Present or Past signification are also formed by annexing to the bare Verbal Root, or to the Participle, the Auxiliary Verbal Particles already dealt with at an earlier stage of this paragraph. The following are all annexed to the Root :—

གི་, གྱི་ ཀྱི་, ཡི་, འི་	....*ing.*	Present signification Periphrastic form.
གིན་, གྱིན་, ཀྱིན་, ཡིན	*ing.*	Present. Sometimes periphrastic.
རེ་, ཏེ་, སྟེ་ ...*ing*	....*ed.*	Present or Past according to root.
ཅིང་, ཞིང་, ཤིང་ ...*ing.*	...*ed.*	Usually Present but sometimes Past.

པས་ and བས་ ...ing. ...ed / *As, when, since.* — Really ས་ annexed to Participle. Usually Past.

ནས་ ...ed. — Past.

ལ་ ...ing. ...ed. — Much like ཅིང་ and དེ་ and their variants.

བཞིན་ and བཞིན་དུ་ ...ing. — Present.

ཙང་ ...ing. ...ed. — Present or Past.

དུས་ ...ing. ...ed. / *While when.* — Present or Past.

The following are annexed to the Participle :—

ཡས་ ...ing. ... ed. / *As, since*, etc. — Usually Past, but sometimes Present.

ཏང་ ...ed. / *As, since*, etc. — Past.

དུས་ལ་ ...ing. ...ed. / *While, when.* — Used with genitive. Present or Past.

ལ་ ....ing. / *As. since.* — Usually Present.

E.—Gerunds.

This name is another instance of the attempt that has somewhat unfortunately been made to present the mysteries of Tibetan in the guise of western nomenclature. What has already been dealt with under the heading *Verbal Noun* was really the Gerund in the Nominative case (equivalent to the Present Infinitive) and the constructions usually called Gerunds in Tibetan Grammars are really a kind of Participial expressions, none other, in fact, than those which we have just been considering.

Here reference may be made to a form of the Gerund in the genitive case which is common in Literary and Colloquial Tibetan, though it might equallv well have apppeared under the heading Verbal Noun.

EXAMPLES :—

སྤུན་རྣམས། དེ་ལྟར་འགྱུར་བའི་མི་རིགས་སོ། *Brethren, these things ought not so to be (of the being so there is not propriety).* (James iii. 10).

ངེད་ཀྱིས་ཐོས་པའི་གནས་ལ་ལྷག་པར་བརྩོན་པའི་རིགས་སོ། *We ought to give the more earnest heed to the things that were heard (of the taking pains by us as regards the heard-things there is the more propriety or necessity).* (Heb. ii. 1).

ད་ལྟ་ཉོ་བའི་ (or ཉོ་ཡའི་ or ཉོ་རྒྱུའི་) དུས་རེད། *Now is the time to buy,* i.e. *of buying = for buying.*

(*N.B.*—This last is Colloquial.)

F.—Indicative.

(*a*) PRESENT.

In Literary Tibetan this is formed with the Present Root in several ways, some of which are as follows:—

1.—By the simple Root for all persons, singular and plural; as ང་འགྲོ *I go;* ཁྱེད་འགྲོ *Thou goest;* ཁོང་འགྲོ *He goes;* ང་རྣམས་འགྲོ *We go,* etc.; ངས་གཏོང་ *I send,* ཁྱེད་ཀྱིས་གཏོང་ *Thou sendest,* etc.

2.—At the end of sentences, by the simple Root as above, with the addition of འོ̃ in the case of verbs like འགྲོ, the root of which ends in a vowel, and, in the case of other verbs, reduplicating the final letter of the root, and putting ~ over it; as ང་འགྲོའོ̃ *I go;* ངས་གཏོང་ངོ̃ *I send,* and so for all persons, singular and plural.

In fact, throughout all conjugations the singular and plural are alike.

Where, however, the Root ends in འ, another འ with ~ superposed is not added, but the ~ is put over the first འ Thus ངདའོ̃ *I drive.*

3.—By putting the Infinitive into the Terminative case with ར་ and adding the auxiliary བྱེད་ or བྱེད་དོ̃ *Do,* or *Does,* for all persons; as ང་འགྲོ་བར་བྱེད་ or ང་འགྲོ་བར་བྱེད་དོ̃ *I do walk;* ཁྱེད་འགྲོ་བར་བྱེད་ *Thou dost walk;* ཁོང་འགྲོ་བར་བྱེད་ *He does walk;* ངས་ཤེས་པར་བྱེད་ *I do know,* etc. An intensive form.

4.—A rather obsolete form is to add the བྱེད་ or བྱེད་དོ་ direct to the Root; as ང་འགྲོ་བྱེད་ *I do go*, etc., ངས་ཤེས་བྱེད་ *I do know*, etc.

5.—Periphrastically, by the simple Participle Present, combined with the appropriate conjugation of འདུག་པ་ or ཡོད་པ་ *To be*, or any of their elegant or honorific forms. But this is rather a doubtful form and in any case old.

EXAMPLES :—

ང་འགྲོ་བ་ཡོད་, or མཆིས། — *I am going.*

ཁྱོད་འགྲོ་བ་འདུག, or གདའ། — *Thou art going.*

ཁོང་འགྲོ་བ་ཡོད་, or མཆིས, or འདུག, or གདའ, or ཡོད་པ་རེད, or མཆིས་པ་རེད། — *He is going.*

6.—Periphrastically, by connecting the root with the appropriate conjugation of ཡོད་པ་ *To be*, the link being one of the auxiliary particles གིན་, གྱིན་, ཀྱིན་ or ཡིན་ according to the rule relating to the final letter of the root, as :—

ངས་གཏོང་གིན་ཡོད། — *I am sending.*

ཁྱོད་འཐོན་གྱིན་འདུག། — *Thou art starting.*

ཁོང་གིས་འདེབས་ཀྱིན་ཡོད་, or འདུག, or ཡོད་པ་རེད། — *He is throwing, offering.*

ང་འགྲོ་ཡིན་ཡོད། — *I am going.*

7.—Periphrastically, by connecting the root with the appropriate elegant or honorific form of ཡོད་པ་ or འདུག་པ, the link being the auxiliary particle བཞིན་ or ཞིང་ This is, however, obsolete.

EXAMPLES :—

ངས་གཏོང་བཞིན་མཆིས། — *I am sending.*

ཁྱེད་ཀྱིས་གཏོང་བཞིན་གདའ། — *Thou art sending.*

ཁོང་གིས་གཏོང་བཞིན་མཆིས་, or གནང་, or མཆིས་པ་རེད། } *He is sending.*

And :—

ངས་གཏོང་བཞིན་བཞུགས།

ཁྱེད་ཀྱིས་གཏོང་བཞིན་མངའ།

ཁོང་གིས་གཏོང་བཞིན་བཞུགས་, or མངའ་, or བཞུགས་པ་རེད།

As regards the Colloquial, when the Present Root of a verb ends in an inherent ཨ་, or འ་, or in ུ or ོ, that Present Root is generally used for the Present Indicative. With all other verbs the Colloquial, according to Mr. Bell, usually adopts the Perfect Root, if any; or, as seems more likely, at least the sound of it. When *writing* the Colloquial it is advisable, or allowable, to employ the proper root.

The formation of the tense then proceeds thus :—

1.—The Root (Present or Perfect) for all persons, as ངས་བལྟ་ *I see* or *look;* ངས་བཙའ་ *I bring forth;* ངས་ཞུ་ *I request;* but either ངས་གཏོང་ or ངས་བཏང་ *I send.*

2.—Periphrastically. The Root (Present or Perfect) combined with the appropriate conjugation of ཡོད་པ་ *To be;* the connecting link being གི་, གྱི་, ཀྱི་, or ཡི་, or འི་ (though གི་ generally takes the place of these last two), agreeably to the final letter of the root.

EXAMPLES :—

ངས་ལྟ་གི་ཡོད། *I am looking.*

ཁྱེད་འཐོན་ (or ཐོན་) གྱི་འདུག། *Thou art starting.*

ཁོ་སླེབ་ (or སླེབས་) ཀྱི་ཡོད་, or འདུག་, or ཡོད་པ་རེད། *He is arriving.*

(b)—Imperfect.

This expresses the idea of the Periphrastic Past: *Was, wast, were . . . . . ing.*

In Literary Tibetan it may be rendered by the Perfect root (if any), with པ་ or བ་ annexed, combined with the Indicative Present of Literary ཡིན་པ་ *To be.* Thus:—

ཡང་ཤ་ཨུལ་དེ་ནི་ཁོང་བསད་པ་ལ་ཁས་མཐུན་པ་ཡིན་ནོ། *And Saul was consenting unto his death.* (Acts viii. 1.)

Or it may take the form of the Perfect Root (if any) with one of the auxiliary Verbal Particles or Suspensives annexed, and combined with ཡོད་པ་ཡིན།

Examples:—

མི་མང་པོ་འཛོམས་ནས་སྨོན་ལམ་བཏབ་ཅིང་ཡོད་པ་ཡིན། *Many were (being) gathered together and were praying.* (Acts xii. 12.)

Probably however, it would generally be found put participially. Thus:—

དེའི་དུས་སུ་ཉེ་གནས་རྣམས་ཀྱི་གྲངས་འཕེལ་བ་ལས། *In those days, when the number of the disciples was multiplying (the number, etc. multiplying)* (Acts vi. 1.)

This almost endlessly Suspensive Construction, as the ordinary feature of a Tibetan sentence, which really only contains an absolute statement at the end, must never be forgotten.

In the Colloquial the *Imperfect Indicative* has no special form. It simply employs the Present Tense construction, leaving the context (generally some adverb like ཁས་ས་ *Yesterday*, སྔོན་ལ་ *Recently*, or སྔར་ *Long ago*), to indicate the Past idea, if it exists.

Examples:—

ཁས་ས་ང་ཁྲིམས་ཁང་ལ་འགྲོ་གི་ཡོད་པ་ཡིན། *Yesterday I was going to Court.*

སྤྱན་ལ་ཁྱུ་དེ་ནགས་གསེབ་ནང་ལ་རྒྱུ་གི་ཡོད་པ་རེད། — *The herd was roving about in the forest.*

སྔར་མི་སྤྲེའུ་དང་འདྲ་གི་ཡོད་པ་འདུག། — *Anciently man resembled a monkey.*

(*c*)—PERFECT.

This, which expresses the idea *Have, hast* or *has . . . . ed*, is rendered, in both Literary and Colloquial Tibetan, by the Perfect Root combined with the appropriate elements of ཡིན་པ་ *To be*, which, it will be remembered, are not quite the same in the two modes. Thus, in Literary Tibetan the construction is as follows:—

ངས་གསུངས་པ་ཡིན་ནོ། — *I have spoken.*

ཁྱོད་ཀྱིས་གསུངས་པ་འདུག་གོ་ or, occasionally, ཡིན་ནོ། — *Thou hast spoken.*

ཁོང་གིས་གསུངས་པ་ཡིན་ནོ། — *He has spoken.*

This tense is not infrequently used for our Past Indefinite. Thus:—

ང་ནི་དོན་འདི་ལ་ཡོངས་པ་ཡིན་ནོ — *To this end came I forth.* (Mark i. 39.)

In Colloquial the construction is as follows:—

ངས་གསུངས་པ་ཡིན། — *I have spoken.*

ཁྱོད་ཀྱིས་གསུངས་པ་འདུག་ or རེད། — *Thou hast spoken.*

ཁོས་གསུངས་པ་རེད་ or, occasionally, འདུག། — *He has spoken.*

This also is often used for our Past Indefinite. Thus:—

ཁ་སང་ངས་རྟ་འདི་ཉོས་པ་ཡིན། — *I bought this horse yesterday.*

Another Colloquial rendering of the Perfect Tense is to add བྱུང་ or སོང་ or ཡོད་ or འདུག་, or even སོང་འདུག་ or བྱུང་སོང་, to the Perfect Root, if any: the construction being the same for all persons.

Thus :—

ངས་སྒམ་འཁྱེར་མོངས་ཡོད།	*I have brought the box.*
ངས་དཔེ་ཆ་བཀླགས་འདུག།	*I have read the book.*
ཁོས་ཡི་གེ་ཐོབ་བྱུང་།	*He has received the letter.*
ཁྱི་དེ་ཤི་སོང་།	*The dog has died.*
ཁ་མཆུ་དེ་ཐག་བཅད་སོང་འདུག།	*The suit has been decided.*

Certain verbs usually take བྱུང་ in preference to སོང་, and others སོང་ in preference to བྱུང་ In this connection practice will make perfect. The following are a few that take སོང་, namely, བྱེད་པ་ *To do ;* བཟོ་བ་ *To build ;* ཞེད་པ་ *To fear ;* ཤི་བ་ *To die ;* འཐོན་པ་ *To set out, depart, start ;* ཧ་གོ་བ་ *To understand ;* ཀུན་མ་ཀུ་བ་ *To steal ;* འཚར་བ་ *To be finished ;* སླེབ་པ་ and ཕེབ་པ་ *To come, arrive ;* འཚིག་པ་ *To burn ;* and the following are a few that take བྱུང་, namely, ཐོབ་པ་ *To receive, get, obtain ;* གོ་བ་ *To hear ;* མཐོང་བ་ *To see ;* དབྱུག་པ་ *To throw ;* ཐོས་པ་ *To hear.* བྱུང་ is generally seen with the 1st person, and where this is so the other persons usually take འདུག།

(*d*) Past Indefinite.

In Literary Tibetan, at the end of sentences, this consists of the plain Perfect Root for all persons, with the final letter generally reduplicated.

Examples :—

དེ་ནས་ དེ་དག་ དྲུང་ དུ་ མོངས་ ནས་ ཡེ་ ཤུ་ བཟུང་ངོ་།	*Then they came up to Jesus and took him.* (Matt. xxvi. 50.)
ཁོང་རྒྱལ་ཞིང་རྒྱལ་བའི་ཕྱིར་དུ་ཐོན་ནོ།	*He came forth conquering and to conquer.* (Rev. vi. 2.)

When the verb possesses no Perfect Root the Present Root is used.

Examples :—

ཡང་ངས་ཕོ་ཉ་གཞན་ཞིག་ཤར་ཕྱོགས་ནས་འཕྱོན་པར་མཐོང་ངོ་།	*And I saw another angel ascend from the sun rising.* (Rev. vii. 2.)

But in phrases like the following, introductory to what a speaker has said, the Perfect Participle is always used :—

ཡེ་ཤུས་གསུངས་པ།	*Jesus said.* (John xx. 17.)
མིར་ཡམ་མག་དལ་ན་འོངས་དེ་ཉེ་གནས་རྣམས་ལ་ཟེར་པ།	*Mary Magdalene came and said to the disciples.* (John xx. 18.)
ཉེ་གནས་གཞན་མ་རྣམས་ཀྱིས་ཁོ་ལ་སྨྲས་པ།	*The other disciples said unto him.* (John xx. 25.)
དེའི་ལན་དུ་ཐོ་མས་ཞུས་པ།	*Thomas answered and said.* (John xx. 28.)

But note the following construction where the verb, being at the end of the sentence, is not put participially, but in the form of the plain Perfect Root again :—

ཡེ་ཤུས་ཁོ་ལ། ···ང་མི་མཐོང་ཡང་དད་པ་བྱས་པ་རྣམས་བདེའོ་ཞེས་གསུངས་སོ།	*Jesus to him....blessed are they that have not seen and yet have believed. Thus he said.* (John xx. 29.)

Sometimes one sees :—

ཞེས་གསུངས་པ་བཞིན་ནོ།	*Thus it has been said.* (1 Cor. x. 7.)

Note also the following construction, where ཐུབ་པ for *she could* does not occur at the end of a sentence, and is put participially :—

བུད་མེད་ཀྱིས་གང་ཐུབ་པ་བྱས་པ་ཡིན།	*The woman hath done what she could.* (Mark xiv. 8.)

In the Colloquial the Past Indefinite is rendered by the plain Perfect Root, if any, or, if none, then by the Present Root, with བྱུང་ or སོང་ added ; and this holds for all persons.

EXAMPLES :—

ངས་དེ་རིང་ངའི་དྲུང་ཡིག་ཁྲིམས་ཁང་ལ་བཏང་སོང་།	*I sent my clerk to Court to-day.*
ལགས་སོ། ངས་ཡི་གེ་ཐོབ་བྱུང་།	*I received the letter all right.*

In these cases, however, it would be just as correct to use the Perfect Tense : བཏང་བ་ཡིན་ instead of བཏང་སོང་, and ཐོབ་པ་ཡིན་ instead of ཐོབ་བྱུང་།

(*c*) PLUPERFECT.

This tense, which expresses the idea *Had....ed*, is seldom or never seen in Literary Tibetan at the end of a sentence, i.e. as an absolute statement. It is usually met with in an introductory or suspensory clause, and is then rendered participially with a past signification. Thus :—

ཡང་དེ་ལ་བསམ་བློ་བཏང་ནས།	*And when he had considered the thing ;* i.e. *Having considered,* etc. (Acts xii. 12.)
ཞེས་ཟེར་ནས།	*When she had thus said ;* i.e. *Having thus said.* (John xx. 14.)

Sometimes it is turned into an adjective phrase, i.e. the Past Participle is put in the genitive case. Thus :—

ཡེ་ཤུའི་སྐུ་སྤུར་བཞག་པའི་གནས་ལ།	*Where the body of Jesus had lain.* (John xx. 12.)

In phrases like the following it is constructed by combining ཡིན་པ་ with the Perfect Participle, thus making a sort of Past Infinitive.

EXAMPLES :—

ཁྱེད་རྡོ་རྗེ་གླིང་ལ་ཕྱིན་པ་ཡིན་པ་ངས་ཐོས་བྱུང་།	*I heard you had gone (you to have gone) to Darjeeling.*
ཁྱེད་ཀྱིས་ཆིབས་པ་གཟིགས་པ་ཡིན་པ་ངས་བསམས་སོ།	*I thought you had bought (to have bought) the horse.*

ཁོང་རྣམས་ཀྱིས་ལས་ཀ་ང་ལ་ བཅོལ་བ་ཡིན་ པ་མཐོང་ནས། — *When they saw that the work had been entrusted (to have been entrusted) to me.*

When it does appear at the end of a sentence, it may take the form of the Perfect Root, followed by ནས་, and combined with the Present Indicative of ཡོད་པ་. Thus:—

ངས་བཏང་ནས་ཡོད། — *I had sent.*

ཁྱོད་ཀྱིས་བཏང་ནས་འདུག། — *Thou hadst sent.*

ཁོས་བཏང་ནས་ཡོད་ or འདུག་ or ཡོད་པ་རེད། — *He had sent.*

Or better:—

ངས་བཏང་ཡོད།
ཁྱོད་ཀྱིས་བཏང་འདུག།
ཁོས་བཏང་ཡོད་ or འདུག་ or ཡོད་པ་རེད། — *Ditto.*

Sometimes, e g. in cases in which the direct mode of speech is adopted, the Pluperfect is avoided in favour of the Perfect.

EXAMPLES :—

མིར་ ཡཨམ་ མག་ དལ་ མ་འོངས་ དེ་ཉེ་གནས་ རྣམས་ལ་ཟེར་པ། ངས་གཙོ་བོ་མཐོང་སྟེ། ཁོང་གིས་ དེ་སྐད་ ཅེས་ང་ ལ་ གསུངས་པ་ ཡིན། — *Mary Magdalene cometh (having come) and telleth (told) the disciples, I have seen the Lord; and how that he had (has) said these things unto her (me).* (John xx. 18.)

The Colloquial has no special Pluperfect Tense. Any of the preceding Past Tenses belonging to it may be used (whichever is the more convenient), or even perhaps the Literary construction in ནས་ attached to the Perfect Root and combined with ཡོད་པ།

EXAMPLES :—

ཁོ་སླེབས་པ་དང་ང་བྲོན་སོང་།	*When he arrived I had gone.*
ངས་དཔེ་ཆ་ཁོ་ལ་ད་གི་ནས་བཏང་ནས་ཡོད།	*I had already sent him the book.*
ཁོ་ལྷ་ས་ལ་ནམ་ཡང་འགྲོ་མ་མྱོང་།	*He had never been to Lhasa.*

(NOTE.—མྱོང་ (pron. *nyúng*) *Ever*, or, with a negative, *Never*, is in all tenses attached to the root, and treated as part of the verb.)

In other respects the Colloquial constructions are much like the Literary.

EXAMPLES :—

ཁོས་མནའ་མ་བླངས་པ་ or ལེན་པ་ཡིན་པ་ངས་ཤེས་མ་སོང་།	*I did not know that he had married.*
ཁོ་སོང་བ་དང་།	*When he had gone.*

(*f*) FUTURE.

The Literary construction of this tense is either with the plain Future Root (if any) of the verb, or with the Present Infinitive in the Terminative case, combined with the auxiliary verbs འགྱུར་བ་ *To become*, or *be*; བྱ་བ་ *To become* or *do*; and འོང་བ་, or ཡོང་བ་ *To come*. The construction with བྱ་བ་ is Intensive. There is also another construction with the Present or Future Root combined with རྒྱུ་ and the auxiliary verb ཡིན་པ་ *To be*. This carries the meaning *I am to*, or *I have to*. All these constructions, save the last, are used with all persons.

EXAMPLES :—

ངས་དཔེ་ཆ་དེ་ཁྱེད་ལ་གཏང་ངེ་། ངས་དཔེ་ཆ་དེ་ཁྱེད་ལ་གཏོང་བར་འགྱུར་རོ། ངས་དཔེ་ཆ་དེ་ཁྱེད་ལ་གཏོང་བར་བྱའོ།	*I shall send thee the book.*

ངས་དཔེ་ཆ་དེ་ཁྱེད་ལ་གཏོང་བར་ཡོང་། ངས་དཔེ་ཆ་དེ་ཁྱེད་ལ་གཏོང་འོང་།	*I shall send thee the book.*
ངས་དཔེ་ཆ་དེ་ཁྱེད་ལ་གཏོང་རྒྱུ་ཡིན།	*I am* (or *have*) *to send thee the book.*
ཁྱེད་ཀྱིས་དཔེ་ཆ་དེ་ང་ལ་གཏོང་རྒྱུ་འདུག།	*Thou art* (or *hast*) *to send me the book.*
ཁོང་གིས་དཔེ་ཆ་དེ་ཁྱེད་ལ་གཏོང་རྒྱུ་ཡིན།	*He is* (or *hath*) *to send thee the book.*

In the Colloquial the Simple Future is formed either with ཡོང་ (for all persons) annexed to the Perfect Root (or probably more correctly to the Future Root), or with the Present Root combined with the Present Indicative of ཡིན་པ་ *To be*, the link between them being གི་, གྱི་, or ཀྱི་, according to rule with reference to the last letter of the Root.

EXAMPLES :—

ངས་དཔེ་ཆ་དེ་ཁྱོད་ལ་གཏང་ཡོང་།	*I shall send thee the book.*
ཁྱོད་ཀྱིས་དཔེ་ཆ་དེ་ང་ལ་གཏང་ཡོང་།	*Thou wilt send me the book.*
ཁོས་དཔེ་ཆ་དེ་ཁྱོད་ལ་གཏང་ཡོང་།	*He will send thee the book.*

Or :—

ངས་གཏོང་གི་ཡིན།	*I shall send.*
ཁྱོད་ཀྱིས་གཏོང་གི་རེད།	*Thou wilt send.*
ཁོས་གཏོང་གི་རེད།	*He will send.*

The other Future tenses, as known to Tibetan, are only found in connection with the Subjunctive and Conditional Moods. The first is similar to the Perfect tense. Thus :—

ངས་བཏང་བ་ཡིན།	*I would send.*
ཁྱོད་ཀྱིས་བཏང་བ་འདུག, or རེད།	*Thou wouldst send.*
ཁོས་བཏང་བ་རེད, or འདུག།	*He would send.*

However, with this the Simple Future may also be used.

The second is formed with the Perfect Participle combined with the Indicative Present of ཡོད་པ་. Thus:—

ངས་བཏང་བ་ཡོད།	*I would have sent.*
ཁྱོད་ཀྱིས་བཏང་བ་ཡོད་ or འདུག།	*Thou wouldst have sent.*
ཁོས་བཏང་བ་ཡོད་, or བཏང་བ་འདུག, or བཏང་ཡོད་པ་རེད།	*He would have sent.*

Or even thus:—

ངས་	བཏང་ཡོད་ or འདུག་	*I would have sent.*
ཁྱོད་ཀྱིས་		*Thou wouldst have sent.*
ཁོས་	or བྱུང་།	*He would have sent.*

N.B.—The Future Root is seldom used in the Colloquial, unless, in the case of verbs like གཏོང་བ་, it really lurks in the *sound* of བཏང་བ་ as said to be sometimes used in the Future tense, and in the Participles, etc. Even in Literary Tibetan it is not met with very much.

G.—Subjunctive or Conditional.

When the sentence consists of a *conditional clause* dependent upon a preceding *hypothetical clause* in the Present Tense with གལ་ཏེ་ . . . ན་, *If*, or ན་ alone, the conditional clause takes the Indefinite Future in Literary འགྱུར་ or Colloquial ཡོང་ for all persons. In this Literary and Colloquial Tibetan are the same.

EXAMPLES :—

གལ་ཏེ་ཁྱོད་ཚག་གིས་ང་ལ་གཅེས་པར་འཛིན་ན་ངའི་བཀའ་རྣམས་སྲུང་བར་འགྱུར་རོ།	*If ye love me ye will keep my commandments.*

ཁྱོད་ཀྱིས་ཁོ་ལ་དྲི་ན་ཁོས་བསྟེར་ཡོང་ (or སྟེར་གྱི་རེད)། *If thou askest him he will give.*

When the preceding clause is in the Past Tense, and the conditional clause signifies *I*, *Thou*, *He*, etc., *would*.., this last clause, both in Literary and Colloquial Tibetan, takes the Perfect Participle, combined with ཡིན་པ་ in the Present Indicative, which, it will be remembered, is not quite the same in the two languages. Thus, in Literary Tibetan :—

ཁྱོད་རྣམས་ཀྱིས་ང་ངོ་ཤེས་པ་ཡིན་ན། ངའི་ཡབ་ཀྱང་ངོ་ཤེས་པ་ཡིན་ནོ་ or འདུག་གོ། *If ye knew me ye would know my Father also.* (John xvi. 7.)

ཁྱེད་ཀྱིས་ང་གཅེས་པར་བཟུང་ན། སེམས་དགའ་བར་གྱུར་པ་ཡིན་ནོ་ or འདུག་གོ། *If ye loved me ye would rejoice* (i.e. *be glad.*) (John xiv. 28.)

This construction may also apparently be used when the conditional clause signifies *Would have*.. .*d*, e.g. ཤི་བ་མ་ཡིན་ *Would not have died* (John xi. 21); བརྐྱང་བ་མ་ཡིན་ *Would not have crucified.* (1 Cor. ii. 8); but the construction in ཡོད་པ་ (to which we shall come presently) is better.

The Colloquial is much the same as the above.

Examples :—

ཁྱོད་ཚོས་ང་ངོ་ཤེས་པ་ཡིན་ན། ངའི་ཡབ་ཀྱང་ངོ་ཤེས་པ་འདུག་ or ཡོད། *If you knew me you would also know my Father.*

Or, for all persons :—

ངས་ངོ་ཤེས་པ་ཡིན། *I would know.*

ཁྱོད་ཀྱིས་ངོ་ཤེས་པ་འདུག, or རེད། *Thou woulds know.*

ཁོས་ངོ་ཤེས་པ་རེད, or འདུག། *He would know.*

But, when the preceding clause is in the Past Tense, and the conditional clause signifies *Would have....d*, then, both in Literary and Colloquial Tibetan, this last clause ought to be constructed with the Perfect Participle combined with the appropriate forms of ཡོད་པ་ in the Present Indicative. Thus, in Literary Tibetan:—

དེ་ལྟར་མ་ཡིན་ན་ངས་ཁྱོད་རྣམས་ལ་སྨྲས་པ་ ཡོད།	*If it were not so, I would have told you.* (John xiv. 2.)
ངས་སྨྲས་པ་ཡོད།	*I would have told.*
ཁྱོད་ཀྱིས་སྨྲས་པ་འདུག།	*Thou wouldst have told.*
ཁོས་སྨྲས་པ་ཡོད་, or འདུག་, or ཡོད་ པ་རེད།	*He would have told.*

The Colloquial construction is similar.

EXAMPLES :—

འདི་འདྲས་མ་ཡིན་ན་ངས་ཁྱོད་ ཚོ་ལ་བཤད་པ་ཡོད་ or བཤད་ཡོད་ or བཤད་འདུག།	*Were it not so I would have told you.*
ངས་ཁྱོད་ལ་ དྲིས་ ན་ ཁྱོད་ཡོངས་ པ་ འདུག་ གས་ or ཡོངས་ཡོད་པས་ etc.	*If I had asked you, would you have come?*
ཁོས་ང་ལ་དྲིས་པ་མེད་ or མི་འདུག་ or ཡོད་པ་མ་རེད་ or དྲིས་མེད་ etc.	*He would not have asked me.*

H.—Potential.

In the Colloquial this is formed by adding the auxiliary ཐུབ་པ་ *To be able*, properly conjugated, to the Present Root of the verb it governs. Thus:—

PRESENT.

(ངས་) གཏོང་ཐུབ་ (for all persons). Or :— (ངས) གཏོང་ཐུབ་ཡོང་ (for all persons).	*(I) can send.*

Or —

ངས་གཏོང་ཐུབ་ཀྱི་ཡོད།	*I can send.*
ཁྱོད་ཀྱིས་གཏོང་ཐུབ་ཀྱི་འདུག།	*Thou canst send.*
ཁོས་གཏོང་ཐུབ་ཀྱི་ཡོད་ or འདུག་ or ཡོད་པ་རེད།	*He can send.*

PAST.

(ངས་) གཏོང་ཐུབ་སོང་། (for all persons).	*(I) could send.*

Or :—

ངས་གཏོང་ཐུབ་པ་ཡིན།	*I could send.*
ཁྱོད་ཀྱིས་གཏོང་ཐུབ་པ་འདུག་ or རེད།	*Thou couldst send.*
ཁོས་གཏོང་ཐུབ་པ་རེད་ or འདུག།	*He could send.*

ངས་གཏོང་ཐུབ་པ་ཡོད།	or ཐུབ་ཡོང་,	*I could have sent.*
ཁྱོད་ཀྱིས་གཏོང་ཐུབ་པ་འདུག།	ཐུབ་འདུག་,	*Thou couldst have sent.*
ཁོས་གཏོང་ཐུབ་པ་ཡོད་ or འདུག་ or ཡོད་པ་རེད།	or ཐུབ་བྱུང་ (for all persons).	*He could have sent.*

The Literary construction with ཐུབ་པ་ is as follows :—

PRESENT.

ངས་	གཏོང་ཐུབ་བོ་	*I can*	*send.*
ཁྱོད་ཀྱིས་		*Thou canst*	
ཁོང་གིས་		*He can*	

PAST.

ས་	གཏོང་ཐུབ་སོང་ངོ་།	*I could*	send.
ད་ཀྱིས་		*Thou couldst*	
ང་གིས་		*He could*	

Or :—

ས་གཏོང་ཐུབ་པ་ཡིན་ནོ། — *I could send.*

ད་ཀྱིས་གཏོང་ཐུབ་པ་འདུག་གོ་ or ཡིན་ནོ། — *Thou couldst send.*

ང་གིས་གཏོང་ཐུབ་པ་ཡིན་ནོ། — *He could send.*

ས་གཏོང་ཐུབ་པ་ཡོད་དོ། — *I could have sent.*

(And so on as in the Colloquial.)

But the Literary construction may also be with the auxiliary ནུས་པ་ *o be able*, which, unlike ཐུབ་པ་, governs the Infinitive put in the erminative case. Thus :—

PRESENT.

ས་གཏོང་བར་ནུས་སོ། — *I can send.*

(And so throughout.)

PAST.

ས་གཏོང་བར་ནུས་པ་ཡིན་ནོ། — *I could send.*

ད་ཀྱིས་གཏོང་བར་ནུས་པ་འདུག་གོ་ or ཡིན་ནོ། — *Thou couldst send.*

ང་གིས་གཏོང་བར་ནུས་པ་ཡིན་ནོ། — *He could send.*

ས་གཏོང་བར་ནུས་པ་ཡོད་དོ། — *I could have sent.*

ད་ཀྱིས་གཏོང་བར་ནུས་པ་འདུག་གོ། — *Thou couldst have sent.*

ང་གིས་གཏོང་བར་ནུས་པ་ཡོད་དོ་ or འདུག་གོ་ or ཡོད་པ་ཡིན་ནོ། — *He could have sent.*

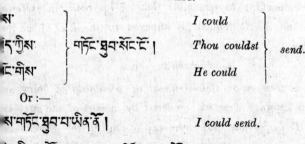

N.B.—It is important to remember that ཐུབ་, both in Literar[y] Tibetan and the Colloquial, is annexed to the *Root* of the ver[b] it governs.

I.—Probability, etc.

Phrases expressive of the *likelihood* or *possibility* of doing an[y]thing are, in Literary Tibetan, rendered by means of the auxiliar[y] verb སྲིད་པ་ *To be possible,* or by the expression སུ་ཤེས་ *Who know[s]* =*May be.*

EXAMPLES :—

སུ་ཤེས་ང་འགྲོ་འོ་ or འགྲོ་བར་འགྱུར་རོ།	*I may go ; perhaps, possibly, pro[b]ably I shall go.*
ངས་གཏོང་ (or even གཏོང་བར་) སྲིད་དོ།	*I may send.*
ཁྱེད་ཀྱིས་གཏོང་ (or གཏོང་བར་) སྲིད་དོ།	*Thou mayest send.*
ཁོང་གིས་གཏོང་ (or གཏོང་བར་) སྲིད་དོ།	*He may send.*
ངས་གཏོང་སྲིད་པ་ཡིན་ནོ།	*I might send.*
ཁྱོད་ཀྱིས་གཏོང་སྲིད་པ་འདུག་གོ, or ཡིན་ནོ།	*Thou mightest send.*
ཁོང་གིས་གཏོང་སྲིད་པ་ཡིན་ནོ།	*He might send.*
ངས་གཏོང་སྲིད་པ་ཡོད་དོ།	*I might have sent.*
ཁྱེད་ཀྱིས་གཏོང་སྲིད་པ་འདུག་གོ།	*Thou mightest have sent.*
ཁོང་གིས་གཏོང་སྲིད་པ་འདུག་གོ, or ཡོད་དོ།	*He might have sent.*

The auxiliary འདུག་པ་ *To be*, combined with the Root or t[he] Infinitive, put in the Terminative case, also conveys the idea [of] *probability* or *likelihood*. Thus :—

་འདི་འགྲོར་འདུག།	*This man is probably going.*
ས་དེ་སྟེར་དགོས་པར་འདུག།	*I shall probably have to give it.*
མ་པ་དེ་འགས་སུ་འདུག།	*That bottle is likely to crack.*

In the Colloquial སུ་ཞེས་, or གཅིག་བྱེད་ན་ *Perhaps*, or the auxiliaries ཡིན་བ་འདྲ་, or ཡིན་གྲྭ་, may be used instead of སྲིད་པ།

N.B.—ཡིན་གྲྭ་ is sometimes written ཡིན་འགྲྭ. Which of these two is the more correct form is somewhat uncertain.

EXAMPLES :—

ུ་ཞེས་ང་འགྲོ་གི།	*I may go, or be going.*
ུ་ཞེས་ཁྱོད་འགྲོ་གི་འདུག, or རེད།	*Probably thou wilt go.*
ུ་ཞེས་ཁོ་འགྲོ་གི་རེད་, or འདུག།	*It is likely he will go.*
ཅིག་བྱེད་ན་ང་འགྲོ་གི།	*Perhaps I shall go.*

(And so on, as above.)

་འགྲོ་གི་ཡིན་པ་འདྲ་, or ཡིན་གྲྭ།	*I may be going.*

(And so throughout.)

་སོང་བ་ཡིན་པ་འདྲ་, or ཡིན་གྲྭ།	*I might be going.*

(And so throughout.)

་སོང་བ་ཡོད་པ་འདྲ་, or ཡོད་གྲྭ།	*I might have been going.*

(And so throughout.)

ཅིག་བྱེད་ན་ང་སོང་བ་ཡིན།	*I might go.*
ཅིག་བྱེད་ན་ཁྱོད་སོང་བ་འདུག, or རེད།	*Thou mightest go.*
ཅིག་བྱེད་ན་ཁོ་སོང་བ་རེད་, or འདུག།	*He might go.*
ཅིག་བྱེད་ན་ང་སོང་བ་ཡོད།	*I might have gone.*

གཅིག་བྱེད་ན་ཁྱོད་སོང་བ་འདུག། — *Thou mightest have gone.*

གཅིག་བྱེད་ན་ཁོ་སོང་བ་ཡོད་, or འདུག་ or ཡོད་པ་རེད། — *He might have gone.*

J.—Hortative.

In the Colloquial this is rendered by དགོས་པ་ or vulgarly དགོ་ *To need, To be necessary, To be obliged* or *compelled*; also where w use *Must, Ought, Should, Have to.* Like ཐུབ་པ་ *To be able*, it annexed to the Root, not to the Infinitive, and is used with or withou the auxiliaries ཡོད་པ་ and ཡིན་པ་ With this verb the subject shou be put in the Nominative or Dative (not the Agentive) case.

EXAMPLES :—

ད་ལྟ་ང་འཐོན་དགོས་, or དགོ་གི་ཡོད། — *Now I must start.*

ང་དཔེ་ཆ་ཁོ་ལ་གཏོང་དགོས་ or དགོ་གི་ ཡོད། — *I have to send him the book.*

ང་དཔེ་ཆ་ཁོ་ལ་གཏོང་དགོས་པ་ཡིན། — *I had to send him the book.*

ང་དཔེ་ཆ་ཁོ་ལ་གཏོང་དགོ་གི་ཡིན། — *I shall have to send him the book*

ང་ལ་རྡོ་རྗེ་གླིང་ལ་འགྲོ་དགོས་ or དགོ་གི་ ཡོད། — *I want to go to Darjeeling.*

ཁྱེད་ང་དང་མཉམ་དུ་ཡོང་དགོ་གི་འདུག། — *You ought to come with me.*

In Literary Tibetan the construction for all persons is in དགོས་ང not added to the Root, but to the Infinitive put in the Terminati case. Thus :—

ཁོང་ནི་འཕེལ་བར་དགོས་ཀྱི།
ང་ནི་འགྲིབ་པར་དགོས་སོ། — *He must increase but I mu decrease.* (John iii. 30).

There is, however, another construction for all persons in བྱ་ བྱའོ་ (Future Root of བྱེད་པ་), added to the Infinitive in t Terminative case, or to the Root, but sometimes used by itself.

EXAMPLES :—

ངེད་ རྣམས་ བཟང་ བ་ བྱེད་ པ་ལ་ སྐྱོ་བ་སྐྱེད་ པར་མི་བྱའོ།	*Let us not* (i.e. *we should, ought, must not*) *be weary in well-doing.* (Gal. vi. 9).
ཐམས་ཅད་ཆོས་ནི་ཉན་པར་བྱ།	*All should hear this precept ;*
ཐོས་ནས་རབ་ཏུ་གཟུང་བྱ་སྟེ།	*Having heard, should keep it well ;*
གང་ཞིག་བདག་ཉིད་མི་འདོད་པ།	*Whatever things we do not ourselves like ;*
དེ་དག་གཞན་ལ་མི་བྱའོ།	*Should not be done to others.*
(བསྟན་འགྱུར་མདོ་ Vol. གོ་ leaf 174).	(*Tangyur*).
བརྩམ་པར་བྱ་ཞིང་འབྱུང་བར་བྱ།	*You must exert yourself and arise ;*
སངས་རྒྱས་བསྟན་པ་ལ་འཇུག་པར་བྱ། (Dulva, Vol. 5, Leaf 30).	*And walk according to Buddha's teaching.*

There may be said to be still another construction in རྒྱུ་ added to the Future Root (or to the Present Root if there is no Future Root) combined with ཡིན་པ་ in the Present Indicative. This expresses the idea of *I am to*, or *I have to*. Thus :—

ངས་གཏང་རྒྱུ་ཡིན།	*I have to send.*
ཁྱོད་ཀྱིས་གཏང་རྒྱུ་འདུག།	*Thou hast to send.*
ཁོས་གཏང་རྒྱུ་ཡིན།	*He has to send.*
ང་འགྲོ་རྒྱུ་ཡིན།	*I am to go.*
ཁྱོད་འགྲོ་རྒྱུ་འདུག།	*Thou art to go.*
ཁོང་འགྲོ་རྒྱུ་ཡིན།	*He is to go.*

And also another in ཡ་ Thus :—

ང་ལ་གཏང་ཡ་རེད།	*I have* (or *am*) *to send.*
ང་ལ་འགྲོ་ཡ་རེད།	*I have* (or *am*) *to go.*

K.—Purposive.

To express *In order that, In order to, With the object of*, or other similar phrase, the Infinitive is put in the Genitive case, followed, in the Colloquial, by དོན་ལ་, and, in Literary Tibetan, by ཕྱིར་དུ་ or དོན་དུ་, the construction being the same for all persons.

EXAMPLES :—

ངས་གཏོང་ (or བཏང་) བའི་དོན་ལ་ or ཕྱིར་དུ་ or དོན་དུ།	*So that I may* (or *might*) *send.*
ངས་ཤེས་པའི་དོན་ལ་ཁོས་ང་ལ་བྲིས་པ་རེད།	*He wrote to me in order that I might know.*
ཁྱོད་དགའ་བར་བྱེད་པའི་ཕྱིར་དུ་ངས་དེ་ལྟར་གསུངས་སོ།	*I spoke thus with the object of pleasing you.*
ཁོས་ཁྲིམས་སློབ་པའི་དོན་ལ་དཔེ་ཆ་དེ་ཀློག་གི་འདུག།	*He is reading the book in order to learn law.*

L.—Precative.

In Literary Tibetan the construction is in ཆུག་ or གནོང་, Imperatives of འཇུག་པ་ and གནང་བ་ *To allow*; the verb it governs being put in the Terminative case of the Root or of the Infinitive.

EXAMPLES :—

འདི་དག་འགྲོར་ཆུག་ཅིག།	*Let these go their way.* (John xviii. 8.)
ངས་ཁྱོད་ལ་གསོལ་ཇ་ཏོག་ཙོ་གཏོང་བར་ཆུག་རོགས་གནང་།	*Let me send thee some tea.*

If the governed verb is active and transitive, the subject is in the Agentive.

གཤིན་པོ་རྣམས་ཀྱིས་རང་གི་གཤིན་པོ་རྣམས་དུར་དུ་འཇུག་པར་ཆུག་ཅིག།	*Let the dead bury their dead.* (Matt. viii. 22.)

The Colloquial construction may also be in ཆུག་, but it is usually in བཅུག་ (the Perfect Root used as an Imperative); but in either case only the Root of the governed verb is used.

EXAMPLE :—

ང་ཚོ་ཐམས་ཅད་རྡོ་རྗེ་གླིང་ལ་འགྲོ་བཅུག་དང་, or བཅུག་རོགས་གནང་།	*Let us all go to Darjeeling.*

N.B.— རོགས་ in the polite expression རོགས་གནང་, is merely the Colloquial way of pronouncing གྲོགས་ in the polite Literary expression གྲོགས་གནང་ *Please, Be so good as*, etc.

M.—Permissive.

In Literary Tibetan the construction is in ཆོག་པ་ *To be allowed* or *permitted*; the governed verb being generally put in the Instrumental case of the Infinitive, and the subject in the Agentive, if connected with a Transitive verb.

EXAMPLES :—

ངས་གཏོང་བས་ཆོག་གོ།	*I may (or am allowed to) send.*
ཁྱོད་ཀྱིས་གཏོང་བས་ཆོག་གོ།	*Thou mayest send.*
ཁོས་གཏོང་བས་ཆོག་གོ།	*He may send.*
ངས་གཏོང་བས་ཆོག་པ་ཡིན་ནོ།	*I was allowed to send.*
ངས་གཏོང་བས་ཆོག་པར་འགྱུར་རོ།	*I shall be allowed to send.*

(*N.B.*—This construction in བས་, or པས་, is generally used in books only.)

Sometimes the construction in རུང་བ་ *To be suitable*, or *proper*, is used idiomatically instead of the above.

EXAMPLE :—

གང་བྱས་ཀྱང་རུང་ངོ་།	*Whatever has been done is proper*, which is the ordinary idiom for *You may do as you please*, or *whatever you like*.

The Colloquial construction is in ཆོག་པ་ added to the Root of the governed verb. Subject in Nominative for Intransitive verbs.

EXAMPLES :—

ང་འགྲོ་ཆོག་, or ཆོག་གི་ཡོད།	*I may* (or *am permitted to*) *go.*
ཁྱོད་འགྲོ་ཆོག་, or ཆོག་གི་འདུག།	*Thou mayest go.*
ཁོ་འགྲོ་ཆོག་, or ཆོག་གི་ཡོད་, or འདུག་, or ཡོད་པ་རེད།	*He may go.*
ང་འགྲོ་ཆོག་པ་ཡོད་, or ཆོག་ཡོད།	*I might have gone*, or *would have been permitted to go.*
ང་འགྲོ་ཆོག་གི་ཡིན་, or ཆོག་ཡོང་།	*I shall be allowed to go.*
ཁྱོད་འགྲོ་ཆོག་གི་འདུག་, or རེད་, or ཆོག་ཡོང་།	*Thou wilt be allowed to go.*
ཁོ་འགྲོ་ཆོག་གི་རེད་ or ཆོག་ཡོང་།	*He will be allowed to go.*

But with Transitive verbs the subject is in the Agentive.

EXAMPLES :—

ངས་གཏང་ཆོག།	*I may* (or *am allowed to*) *send.*
ངས་བཏང་ཆོག་, or ཆོག་པ་ཡིན།	*I was allowed to send.*
ངས་གཏང་ཆོག་, or བཏང་ཆོག་ཡོང་།	*I shall be allowed to send.*

Also note :—

ང་ཚོས་ ཁང་ མིག་ འདིའི་ ནང་ ལ་ ཐ་ མག་ འཐེན་ཆོག་གི་རེད་དམ་ or ཆོག་གམ།	*Are we allowed to smoke in this room?*

N.—Optative.

In Literary Tibetan this may be formed by putting the verb in the Terminative case of the Infinitive and adding གྱུར་, the Imperative of འགྱུར་བ་ *To be, To become*, followed by ན་ *If*, and ཨང་ an interjection.

EXAMPLE :—

ངས་གཏོང་བར་གྱུར་ན་ཨང་། *Would*, or *Oh, that I might send.*

Another Literary construction is in ཤོག, the Imperative of ཡོང་བ་ or འོང་བ་ *To come*; the verb being similarly put in the Terminative case of the Infinitive.

EXAMPLES :—

ངས་གཏོང་བར་ཤོག་ཅིག། *Would that I might send.*

ཁྱེད་མི་ངལ་བ་བདེ་བླག་འདོང་བར་ཤོག། *May you without fatigue proceed happily.* (Das.)

Another Literary construction is in ན་ *If*, combined with the expression ཅི་མ་རུང་ *How suitable*, or *excellent.*

EXAMPLES :—

ང་འགྲོ་ན་ཅི་མ་རུང་། *Oh that*, or *would that, I were going.*

ང་མ་སོང་ན་ཅི་མ་རུང་། *Would that I had not gone.*

ངས་དཔེ་ཆ་དེ་ཁྱོད་ལ་སྟེར་ཆོག་པ་ཡིན་ན་ཅི་མ་རུང་། *Would I were permitted to give you the book.*

In the Colloquial the Root or the Infinitive of the verb is used, followed by ཤོག།

EXAMPLES :—

ང་འགྲོ་ (བ་) ཤོག། *Would I were going.*

ངས་གཏོང་ (བ་) ཤོག། *Oh that I might send.*

The following Colloquialism is also heard :—

ང་གཏོང་ན་ཆོག་པ་ཨ། *Oh that I might send.*

ང་འགྲོ་ན་ཆོག་པ་ཨ། *Would I were going.*

O.—*Imperative.*

It will be remembered that many verbs have no distinctively Imperative Roots. Such, for instance, are མཐོང་བ་ *To see*, and ཐོབ་པ་ *To receive*, each of which has only one Root throughout ; and ངུ་བ་ *To weep* and འཚོར་བ་ *To flee*, each of which has only a Present and a Perfect Root. In all such cases the Present Root is used in Literary Tibetan for the Imperative, with the addition of the Imperative sign ཅིག་, ཞིག་, or ཤིག་, agreeably to the final letter of the Root. The further addition of དང་ has a softening effect, and so has ཨང་ A politer form adds རོགས་བྱེད་ to the Root, and a still more respectful form adds རོགས་གནང་ to the Root.

Rules, it is true, are given in some grammars for the formation of the Imperative Root, but, as they are somewhat complex, and, moreover, do not always work, it is just as easy and much safer to look up in the dictionary the Imperative Root of each individual verb, and remember it as well as one can.

Prohibitives are formed with མ་ (never མི་ except in the case of དགོས་ and བྱ་) preceding either the Imperative Root or the other part of the verb, if a compound one, e.g. མ་རྗེད་, or མ་རྗེད་པ་བྱེད་, or རྗེད་པ་མ་བྱེད་ *Do not forget.*

With some verbs, even though they have Imperative Roots of their own, the Present Roots, and not the Imperative Roots, are used for Prohibitions.

EXAMPLES :—

འགྲོ་བ་ *To go ;* Present Root འགྲོ་ ; Imperative Root སོང་ *Go ,* Prohibitive མ་འགྲོ་ (pron. MAN-ḌO.) *Do not go.*

བྱེད་པ་ *To do ;* Present Root བྱེད་ ; Imperative Root བྱོས་ or sometimes བྱེད་ *Do ;* Prohibitive མ་བྱེད་ *Don't do.*

འོང་བ་ *To come;* Present Root འོང་; Imperative Root ཤོག་ *Come;* Prohibitive མ་འོང་ *Don't come.*

In the case of Double Imperatives, the two Roots are united by ལ།

EXAMPLES :—

ཤོག་ལ་ལྟོས་ཤོག། *Come and see.* (John i. 39.)

In the Colloquial, if one is using the different Roots properly, the true Imperative Root, or, if none, then the Present Root, is adopted for the Imperative, as in Literary Tibetan.

EXAMPLES :—

ཁྱོད་ཀྱིས་རྟ་འདི་ཙག་ག་ (for པ་) བྱོས། *Take charge of this horse.*

མ་བརྗེད་པ་བྱེད། *Don't forget.*

Or, if the Colloquial has a special Root of its own, it may be used

EXAMPLES :—

རྟ་འདི་ཙག་ག་བྱེད་, or elegantly གྱིས་, or vulgarly བྱས། } *Take charge of this horse.*

But if, as may often be done, one is using the Perfect Root for all moods and tenses, then that Root is also used for the Imperative, with or without ཅིག་, ཞིག་, or ཤིག།

If this latter Imperative sign is used at all, the Colloquial usually adopts the form ཅིག།

ཅིག་, however, is only used in the case of stern or urgent orders or injunctions, or when talking to coolies and the like.

The Colloquial equivalents for གྲོགས་བྱེད་, གྲོགས་གནང་, and ཨང་ are རོགས་བྱེད་, རོགས་གནང་, and ཨ།

དང་ is also largely used in the Colloquial instead of ཅིག་, and has a softening effect.

The following are some of the commoner Colloquial Imperatives and Prohibitives :—

Infinitive.	*Imperative.*
འགྲོ་བ་ *To go.*	སོང་ or རྒྱུག *Go.*
བྱེད་པ་ *To do.*	བྱོས་ or བྱས་ or གྱིས་ *Do.*
ཡོང་བ་ or འོང་བ་ *To come.*	ཤོག *Come.*
འཁྱེར་ཡོང་བ་ or འཁྱེར་བ་ or འཁུར་བ་ *To bring (in hand).*	འཁྱེར་ཤོག or འཁུར་ཤོག *Bring.*
བཏང་བ་ (གཏོང་བ་) *To send.*	ཐོང་ or གཏོང་ (ཅིག) *Send.*
བླུགས་པ་ (བླུག་པ་) *To pour.*	བླུགས་ (ཤིག) *Pour.*
སྐྱོལ་བ་ *To lay* or *put down.*	སྐྱོལ་ (ཞིག) *Put down.*

Negative.

མ་འགྲོ་ *Don't go.*

མ་བྱེད་ *Don't do.*

མ་ཡོང་ or མ་འོང་ *Don't come.*

འཁྱེར་མ་ཡོང་ *Don't bring.*

མ་གཏོང་ or མ་བཏང་ *Don't send.*

མ་བླུག, or མ་བླུགས་ *Don't pour.*

མ་སྐྱོལ་ or མ་བསྐྱལ་ *Don't put down.*

As a matter of fact, in these matters there is no rule save custom; for, according as a man is more or less educated, so he will mix up in his speech literary with vulgar forms, and the only way to learn is to keep one's ears open and observe what the prevailing custom is amongst different classes of Tibetans; for some will prefer to use the roots properly, while others, knowing little or nothing of them, will adopt the sound of the perfect root. So far as *speaking* is concerned, it will not much matter which method is adopted, unless of course one is talking to a cultured Tibetan; but, when *writing* in Tibetan, the roots should be used properly, and the usage with the perfect root discarded.

VI.—The Passive Voice.

In Literary Tibetan, as a rule, the subject of a transitive active verb, or of a causative verb, is put in the agentive case, and the subject of a neuter or of a passive verb is put in the nominative or the accusative (objective) case When, however, the active verb is intransitive, the subject is put in the nominative case. Moreover, when the subject, even of a transitive verb, is a pronoun emphatically used (as, for instance, with the particle ཉི་ annexed to it), the subject is put in the nominative case. Further, when the subject is obviously the agent or instrument, as, for example, when the postposition ལ་ is expressly used with the objective, then it is not necessary, though quite allowable, for the subject to be put in the agentive case; in other words, it may appear in the nominative case.

Examples:—

ཡབ་ཀྱིས་སྲས་ལ་བྱམས་སོ།	*The father loveth the son*, or, *The son is loved by the father.*
བཀའ་བློན་གྱིས་དམག་ཚོ་རུབ་དུ་བཅུག་གོ།	*The governor ordered the soldiers to attack.*
ང་ཕྱུག་པོ་མེད།	*I am not rich.*
དཔེ་ཆ་འདི་ཏ་ལམ་ཚར་ར་ (for བ་) རེད།	*This book is nearly finished.*
ང་ཁྲིམས་ཁང་ལ་འགྲོ་ནོ།	*I am going to court.*
ང་ཉི་ཅི་ཡང་བྱེད་མི་ཐུབ་བོ།	*I can do nothing.*

But what is a Passive Verb in Tibetan? How does the construcion of the Passive Voice differ from that of the Active Voice? In a ense every Tibetan sentence, even when the verb is what we call ctive, is permeated with the Passive idea. For, even such a sentence s ཡབ་ཀྱིས་སྲས་ལ་བྱམས་སོ། *The father loveth the son*, may be rendered qually correctly *The son is loved by the father*; for, literally translated, is *By the father, to*, or *as regards the son, a loving is*. It practically erefore comes to this, that, when the subject is in the agentive case, e Active Voice is intended; but, when the subject of a transitive verb is in the nominative or objective case, the Passive Voice is intended, unless some other structural peculiarity in the sentence indicates otherwise.

The same remarks hold as regards the Colloquial. The subject in the agentive case indicates the Active Voice; the subject in the objective (with or without ལ་) indicates the Passive Voice. As a matter of fact, the Tibetan language strongly favours the agentive construction; and therefore the Passive Voice, or what passes as such, should be avoided as much as possible.

The Infinitive of the Passive Voice is, in Literary Tibetan, the same as the Participle Future of the Active Verb, i.e. the Future Root with the particle, e.g བྱ་བ་ *To be done.*

In the Colloquial it is the Root with རྒྱུ་, or གྱི་ added. These, however, may also be used in Literary Tibetan.

VII.—Compound Verbs.

In Literary Tibetan these are of several kinds.

(*a*) A Substantive combined with an Active Verb.

Example :—

ཉེས་པ་བྱེད་པ་ *To make a mistake,* or *commit a fault,* i.e. *to err.* In such cases the Substantive remains constant, and བྱེད་པ་ is conjugated regularly as an Active 4-Rooted verb; Present Root བྱེད་ Perfect བྱས་, Future བྱ་, Imperative བྱོས།

(*b*) An Adjective in the Terminative case with ར་ combined with an Active Verb.

Example :—

དཀར་པོར་བྱེད་པ་ *To whiten.* In such cases the Adjective in the Terminative case remains constant, and the Active Verb is conjugated regularly, or according to its nature with reference to the Roots it possesses.

(*c*) A Principal Verb in the Terminative case of the Infinitive with ར་ combined with an Active Auxiliary Verb.

EXAMPLES :—

གཏོང་བར་འཇུག་པ། *To permit to send.*

གཉིད་སད་པར་བྱེད་པ། *To awake ; To rouse.*

In such cases the Principal Verb so formed remains constant, and the auxiliary is conjugated according to its nature.

(*d*) The Root of a Principal Verb put in the Terminative case with དུ་ ཏུ་ སུ་ རུ་ or ར་, agreeably to the final letter of the Root, combined with a Causative Verb.

EXAMPLE :—

བྱེད་དུ་འཇུག་པ། *To bid to do.*

In such cases the Principal Verb so formed remains constant, and the Causative is conjugated according to its nature.

(*e*) The Present, Perfect, or Future Infinitive of a Principal Verb put in the Instrumental case and followed by the Root of an auxiliary.

EXAMPLES :—

ངས་གཏོང་བས་ཆོག། *I am allowed to send.*

ངས་བཏང་བས་ཆོག། *I was allowed to send.*

ངས་གཏང་བས་ཆོག། *I shall be allowed to send.*

Or, Present Infinitive of Principal Verb in Instrumental case, declining the auxiliary regularly in ཡོད་པ།

EXAMPLES :—

གཏོང་བས་ཆོག་གི་ཡོད། *I am allowed to send.*

གཏོང་བས་ཆོག་པ་ཡིན། *I was ,, ,, ,,*

གཏོང་བས་ཆོག་པར་འགྱུར་ or བྱེའོ། *I shall be ,, ,, ,,*

Here the auxiliary alone is conjugated.

(*f*) A Principal Verb (itself consisting of the Root of one verb added to the Root of another) combined with an Active Verb. EXAMPLE— not very idiomatic, but merely adduced by way of illustration :—

འགྲོ་འདུག་བྱེད་པ། *To stroll about.*

Here the two Roots remain constant, and the Active Verb is conjugated according to its nature.

(*g*) A Principal Verb (itself consisting of two Roots as above, combined with the Root of an Active Verb in the Terminative case with དུ་, ཏུ་ etc.), combined with a Causative Verb.

EXAMPLE :—

འགྲོ་འདུག་བྱེད་དུ་འཇུག་པ། *To cause to stroll about.*

Here all except the Causative remains constant, and the Causative is conjugated according to its nature.

In the Colloquial the Infinitive and the Root of a verb are never put in the Terminative case as they are in Literary Tibetan.

Moreover, the Infinitive may represent the Substantive or Noun as well as the Verb.

Hence, when the Infinitive, in form, is combined with an auxiliary verb, it may be regarded either as a Substantive or as a Verb.

Thus ཉེས་པ་ may mean either *A mistake* or *To make a mistake* ; and hence the Colloquial phrase ཉེས་པ་བྱེད་པ་ may be rendered either *To make a mistake* or *To mistake*, *To err*.

However regarded, the tendency of Colloquial Tibetan, when a Substantive or a Verb is combined with an auxiliary verb, is to drop the Infinitive form of the verb, or the full form of the Substantive, and to use only the Root, though this is not always done.

For instance the Literary གྲལ་ (དུ་) སྒྲིག་པ་ *To arrange* or *prepare* (literally *To place in rows*) is used Colloquially with བྱེད་པ་, thus :— གྲལ་ (or even གྲ་) སྒྲིག་བྱེད་པ།

When, however, ཡོད་པ་ *To have*, is the auxiliary, what looks like a formal Infinitive is obviously a Substantive, e.g. འདོད་པ་ in འདོད་པ་ཡོད་པ་ *To have a*, or *the*, *wish* or *desire*, i.e. *to wish* or *desire*.

In short, the tendency to use the Root of the Principal Verb, or of the Substantive, holds, whether the auxiliary is an Active or a Causative Verb, though not where it is a verb like ཡོད་པ་ *To have.*

The ordinary Colloquial Honorific auxiliary verb is གནང་བ་ *To be pleased, good enough, so kind as.* It is combined either with Infinitives, or Roots followed by རྒྱུ་, or bare Roots.

EXAMPLES :—

འབུལ་ར་ (for བ་) གནང་བ།	*To give.*
ཚུར་འཆིབ་རྒྱུ་གནང་བ།	*To return*, or *come* or *go back.*
ཐུགས་འདོད་གནང་བ།	*To desire.*

VIII.—In Literary Tibetan VERBS OF BECOMING, GROWING, CHANGING, TURNING, GETTING, and the like, are often expressed with the aid of the auxiliaries འགྱུར་བ་ *To become,* etc. or འགྲོ་བ་ *To go*, the latter being the more modern. The noun or adjective governed by such auxiliary is put in the Terminative case, e.g. བླ་མར་འགྱུར་བ or འགྲོ་བ་ *To become a Lama ;* ཕྱུག་པོར་འགྱུར་བ་ or འགྲོ་བ་ *To get rich.* But sometimes the Literary Tibetan has in these cases a special verb, e.g. བགྲེ་བ་ *To grow old.*

The Colloquial, when it does not have a special verb, uses འགྲོ་བ་ and does not put the noun or adjective in the Terminative case.

EXAMPLE :—

ཕྱུག་པོ་འགྲོ་བ: *To get rich ;* but རྒས་པ་ *To grow old.*

IX.—INCEPTION is expressed in Literary Tibetan with the aid of the verb འཛུགས་པ or ཛུག་པ་ (*Perfect Root* བཙུགས་ or ཛུགས་ *Future Root* གཛུགས་ *Imperative Root* ཛུག་ or ཛུགས་) *To begin.* It is used with or without the prefixed word མགོ། When used as an auxiliary the construction is that described under Compound Verbs, No. VII.

The Colloquial equivalent is (མགོ་) བཙུག་པ་ *To begin*, which when used as an auxiliary, may be combined either with the Infinitive or the Root (generally the Root) of the Principal Verb.

Inception may also be expressed by the verb next-noticed.

X.—Imminence is expressed in Literary Tibetan (amongst other ways) by the verb གཟས་པ་ *To be about to, To be on the point of, To be just going to.* When used as an auxiliary the Principal Verb is generally put in the Terminative case of the Infinitive.

Example :—

ངས་འབྲི་བར་གཟས་པ་ལས། — *I was about to write ;* or *as I was about to write.* (Rev. x. 4.)

In the Colloquial the same idea is expressed by means of the auxiliary verb འགྲོ་བ་ *To go*, combined with the Root of the Principal Verb.

Examples :—

ངས་ཡི་གེ་འབྲི་འགྲོ་ཡོད། — *I am just about to write.*

ངས་ཡི་གེ་འབྲི་འགྲོ་ཡོད་པ་ཡིན། — *I was just about to write.*

ཁ་སང་ངས་ཡི་གེ་འབྲི་འགྲོ་ཡོད། — *Yesterday I was just about to write.*

XI.—In Literary Tibetan Verbal Continuatives are expressed with the aid of some adverb like རྒྱུན་དུ་ or རྟག་ཏུ་ *Always, Continually, Perpetually*, or of a phrase like རྒྱུན་ཆད་མེད་པར་ *Without ceasing.*

Examples :—

ཁོང་གིས་རྟག་ཏུ་ (or རྒྱུན་དུ་) རེའོ། — *He hopes on, keeps on hoping, hopes continually.*

རྟག་ཏུ་དགའ་བར་གྱུར་ཅིག། — *Go on rejoicing ; Rejoice always.* (1 Thess. v. 17.)

རྒྱུན་ཆད་མེད་པར་སྨོན་ལམ་ཐོབ་ཅིག། — *Pray on ; keep on praying ; Pray without ceasing.* (1 Thess. v. 18.)

Colloquially they are formed by repeating the Root of the verb, with གི་, གྱི་, or ཀྱི་ added to each Root, and combining the whole with བྱེད་པ་ *To do*, as an auxiliary.

EXAMPLES :—

ངས་ཟ་གི་ཟ་གི་བྱེད་ཡོང་ or བྱེད་ཀྱི་ཡིན།	*I shall go on eating.*
དཔེ་ཆ་འདི་ཀློག་གི་ཀློག་གི་བྱེས་ or བྱོས་ or གྱིས།)	*Go on reading this book.*

XII.—FINALITY OR COMPLETE ACCOMPLISHMENT.

In earlier Literature this is expressed by putting the verb in the Terminative case of the Infinitive with ར་, and adding ཟིན་, the Root of ཟིན་པ་ *To be finished*, and then conjugating regularly.

In later Literature the same construction is adopted, but, instead of ཟིན་, use is made of ཚར་ Perfect Root of འཚར་བ་ *To be completed, terminated, finished*, with or without the preceding adverb ཡོངས་སུ་ *Wholly, Entirely*.

The Colloquial custom is simply to add ཚར་ to the Root of the verb, and then conjugate regularly.

EXAMPLES :—

ངས་དཔེ་ཆ་འདི་ཀློག་ཚར་གྱི་ཡོད།	*I am reading this book right through.*
ངས་དཔེ་ཆ་འདི་བཀླགས་ཚར་སོང་།	*I have read this book right through.*
ངས་དཔེ་ཆ་འདི་བཀླག་ཚར་ཡོང་།	*I shall read this book right through.*

XIII.—DESIDERATIVES are expressed, both in Literary Tibetan and in the Colloquial, with the aid of the auxiliary verbs འདོད་པ་ *To wish*, *To desire*, and དགོས་པ་ (the vulgar Colloquial form of which is དགོ་བ་) *To wish*, *want*, etc.

In Literary Tibetan འདོད་པ་ is combined with the Infinitive of the

Principal Verb put in the Terminative case with ར་, e.g. ང་མཐོང་བར་འདོད་དོ་ *I wish to see*, but sometimes only the Root of the Principal Verb is used. Thus: ང་འགྲོ་འདོད་དོ་ or even the Infinitive, ང་འགྲོ་བ་འདོད་དོ།

When དགོས་པ་ or དགོ་བ་ (which latter is never *written*) is used, the subject of course is put in the Dative case. Thus: in Literary Tibetan:—

ང་ལ་མཐོང་བར་དགོས་སོ། *I wish to see.*

Or, in Colloquial:—

ང་ལ་མཐོང་བ་དགོས།

Or:—

ང་ལ་མཐོང་དགོས་ཀྱི་ཡོད།

Or:— } *I wish to see.*

ང་ལ་མཐོང་དགོ་གི་ཡོད།

Or:—

ང་མཐོང་རྒྱུ་འདོད།

An Intensive form of འདོད་པ་ is སྙིང་འདོད་པ་ *To long, to yearn, to crave.*

EXAMPLE:—

ང་རྡོ་རྗེ་གླིང་ལ་འགྲོ་སྙིང་འདོད། *I long to go to Darjeeling.*

Instead of འགྲོ་འདོད་དོ་ *I wish to go*, another Literary form is འགྲོ་བའི་འདོད་པ་ཡོད་ *I have a desire for going*, i.e. *to go*.

XIV.—FREQUENTATIVES may be formed, not by repeating the Root of the Verb, but by the Periphrastic Present.

EXAMPLE:—

ཁྱོད་ཁྲིམས་ཁང་ལ་འགྲོ་གི་འདུག་གམ། *Do you often go to Court (i.e. Law Courts)?*

Or the adverb མཚམས་མཚམས་ *Often*, may be added. Thus :—

ཁྱོད་ཁྲིམས་ཁང་ལ་མཚམས་མཚམས་འགྲོ་གི་འདུག་གམ། } *Do you often go to Court?*

XV.—Use of the Perfect Root in the Colloquial.

When the Present Root of a Verb ends in an inherent ཨ་ (e.g. ལྟ་བ་ *To look*), or in an inherent འ་ (e.g. བཙའ་བ་ *To bear*, or *bring forth*), or in ུ (e.g. ཞུ་བ་ *To request, to ask*), or in ོ (e.g. ཚོ་བ་ *To live, feed, nourish*), that Present Root is generally used for the Present Indicative, the Future Indicative in གི་ཡིན་ etc., the Present Participle, Periphrastic Present Participle, Present Infinitive, Supine and Verbal Noun. Of course, it is quite allowable, and even proper, both when speaking and writing, and especially when writing the Colloquial, to use the Roots that are assigned to particular moods and tenses for those moods and tenses. It is said, however, that as a matter of fact this is seldom or never done, at least in Vulgar Colloquial. It is also said that if, in the verbs above referred to, the Future is formed with ཡོང་ for all persons, instead of with གི་ཡིན་ etc., the Perfect Root should be used; and that for all other verbs the Colloquial usually adopts the Perfect Root, if any, for all moods and tenses. This is very doubtful, except perhaps in vulgar Colloquial. The idea, especially as connected with the Future Tense, probably arises from the fact that the Perfect Root often has the same, or nearly the same, *sound* as the Future Root. For instance, in the Verb གཏོང་བ་ *To send,* the Perfect Root བཏང་ and the Future Root གཏང་ sound alike or nearly alike. In this case, the better course would be to use གཏང་ instead of བཏང་ for the Future in ཡོང་ The best coarse would be to use the Roots properly, in all cases.

CHAPTER III.

SYNTAX.

§ 39.—Most of what the student will desire to know under this head has already been dealt with in Chapter II, Etymology, in connection with each of the different parts of speech, but a brief *résumé* of the main rules will doubtless be appreciated.

1.—Every Tibetan sentence is ordered thus: Subject, Object, Predicate.

Examples :—

ངས་དཔེ་ཆ་འདི་ཀློག་གི་ཡོད།	*I am reading this book.*
ང་ or ང་ལ་རྡོ་རྗེ་གླིང་ལ་འགྲོ་དགོས་ཀྱི་ ཡོད་ (or འགྲོ་སྙིང་འདོད་ or འགྲོ་བའི་འདོད་པ་ཡོད་)།	*I want to go to Darjeeling.*

2.—As regards the component parts of the subject, or of the object, if the student thinks more or less *backwards*, he will get a very fair idea of the order in which they should be spoken or written. That order is as follows :—

(*a*) The principal substantive; unless it is qualified by an adjective in the genitive case, in which event the adjective comes first.

(*b*) The adjective when in any case other than the genitive.

(*c*) Participial clauses containing relative or correlative pronouns, and auxiliary to the principal substantive. These follow the rule of the adjective.

(*d*) The numeral, or the definite or indefinite article, and then the postposition.

3.—Adverbs precede, and interrogative pronouns, immediately precede, the verb which they qualify or with which they are connected.

4.—As regards the predicate, the verb comes last, every extension of the predicate preceding it. As regards the verb itself, the principal verb comes first, either in the shape of an infinitive in the terminative case, or of a simple infinitive, or of a root, and then comes the active, auxiliary, or causative verb, these last alone being conjugated with reference to mood and tense.

5.—The general aspect of a Tibetan sentence, particularly if long and complex, is a series of subordinate clauses in a state of suspense, winding up with a definite statement.

EXAMPLE :—

དེ་ནས་ཁོང་གིས་མི་ཚོགས་རྣམས་གཟིགས་དེ། རི་ལ་ཕེབས་ནས་བཞུགས་པ་ལས།
ཉེ་གནས་རྣམས་ཁོང་གི་མདུན་དུ་ཡོངས་པ་དང་། ཁོང་གིས་ཞལ་ཕྱེས་དེ་དག་ལ་
ཆོས་བསྟན་ཅིང་གསུངས་པ། (Matt. v. 1, 2.)

And seeing the multitudes he went up into the mountain : and when he had sat down, his disciples came unto him : and he opened his mouth and taught them, saying.

But the literal Tibetan is :—

Then by him the crowds seeing, into the mountain having gone, having sat down, the disciples into his presence having come, by him mouth having opened, to them teaching was said.

APPENDIX.

CONJUGATIONS.

Note.—These are intended for ready reference; and, to economize spaco, pronouns have been omitted, except at the beginning. The plural is the same as the singular. They are not to be regarded as rigid, immutable expressions, but as forms which take on a moulding according to the structural necessities of the sentence.

I.—Colloquial ཡོད་པ་ *To be present; To exist; To be.*

Indicative Mood.

Present.

ང་ཡོད། *I am*, or *We are.*

ཁྱོད་ཡོད་ or འདུག། *Thou art*, or *You are.*

ཁོ་ཡོད་ or འདུག་ or ཡོད་པ་རེད། *He* or *it is*, or *They are.*

Or, with an Indefinite signification :—

ཡོང་ for all persons.

Past.

Same as Present, context shewing Tense.

Or :—

ང་ཡོད་པ་ཡིན། *I was.*

ཁྱོད་ཡོད་པ་འདུག་ or occasionally ཡོད་པ་རེད་ or (rarely, chiefly interrogatively) ཡོད་པ་ཡིན། *Thou wast.*

ཁོ་ཡོད་པ་རེད་ or occasionally ཡོད་པ་འདུག་ or rarely ཡོད་པ་ཡིན། He was.

Imperfect: *I was existing.*
Perfect: *I have existed.*
Pluperfect: *I had existed.*
} Same as Present, context shewing Tense; or same as above form of Past.

Future.

ཡོང་ for all persons : *I shall exist.*

SUBJUNCTIVE AND CONDITIONAL MOODS.

Present : *If (so and so)....(then) I shall exist.*

(Present Root)....ན་ ....ཡོང་ for all persons.

Past : *If .... I would exist.*

(Perfect Root)....ན་ ....ཡོད་པ་ཡིན་ and so on as in Past Tense, Indicative Mood.

Or :—

(Perfect Root)....ན་ ....ཡོང་ f. a. p. (= for all persons).

Perfect : *If .... I would have existed.*

(Perfect Root)....ན་ ....ཡོད་ or ....བྱུང་ or ....འདུག་ f. a. p.

POTENTIAL MOOD.

Present : *I can exist.*

ཡོད་ཐུབ་ or ཡོད་ཐུབ་ཡོང་ f. a. p.

Or :—

ཡོད་ཐུབ་ཀྱི་ཡིན།

ཡོད་ཐུབ་ཀྱི་འདུག་ (or རེད་ or rarely, chiefly interrogatively, ཡིན་)།

ཡོད་ཐུབ་ཀྱི་རེད་ (or འདུག་ or rarely ཡིན་)།

Past : *I could exist.*

ཡོད་ཐུབ་སོང་། f. a. p.

Or :—

ཡོད་ཐུབ་པ་ཡིན། and so on, as in Past Indicative.

PROBABILITY.

Present : *Perhaps I shall exist ; I may exist ; It is likely*, etc.

གཅིག་བྱེད་ན་ ..ཡོང་། f. a. p.

Or :—

ཡོང་གི་ཡིན་པ་འདྲ། f. a. p.

Or :—

ཡོང་གི་ཡིན་གྲ་ (or འགྲོ་)། f. a. p.

Past: *I might exist.*

གཅིག་བྱེད་ན་···ཡོད་པ་ཡིན། and so on, as in Past Indicative.

Or :—

གཅིག་བྱེད་ན་··ཡོད་ or འདུག། f. a p.

Or :—

ཡོད་ (or འདུག་) པ་ཡིན་པ་འདྲ། f. a. p.

Or :—

ཡོད་ (or འདུག་) པ་ཡིན་གྱི་ or འགྱི། f a. p.

HORTATIVE MOOD.

Present: *I must exist; I ought to exist.*

ཡོད་དགོས། f. a. p., or ཡོད་དགོས་ཡོང་། f. a. p.

Or :—

ཡོད་དགོས་ཀྱི་ཡིན། and so on, as in Indicative Present of Colloquial ཡིན་པ།

Or vulgarly :—

ཡོད་དགོ་གི་ཡིན། and so on, as next above.

Past: *I ought to have existed.*

ཡོད་དགོས་པ་ཡིན། and so on, as in Indicative Past

Or :—

ཡོད་དགོས་བྱུང་། f. a. p.

Or vulgarly :—

ཡོད་དགོ་བ་ཡིན། and so on, as in Indicative Past, but with བ་ instead of པ།

PURPOSIVE MOOD.

Present and **Past**: *That*, or *In order that*, or *So that I may* or *might exist.*

ཡོད་པའི་དོན་ལ། f. a. p.

IMPERATIVE MOOD.

Be; exist.

བྱུང་, or ཡོད་པ་བྱོས་, or ཡོད་པ་བྱིས་, or ཡོད་པ་བྱེད་, or ཡོད་པ་གྱིས་, or ཡོད་པ་མཛོད། f. a. p.

If Attributive only, then བྱོས་, or བྱིས་ (Coll.), or བྱེད་ or གྱིས་, or མཛོད།

Prohibitive: མ་འབྱུང་, or མ་ (ཡོད་པ་) བྱེད་, or མ་ (ཡོད་པ་) བགྱིད་, or མ་ (ཡོད་པ་) མཛད། f. a. p.

Note.— ཅིག་, or རོགས་བྱེད་, or རོགས་གནང་, or དང་, or ཨ་ may be added according to rule.

PRECATIVE MOOD.

Let me exist.

ཡོད་བཅུག། (with or without ཅིག་ etc.) f. a. p.

PERMISSIVE MOOD.

I may exist; I am allowed to exist.

ཡོད་ཆོག། f. a. p.

Or:—

ཡོད་ཆོག་གི་ཡོད།

ཡོད་ཆོག་གི་ཡོད་ or འདུག།

ཡོད་ཆོག་གི་ཡོད་ or འདུག་ or ཡོད་པ་རེད།

(This last may be conjugated on, according to mood and tense.)

OPTATIVE.

Oh that I existed; Would that I existed.

ཡོད་ཞིག་, or ཡོད་པ་ཞིག། f. a. p.

Participles.

Present: ཡོད་པ། *Existing; Being.*

Past: ཡོད་པ། *Existed; Been.*

Com. Perfect: ཡོད་པ་ཡིན་པ། *Having existed; having been.*

Future: ཡོང་རྒྱུ་, or ཡོང་གྱི། *About to exist* or *be.*

Periphrastic Expressions.

ཡོད་མཁན། *Who* or *which exists* or *existed.*

ཡོད་པ། *Which exists* or *existed.*

ཡོང་གྱི་ (or ཡོང་རྒྱུ་) མཁན། *Who is to,* or *will, exist.*

ཡོང་གྱི་ (or ཡོང་རྒྱུ་) ཡིན་པ་དེ། *Which is to,* or *will, exist.*

ཡོང་གྱི་ (or ཡོང་རྒྱུ་) དེ། Ditto.

Other Participial Expressions.

Present.

ཡོད་ཙང་། *As, since, because,* etc. .... *exists, exist.*

ཡོད་དུས། }
ཡོད་པའི་དུས་ལ། } *At the time of existing; when, while* .... *exists, exist.*

ཡོད་ན། *In* or *by existing; if, when,* .... *exists, exist.*

ཡོད་ལ། *Existing.*

ཡོད་ཀྱིས། *Though, because existing.*

ཡོད་པའི་དོན་ལ། *For existing.*

Past.

ཡོད་པས། }
ཡོད་པ་དང་། }
ཡོད་པ་ལས། } *As, since, because, when, after,* etc. .... *existed.*

ཡོད་ཀྱིས། *Though, because* .... *existed.*

VERBAL NOUNS.

ཡོད་པ, or ཡོད་པ་དེ། *The existing.*

SUPINES.

ཡོད་པ, or ཡོད་རྒྱུ། *To exist ; To be.*

ཡོད་པའི་དོན་ལ།
ཡོད་རྒྱུའི་དོན་ལ།
ཡོད་ཡའི་དོན་ལ།
} *For existing ; For being.*

INFINITIVE MOOD.

ཡོད་པ། *To exist ; To be.*

ཡོད་པ་ཡིན་པ། *To have existed ; To have been.*

ཡོང་གྱི (or ཡོང་རྒྱུ) ཡིན་པ། *To be about to exist.*

N.B.—ཡོད་པ may always be used for ཡིན་པ but ཡིན་པ may not be used for ཡོད་པ།

II.—LITERARY ཡོད་པ *To exist ; To be present ; To be.*

(*N.B.*—The forms in འགྱུར་བ are only used when that verb is being used as a mere copula.)

INDICATIVE MOOD.

Present : *I exist ; I am existing ; I am present ; I am.*

(Same as in Colloquial.)

Or, elegantly but rather obsoletely :—

ང་མཆིས། *I exist.*

ཁྱེད་གདའ། *Thou existest.*

ཁོང་མཆིས, or གདའ, or མཆིས་པ་ཡིན། *He exists.*

Or respectfully :—

བདག་ཡོད།

ཁྲིད་མངའ།

ཁོང་བཞུགས, or མངའ, or བཞུགས་པ་ཡིན།

N.B.—

མཆིས་པ་ is an elegant form for ཡོད་པ།

གདའ་བ་ ,, ,, ,, ,, འདུག་པ།

ལགས་པ་ ,, ,, ,, ,, ཡིན་པ།

མངའ་བ་ ,, a respectful ,, ,, ཡོད་པ།

བཞུགས་པ་ ,, ,, ,, ,, ཡོད་པ།

Past : *I existed.*

(Same as in Colloquial.)

Or :—

ཡོད་པར་གྱུར་ཏོ། f. a. p.

Or :—

གྱུར་ཏོ། f. a. p. *I was....*

Or :—

ཡོད་པར་གྱུར་པ་ཡིན། and so on, as in second form of Indicative Past of Literary ཡིན་པ།

Or :—

གྱུར་པ་ཡིན། Ditto.

Imperfect : *I was existing.*

(Same as Present, context showing tense.)

Perfect : *I have existed ;* **Pluperfect** : *I had existed.*

(Same as Past.)

Future : *I shall exist.*

ཡོད་པར་འགྱུར་རོ། f. a. p.

Or :—

འགྱུར་རོ། f. a. p. *I shall be....*

Subjunctive and Conditional Moods.

Present: *If......I shall exist.*

(Present Root) ···ན··· (any Future form as above).

Past: *If......I would exist.*

(Perfect Root) ···ན···ཡོད་པ་ཡིན། and so on.

Or :—

···ན···ཡོད་པར་གྱུར་པ་ཡིན། and so on.

Or :—

···ན···གྱུར་པ་ཡིན། and so on. *I would be...*

Or :—

···ན···ཡོད་པར་གྱུར་ཏོ། f. a. p

Or :—

···ན···གྱུར་ཏོ། f. a. p *I would be....*

Perfect: *If....I would have existed.*

(Perfect Root) ···ན···ཡོད, or ···འདུག, or ···བྱུང། f. a. p.

Or :—

···ན···ཡོད་པར་གྱུར་པ་ཡོད། and so on.

Or :—

···ན···གྱུར་པ་ཡོད། and so on. *I would have been.*

Potential Mood.

Present: *I can exist.*

ཡོད་པར་ནུས་སོ། f. a. p

Past: *I could exist.*

ཡོད་པར་ནུས་པ་ཡིན།

ཡོད་པར་ནུས་པ་འདུག, or occasionally, chiefly interrogatively, ཡིན།

ཡོད་པར་ནུས་པ་ཡིན།

Perfect: *I could have existed.*

ཡོད་པར་ནུས་པ་ཡོད། and so on.

Probability.

Present : *Perhaps I shall exist : I may exist.*

སྲུ་ཞིས་·· ཡོད་པར་འགྱུར་རོ། f. a. p.

Or :—

ཡོད་པར་སྲིད་དོ། f. a. p.

Or :—

ཡོད་པར་འདུག་གོ། f. a. p.

Past : *Perhaps I would exist : I might exist.*

སྲུ་ཞིས་·· ཡོད་པར་གྱུར་པ་ཡིན། and so on.

Or :—

ཡོད་པར་སྲིད་པ་ཡིན། and so on.

Or :—

སྲུ་ཞིས་·· ཡོད་པར་གྱུར་ཏོ། f. a. p.

Perfect : *I would have existed : I might have existed.*

སྲུ་ཞིས་·· ཡོད་པར་གྱུར་པ་ཡོད། and so on.

Or :—

ཡོད་པར་སྲིད་པ་ཡོད། and so on.

Hortative Mood.

Present : *I must exist ; I ought to exist.*

ཡོད་པར་དགོས་སོ་ or ཡོད་པར་བྱ། f. a. p.

Past : *I must have existed ; ought to have existed.*

ཡོད་པར་དགོས་པ་ཡིན། and so on.

Purposive Mood.

Present and Past : *In order that I may* or *might exist.*

ཡོད་པར་འགྱུར་བའི་ཕྱིར། f. a. p.

Or :—

ཡོང་རྒྱུའི་ཕྱིར། f. a. p.

Imperative Mood.

བཞུགས་ཤིག or ཡོད་པར་གྱུར་ཅིག། *Exist.*

Precative Mood.

Let me etc., *exist.*

ཡོད་དུ་ཚུག་ཅིག་ or ཡོད་པར་ཚུག་ཅིག། f. a. p.

Permissive Mood.

Present : *I am allowed to exist.*

ཡོད་པས་ཆོག་གི། f. a. p.

Or :—

ཡོད་པར་རུང་ངོ་། f. a. p., or ཡོད་པའི་རིགས་སོ། f. a. p.

Past : *I was allowed to exist.*

ཡོད་པས་ཆོག་པ་ཡིན། and so on.

Future : *I shall be allowed to exist.*

ཡོད་པས་ཆོག་པར་འགྱུར་རོ། f. a. p.

Optative Mood.

Oh that I might exist.

ཡོད་པར་གྱུར་ན་ཨང་།

Or :—

ཡོད་པར་ཤོག་ཅིག།

Or :—

ཡོད་ན་ཅི་མ་རུང་།

} f. a. p.

Participles.

(Same as in Colloquial.)

Periphrastic Expressions :—

Same as in Colloquial. Also :—

ཡོད་བྱེད་མཁན་ or ཡོད་བྱེད་པ་པོ། *He who exists* or *existed.*

ཡོད་བྱེད་པ། *That which exists* or *existed.*

OTHER PARTICIPIAL EXPRESSIONS.

Present : *Existing.*

ཡོད་དེ་, ཡོད་ལ་, ཡོད་པ་ལ་, ཡོད་ཀྱིན་, ཡོད་ཅིང་, ཡོད་པའི་ཚེ་ལ་, ཡོད་ན་, ཡོད་པའི་དོན་དུ, ཡོད་པའི་ཕྱིར་དུ། etc.

Past : *Having existed.*

ཡོད་དེ་, ཡོད་པས་, ཡོད་ནས་, ཡོད་པ་ལས་, ཡོད་པ་དང་། etc.

VERBAL NOUN.

ཡོད་པ་ or ཡོད་པ་ནི། *Existing, To exist.*

SUPINE.

ཡོད་པར་ or ཡོད་དུ། *To exist.*

INFINITIVES.

(As in Colloquial.) Also :—

ཡོད་པར་འགྱུར་བ། *To be about to exist.*

N.B.—ཡོད་པ་ may always be used instead of ཡིན་པ་, but ཡིན་པ་ may never take the place of ཡོད་པ་ when the latter means *To be present, To exist.*

III.—COLLOQUIAL ཡིན་པ་ *To be.*

INDICATIVE MOOD.

Present.

ཡིན་ *I am.*

འདུག་ or occasionally རེད་, or rarely, chiefly interrogatively ཡིན། } *Thou art.*

རེད་ or occasionally འདུག་ } *He is.*
or rarely ཡིན།

Past:	*I was.*	Same as Present, context showing Tense.
Imperfect:	*I was being.*	
Perfect:	*I have been.*	
Pluperfect:	*I had been.*	

Future: *I shall be.*

ཡོང་། f. a. p. (*N.B.*—Also used for *Indefinite Present.*)

Or :—

···གི་ཡིན།

···གི་འདུག་ or ···གི་རེད་ or ···གི་ཡིན།

···གི་རེད་ or ···གི་འདུག་ or ···གི་ཡིན།

SUBJUNCTIVE AND CONDITIONAL MOODS.

Present: *If ... I shall be.*

(Present Root with ···ན་ followed by either of above Future forms.)

Past: *If .... I would be.*

(Perfect Root) ···ན་··པ་ཡིན།

,, ,, ···ན་···པ་འདུག་ or ···པ་རེད་ or ···པ་ཡིན།

,, ,, ···ན་···པ་རེད་ or པ་འདུག་ or པ་ཡིན།

Or :—

(Perfect Root) ···ན་··ཡོང་། f. a. p.

Perfect: *If .... I would have been.*

(Perfect Root) ···ན་···པ་ཡོད། and so on.

Or :—

(Perfect Root) ···ན་··ཡོད་ or ···འདུག་ or ···བྱུང་། each f. a. p.,

save that བྱུང་ is confined to 1st person.

POTENTIAL MOOD.

Present: *I can be.*

ཡིན་ཐུབ་ or ཡིན་ཐུབ་ཡོང་། f. a. p.

Past: *I could be.*

ཡིན་ཐུབ། f. a. p. context showing Tense.

Or :—

བྱུང་ཐུབ། f. a. p.

Or :—

ཡིན་ཐུབ་པ་ཡིན། and so on.

PROBABILITY.

Present and **Past**: *I may* or *might be ; Perhaps I shall* or *would be.*

གཅིག་བྱེད་ན་ ·· ཡོང་། f. a. p.

Or :—

ཡོང་གི་ཡིན་པ་འདྲ། f. a. p.

Or :—

ཡོང་གི་ཡིན་གྲོ། f. a. p.

HORTATIVE MOOD.

Present: *I ought to be : I must be.*

ཡིན་དགོས། f. a. p.

Past: *I ought to have been ; must have been.*

ཡིན་དགོས་བྱུང་། for 1st person, others taking འདུག།

PURPOSIVE MOOD.

In order that I may or *might be.*

ཡིན་པའི་དོན་ལ། f. a. p.

IMPERATIVE MOOD.

བྱོས་, གྱིས་, བྱེད་, or བྱིས། *Be.*

མ་བྱེད། *Do not be.*

PRECATIVE MOOD.

Let me, etc. *be.*

ཡིན་བཅུག། f. a. p. with ཅིག་ or དང་ or ཨ་ or རོགས་བྱེད་ or

རོགས་གནང་། added according to rule.)

PERMISSIVE MOOD.

Present: *I am allowed to be.*

ཡིན་ཆོག། f. a. p.

Or:—

ཡིན་ཆོག་གི་ཡོད། and so on.

Past: *I was allowed to be.*

ཡིན་ཆོག་སོང་། f. a. p.

Or:—

ཡིན་ཆོག་པ་ཡིན། and so on.

OPTATIVE MOOD.

Oh that I were: Would that I were.

ཡིན་ཤོག་ or ཡིན་པ་ཤོག། f. a. p.

PARTICIPLES.

Present:	ཡིན་པ།	*Being.*
Past:	ཡིན་པ།	*Been.*
Com. Perfect:	ཡོད་པ་ཡིན་པ།	*Having been.*
Future:	ཡོང་རྒྱུ་ or ཡོང་གྱི།	*About to be.*

PERIPHRASTIC EXPRESSIONS.

ཡིན་པ་ or ཡིན་པ་དེ། — *Who* or *which is* or *was.*

ཡོང་རྒྱུ་མཁན།
ཡོང་རྒྱུ་དེ།
ཡོང་གྱི་མཁན།
ཡོང་གྱི་དེ།
} *Who* or *which will be,* or *is* or *are to be.*

Other Participial Expressions.

Present.

ཡིན་དུས། ཡིན་པའི་དུས་ལ།	*At the time of being ; when, while . . am, is, are.*
ཡིན་ན།	*By, if, when . . am, is, are.*
ཙང་ or ཡིན་ཙང་།	*As, since, because . . am, is, are.*
ཡིན་ལ།	*Being.*
ཡིན་པ་ལ།	*As . . am, is, are.*
ཡིན་པའི།	*Of* or *for being.*

Past.

ཡིན་དུས། ཡིན་པའི་དུས་ལ།	*When, while . . was, were.*
ཡིན་པ་ལ།	*As . . . . . was, were.*
ཡིན་ནས། ཡིན་པས།	*Having been ; as, since, when, because . . . . was, were.*
ཡིན་པ་ལས། ཡིན་པ་དང་། ཙང་། ཡིན་ཙང་།	*As, since, because, when . . . was, were.*

Verbal Noun.

ཡིན་པ། ཡིན་པ་དེ།	*Being ; The being ; To be.*

Supines.

ཡིན་པ།	To be.
ཡིན་ཡ།	
ཡིན་རྒྱུ།	

Infinitives.

ཡིན་པ།	*To be.*
ཡོད་པ་ཡིན་པ།	*To have been.*
ཡོང་རྒྱུ་ཡིན་པ།	*To be about to be.*
ཡོང་གྲོ་ཡིན་པ།	

N.B.—ཡིན་པ། is only a copula, and may not be used for ཡོད་པ་, but ཡོད་པ་ may be used for ཡིན་པ།

Moreover, it must always be remembered that ཡིན་པ་, whether Colloquial or Literary, is never used substantively, but always in connection with some noun, adjective, or substantive or auxiliary verb, into which its forms have to be moulded.

IV.—Literary ཡིན་པ། *To be.*

Indicative Mood.

Present : *I am.*

ཡིན་ (ནོ)།

འདུག་ (གོ་) or occasionally, chiefly interrogatively, ཡིན།

ཡིན་ (ནོ)།

Or, honorifically :—

(Not used : ordinary ཡིན་ with བདག་ instead of ང་)།

གདའོ།

ལགས་ (སོ་) or ལགས་པ་ཡིན་ (ནོ)།

Past : *I was.*

Same as first Present form, context showing Tense.

Or :—

···པ་ཡིན་ (ནོ)།

···པ་འདུག་ (གོ) or occasionally, chiefly interrogatively ཡིན།

···པ་ཡིན་ (ནོ)།

Imperfect :	*I was being.*	Same as first Present form, context showing Tense; or same as Past.
Perfect :	*I have been*	
Pluperfect :	*I had been.*	

Future : *I shall be.*

···བར་འགྱུར་ (རོ)།
···པར་འགྱུར་ (རོ)།
···བོར་འགྱུར་ (རོ)།
each f. a. p.

Conditional and Subjunctive Moods.

Present : *If ....I shall be.*

(Present Root) ···ན་···འགྱུར་ (རོ)། f. a. p.

Past : *If ....I would be.*

(Perfect Root) ···ན་···གྱུར་པ་ཡིན་ (ནོ)། and so on.

Or :—

,, ,, ···ན་···གྱུར་ཏེ། f. a. p.

Perfect : *If....I would have been.*

(Perfect Root) ···ན་···གྱུར་པ་ཡོད་ (དོ)། and so on.

Potential Mood.

Present : *I can be.*

ཡིན་ཐུབ་ (བོ)། f. a. p.

Or :—

ཡིན་པར་ནུས་ (སོ)།

Past : *I could be.*

ཡིན་ཐུབ་པ་ཡིན་ (ནོ)། and so on.

Or :—

ཡིན་པར་ནུས་པ་ཡིན་ (ནོ)། and so on.

Perfect : *I could have been.*

ཡིན་ཐུབ་པ་ཡོད་ (དོ)། and so on.

Or :—

ཡིན་པར་ནུས་པ་ཡོད་ (དོ)། and so on.

Or :—

ཡིན་ཐུབ་སོང་ (ངོ་)། f. a. p.

Or :—

ཡིན་པར་ནུས་བྱུང་ (ངོ་)། f. a. p.

Probability.

Present : *I may be ; Perhaps I shall be.*

སུ་ཞིག་···བར་ (or ···པར་ or ···མོར་) འགྱུར་ (རོ)། f. a. p.

Or :—

ཡིན་པར་སྲིད་ (དོ)། f. a. p.

Or :—

ཡིན་པར་འདུག་ (གོ)། f. a. p.

Past : *I might be : Perhaps I would be.*

སུ་ཞིག་···བར་ (or ···པར་ or ···མོར་) གྱུར་པ་ཡིན་ (ནོ)། and so on.

Or :—

ཡིན་པར་སྲིད་པ་ཡིན་ (ནོ)། and so on.

Perfect : *I might have been ; Perhaps I would have been.*

སུ་ཞིག་···བར་ (or ···པར་ or མོར་) གྱུར་པ་ཡོད་ (དོ)། and so on.

Or :—

ཡིན་པར་སྲིད་པ་ཡོད་ (དོ)། and so on.

Hortative Mood.

Present : *I must be ; I ought to be.*

ཡིན་པར་དགོས་ (སོ)།

Or :—

ཡིན་པར་བྱའོ།

Or :—

ཡིན་པར་རུང་ (ངོ)།

Or :—

ཡིན་པའི་རིགས་ (སོ)།

} f. a. p.

Past : *I must have been ; I ought to have been.*

ཡིན་པར་དགོས་པ་ཡིན་ (ནོ)། and so on.

Or :—

ཡིན་པར་དགོས་བྱུང་ (ངོ)། f. a. p.

Or :—

ཡིན་པར་རུང་བ་ཡིན་ (ནོ)། and so on.

Or :—

ཡིན་པའི་རིགས་པ་ཡིན་ (ནོ)། and so on.

Purposive Mood.

In order that I may or *might be.*

ཡིན་པར་འགྱུར་བའི་ཕྱིར་ (རོ), or ཕྱིར་དུ, or དོན་ལ། f. a. p.

Or :—

ཡོང་རྒྱུའི་ཕྱིར་ (རོ)། f. a. p.

Or :—

…བར་ (or པར་ or …ཏུ་ or …དུ་ or …སུ་ or …རུ་) འགྱུར་བའི་ ཕྱིར། f. a. p.

IMPERATIVE MOOD.

···དུ་ (or ···ཏུ་ or ···སུ་ or ···རུ་) གྱུར་ཅིག། } *Be.*

Or :—

···པར་ or ···བར་ or ···པོར་གྱུར་ཅིག། } *Be.*

PRECATIVE MOOD.

Let me, etc. be.

ཡིན་པར་རྩུག་ཅིག། f. a. p.

PERMISSIVE MOOD.

Present : *I am allowed to be.*

ཡིན་པས་ཆོག་ (གོ)། f. a. p.

Or :—

ཡིན་པས་ཆོག་གི་ཡོད་ (དོ)། and so on throughout.

OPTATIVE MOOD.

Would that I were ; Oh that I were

ཡིན་པར་གྱུར་ཅིག། f. a. p.

VERBAL NOUN.

ཡིན་པ་ or ཡིན་པ་ནི། *Being ; The being ; To be.*

SUPINE.

ཡིན་པར་ or ཡིན་དུ། *Tc be.*

PARTICIPLES.

Present :	ཡིན་པ།	*Being.*	མིན་པ།	*Not being.*
Past :	ཡིན་པ།	*Been.*	མན་པ།	*Not been.*
Com. Perfect :	ཡོད་པ་ཡིན་པ།	*Having been.*	མེད་པ་ཡིན་པ།	*Not having been.*
Future :	ཡོང་རྒྱུ་ or ཡོང་གྲོ།	*About to be*	མི་ཡོང་རྒྱུ་ or མི་ཡོང་གྲོ།	*Not about to be.*

Periphrastic Expressions.

ཡིན་པ་ or ཡིན་པ་དེ་ or ནི།	*Who* or *which is* or *was.*
ཡོང་རྒྱུ་མཁན་དེ་ or ནི།	*Who will be*, or *is* or *are to be.*
ཡོང་གྲོ་མཁན་དེ་ or ནི།	
…ར་ཇུ་བ་དེ་ or ནི།	
ཡོང་རྒྱུ་དེ་ or ནི།	*Which will be*, or *is* or *are to be.*
ཨོང་གྲོ་དེ་ or ནི།	
…ར་བྱུ་བ་དེ་ or ནི།	

Other Participial Expressions.

Present.

ཡིན་པའི་ཚེ་ལ།	*At the time of being ; when, while, as .. am, is, are.*
ཡིན་པའི་དུས་ལ།	
ཡིན་པ་ལ།	
ཡིན་ཏེ།	*Being ; as, since, when, after, while .. am, is, are.*
ཡིན་ཞིང་།	
ཡིན་ན།	*In* or *by being ; if, when .. am, is, are.*
ཡིན་ལ།	*Being.*
ཡིན་གྱིས།	*Though, since, because ... am, is, are.*
ཡིན་པའི།	*Of* or *for being.*

Past.

ཡིན་ཏེ།	*Having been ; as, since, when, after ... was, were.*
ཡིན་ནས།	
ཡིན་པས།	*Because, since, when...was, were.*

ཡིན་པ་ལ། — *As ... was, were.*

ཡིན་པ་ལས།
ཡིན་པ་དང་། — *After, since, because, when ..was, were.*

ཡན་ན། — *If, when ... was, were.*

INFINITIVES.

ཡིན་པ། — *To be.*

ཡོད་པ་ཡིན་པ། — *To have been.*

ཡིན་པར་འགྱུར་བ།
ཡོང་རྒྱུ་ཡིན་པ།
ཡིན་པར་འགྲོ་བ། — *To be about to be ; going to be.*

V.—ཡོད་པ་ *To have ; To possess.*

Same as Colloquial or Literary ཡོད་པ་ *To be present, To exist,* save that it is conjugated with the subject in the Dative case with ལ་ Thus :—

INDICATIVE MOOD.

Present : *I have ; I possess.*

ང་ལ་ཡོད། — *To me there is.*

ཁྱེད་ལ་འདུག། — *To thee there is.*

ཁོ་ལ་ཡོད་ or འདུག or ཡོད་པ་རེད། — *To him there is.*

And so on throughout.

VI.—Active, Transitive, 4-rooted COLLOQUIAL verb.

གཏོང་བ་ *To send.*

ROOTS.

Present : གཏོང་ **Perfect :** བཏང་ **Future :** གཏང་ **Imperative :** ཐོང་།

INDICATIVE MOOD.

Present : *I send.*

ངས་གཏོང་།

ཁྱེད་ཀྱིས་གཏོང་།

ཁོས་གཏོང་།

Periphrastic Present : *I am sending.*

ངས་གཏོང་གི་ཡོད།

ཁྱེད་ཀྱིས་གཏོང་གི་ཡོད་ or འདུག།

ཁོས་གཏོང་གི་ཡོད་ or འདུག་ or ཡོད་པ་རེད།

N.B.—Pronouns are henceforth omitted, except where necessary to make the construction clear.

The construction is in the AGENTIVE, save where otherwise indicated.

Past : *I sent.*

བཏང་། f. a. p.

Or :—

བཏང་བ་ཡིན།

བཏང་བ་འདུག་ or occasionally རེད་ or rarely (interrogatively) ཡིན།

བཏང་བ་རེད ,, ,, འདུག ,, ,, ཡིན།

Or :—

བཏང་སོང་། f. a. p.

Imperfect : *I was sending.*

Same as Periphrastic Present, context showing Tense; or བཏང་བ་ཡིན། and so on, as in Past.

Perfect : *I have sent.*

Same as Past.

Pluperfect : *I had sent.*

Same as Past or Perfect.

Or, seldom used save at end of sentences :—

བཏང་ནས་ཡོད།

བཏང་ནས་ཡོད་ or འདུག།

བཏང་ནས་ཡོད་ or འདུག་ or ཡོད་པ་རེད།

Future : *I shall send.*

གཏོང་ (or གཏང་) ཡོང་། f. a. p.

Or :—

གཏོང་གི་ཡིན།

གཏོང་གི་འདུག་ or རེད་ or ཡིན།

གཏོང་གི་རེད་ or འདུག་ or ཡིན།

Or :—

གཏང་ཡ་རེད། *I am* (or *have*) *to send.*

And so f. a. p.

SUBJUNCTIVE AND CONDITIONAL MOODS.

Present : *If....I shall send.*

(Present Root) ...ན...གཏོང་ (or གཏང་) ཡོང་། f. a. p.

Or :—

(Present Root) ...ན...གཏོང་གི་ཡིན། and so on.

Past : *If....I would send.*

(Perfect Root) ...ན...བཏང་བ་ཡིན། and so on.

Or :—

(Perfect Root) ...ན...གཏོང་ (or གཏང་) ཡོང་། f. a. p.

Perfect : *If....I would have sent.*

(Perfect Root) ...ན...བཏང་བ་ཡོད། and so on.

Or :—

(Perfect Root) ...ན...བཏང་ཡོད་ or བཏང་འདུག་ or བཏང་བྱུང་། f. a. p.

except that བྱུང་ is usually confined to the first person, and འདུག་ used with the others.

Potential Mood.

Present: *I can send ; am able to send.*

གཏོང་ཐུབ། f. a. p.

Or :—

གཏོང་ཐུབ་ཡོང་། f. a. p.

Or :—

གཏོང་ཐུབ་ཀྱི་ཡོད། and so on.

Past: *I could send.*

གཏོང་ཐུབ་པ་ཡིན། and so on.

Perfect: *I could have sent.*

གཏོང་ཐུབ་པ་ཡོད། and so on.

Or :—

གཏོང་ཐུབ་པ་འདུག། f. a. p.

Probability.

Present: *Perhaps I shall send ; I may send ; It is likely that I shall send.*

གཅིག་བྱེད་ན། ... (Either form of Simple Future).

Or :—

གཏོང་གི་ཡིན་པ་འདྲ། f. a. p.

Or :—

གཏོང་གི་ཡིན་འགྲོ། f. a. p.

Past: *Perhaps I should send ; I might send.*

གཅིག་བྱེད་ན་ . . བཏང་བ་ཡིན། and so on.

Or :—

གཅིག་བྱེད་ན་ . . གཏོང་ཡོང་། f. a. p.

Or :—

བཏང་བ་ཡིན་པ་འདྲ། f. a. p.

Or :—

བཏང་བ་ཡིན་འགྲོ། f. a. p.

Perfect : *Perhaps I would have sent ; I might have sent.*

གཅིག་བྱེད་ན་ ··· བཏང་བ་ཡོད། and so on.

Or :—

བཏང་བ་ཡོད་པ་འདྲ། f. a. p.

Or :—

བཏང་བ་ཡོད་འགྲོ། f. a. p.

HORTATIVE MOOD

Present : *I must send* : *I ought to send*

··· ལ་གཏོང་དགོས། f. a. p.

Or :—

··· ལ་གཏོང་དགོས་ཀྱི་ཡོད། and so on.

Or :—

··· ལ་གཏོང་དགོས་ཀྱི་ཡིན། and so on.

Or vulgarly :—

··· ལ་གཏོང་དགོ་གི་ཡོད། and so on.

Also the following, sometimes used :—

··· ལ་གཏང་ཡ་རེད། *I am* (or *have*) *to send.*

··· ལ་གཏང་ཡ་རེད། *Thou art* (or *hast*) *to send.*

··· ལ་གཏང་ཡ་རེད། *He is* (or *has*) *to send.*

Past : *I must have sent ; ought to have sent.*

··· ལ་གཏོང་དགོས་པ་ (or vulgarly དགོ་བ་) ཡིན། and so on.

Or :—

··· ལ་གཏོང་དགོས་བྱུང་། f. a. p., except that བྱུང་ is usually confined to the 1st person, and འདུག་ used with the others.

Purposive Mood.

Present: *In order that I may send.*

གཏོང་བའི་དོན་ལ། f. a. p.

Past: *In order that I might send.*

བཏང་བའི་དོན་ལ། f. a. p.

Imperative Mood

ཐོང་ or གཏོང་། *Send.*

N.B.—ཞིག་ (commonly but improperly ཅིག་), or རོགས་བྱེད་, or རོགས་གནང་, or དང་, or ཤོག་, may be added according to rule.

མ་གཏོང་ or vulgarly མ་བཏང་། *Do not send.*

Precative Mood.

Let me, etc. *send.*

ངས་གཏོང་བཅུག་ (ཅིག་)།

ཁྱོད་ཀྱིས་གཏོང་བཅུག་ (ཅིག་)།

ཁོས་གཏོང་བཅུག་ (ཅིག་)།

N.B.—The construction here is, "By me (or thee or him) a sending permit"

Permissive Mood.

Present: *I am allowed to send ; I may send.*

ངས་གཏོང་ཆོག། f. a. p., or གཏོང་ཆོག་གི་ཡོད། and so on.

Past: *I was allowed to send ; I might send.*

ངས་གཏོང་ཆོག་པ་ཡིན། and so on.

Future: *I shall be allowed to send.*

ངས་གཏོང་ཆོག་ཡོང་། f. a. p.

Or :—

ངས་གཏོང་ཆོག་གི་ཡོང་། and so on.

N.B.—Here the construction is, " A sending by me is allowed, or was allowed, or will be allowed."

The following is more Bookish :—

ངས་གཏོང་བས་ཆོག། *I may send.*

ཁྱོད་ཀྱིས་གཏོང་བས་ཆོག། *Thou mayest send.*

ཁོས་གཏོང་བས་ཆོག། *He may send.*

Optative Mood.

Present : *Oh that I*, etc. *were sending*, or **might send.**

ངས་གཏོང་ཤིག་ or ངས་གཏོང་བ་ཤིག།

Or, better :—

ངས་གཏོང་ན་ཆོག་པ་ཨ།

Past : *Oh that I*, etc. *had sent.*

ངས་བཏང་ཤོག་ or བཏང་བ་ཤོག།

Or, better :—

ངས་བཏང་ན་ཆོག་པ་ཨ།

Participles.

Present :	གཏོང་བ།	*Sending.*
Perfect :	བཏང་བ།	*Sent.*
Com. Perfect :	བཏང་བ་ཡིན་པ།	*Having sent.*
Future :	གཏོང་རྒྱུ་ or གཏང་རྒྱུ་ཡིན་པ། གཏོང་འགྲོ་ or གཏང་འགྲོ་ཡིན་པ།	*About to send.*

Active or Periphrastic.

གཏོང་མཁན་ or གཏོང་བ་དེ་ or གཏོང་བ་པོ། *He who sends.*

བཏང་མཁན་ or བཏང་བ་དེ། *He who sent.*

གཏང་མཁན། }
གཏང་བ་དེ། } *He who will send*, or *is to send*.
གཏང་རྒྱུ་དེ་ or གཏོང་རྒྱུ་དེ། }

Or the following constructions may be used :—

གཏོང་མཁན་གྱི་མི། }
Or :— } *The man who sends.*
གཏོང་བའི་མི་དེ། }

བཏང་མཁན་གྱི་མི། }
Or :— } *The man who sent.*
བཏང་བའི་མི་དེ། }

གཏང་མཁན་གྱི་མི། }
Or :— } *The man who will send* or *is to send.*
གཏང་བའི་མི་དེ། }

See regarding Active and Periphrastic Participles generally, § 38, V. D.

OTHER PARTICIPIAL EXPRESSIONS.

Present.

གཏོང་སྟེ། *Sending.*

གཏོང་བས། *Sending ; Because, since, when, while..sending.*

གཏོང་ལ། *Sending ; at, for, though.... sending.*

གཏོང་གིས། *Though, because..sending.*

གཏོང་བ་ལ། }
གཏོང་བ་ལས། } *As, since..sending.*

གཏོང་གཏོང་ལ།	*Whilst sending.*
གཏོང་ན།	*If, when, though..send, sending.*

etc., etc.

Past.

བཏང་སྟེ།	*Having sent.*
བཏང་བས།	*Sent ; because, since, when..sent.*
བཏང་ནས། བཏང་བ་ལས།	*Having sent.*
བཏང་གིས།	*Because, though... sent.*
བཏང་ན།	*If, when, though... sent.*
བཏང་བ་ལ། བཏང་བ་དང་། བཏང་བ་ལས།	*As, since, because, having... sent.*

etc., etc.

SUPINES.

གཏོང་བ། གཏོང་རྒྱུ།	*To send.*
གཏོང་ལ། གཏོང་ཡ། གཏོང་བའི་དོན་ལ། གཏོང་རྒྱུའི་དོན་ལ། གཏོང་ཡའི་དོན་ལ།	*For sending.*

Verbal Nouns.

གཏོང་བ། ⎫
གཏོང་བ་དེ། ⎬ *Sending ; the sending ; a sending.*
གཏོང་ཡ། ⎭

བཏང་བ། ⎫
བཏང་བ་དེ། ⎬ *The having sent.*

གཏོང་རྒྱུ། ⎫
གཏང་རྒྱུ། ⎪
གཏོང་རྒྱུ་དེ། ⎬ *The being about to send.*
གཏང་རྒྱུ་དེ། ⎭

Infinitives.

Present : གཏོང་བ། *To send.*

བཏང་བ། ⎫
བཏང་ཆར་བ། ⎪
Perfect : བཏང་བ་ཡིན་པ། ⎬ *To have sent.*
བཏང་ཡོད་པ། ⎭

གཏང་བ། ⎫
གཏོང་རྒྱུ་ཡིན་པ། ⎪
Future : གཏོང་རྒྱུ་ཡིན་པ། ⎬ *To be about to send,*
གཏང་འགྲོ་ཡོད་པ། ⎪ *or to be sent.*
གཏོང་གྲབ་ཡིན་པ། ⎭

VII.—Active, Transitive, 4-Rooted Literary Verb གཏོང་བ་
To send.

Roots.

Present: གཏོང་། **Perfect:** བཏང་། **Future:** གཏང་།

Imperative: ཐོང་ or གཏོང་ཞིག།

N.B.—Pronouns are omitted, but the construction is in the AGENTIVE, save where otherwise indicated.

The སྐྱར་བསྐྱུ་བ་ or ͝ placed over the reduplicated final consonant, or final vowel of a verb, is also omitted.

Indicative Mood.

Present: *I send.*

གཏོང་། f. a. p.

Or, Intensively :—

གཏོང་བར་བྱེད། f. a. p.

Periphrastically :—

གཏོང་གིན་ཡོད།	*I am* } *sending.*
གཏོང་གིན་ཡོད་ or འདུག།	*Thou art* } *sending.*
གཏོང་གིན་ཡོད་ or འདུག་ or ཡོད་པ་རེད།	*He is* } *sending.*

Elegant but obsolete form :—

གཏོང་བཞིན་མཆིས།

གཏོང་བཞིན་གདའ།

གཏོང་བཞིན་མཆིས་ or གདའ་ or མཆིས་པ་ཡིན།

Or :—

Same, substituting ཞིང་ for བཞིན།

Or, Respectfully :—

བདག་གཏོང་གིན་ཡོད།

ཁྱེད་གཏོང་གིན་མངའ།

ཁོང་གཏོང་གིན་གཞུགས་ or མངའ་ or བཞུགས་པ་ཡིན།

Past : *I sent.*

བཏང་། f. a. p.

Or :—

བཏང་བ་ཡིན།

བཏང་བ་འདུག་ or occasionally and chiefly interrogatively ཡིན།

བཏང་བ་ཡིན།

Or :—

བཏང་སོང་། f. a. p.

Imperfect : *I was sending.*

Same as Periphrastic Present, the context showing Tense.

Or :—

བཏང་བ་ཡིན། and so on, as in Past.

Or :—

བཏང་ཞིང་ཡོད་པ་ཡིན། f. a. p.

Perfect : *I have sent.*

Same as Past.

Pluperfect : *I had sent.*

Same as Past, or :—

བཏང་ཡོད།

བཏང་ཡོད་ or འདུག།

བཏང་ཡོད་ or འདུག or ཡོད་པ་རེད།

Also, but seldom used, and only at end of sentences :—

བཏང་ནས་ཡོད།

བཏང་ནས་ཡོད་ or འདུག།

བཏང་ནས་ཡོད་ or འདུག་ or ཡོད་པ་རེད།

Future : *I shall send.*

གཏང་། f. a. p.

Or :—

གཏོང་བར་འགྱུར། f. a. p.

Or :—

གཏོང་བར་བྱ། f. a. p.

Or :—

གཏང་ཡོང་། f. a. p.

And note the following :—

གཏང་རྒྱུ་ཡིན། *I am* (or *have*) *to send.*

གཏང་རྒྱུ་འདུག། or interrogatively ཡིན། *Thou art* (or *hast*) *to send.*

གཏང་རྒྱུ་ཡིན། *He is* (or *has*) *to send.*

Subjunctive and Conditional Moods.

Present : *If . . . I shall send.*

(Present Root) ···ན··· (any of the above Future forms), f. a. p.

Past : *If . . . I would send.*

Same as Present, save that in the Introductory Clause the Perfect Root is used : or :—

(Perfect Root) ···ན···བཏང་བ་ཡིན། and so on.

Perfect : *If . . I would have sent.*

Same as Past.

Or :—

(Perfect Root) ···ན···བཏང་བ་ཡོད། and so on.

Potential Mood.

Present : *I can send.*

གཏོང་ཐུབ། f. a. p.

Or :—

གཏོང་བར་ནུས། f. a. p.

Or :—

གཏོང་ཐུབ་ཡོང་། f. a. p.

Past : *I could send.*

གཏོང་ཐུབ་སོང་། f. a. p.

Or :—

གཏོང་བར་ནུས་སོང་། f. a. p.

Or :—

གཏོང་ཐུབ་པ་ཡིན། and so on.

Or :—

གཏོང་བར་ནུས་པ་ཡིན། and so on.

Perfect : *I could have sent.*

གཏོང་ཐུབ་པ་ཡོད། and so on.

Or :—

གཏོང་བར་ནུས་པ་ཡོད། and so on.

PROBABILITY.

Present : *I may send ; Perhaps I shall send.*

སུ་ཤེས་ ·· གཏང་། f. a. p., or གཏོང་ཡོང་། f. a. p.

Or :—

སུ་ཤེས་ ·· གཏོང་བར་འགྱུར། f. a. p.

Or :—

གཏོང་བར་སྲིད། f. a. p.

Or :—

གཏོང་སྲིད། f. a. p.

Past : *I might send.*

གཏོང་སྲིད་པ་ཡིན། and so on.

Or :—

As in Past Tense, Potential Mood.

Perfect : *I might have sent.*

གཏོང་ཐུབ་སོང་། f. a. p.

Or :—

གཏོང་ཐུབ་པ་ཡོད། and so on.

Or :—

གཏོང་སྲིད་པ་ཡོད། and so on.

Hortative.

Present: *I ought to send*: *I must send.*

···ལ་གཏོང་བར་དགོས། f. a. p.

Or :—

གཏོང་བར་བྱའོ། f. a. p.

Or :—

གཏང་རྒྱུ་ཡིན། — *I am* (or *have*) — to send.

གཏང་རྒྱུ་འདུག or interrogatively ཡིན། — *Thou art* (or *hast*) — to send.

གཏང་རྒྱུ་ཡིན། — *He is* (or *has*) — to send.

Past: *I ought to have sent.*

···ལ་གཏོང་བར་དགོས་པ་ཡིན། and so on.

Purposive Mood.

So that I may send, or might send.

གཏོང་བའི་དོན་དུ།

གཏོང་བའི་དོན་ལ།

གཏོང་བའི་ཕྱིར་དུ།

Each f. a. p.

Precative Mood.

Let me, etc. *send.*

གཏོང་བར་ཚུག་ or གནང་།

Or :—

གཏོང་དུ་ཚུག་ or གནང་།

Permissive Mood.

Present: *I am allowed to send* : *I may send.*

གཏོང་བུས་ཆོག། f. a. p.

Or :—

གཏོང་བས་ཆོག་གི་ཡོད། and so on.

Past : *I was allowed to send : I might send.*

གཏོང་བས་ཆོག་པ་ཡིན། and so on.

Or :—

གཏོང་བས་ཆོག་པ་ཡོད། and so on.

Future : *I shall be allowed to send.*

གཏང་བས་ཆོག།

Or :—

གཏོང་བས་ཆོག་པར་འགྱུར། f. a. p.

Or :—

གཏོང་བས་ཆོག་པར་བྱ། f. a. p.

Optative Mood.

Present : *Oh that I*, etc. *were sending*, or *might send.*

གཏོང་ན་ཅི་མ་རུང་། f. a. p.

Or :—

གཏོང་བར་ཤོག་ཅིག། f. a. p.

Past : *Oh that I*, etc. *had sent.*

གཏོང་བར་གྱུར་ན་ཨང་། f. a. p.

Or :—

བཏང་བར་ཤོག་ཅིག། f. a. p.

Imperative Mood.

ཐོང་།	*Send.*
ཐོང་ཞིག།	
གཏོང་།	
གཏོང་ཞིག།	
···ལ་གཏོང་བར་དགོས།	

མ་གཏོང་ (ཞིག)།	Do not send.
... ལ་གཏོང་བར་མི་དགོས།	

N.B.— ཞིག་ is not used with དགོས།

PARTICIPLES.

Present:	གཏོང་བ།	*Sending.*
Perfect:	བཏང་བ། བཏང་ཚར་བ། བཏང་ཟིན་པ། བཏང་སོང་བ།	*Sent.*
Com. Perfect:	བཏང་བ་ཡིན་པ།	*Having sent.*
Future:	གཏོང་བར་འགྱུར་བ། གཏོང་བར་བྱ་བ། གཏོང་བྱ། གཏོང་བར་གཟམས་པ།	*About to send.*

ACTIVE, PERIPHRASTIC, OR SUBSTANTIVE.

གཏོང་མཁན། གཏོང་བྱེད་མཁན། གཏོང་བ་པོ། གཏོང་བྱེད་པ། གཏོང་བྱེད་པ་པོ།	*He who sends ; the sender ; the sending person.*
བཏང་ .. མཁན།	*He who sent. The sent.*

(Matt. xi. 3) གཏོང་བར་འགྱུར་བ་དེ།
གཏང་མཁན།
(Matt. xi. 14) གཏང་རྒྱུ་ཡིན་པ་དེ།
གཏང་བྱ་མཁན།
(Rom. viii. 36) གཏོང་བར་བྱ་བ་དེ།

} *He who will send, or is to send. The sender.*

Or the following simple construction may be used :—

ང་གཏོང་བའི་ཡབ་ཉིད། *The Father who sends me.*

ང་བཏང་བའི་ཡབ་ཉིད། ,, ,, ,, *sent me.*

ང་གཏང་བའི་ཡབ་ཉིད། ,, ,, ,, *will send me.*

See generally, § 38, V. D.

Other Participial Expressions.

As in Colloquial.

Verbal Noun, or Adjective.

གཏོང་བ་ (ཉི)། *Sending ; a or the sending.*

བཏང་བ་ (ཉི)། *The having sent.*

གཏང་བ་ (ཉི)།
གཏོང་བར་བྱ་བ་ (ཉི)།
གཏོང་བར་འགྱུར་བ་ (ཉི)།
གཏོང་རྒྱུ་ཡིན་པ་ (ཉི)།

} *The being about to send.*

Supines.

གཏོང་བར།
གཏོང་དུ།

} *To send.*

གཏོང་བའི་དོན་དུ། }
གཏོང་བའི་དོན་ལ། } *For sending.*
གཏོང་བའི་ཕྱིར་དུ། }

Infinitive Mood.

Present: གཏོང་བ། *To send.*

Past:
བཏང་བ། }
བཏང་ཚར་བ། }
བཏང་བ་ཡིན་པ། } *To have sent.*
བཏང་བ་ཟིན་པ། }

Future:
གཏང་བ། }
གཏོང་བར་བྱ་བ། }
གཏོང་བྱ། }
གཏོང་བར་གཟས་པ། } *To be about to send ; to be sent.*
གཏོང་བར་འགྱུར་བ། }
གཏོང་རྒྱུ་ཡིན་པ། }

VIII.—Passive, 4-Rooted Colloquial Verb གཏང་བ་, གཏོང་རྒྱུ་, གཏང་རྒྱུ་, བཏང་རྒྱུ་, or གཏང་གྲོ། *To be scnt.*

Roots.

As in Active Verb No. VI.

N.B.—The construction throughout is in the Objective or Accusative case, with or without ལ།

Indicative Mood.

Present: *I am being sent.*

གཏོང་གི་ཡོད།

གཏོང་གི་ཡོད་ or འདུག།

གཏོང་གི་ཡོད་ or འདུག་ or ཡོད་པ་རེད།

Past: *I was sent.*

བཏང་བ་ཡིན།

བཏང་བ་འདུག་ or occ. རེད་ or interr. ཡིན།

བཏང་བ་རེད་ or འདུག་ or rarely ཡིན།

Or :—

བཏང་སོང་། f. a. p.

Imperfect: *I was being sent.*

Same as Present, but with adverb or other context showing Tense.

Perfect: *I have been sent.*

བཏང་ཡོད་། and so on.

Or, same as Past.

Or the following, though seldom used save at end of sentence :—

བཏང་ནས་ཡོད། and so on.

Pluperfect: *I had been sent.*

Same as Perfect.

Future: *I shall be sent.*

As in Active Verb No. VI.

Subjunctive and Conditional Moods.

Present: *If..I shall be sent.*
Past: *If..I would be sent.*
Perfect: *If..I would have been sent.*
} As in Active Verb No. VI.

Potential Mood.

Present: *I can be sent.*
Past: *I could be sent.*
Perfect: *I could have been sent.*
} As in Active Verb No. VI.

Probability.

Present: *I may perhaps be sent.*
Past: *I might* ,, ,, ,,
} As in Active Verb No. VI.

Hortative Mood.

Present : *I ought to be sent ; I must be sent.*

བཏང་དགོས་ཀྱི་ཡོད། and so on.

Or :—

བཏང་དགོས་ཀྱི་ཡིན། and so on.

Or :—

བཏང་དགོས། f. a. p.

Or :—

བཏང་དགོས་ཡོང་། f. a. p.

Past : *I ought to have been sent.*

བཏང་དགོས་པ་ཡིན། and so on.

Or :—

བཏང་དགོས་བྱུང་། and so on.

Purposive Mood.

Present : *In order that I may be sent.*
Past : *In order that I might be sent.*

As in Active Verb No. VI.

Imperative Mood.

གཏོང་ཞིག།
གཏོང་བ་གྱིས།
བཏང་བ་གྱིས། } *Be sent.*

མ་གཏོང་བ་གྱིས། *Do not be sent.*

Precative Mood.

གཏོང་ (or བཏང་) བཅུག། *Let me, etc., be sent.*

Permissive Mood.

Present : *I am allowed to be sent.*

གཏང་ (or བཏང་) ཆོག་གི་ཡོད། and so on

And so on conjugating ཆོག་པ་ regularly.

Or :—

གཏོང་ (or བཏང་) ཆོག། f. a. p.

Optative Mood.

Present : *Oh that I were being sent.*

གཏོང་ (བ་) ཤོག། f. a. p.

Or, better :—

གཏོང་ན་ཆོག་པ་ལ། f. a. p.

Past : *Oh that I had been sent.*

བཏང་ (བ་) ཤོག། f. a. p.

Or, better :—

བཏང་ན་ཆོག་པ་ལ། f. a. p.

Participles.

Present :	གཏོང་བ།	*Being sent.*
Past :	བཏང་བ།	*Been sent.*
Com. Perfect :	བཏང་བ་ཡིན་པ།	*Having been sent.*
Future :	གཏོང་རྒྱུ། གཏང་རྒྱུ། བཏང་རྒྱུ།	*About to be sent.*

Periphrastic.

བཏང་མཁན། བཏང་བ་དེ།	*He who is* or *was sent.*
གཏང་མཁན། བཏང་རྒྱུ་དེ།	*He who will be sent.*

Or the following simple construction may be used :—

ངས་བཏང་མཁན་གྱི་མི་དེ། Or :— ངས་བཏང་བའི་མི་དེ།	*The man who is* or *was sent by me.*
ཁྱོད་ཀྱིས་གཏང་མཁན་གྱི་དཔེ་ཆ་དེ། Or :— ཁྱོད་ཀྱིས་གཏང་རྒྱུའི་དཔེ་ཆ་དེ།	*The book which will be*, or *is to be, sent by thee.*

OTHER PARTICIPIAL EXPRESSIONS.

བཏང་སྟེ།	*Being sent, having been sent.*
བཏང་བས།	*Because, since, when..was* or *were sent.*
བཏང་ནས། བཏང་བ་ལས།	*Having been sent.*
བཏང་ན།	*If, when, though..was* or *were sent.*
བཏང་བ་ལ། བཏང་བ་དང་། བཏང་བ་ལས།	*As, since, because..was* or *were sent ; having been sent.*
བཏང་གིས།	*Because, though..was* or *were sent.*

SUPINES.

གཏོང་རྒྱུ། གཏང་རྒྱུ། བཏང་རྒྱུ། གཏང་གྲོ།	*To be sent.*
གཏོང་རྒྱུའི་དོན་ལ།	*For being sent.*

Verbal Nouns.

བཏང་བ་དེ། — *The being sent.*

བཏང་བ་ཡིན་པ་དེ། — *The having been sent.*

གཏོང་རྒྱུ་དེ།
གཏང་རྒྱུ་དེ། } *The being about to be sent.*

Infinitive Mood.

གཏོང་རྒྱུ་ཡིན་པ།
གཏང་རྒྱུ་ཡིན་པ།
བཏང་རྒྱུ་ཡིན་པ།
གཏང་གྲོ་ཡིན་པ། } *To be sent.*

The same or :—
གཏང་གྲོ་ཡོད་པ། } *To be about to be sent.*

IX.—Active, one-rooted Colloquial Verb མཐོང་བ། *To see.*

Root throughout མཐོང་།

N.B.—The construction is in the Agentive, except where otherwise indicated.

Indicative Mood.

Present : *I see.*

མཐོང་། f. a. p.

Periphrastic : *I am seeing.*

མཐོང་གི་ཡོད།

མཐོང་གི་ཡོད་ or འདུག།

མཐོང་གི་ཡོད་ or འདུག or ཡོད་པ་རེད།

Past : *I saw.*

མཐོང་བྱུང་ * or མཐོང་སོང་། f. a. p.

* *N.B.*—བྱུང་ for first person, འདུག་ for the others.

Or :—

མཐོང་བ་ཡིན།

མཐོང་བ་འདུག་ or occ. རེད་ or rarely, chiefly interr. ཡིན།

མཐོང་བ་རེད་ ,, འདུག ,, ཡིན།

Imperfect : *I was seeing.*

Same as Periphrastic Present, context showing Tense.

Perfect : *I have seen.*

Same as Past.

Pluperfect : *I had seen.*

Same as Past or Perfect.

Or, seldom used save at end of sentence :—

མཐོང་ནས་ཡོད། and so on.

Future : *I shall see.*

མཐོང་ཡོང་། f. a. p.

Or :—

མཐོང་གི་ཡིན། and so on.

Note also the following :—

མཐོང་རྒྱུ་ཡིན། *I am* (or *have*) *to see.*

And so on.

Also :—

མཐོང་ཡ་རེད། *I am* (or *have*) *to see.*

And so f. a. p.

SUBJUNCTIVE AND CONDITIONAL MOODS.

Present : *If..I shall see.*

(Present Root) ···ན་··· མཐོང་གི་ཡིན། and so on.

Or :—

(Present Root) ···ན་··· མཐོང་ཡོང་། f. a. p.

Past : *If..I would see.*

(Perfect Root) ···ན་··· མཐོང་ཡོང་། f. a. p.

Or :—

(Perfect Root) ···ན···མཐོང་བ་ཡིན། and so on.

Perfect : *If..I would have seen.*

(Perfect Root) ···ན···མཐོང་བ་ཡོད། and so on.

Or :—

(Perfect Root) ···ན···མཐོང་བ་འདུག། f. a. p.

Potential Mood.

Similar to construction in གཏོང་བ། *To send*, No. VI.

Probability.

Present : *Perhaps I shall see : I may see.*

Same as in གཏོང་བ། *To send*, No. VI.

Past : *Perhaps I would see : I might see.*

མཐོང་བ་ཡིན་པ་འདྲ། f. a. p.

Or :—

མཐོང་བ་ཡིན་འགྲོ། f. a. p.

Or :—

གཅིག་བྱེད་ན···མཐོང་ཡོང་། f. a. p.

Or :—

གཅིག་བྱེད་ན···མཐོང་བ་ཡིན། f. a. p.

Or :—

Perfect : *Perhaps I would* or *might have seen.*

མཐོང་བ་ཡོད་པ་འདྲ། f. a. p.

Or :—

མཐོང་བ་ཡོད་འགྲོ། f. a. p.

Or :—

གཅིག་བྱེད་ན···མཐོང་བ་ཡོད། and so on.

Hortative.

Present : *I ought to see : I must see.*

ང་ལ་མཐོང་དགོས་ཀྱི་ཡོད། and so on.

Or :—

ང་ལ་མཐོང་དགོས་ཀྱི་ཡིན། and so on.

Or :—

... ལ་མཐོང་དགོས་ཡོང་། f. a. p.

Or :—

མཐོང་རྒྱུ་ཡིན། *I am* (or *have*) *to see.*

And so on.

Or :—

མཐོང་ཡ་རེད། *I am* (or *have*) *to see.*

And so, f. a. p.

Past : *I ought to have seen ; must have seen.*

ང་ལ་མཐོང་དགོས་པ་ཡིན། and so on.

Or :—

... ལ་མཐོང་དགོས་བྱུང་། f. a. p. But see note *re* བྱུང་ on p. 354.

PURPOSIVE MOOD.

Present and Past : *In order that I may* or *might see.*

མཐོང་བའི་དོན་ལ། f. a. p.

IMPERATIVE MOOD.

མཐོང་ (ཞིག)། *See.*

མ་མཐོང་ (ཞིག)། *Do not see.*

PRECATIVE MOOD.

མཐོང་བཙུག་ (ཅིག)། *Let me, etc. see.*

PERMISSIVE MOOD.

Present : *I am allowed to see ; I may see.*

མཐོང་ཆོག། f. a. p. and tenses.

Or :—

མཐོང་ཆོག་གི་ཡོད། and so on.

And so on, conjugating ཆོག་པ་ regularly.

The following is more Bookish :—

མཐོང་བས་ཆོག། f. a. p.

Optative Mood.

Present and **Past** : *Oh that I were seeing*, or *had seen.*

མཐོང་ཤོག། Or :— མཐོང་བ་ཤོག། Or better :— མཐོང་ན་ཆོག་པ་ཨ།	f. a. p.

Participles.

Present :	མཐོང་བ།	*Seeing.*
Perfect :	མཐོང་བ།	*Seen.*
Com. Perfect :	མཐོང་བ་ཡིན་པ།	*Having seen.*
Future :	མཐོང་རྒྱུ།	*About to see.*

Active, Periphrastic, or Substantive.

མཐོང་མཁན་ (དེ)། མཐོང་བ་ (དེ)། མཐོང་བ་པོ།	*He who sees* or *saw. The seer.*
མཐོང་རྒྱུ་དེ། མཐོང་མཁན་ (དེ)།	*He who will see. The seer.*

See also the other examples under this head in གཏོང་བ། *To send,* No. VI.

Other Participial Expressions.

Present.

མཐོང་སྟེ།	*Seeing.*
མཐོང་བས།	*Seeing ; because, since, when, while..am, is,* or *are seeing.*
མཐོང་བ་ལ།	*Seeing ; at, for, though..am, is,* or *are seeing.*
མཐོང་བ་ལས། མཐོང་བ་ལ།	*As, since..am, is* or *are seeing.*
མཐོང་ལ། མཐོང་མཐོང་ལ།	*Whilst seeing.*
མཐོང་གིས།	*Though seeing.*
མཐོང་ན།	*If, when, though..am, is* or *are seeing.*

Past.

མཐོང་ནས། མཐོང་བྱུང་སྟེ།	*Having seen.*
མཐོང་བྱུང་བས།	*Seen ; because, since, when..was* or *were seen.*
མཐོང་བྱུང་ནས། མཐོང་བྱུང་བ་ལས།	*Having seen.*
མཐོང་བྱུང་ན།	*If, when, though..was* or *were seen.*
མཐོང་བྱུང་གིས།	*Because, though..was* or *were seen.*
མཐོང་བྱུང་བ་ལ། མཐོང་བྱུང་བ་དང་། མཐོང་བྱུང་བ་ལས།	*Having seen ; as, since, when, because..was* or *were seen.*

Supines.

མཐོང་བ།	To see.
མཐོང་རྒྱུ།	
མཐོང་ཡ།	For seeing.
མཐོང་བ་ལ།	
མཐོང་བའི་དོན་ལ།	
མཐོང་རྒྱུའི་དོན་ལ།	

Verbal Nouns or Adjectives.

མཐོང་བ།	Seeing ; a or the seeing.
མཐོང་ཡ།	
མཐོང་བ་དེ།	
མཐོང་བྱུང་བ་དེ།	*A* or *the having seen.*
མཐོང་རྒྱུ་དེ།	*The being about to see.*

Infinitive Mood.

Present : མཐོང་བ། *To see.*

Perfect : མཐོང་བྱུང་བ། *To have seen.*

Future : མཐོང་རྒྱུ་ཡིན་པ། *To be about to see ; To be seen.*

X.—Neuter, One-Rooted COLLOQUIAL Verb དགའ་བ། *To be glad, To rejoice.*

Root དགའ། throughout.

Conjugated throughout like Colloquial མཐོང་བ་ *To see,* save that in the forms in ཡོད་པ་ and ཡིན་པ་ the auxiliary particle is ཡི་ instead of གི་, while the Imperative is དགའ་བོ་བྱེད་ (ཅིག་) or དགའ་བོ་བྱིས་ (ཤིག), or the Literary གདའ་བར་གྱུར་ཞིག། *Rejoice, Be glad.*

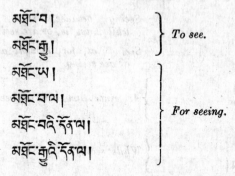

The construction throughout is in the NOMINATIVE, save that in the *Hortative Mood* it is in the DATIVE with ལ་, as in མཐོང་བ། *To see*, No. IX.

XI.—Neuter, One-Rooted LITERARY Verb དགའ་བ། *To be glad, To rejoice.*

Root དགའ། throughout.

N.B.—The construction is in the NOMINATIVE case, except where otherwise indicated. The སྒྲར་བསྒྱུ་བ། is omitted.

INDICATIVE MOOD.

Present : *I am glad : I rejoice.*

དགའ། f. a. p.

Or, intensively :—

དགའ་མགྱུ་རངས། f. a. p.

Periphrastic : *I am rejoicing.*

དགའ་བ་ཡོད།

དགའ་བ་ཡོད་ or འདུག།

དགའ་བ་ཡོད་ or འདུག་ or ཡོད་པ་རེད།

Or :—

དགའ་ཡི་ཡོད་ and so on ; or དགའ་གི་ཡོད། and so on.

Or :—

དགའ་བ་ཡིན།

དགའ་བ་འདུག་ or occ. chiefly interr. ཡིན།

དགའ་བ་ཡིན།

Or :—

དགའ་ཡི་ཡིན། and so on.

Or, seldom used now :—

དགའ་བཞིན་ (or ཞིང་) མཆིས།

དགའ་བཞིན་ (or ཞིང་) གདའ།

དགའ་བཞིན་ (or ཞིང་) མཆིས་ or གདའ་ or མཆིས་པ་ཡིན།

Past: *I rejoiced*: *I was glad.*

དགའ་སོང་། f. a. p.

Or :—

དགའ་བར་གྱུར་ཏོ། f. a. p.

Or :—

དགའ་བར་གྱུར་པ་ཡིན། and so on.

Imperfect: *I was rejoicing.*

Same as Present, context indicating Tense.

Perfect: *I have rejoiced.*

Same as Past.

Pluperfect: *I had rejoiced.*

དགའ་བར་གྱུར་ཏོ། f. a. p.

Or, though not common :—

དགའ་ཚར་ནས་ཡོད། and so on.

Future: *I shall rejoice*: *I shall be glad.*

དགའ་ཡོང་། f. a. p.

Or :—

དགའ་བར་འགྱུར། f. a. p.

Or :—

དགའ་གྱུ་ཡིན། *I am* (or *have*) *to rejoice.*

And so on.

SUBJUNCTIVE AND CONDITIONAL MOODS.

Present: *If..I shall rejoice.*

(Present Root) ...ན་... དགའ་བར་འགྱུར། f. a. p.

Or :—

(Present Root) ...ན་... དགའ་བར་ཏུ། f. a. p.

Or :—

(Present Root) ···ན···དགའ་ཡོང་། f. a. p.

Past : *If..I would rejoice.*

(Perfect Root) ···ན···དགའ་བར་གྱུར་པ་ཡིན། and so on.

Or :—

(Perfect Root) ···ན···དགའ་བར་གྱུར་དོ། f. a. p.

Perfect : *If..I would have rejoiced.*

(Perfect Root) ···ན···དགའ་བར་གྱུར་པ་ཡོད། and so on.

POTENTIAL MOOD.

Present : *I can rejoice* or *be glad.*

དགའ་ཐུབ། f. a. p.

Or :—

དགའ་བར་ནུས། f. a. p.

Or :—

དགའ་ཐུབ་ཡོང་། f. a. p.

Past : *I could rejoice.*

Same as Present.

Or :—

དགའ་བར་ནུས་པ་ཡིན། and so on.

Or :—

དགའ་ཐུབ་པ་ཡིན། and so on.

Or :—

དགའ་ཐུབ་སོང་། f. a. p.

Or :—

དགའ་བར་ནུས་སོང་། f. a. p.

Perfect : *I could have rejoiced.*

དགའ་ཐུབ་པ་ཡོད། and so on.

Or :—

དགའ་བར་ནུས་པ་ཡོད། and so on.

Or :—

དགའ་ཐུབ་པ་འདུག། f. a. p.

Or :—

དགའ་བར་ནུས་པ་འདུག། f. a. p.

Probability.

Present : *Perhaps I shall rejoice : I may rejoice.*

ཕུ་ཞེས་ ·· དགའ་བར་འགྱུར། }

Or :—

ཕུ་ཞེས་ ·· དགའ་བར་བྱ། }

Or :—

ཕུ་ཞེས་ ·· དགའ་ཡོང་། } f. a. p.

Or :—

དགའ་བར་སྲིད། }

Or :—

དགའ་སྲིད། }

Past : *Perhaps I would* or *might rejoice.*

དགའ་སྲིད་པ་ཡིན། and so on.

Perfect : *Perhaps I would* or *might have rejoiced.*

དགའ་སྲིད་པ་ཡོད། and so on.

Hortative Mood.

Present : *I ought to rejoice ; I must rejoice.*

··ལ་དགའ་བར་དགོས། f. a. p.

Or :—

དགའ་བར་བྱ། f. a. p.

Past : *I ought to have rejoiced.*

···ལ་དགའ་བར་དགོས་པ་ཡིན། and so on.

PURPOSIVE.

Present : *In order that I may rejoice.*

དགའ་བའི་དོན་དུ།

Or :—

དགའ་བའི་དོན་ལ།

Or :—

དགའ་བའི་ཕྱིར་དུ།

Or :—

དགའ་བར་འགྱུར་བའི་དོན་དུ། } f. a. p.

Past : *In order that I might rejoice.*

Same as first three forms of Present.

Or :—

དགའ་བར་གྱུར་པའི་དོན་དུ། f. a. p.

PRECATIVE MOOD.

Let me, etc. *rejoice.*

དགའ་བར་ཆུག།

Or :—

དགའ་ཏུ་ཆུག། } f. a. p.

Or :—

དགའ་བར་གནང་།

Or :—

དགའ་ཏུ་གནང་།

Or :—

དགའ་བར་གྱུར་ཅིག། } f. a. p.

PERMISSIVE MOOD.

Present : *I am allowed to rejoice ; I may rejoice.*

···ལ་དགའ་བས་ཆོག། f. a. p.

Past : *I was allowed to rejoice ; I might rejoice.*

···ལ་དགའ་བས་ཆོག་པ་ཡིན། and so on.

Optative Mood.

Oh that I were glad or *rejoicing.*

དགའ་ན་ཅི་མ་རུང་།

Or :—

དགའ་བར་གྱུར་ན་ཨང་།

Or :—

དགའ་བར་ཤོག་ཅིག།

f. a. p

Imperative.

དགའ་བར་གྱུར་ཞིག།

Or :—

དགའ་བར་བྱ།

Or :—

··· ལ་དགའ་བར་དགོས།

Rejoice, Be glad.

མ་དགའ།

Or :—

དགའ་བར་མ་འགྱུར་ཞིག།

Or :—

དགའ་བར་མི་བྱ།

Or :—

··· ལ་དགའ་བར་མི་དགོས།

Do not rejoice. Be not glad.

Participles.

Present: དགའ་བ། *Rejoicing.*

Perfect: དགའ་ཚར་བ། / དགའ་སོང་། *Rejoiced.*

Com. Perfect: དགའ་ཚར་བ་ཡིན་པ། *Having rejoiced.*

Future:	དགའ་བར་འགྱུར་བ།	*About to rejoice.*
	དགའ་བར་གཟས་པ།	
	དགའ་བར་བྱ་བ།	
	དགའ་རྒྱུ་ཡིན་པ།	

ACTIVE, PERIPHRASTIC, OR SUBSTANTIVE.

དགའ་མཁན།	*He who rejoices* or *is glad. The rejoicer.*
དགའ་བ་ཡོད་མཁན།	
དགའ་བ་ཡོད་པ།	
དགར་ཚར་མཁན།	*He who rejoiced*, or *was glad.*
དགའ་བ་ཡོད་པ་ཡིན་པ་དེ།	
Matt. xi. 14. དགར་རྒྱུ་ཡིན་པ་དེ།	*He who is about to rejoice*, or *will*, or *is to, rejoice.*
Matt. xi. 3. དགའ་བར་འགྱུར་བ་དེ།	
Rom. viii. 36. དགའ་བར་བྱ་བ་དེ།	

OTHER PARTICIPIAL EXPRESSIONS.

Present.

Same as in མཐོང་བ་ *To see*, No. IX.

Past.

Same as in མཐོང་བ་ *To see*, No. IX, substituting ཚར་ for བྱུང་, and ཚར་ taking ཏེ་ instead of སྟེ།

VERBAL NOUN OR ADJECTIVE.

དགའ་བ་ (ནི)།	*Rejoicing; A*, or *the rejoicing.*
དགའ་ཚར་བ་ (ནི)།	*The having rejoiced.*
དགའ་བར་བྱ་བ་ (ནི)།	*The being about to rejoice.*

SUPINES.

དགའ་བར། Or :— དགའ་རུ།	To rejoice or be glad.
དགའ་བའི་དོན་དུ་ (or དོན་ལ་ or ཕྱིར་དུ)།	*For rejoicing.*

INFINITIVE MOOD.

Present :	དགའ་བ།	*To rejoice* or *be glad.*
Past :	དགའ་ཚར་བ། དགའ་ཚར་བ་ཡིན་པ།	*To have rejoiced* or *been glad.*
Future :	དགའ་བར་འགྱུར་བ། དགའ་བར་གཟམས་པ། དགའ་བར་བྱ་བ།	*To be about to rejoice* or *be glad.*

XII.—Passive 4-Rooted, LITERARY Verb གཏོང་བར་བྱ་བ or གཏོང་བྱ། *To be sent.*

N.B.—The construction throughout is in the OBJECTIVE or DATIVE case in ལ།

Otherwise it is the same as the Active Literary Verb གཏོང་བ་ *To send*, No. VII. as far as and including the Potential Mood.

HORTATIVE MOOD.

Present : *I ought to be sent ; I must be sent.*

བཏང་ (or གཏོང་) བར་དགོས། f. a. p.

Or :—

གཏོང་བར་བྱ། f. a. p.

Past : *I ought to have been sent.*

བཏང་ (or གཏོང་) བར་དགོས་པ་ཡིན། and so on.

Then it is again similar to Verb No. VII. as far as and including the Optative Mood.

IMPERATIVE MOOD.

གཏོང་བར་གྱུར་ཅིག ། གཏོང་བར་བྱ ། ...ལ་གཏོང་བར་དགོས །	*Be sent.*
གཏོང་བར་མ་འགྱུར་ཅིག ། གཏོང་བར་མི་བྱ ། ...ལ་གཏོང་བར་མི་དགོས །	*Do not be sent.*

PARTICIPLES.

Present:	གཏོང་བ ། གཏོང་གི་ཡོད་པ །	*Being sent.*
	བཏང་བ ། བཏང་ཚར་བ ། བཏང་ཟིན་པ །	*Been sent.*
Com. Perfect:	བཏང་བ་ཡིན་པ ། བཏང་ཚར་བ་ཡིན་པ ། བཏང་ཟིན་པ་ཡིན་པ །	*Having been sent.*
Future:	གཏོང་བར་བྱ་བ ། གཏོང་བར་འགྱུར་བ ། གཏོང་བྱ ། གཏོང་རྒྱུ་ཡིན་པ ། གཏོང་རྒྱུ །	*About to be sent.*

Periphrastic.

	བཏང་བ་ (དེ་ or ནི)།	*He who* or *that which is* or *was sent.*
	གཏོང་བར་བྱས་པ་ (དེ་ or ནི)།	
Matt. xi. 3.	གཏོང་བར་འགྱུར་བ་ (དེ་ or ནི)།	*He who* or *that which, will be,* or *is to be sent.*
	གཏང་བ་ (དེ་ or ནི)།	
Rom. viii. 36.	གཏོང་བར་བྱ་བ་ (དེ་ or ནི)།	
	གཏོང་བྱ་ (དེ་ or ནི)།	
Matt. xi. 14.	གཏོང་རྒྱུ་ཡིན་པ་ (དེ་ or ནི)།	

Participial Expressions.

Same as in Colloquial Passive Verb གཏོང་རྒྱུ་ *To be sent,* **No. VIII.**

Supines.

གཏོང་བར།	*To be sent.*
གཏོང་བར་བྱ་བ།	
གཏོང་བར་བྱ་བའི་དོན་དུ།	*For being sent.*
གཏོང་བར་བྱ་བའི་དོན་ལ།	
གཏོང་བར་བྱ་བའི་ཕྱིར་དུ།	
གཏང་བྱའི་དོན་ལ།	
གཏང་བྱའི་དོན་དུ།	
གཏང་བྱའི་ཕྱིར་དུ།	

Verbal Nouns.

གཏོང་བར་བྱ་བ་ནི།	*The being about to be sent.*
གཏོང་བར་འགྱུར་བ་ནི།	
གཏོང་རྒྱུ་ཡིན་པ་ནི།	

INFINITIVE MOOD.

གཏོང་རྒྱུ་ཡིན་པ། གཏོང་བར་འགྱུར་བ། གཏོང་བར་བྱ་བ། གཏོང་བྱ།	*To be sent.*
གཏོང་བར་བྱས་པ།	*To have been sent.*

XIII.—Active, 2-Rooted COLLOQUIAL Verb འགྲོ་བ། *To go*

ROOTS.

Present: འགྲོ།

Perfect: སོང་ or ཕྱིན།

Future: འགྲོ།

Imperative: སོང་ or སོངས་ or རྒྱུག། ཤིག་ or ཞིག་ or ཅིག། With Particle when appropriate.

N.B.—The construction throughout is in the NOMINATIVE case.

INDICATIVE MOOD.

Present: *I go.*

འགྲོ། f. a. p.

Periphrastic: *I am going.*

འགྲོ་གི་ཡོད།

འགྲོ་གི་ཡོད་ or འདུག།

འགྲོ་གི་ཡོད་ or འདུག་ or ཡོད་པ་རེད།

Past: *I went.*

སོང་ or ཕྱིན། f. a. p.

Or :—

སོང་བ་ཡིན།

སོང་བ་འདུག་ or occ. རེད་ or rarely, chiefly interr. ཡིན།

སོང་བ་རེད་ ,, འདུག ,, ཡིན།

Or :—

ཕྱིན་པ་ཡིན། and so on.

Imperfect : *I was going.*

Same as Periphrastic Present, context showing Tense.

Perfect : *I have gone.*

Same as Past.

Pluperfect : *I had gone.*

Same as Past.

Or, seldom used save at end of sentences :—

སོང་ནས་ཡོད། and so on.

Or :—

ཕྱིན་ནས་ཡོད། and so on.

Future : *I shall go.*

འགྲོ་ཡོང་། f. a. p.

Or :—

འགྲོ་གི་ཡིན། and so on.

Or :—

··· ལའགྲོ་ཡ་རེད། *I am* (or *have*) *to go.*

f. a. p.

Or :—

འགྲོ་རྒྱུ་ཡིན། and so on. *I am* (or *have*) *to go.*

Subjunctive and Conditional Moods.

Present : *If…I shall go.*

(Present Root) ···ན་·· འགྲོ་ཡོང་། f. a. p.

Or :—

(Present Root) ···ན···འགྲོ་གི་ཡིན། and so on.

Past : *If...I would go.*

(Perfect Root)...Same as Present, context indicating Tense.

Or :—

(Perfect Root) ···ན···སོང་བ་ (or ཕྱིན་པ་) ཡིན། and so on.

Perfect : *If...I would have gone.*

(Perfect Root) ···ན···སོང་བ་ (or ཕྱིན་པ་) ཡོད། and so on.

Or :—

(Perfect Root) ···ན···སོང་ (or ཕྱིན་) ཡོད། f. a. p.

Or :—

(Perfect Root) ···ན···སོང་ (or ཕྱིན་) འདུག། f. a. p.

Potential Mood.

Present : *I can go.*

འགྲོ་ཐུབ། f. a. p.

Or :—

འགྲོ་ཐུབ་ཡོང་། f. a. p.

Or :—

འགྲོ་ཐུབ་ཀྱི་ཡོད། and so on.

Past : *I could go.*

འགྲོ་ཐུབ་པ་ཡིན། and so on.

Perfect : *I could have gone.*

འགྲོ་ཐུབ་པ་ཡོད། and so on.

Or :—

འགྲོ་ཐུབ་པ་འདུག། f. a. p.

Probability.

Present : *Perhaps I shall go ; I may go.*

གཅིག་བྱེད་ན···འགྲོ་ཡོང་། f. a. p.

Or :—

གཅིག་བྱེད་ན་ ·· འགྲོ་གི་ཡིན། and so on.

Or :—

འགྲོ་གི་ཡིན་པ་འདུ། f. a. p.

Or :—

འགྲོ་གི་ཡིན་འགྲོ། f. a. p.

Past : *Perhaps I might go.*

གཅིག་བྱེད་ན་ ·· ཕྱིན་པ་ (or སོང་བ་) ཡིན། and so on.

Or :—

ཕྱིན་པ་ (or སོང་བ་) ཡིན་པ་འདུ། f. a. p.

Or :—

ཕྱིན་པ་ (or སོང་བ་) ཡིན་འགྲོ། f. a. p.

Perfect : *Perhaps I might have gone.*

གཅིག་བྱེད་ན་ ·· ཕྱིན་པ་ (or སོང་བ་) ཡོད། and so on.

Or :—

ཕྱིན་པ་ (or སོང་བ་) ཡོད་པ་འདུ། f. a. p.

Or :—

ཕྱིན་པ་ (or སོང་བ་) ཡོད་འགྲོ། f. a. p.

HORTATIVE MOOD.

Present : *I ought to go ; I must go.*

འགྲོ་དགོས། f. a. p.

Or :—

འགྲོ་དགོས་ཀྱི་ཡོད། and so on.

Or :—

འགྲོ་དགོས་ཡོང་། f. a. p.

Or vulgarly :—

འགྲོ་དགོ་གི་ཡོད། and so on.

Or :—

འགྲོ་དགོ་ཡོང་། f. a. p.

Or :—

འགྲོ་དགོ་གི་ཡིན། and so on.

Past: *I ought to have gone.*

འགྲོ་དགོས་པ་ (or vulgarly དགོ་པ་) ཡིན། and so on.

Or :—

འགྲོ་དགོས་བྱུང་། f. a. p. But see note *re* བྱུང་, p. 354.

PURPOSIVE MOOD.

Present: *In order that*, or *so that*, *I may go.*

འགྲོ་བའི་དོན་ལ། f. a. p.

Past: *In order that*, or *so that*, *I might go.*

ཕྱིན་པའི་ (or སོང་བའི་) དོན་ལ། f. a. p.

IMPERATIVE MOOD.

སོང་ (ཞིག)། }
སོངས་ (ཤིག)། } *Go.*
རྒྱུག་ (ཅིག)། }

མ་འགྲོ། (Pronounced *Mān-ḍo*) *Do not go.*

PRECATIVE MOOD.

འགྲོ་བཅུག་ (ཅིག)། *Let me*, etc. *go.*

PERMISSIVE MOOD.

Present: *I am allowed to go : I may go.*

འགྲོ་ཆོག། f. a. p.

Or :—

འགྲོ་ཆོག་གི་ཡོད། and so on.

(*N.B.*—Other Tenses may be formed by conjugating ཆོག་པ། regularly.)

OPTATIVE MOOD.

Present: *Oh that*, or *would that*, *I were going.*

འགྲོ་ན་ཆོག་པ་ཨ། }
Or :— } f. a. p.
འགྲོ་བར་ཤོག། }

Past: *Oh that*, or *would that*, *I had gone.*

ཕྱིན་ (or སོང་) ན་ཆོག་པ་ཨ། } f. a. p.

Or :—

ཕྱིན་པར་ (or སོང་བར་) ཤོག།

(*N.B.*—The expressions in ཤོག། are not much used in Colloquial, being rather Literary.)

PARTICIPLES.

Present:	འགྲོ་བ།	*Going.*
Perfect:	ཕྱིན་པ། སོང་བ། སོངས་པ།	*Gone.*
Com. Perfect:	ཕྱིན་པ་ཡིན་པ། སོང་བ་ཡིན་པ། སོངས་པ་ཡིན་པ།	*Having gone.*
Future:	འགྲོ་རྒྱུ་ཡིན་པ།	*About to go.*

ACTIVE, PERIPHRASTIC, OR SUBSTANTIVE.

འགྲོ་མཁན། འགྲོ་བ་དེ།	*He who* or *that which goes*; *The goer.*
ཕྱིན་ (or སོང་) མཁན། ཕྱིན་པ་དེ། སོང་བ་དེ།	*He who*, or *that which went.*
འགྲོ་རྒྱུ་མཁན། འགྲོ་རྒྱུ་དེ།	*He who* or *that which will go*, or *is to go.*

OTHER PARTICIPIAL EXPRESSIONS.

As in Colloquial Verb མཐོང་བ་ *To see*, No. IX, འགྲོ་ taking སྟེ་, སོང་ taking སྟེ་, and ཕྱིན་ taking ཏེ་ If སོངས་ be used it would take ཏེ།

SUPINES.

འགྲོ་བ། འགྲོ་རྒྱུ།	*To go.*
འགྲོ་ཡ། འགྲོ་བ་ལ། འགྲོ་བའི་དོན་ལ། འགྲོ་རྒྱུའི་དོན་ལ།	*For going.*

VERBAL NOUNS OR ADJECTIVES.

འགྲོ་བ་ (དེ)། འགྲོ་ཡ།	*Going ; a* or *the going.*
སོང་བ་ (དེ)། ཕྱིན་པ་ (དེ)།	*The having gone.*
འགྲོ་རྒྱུ་ (དེ)།	*The being about to go.*

INFINITIVE MOOD.

Present:	འགྲོ་བ།	*To go.*
Perfect:	སོང་བ་ or ཕྱིན་པ། སོང་ (or ཕྱིན་) ཚར་བ། སོང་ (or ཕྱིན་) ཡོད་པ། སོང་བ་ (or ཕྱིན་པ་) ཡིན་པ།	*To have gone.*
Future:	འགྲོ་རྒྱུ་ཡིན་པ།	*To be about to go.*

XIV.—Active 2-Rooted LITERARY Verb འགྲོ་བ། *To go.*

ROOTS.

Same as in Colloquial Verb, No. XIII, omitting རྒྱུག།

N.B.—The construction throughout is in the NOMINATIVE case.

INDICATIVE MOOD.

Present: *I go.*

འགྲོའོ། f. a. p.

Periphrastic: *I am going.*

འགྲོ་གི་ཡོད་དོ།

འགྲོ་གི་ཡོད་དོ་ or འདུག་གོ།

འགྲོ་གི་ཡོད་དོ་ or འདུག་གོ་ or ཡོད་པ་རེད་དོ།

Or:—

འགྲོ་བ་ཡོད་དོ། and so on.

Past: *I went.*

སོང་ངོ་ or ཕྱིན་ནོ། f. a. p.

Or:—

ཕྱིན་སོང་ངོ། f. a. p.

Or:—

སོང་བ་ཡིན་ནོ།

སོང་བ་འདུག་གོ་ or occ., chiefly interr. ཡིན་ནོ།

སོང་བ་མིན་ནོ།

Or:—

ཕྱིན་པ་ཡིན་ནོ། and so on.

Imperfect: *I was going.*

Same as Periphrastic Present, context showing Tense.

Or:—

སོང་བ (or ཕྱིན་པ་) ཡིན་ནོ། and so on.

Or:—

སོང་ཞིང་ (or ཕྱིན་ཞིང་) ཡོད་པ་ཡིན་ནོ། and so on.

Perfect: *I have gone.*

Same as Past.

Pluperfect: *I had gone.*

Same as Past.

Or, seldom used save at end of sentence:—

སོང་ (or ཕྱིན) ནས་ཡོད་དོ། and so on.

Or:—

སོང་ (or ཕྱིན) ཡོད་དོ། f. a. p.

Future: *I shall go.*

འགྲོ་བར་འགྱུར་རོ། f. a. p.

Or:—

འགྲོ་བར་བྱའོ། f. a. p.

Or:—

འགྲོ་ཡོང་ངོ། f. a. p.

Subjunctive and Conditional Moods.

Present: *If... I shall go.*

(Present Root) ···ན (any simple Future).

Past: *If... I would go.*

(Perfect Root) ···ན··སོང་བ་ (or ཕྱིན་པ་) ཡིན་ནོ། and so on.

Or, same as Present.

Perfect: *If... I would have gone.*

(Perfect Root) ···ན··སོང་བ་ (or ཕྱིན་པ་) ཡོད་དོ། and so on.

Potential Mood.

Same as Potential Mood in Literary གཏོང་བ། *To send*, No. VII using Root འགྲོ། throughout.

Probability.

Present: *Perhaps I shall go; I may go.*

སྲུ་རེམ། ...(simple Future).

Or:—

འགྲོ་བར་སྲིད་དོ། f. a. p.

Or :—

འགྲོ་སྲིད་དོ། f. a. p.

Past: *Perhaps I would go; I might go.*

འགྲོ་སྲིད་པ་ཡིན་ནོ། and so on.

Perfect: *Perhaps I would have gone; I might have gone.*

འགྲོ་སྲིད་པ་ཡོད་དོ། and so on.

HORTATIVE MOOD.

Similar to Literary གཏོང་བ། *To send*, No. VII.

PURPOSIVE MOOD.

Similar to Literary གཏོང་བ། *To send*, No. VII, using Root འགྲོ in Present Tense, and ཕྱིན་ or སོང་ in Past Tense.

PRECATIVE MOOD.

འགྲོ་བར་ཆུག་ or གནང་།

Or :—

འགྲོ་རུ་ཆུག་ or གནང་།

Or :—

འགྲོར་ཆུག་ or གནང་།

} *Let me*, etc., *go.*

PERMISSIVE AND OPTATIVE MOOD.

As in Literary གཏོང་བ། *To send*, No. VII, keeping the construction in the Nominative case and using the appropriate roots.

IMPERATIVE.

སོང་།

Or :—

འགྲོ་བར་དགོས།

Or :—

འགྲོ་བར་གྱུར་ཞིག།

Or :—

འགྲོ་བར་བྱའོ།

} *Go, Begone.*

མ་འགྲོ། Or :— འགྲོ་བར་མི་དགོས། Or :— འགྲོ་བར་མི་གྱུར་ཅིག། Or :— འགྲོ་བར་མི་བྱའོ།	*Do not go.*

PARTICIPLES.

Present :	འགྲོ་བ།	*Going.*
Perfect :	སོང་བ་ or ཕྱིན་པ། སོང་ (or ཕྱིན་) ཚར་བ། སོང་ (or ཕྱིན་) ཟིན་པ།	*Gone.*
Com. Perfect :	སོང་བ་ (or ཕྱིན་པ) ཡིན་པ། སོང་ (or ཕྱིན་) ཚར་བ་ཡིན་པ། སོང་ (or ཕྱིན་) ཟིན་པ་ཡིན་པ།	*Having gone.*
Future :	འགྲོ་བར་འགྱུར་བ། འགྲོ་བར་བྱ་བ། འགྲོ་བྱ། འགྲོ་རྒྱུ།	*About to go.*

ACTIVE OR PERIPHRASTIC OR SUBSTANTIVE.

Same as in Colloquial No. XIII, save for the following :—

འགྲོ་བར་འགྱུར་བ་དེ། འགྲོ་བར་བྱ་བ་དེ། འགྲོ་རྒྱུ་ཡིན་པ་དེ། འགྲོ་བྱ་མཁན། འགྲོ་མཁན།	*He who* or *that which will go*, or *is to go.*

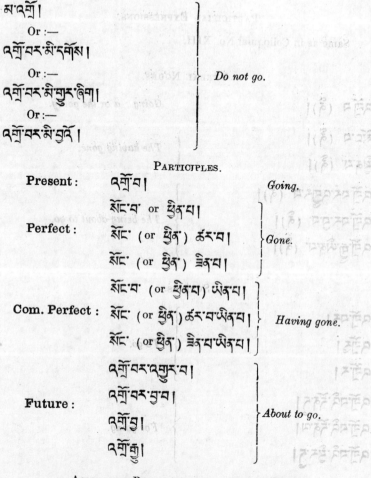

Participial Expressions.

Same as in Colloquial No. XIII.

Verbal Nouns.

འགྲོ་བ་ (ནི)།	*Going ; a or the going.*
སོང་བ་ (ནི)། ཕྱིན་པ་ (ནི)།	*The having gone.*
འགྲོ་བར་འགྱུར་བ་ (ནི)། འགྲོ་བར་བྱ་བ་ (ནི)། འགྲོ་རྒྱུ་ཡིན་པ་ (ནི)།	*The being about to go.*

Supines.

འགྲོ་བར། འགྲོརུ། འགྲོར།	*To go.*
འགྲོ་བའི་དོན་དུ། འགྲོ་བའི་དོན་ལ། འགྲོ་བའི་ཕྱིར་དུ།	*For going.*

Infinitive Mood.

Present:	འགྲོ་བ།	*To go.*
Perfect:	སོང་བ་ or ཕྱིན་པ། སོང་ (or ཕྱིན) ཚར་བ། སོང་ (or ཕྱིན) ཟིན་པ། སོང་བ་ (or ཕྱིན་པ་) ཡིན་པ།	*To have gone.*

	འགྲོ་བར་འགྱུར་བ།	
	འགྲོ་བར་བྱ་བ།	
Future:	འགྲོ་བར་གཟས་པ།	*To be about to go.*
	འགྲོ་རྒྱུ་ཡིན་པ།	
	འགྲོ་བྱ།	

XV.—Two-rooted LITERARY Verb འགྱུར་བ། *To become, To be changed, To be turned, To grow,* etc.

N.B.—This verb is often used as an Auxiliary verb, and the way in, and extent to which, it is so employed, is best seen in the other Literary Conjugations. It is purely classical.

The construction here is in the NOMINATIVE case.

ROOTS.

Present: འགྱུར། **Perfect:** གྱུར། **Future:** འགྱུར།

Imperative: གྱུར། but sometimes ཤོག།

INDICATIVE MOOD.

Present: *I become.*

འགྱུར་རོ། f. a. p.

Periphrastic: *I am becoming.*

འགྱུར་གྱིན་ཡོད་དོ།

འགྱུར་གྱིན་ཡོད་དོ་ or འདུག་གོ།

འགྱུར་གྱིན་ཡོད་དོ་ or འདུག་གོ་ or ཡོད་པ་རེད་དོ།

Past: *I became.*

གྱུར་ or གྱུར་ཏོ། f. a. p.

Or :—

གྱུར་པ་ཡིན་ནོ།

གྱུར་པ་འདུག་གོ་ or occ. chiefly interr. ཡིན་ནོ།

གྱུར་པ་ཡིན་ནོ།

Imperfect : *I was becoming.*

Same as Periphrastic Present, context showing Tense.

Or :—

གྱུར་པ་ཡིན་ནོ། and so on.

Or :—

གྱུར་ཞིང་ཡོད་པ་ཡིན་ནོ། and so on.

Perfect : *I have become.*

Same as Past.

Pluperfect : *I had become.*

Same as Past.

Or, though seldom used :—

གྱུར་ནས་ཡོད་དོ། f. a. p.

Or :—

གྱུར་ཡོད་དོ། f. a. p.

Future : *I shall become.*

འགྱུར་བར་འགྱུར་རོ། f. a. p.

Or :—

འགྱུར་བར་བྱའོ། f. a. p

SUBJUNCTIVE AND CONDITIONAL MOODS.

Present : *If . . . I shall become.*

(Present Root) ···ན··· (simple Future).

Past : *If . . . I would become.*

(Perfect Root) ···ན··· གྱུར་ཏོ། f. a. p.

Or :—

(Perfect Root) ···ན··· གྱུར་པ་ཡིན་ནོ། and so on.

Perfect : *If . . . I would have become.*

(Perfect Root) ···ན··· གྱུར་པ་ཡོད་དོ། and so on.

POTENTIAL MOOD, PROBABILITY, HORTATIVE MOOD.

(As in Literary Verb དགའ་བ། *To be glad*, No. XI.)

Purposive Mood.

Present : *So that I may become.*

འགྱུར་བའི་དོན་དུ་ or ཕྱིར་དུ། f. a. p.

Past : *So that I might become.*

གྱུར་པའི་དོན་དུ་ or ཕྱིར་དུ། f. a. p.

Precative Mood.

འགྱུར་བར་ཚུག་ or གནང་།

Or :—

འགྱུར་དུ་ཚུག་ or གནང་། } *Let me*, etc. *become.*

Permissive and Optative Moods.

As in Literary གཏོང་བ། *To send*, No. VII, keeping the construction in the Nominative Case, and using the appropriate Roots.

Imperative Mood.

གྱུར་ (ཞིག་) or sometimes ཤོག་ (ཅིག)།

Or :—

...ལ་འགྱུར་བར་དགོས། } *Become.*

མ་འགྱུར་ or མ་ཡོང་།

Or :—

...ལ་འགྱུར་བར་མི་དགོས། } *Do not become.*

Participles.

Present : འགྱུར་བ། *Becoming.*

Perfect :

གྱུར་པ།

གྱུར་ཚར་བ།

གྱུར་ཟིན་པ། } *Become.*

49

Com. Perfect:	གྱུར་པ་ཡིན་པ། གྱུར་ཚར་བ་ཡིན་པ། གྱུར་ཟིན་པ་ཡིན་པ།	*Having become.*
Future:	འགྱུར་བར་འགྱུར་བ། འགྱུར་བར་བྱ་བ། འགྱུར་བྱ། འགྱུར་རྒྱུ་ཡིན་པ།	*About to become.*

Periphrastic Expressions.

འགྱུར་བ་ (དེ་ or ནི། འགྱུར་མཁན་ (དེ་ or ནི)།	*He who* or *that which becomes.* *The becomer.*
གྱུར་པ་ (དེ་ or ནི)། གྱུར་མཁན་ (དེ་ or ནི)།	*He who* or *that which became.*
འགྱུར་བར་འགྱུར་བ་ (དེ་ or ནི)། འགྱུར་བར་བྱ་བ་ (དེ་ or ནི)། འགྱུར་རྒྱུ་ཡིན་པ་ (དེ་ or ནི)། འགྱུར་རྒྱུ་ (དེ་ or ནི)། འགྱུར་རྒྱུ་མཁན་ (དེ་ or ནི)། འགྱུར་བྱ།	*He who* or *that which is to*, or *will, become.*

Other Participial Expressions.

Same as in མཐོང་བ་ *To see*, No. XI, using the appropriate Roots.

Both འགྱུར་ and གྱུར་ take ཏེ་ and གྱིས།

Supines.

འགྱུར་བར། འགྱུར་དུ།	*To become.*

འགྱུར་བའི་དོན་དུ། འགྱུར་བའི་དོན་ལ། འགྱུར་བའི་ཕྱིར་དུ།	*For becoming.*

VERBAL NOUNS.

འགྱུར་བ་ (ནི)།	*Becoming. A or the becoming.*
གྱུར་པ་ (ནི)།	*The having become.*
འགྱུར་བར་འགྱུར་བ་ (ནི)། འགྱུར་བར་བྱ་བ་ (ནི)། འགྱུར་རྒྱུ་ཡིན་པ་ (ནི)།	*The being about to become.*

INFINITIVE MOOD.

Present :	འགྱུར་བ།	*To become.*
Perfect :	གྱུར་པ། གྱུར་ཚར་བ། གྱུར་ཟིན་པ། གྱུར་པ་ཡིན་པ།	*To have become.*
Future :	འགྱུར་བར་འགྱུར་བ། འགྱུར་བར་བྱ་བ། འགྱུར་བར་གཟམ་པ། འགྱུར་རྒྱུ་ཡིན་པ།	*To be about to become.*

XVI.—Active, 4-Rooted COLLOQUIAL Verb བྱེད་པ *To do, To make,* etc.

N.B.—The construction is in the AGENTIVE case, save where otherwise indicated.

ROOTS.

Present : བྱེད། Perfect : བྱས། Future : བྱ། Imperative : བྱོས, བྱེད, བྱིས, གྱིས།

The construction is throughout similar to that of Colloquial གཏོང་བ་ *To send*, No. VI, up to and including the Optative Mood, save for the following :—

Imperative Mood.

བྱོས་ཤིག། བྱེས་ཤིག། གྱིས་ཤིག། བྱེད་ཤིག།	*Do*
མ་བྱེད།	*Do not do.*

N.B.—The form བྱེད་ *Do* is probably really བྱས།

Participles.

As in Colloquial གཏོང་བ་ *To send*, No. VI.

Active or Periphrastic Expressions.

As in Colloquial གཏོང་བ་ *To send* No. VI.

Other Participial Expressions.

Present.

བྱེད་དེ། བྱ་སྟེ།	*Doing.*
བྱེད་པས།	*Because, since, when, while.. doing.*

And so on, as in Colloquial གཏོང་བ་ *To send*, No. VI.

Past.

བྱས་དེ།	*Having done.*
བྱས་པས། བྱས་པ་ལས།	*Because, since, when..did*, or *was done*, or *had done.*

And so on, as in Colloquial གཏོང་བ་ *To send*, No. VI.

SUPINES, AND VERBAL NOUNS AND INFINITIVE MOOD.

As in Colloquial གཏོང་བ་ *To send*, No. VI.

XVII.—Active, 4-Rooted LITERARY Verb, བྱེད་པ་ *To do, To make*, etc.

ROOTS.

Present :
Perfect : } As in Active Colloquial Verb, No. XVI.
Future :

Imperative : བྱོས་ (ཤིག)།

INDICATIVE MOOD.

Present : *I do ; I make.*

བྱེད་དོ། f. a. p.

Intensive : *I do do ; I do make.*

བྱེད་པར་བྱེད་དོ། f. a. p.

Periphrastic : *I am making.*

བྱེད་ཀྱིན་ཡོད་དོ།

བྱེད་ཀྱིན་ཡོད་དོ་ or འདུག་གོ།

བྱེད་ཀྱིན་ཡོད་དོ་ or འདུག་གོ་ or ཡོད་པ་རེད་དོ།

Or, elegantly, but seldom used :—

བྱེད་ཅིང་མཆིས་སོ།

བྱེད་ཅིང་གདའོ།

བྱེད་ཅིང་མཆིས་སོ་ or གདའོ་ or མཆིས་པ་ཡིན་ནོ།

Past : *I made.*

བྱས་སོ། f. a. p.

Or :—

བྱས་པ་ཡིན་ནོ།

བྱས་པ་འདུག་གོ་ or occ., chiefly interr. ཡིན་ནོ།

བྱས་པ་ཡིན་ནོ།

Or :—

བྱས་སོང་ངོ། f. a. p.

Imperfect : *I was making.*

Same as Periphrastic Present, context showing Tense.

Or :—

བྱས་པ་ཡིན་ནོ། and so on.

Or :—

བྱེད་ཀྱིན་ཡོད་པ་ཡིན་ནོ། and so on.

Or :—

བྱས་ཤིང་ཡོད་པ་ཡིན་ནོ། and so on.

Perfect : *I have made.*

Same as Past.

Pluperfect : *I had made.*

Same as Past.

Or :—

བྱས་ཡོད་དོ། f. a. p.

Or :—

བྱས་ཚར་སོང་ངོ། f. a. p.

Or, though seldom used :—

བྱས་ནས་ཡོད་དོ། f. a. p.

Future : *I shall make.*

བྱེད་པར་བྱའོ། f. a. p.

Or :—

བྱེད་པར་འགྱུར་རོ། f. a. p.

Or :—

བྱེད་ཡོང་ངོ། f. a. p.

Or :—

བྱའོ། f. a. p.

Subjunctive and Conditional Moods.

Present : *If . . . I shall make.*

(Present Root) . . . ··· ན་ ·· (any simple Future as above).

The rest as in Literary གཏོང་བ། *To send*, No. VII.

The other Moods as in the same Verb No. VII, down to and including the Optative Mood, with appropriate Roots, etc.

IMPERATIVE MOOD.

གྱིས་ (ཤིག)། བྱེད་པར་དགོས། བྱེད་པར་བྱའོ།	*Make.*
མ་བྱེད། བྱེད་པར་མི་དགོས། བྱེད་པར་མི་བྱའོ།	*Do not make.*

PARTICIPLES.

Present :	བྱེད་པ།	*Making.*
Perfect :	བྱས་པ། བྱས་ཚར་བ། བྱས་ཟིན་པ།	*Made.*
Com. Perfect :	བྱས་པ་ཡིན་པ།	*Having made.*
Future	བྱ་བ། བྱེད་རྒྱུ་ཡིན་པ། བྱེད་འགྲོ་ཡིན་པ། བྱེད་པར་འགྱུར་བ། བྱེད་པར་བྱ་བ། བྱེད་པར་གཟས་པ། བྱ་རྒྱུ་ཡིན་པ། བྱ་འགྲོ་ཡིན་པ།	*About to make.*

ACTIVE OR PERIPHRASTIC PARTICIPLES.

བྱེད་མཁན། བྱེད་པ་པོ། བྱེད་པ་དེ།	*He who* or *that which makes* **or** *does ; the maker* or *doer*.
བྱས་མཁན།	*He who* or *that which made* or *did*.
བྱ་མཁན། བྱ་བ་དེ། བྱེད་པར་འགྱུར་བ་དེ། བྱེད་པར་བྱ་བ་དེ། བྱ་རྒྱུ་ཡིན་པ་དེ།	*He who* or *that which will make* or *do*, or *is to make* or *do*.

Or the following simple construction may be used :—

ཤྲུག་སྐྲམ་བྱེད་པའི་དབུ་མཛོད་ལགས་དེ།	*The carpenter who makes the box.*
ཤྲུག་སྐྲམ་བྱས་པའི་དབུ་མཛོད་ལགས་དེ།	*The carpenter who made the box.*
ཤྲུག་སྐྲམ་བྱ་བའི་དབུ་མཛོད་ལགས་དེ།	*The carpenter who will make*, **or** *is to make, the box.*

OTHER PARTICIPIAL EXPRESSIONS.

As in Colloquial བྱེད་པ། *To make*, No. XVI.

SUPINES.

བྱེད་པར། བྱེད་དུ།	*To make.*
བྱེད་པའི་དོན་དུ། བྱེད་པའི་དོན་ལ། བྱེད་པའི་ཕྱིར་དུ།	*For making*

VERBAL NOUNS.

བྱེད་པ་ (ནི)།	*Making; a* or *the making.*
བྱས་པ་ (ནི)།	*The having made.*
བྱེད་པར་འགྱུར་བ་ (ནི)། བྱེད་པར་བྱ་བ་ (ནི)། བྱེད་རྒྱུ་ཡིན་པ་ (ནི)། བྱ་རྒྱུ་ཡིན་པ་ (ནི)། བྱ་བ་ (ནི)།	*The being about to make.*

INFINITIVE MOOD.

Present :	བྱེད་པ།	*To make.*
Perfect :	བྱས་པ། བྱས་ཚར་བ། བྱས་ཟིན་པ། བྱས་པ་ཡིན་པ།	*To have made.*
Future :	བྱེད་པར་འགྱུར་བ། བྱེད་པར་བྱ་བ། བྱེད་པར་གཟས་པ། བྱེད་རྒྱུ་ཡིན་པ། བྱ་རྒྱུ་ཡིན་པ། བྱ་བ། བྱེད་འགྲོ་ཡིན་པ། བྱ་འགྲོ་ཡིན་པ།	*To be about to make.*

XVIII.—Passive, 4-Rooted COLLOQUIAL Verb བྱེད་རྒྱུ་ཡོད་པ་ or ཡིན་པ། *To be made, To be done,* etc.

Conjugated on the lines of Passive Colloquial Verb གཏོང་རྒྱུ། *To be sent*, No. VIII, with the appropriate Roots, etc.

XIX.—Passive, 4-Rooted LITERARY Verb བྱ་བ། *To be made, To be done*, etc.

Conjugated on the lines of Passive LITERARY Verb གཏོང་བར་བྱ་བ། *To be sent*, No. XII, as far as, and including, the Compound Perfect of the Participles, and with the appropriate Roots, etc. Then :—

PARTICIPLES.

Future :
བྱེད་པར་བྱ་བ།
བྱེད་པར་འགྱུར་བ།
བྱེད་རྒྱུ་ཡིན་པ་
བྱ་རྒྱུ་ཡིན་པ།
བྱ་བ།
} *About to be made* or *done*.

OTHER PARTICIPIAL EXPRESSIONS.

Present.

བྱེད་དེ།
བྱ་སྟེ།
} *Being made* or *done*.

བྱེད་པས།
བྱ་བས།
} *Because, since, while, when... being made* or *done*.

And so on as in LITERARY ACTIVE, No. XVII.

Past.

བྱས་ཏེ། *Having been made* or *done*.

བྱས་པས། } *Because, since, when... is* or *was made* or *done*.

And so on as in LITERARY ACTIVE, No. XVII.

Supines.

- བྱ་བར།
- བྱ་རུ།
- བྱེད་པར།
- བྱེད་དུ།

To be made or *done.*

- བྱ་བའི་དོན་དུ་ (or དོན་ལ་ or ཕྱིར་དུ)།
- བྱའི་དོན་དུ་ (or དོན་ལ་ or ཕྱིར་དུ)།
- བྱེད་པའི་དོན་དུ་ (or དོན་ལ་ or ཕྱིར་དུ)།

For being made or *done.*

Verbal Noun.

བྱ་བ་ (ནི)། — *Being made* or *done.* *A* or *the being made* or *done.*

Infinitive Mood.

- བྱ་བ།
- བྱ་རྒྱུ་ཡིན་པ།
- Future: བྱེད་རྒྱུ་ཡིན་པ།
- བྱེད་པར་འགྱུར་བ།
- བྱེད་པར་བྱ་བ།

To be made or *done.*

Past: བྱས་པར་ཡིན་པ། — *To have been made* or *done.*

XX.—Passive Literary Verb བྱེད་པར་འགྱུར་བ། *To be made* or *done*, etc.

In conjugating this Verb, བྱེད་པར་ remains constant throughout, while the rest is in Literary ཡོང་བ་ *Table*, No. II

Or, while keeping བྱེད་པར་ constant throughout, LITERARY འགྱུར་བ་ No. XV may be substituted for LITERARY ཡོད་པ།

But then the meaning is,—*To become made* or *done*, *To be about to become made* or *done.*

FINIS.

ERRATA ET CORRIGENDA.

Page	4, line 1 at	bottom.	For	དོ་		read	ཛོ
,,	8, ,, 5 from	,,	,,	ཁ་		,,	ཁྲ
,,	9, ,, 13 ,,	,,	,,	ī in col. 2		,,	ī.
,,	12, ,, 6 ,,	top.	,,	"affected"		,,	"effected."
,,	12, ,, 12 ,,	bottom.	,,	"affected"		,,	"effected."
,,	14, ,, 2 ,,	top.	,,	*Yata*		,,	*Yatā.*
,,	18, ,, 7 ,,	bottom.	,,	LÉN-PA		,,	LÈN-PA.
,,	19, ,, 2 ,,	,,	,,	CHO		,,	CH'O.
,,	21, ,, 1 at	top.	,,	མག་		,,	མགོ
,,	21, ,, 2 from	,,	,,	*Heda*		,,	*Head.*
,,	22, ,, 7 ,,	bottom.	,,	མ་		,,	མི
,,	22, ,, 6 ,,	,,	,,	ĎA		,,	ḌA.
,,	23, ,, 11 ,,	,,	,,	ǦEB		,,	ǦEB.
,,	25, ,, 7 ,,	top.	,,	Ǧ'Ā		,,	Ǧ'Ā.
,,	27, ,, 8 ,,	bottom.	,,	Ž		,,	Ž.
,,	27, ,, 7 ,,	,,	,,		ditto.		
,,	28, ,, 4 ,,	,,	,,	BAB́		,,	B́AB́.
,,	31, ,, 6 ,,	top.	,,	*m*		,,	*n.*
,,	31, ,, 4 ,,	bottom.	,,	BAR		,,	B́AR, and
			,,	BA		,,	B́A.
,,	33, ,, 3 ,,	top.	,,	ŽHYU		,,	ŽHYU, and
			,,	ŽHYUM		,,	ŽHYUM.
,,	35, ,, 6 ,,	bottom.	,,	ཀྲྀ་		,,	ཀྲི
,,	48, ,, 5 ,,	,,	,,	"lines loping"		,,	"line sloping."
,,	49, ,, 9 ,,	top.	,,	ལ		,,	ཁྱ
,,	49, ,, 14 ,,	,,	,,	"up"		,,	"at."
,,	56, ,, 3 ,,	,,	,,	ཐྱ		,,	ལྷ
,,	68, ,, 1 at	,,	,,	Ś		,,	ś.

Page 89,	line 10	from bottom.		For	Ży̆ı	read	Zhyı.
,, 89,	,, 3	,,	,,	,,			ditto.
,, 89,	,, 4	,,	top	,,			ditto.
,, 89,	,, 5	,,	,,	,,			ditto in both places
,, 91,	,, 3	,,	,,	,,	Zhyı'	read	Żhyı'.
,, 91,	,, 4	,,	,,	,,	Zhyı'	,,	Żhyı'.
,, 91,	,, 4	,,	,,	,,	Zhyıǵ	,,	Żhyıǵ.
,, 106,	,, 11	,,	,,	,,	༥	,,	༡༥.
,, 139,	last line.			,,	ང་རར་	,,	ང་རང་
,, 140,	line 12	from bottom.		,,	ཁོ་	,,	ཁྲོ
,, 151,	,, 12	,,	,,	,,	ག་རི་	,,	ག་རེ
,, 153,	,, 10	,,	,,	,,	Delete OR between བུ་ and Ex.		
,, 169,	,, 1	at	top	,,	*hath*	read	*that.*
,, 243,	,, 10	from	bottom.	,,	གཏོང་བ ར་	,,	གཏོང་བར་
,, 262,	,, 2	,,	top.	,,	ཞིས་	,,	ཞིས
,, 306,	,, 6	,,	bottom.	,,	འགྲོ་པའི་	,,	འགྲོ་བའི
,, 329,	,, 3	,,	,,	,,	མན་	,,	མིན་

,, 347, last line. Delete second and third dot between བདང and མཁན །

,, 351, line 11 from bottom. Read " *might be sent.*"

,, 371, ,, 11 ,, ,, Delete " ཤིག་ or ཞིག་ or ཅིག །" and re-insert after " Particle " on next previous line.

,, 381,	,, 5	,,	top.	For	མི་གྱུར་	read	མ་འགྱུར་
,, 382,	,, 10	,,	bottom.	,,	འགྲོ་ར་	,,	འགྲོར་
,, 386,	,, 8	,,	,,	,,	དི་	,,	དེ་ and for
					ན་	,,	ནི་

CORRIGENDA—(*continued*).

Page 66 (middle of page).

Delete the words "some uncertainty," and substitute the words "personal knowledge and is certain."

Also delete the word "almost."

Also delete the words "at all," and substitute the word "exactly."

Also delete the words "only hazarding the statement," and substitute the words "speaking on information."

Page 207 (bottom of page).

Delete the words "an emphatic or positive statement is intended," and substitute the words "the speaker expresses knowledge derived from information."

After the words "*No there is not,*" insert the words "(*so I am informed*)."

Then add the following:—

"འདུག། is used when the speaker expresses personal knowledge and certainty. Thus:—

ལགས། མི་འདུག་ *No, there is not* (*I know*). (See also p. 66)."

CORRECTIONS—(contd.)

Page [illegible]

Delete the words [illegible] and substitute the words [illegible] are plain [illegible]

[illegible]

Delete the words [illegible] and substitute the words [illegible] only [illegible] the assessment [illegible] regarding the information."

Page 407 (bottom of page)

Delete the words [illegible] and substitute the words [illegible] knowledge derived from interpretation."

After the words [illegible] insert the words [illegible]

Then add the following—

[illegible] when the [illegible] knowledge [illegible] certainty. Thus—

[illegible]